CM

The World Trade Organization in the New Global
Economy

NEW HORIZONS IN INTERNATIONAL BUSINESS

General Editor: Peter J. Buckley
Centre for International Business,
University of Leeds (CIBUL), UK

The New Horizons in International Business series has established itself as the world's leading forum for the presentation of new ideas in international business research. It offers pre-eminent contributions in the areas of multinational enterprise – including foreign direct investment, business strategy and corporate alliances, global competitive strategies, and entrepreneurship. In short, this series constitutes essential reading for academics, business strategists and policy makers alike.

Titles in the series include:

Deepening Integration in the Pacific Economies
Corporate Alliances, Contestable Markets and Free Trade
Edited by Alan M. Rugman and Gavin Boyd

The Global Integration of Europe and East Asia
Studies of International Trade and Investment
Edited by Sang-Gon Lee and Pierre-Bruno Ruffini

Foreign Direct Investment and Economic Growth in China
Edited by Yanrui Wu

Multinationals, Technology and National Competitiveness
Marina Papanastassiou and Robert Pearce

Globalizing America
The USA in World Integration
Edited by Thomas L. Brewer and Gavin Boyd

Information Technology in Multinational Enterprises
Edited by Edward Mozley Roche and Michael James Blaine

A Yen for Real Estate
Japanese Real Estate Investment Abroad – From Boom to Bust
Roger Simon Farrell

Corporate Governance and Globalization
Long Range Planning Issues
Edited by Stephen S. Cohen and Gavin Boyd

The European Union and Globalisation
Towards Global Democratic Governance
Edited by Brigid Gavin

Globalization and the Small Open Economy
Edited by Daniel Van Den Bulcke and Alain Verbeke

Enterpreneurship and the Internationalisation of Asian Firms
An Institutional Perspective
Henry Wai-chung Yeung

The World Trade Organization in the New Global Economy
Trade and Investment Issues in the Millennium Round
Edited by Alan M. Rugman and Gavin Boyd

The World Trade Organization in the New Global Economy

Trade and Investment Issues in the Millennium Round

Edited by

Alan M. Rugman

Leslie Waters Chair in International Business, Kelley School of Business, Indiana University, USA

Gavin Boyd

Honorary Professor, Political Science Department, Rutgers University, Newark, New Jersey, USA and Adjunct Professor, Management Faculty, Saint Mary's University, Halifax, Canada

NEW HORIZONS IN INTERNATIONAL BUSINESS

Edward Elgar

Cheltenham, UK • Northampton, MA, USA

© Alan M. Rugman, Gavin Boyd 2001

Published by
Edward Elgar Publishing Limited
Glensanda House
Montpellier Parade
Cheltenham
Glos GL50 1UA
UK

Edward Elgar Publishing, Inc.
136 West Street
Suite 202
Northampton
Massachusetts 01060
USA

A catalogue record for this book
is available from the British Library

Library of Congress Cataloguing in Publication Data
The World Trade Organization in the new global economy : trade and investment issues in the millenium round / edited by Alan M. Rugman, Gavin Boyd.
  p. cm. -- (New horizons in international business)
  Papers presented at a conference on the World Trade Organization sponsored by the Saint Mary's University, Halifax, Sept. 29–30, 2000.
  Includes index.
    1. World Trade Organization--Congresses. 2. Free trade--Congresses. 3. Investments, Foreign--Congresses. 4. International business enterprises--Congresses. 5. Competition, International--Congresses. I. Rugman, Alan M. II. Boyd, Gavin. III. Saint Mary's University (Halifax, N.S.) IV. Series.

HF1385 .W67 2002
382'.92--dc21

                                                                              2001033980

ISBN 1 84064 507 5

Typeset by Manton Typesetters, Louth, Lincolnshire, UK.
Printed and bound in Great Britain by MPG Books Ltd, Bodmin, Cornwall.

Contents

Figures

Tables

Contributors

Andrey Anishchenko is a graduate student in Law and International Relations at the University of Toronto, Canada.

Gavin Boyd is an Honorary Professor in Political Science at Rutgers University, Newark, New Jersey, USA and Adjunct Professor in Management at Saint Mary's University, Halifax, Canada.

Thomas L. Brewer is Professor in the Business Faculty at Georgetown University, Washington DC and Editor of the *Journal of International Business Studies*.

Joseph P. Daniels is Professor of Economics at Marquette University, Milwaukee, Wisconsin, USA.

John B. Davis is Professor of Economics at Marquette University, Milwaukee, Wisconsin, USA.

Anna Lanoszka is on the staff of the World Trade Organization, Geneva.

Terutomo Ozawa is Professor of Economics at Colorado State University, Fort Collins, Colorado, USA.

Nigel Pain is a staff member of the National Institute of Economic and Social Research, London, UK.

Robin H. Pedler is an Associate Fellow at Templeton College, Oxford University, UK.

J. David Richardson is Professor of Economics at Syracuse University, Rochester, New York, USA.

Alan M. Rugman holds the Leslie Waters Chair in International Business, Kelley School of Business, Indiana University, USA.

Julie Soloway is an international trade and competition policy lawyer with Davies, Ward, Phillips and Vineberg LLP, Toronto, Canada.

Gilbert Winham is Professor of Political Science at Dalhousie University, Halifax, Canada.

Stephen Young is Professor of Marketing at the University of Strathclyde, UK.

Foreword

This volume contains chapters which were discussed at a conference on the World Trade Organization (WTO) sponsored by The Frank H. Sobey Faculty of Commerce, Saint Mary's University, Halifax, 29–30 September, 2000. The University holds an annual international political economy conference arranged by Professor Gavin Boyd. Alliance Capitalism will be the theme in November 2001 and Professor John H. Dunning (University of Reading, UK and Rutgers University, USA) will be a distinguished guest at this conference.

Much of the literature on the world trading system has been the work of economists focusing on trends and issues in arm's length commerce between nation states. The significance of transnational production in the service of international markets has thus been overlooked. However, the volume of this production is much greater than export flows, for which official figures do not distinguish between arm's length and intrafirm trade. Transnational production is increasing, with large expansions of foreign direct investment, especially between the USA and the European Union (EU). Hence the structural foundations of foreign commerce are being substantially altered. Trade policy conflicts, moreover, add to the incentives of multinational firms to produce abroad, especially in major foreign markets.

All this means that the basic concerns of government with the growth and employment effects of trade liberalization endeavours in the World Trade Organization have to take into account the structural linkages which international firms are building across national borders through foreign direct investment. One consequence for policymakers is that the international competition policy issues are becoming more challenging. A concomitant trend is the growth of cross-border portfolio capital flows. One can pose the question then, should the WTO be given a major responsibility in these areas?

While negotiating or preparing to negotiate for multilateral trade liberalization, governments (and in the case of Europe, the EU) tend to see themselves in rivalries to enhance structural competitiveness. Their firms, however, are under pressures to concentrate on strategies to increase their own global market shares, with selective use of foreign location advantages and the investment bidding of host governments. While national trade policies have to respond to the interacting consequences of government measures and corporate activities, the reactions of diverse groups demand attention. This was dramatized by the Seattle 'riots', which disrupted the 1999 Ministerial meeting of the World Trade Organization. The protests in Prague in the summer of 2000 at the IMF meetings confirm the changing environment in which supranational agencies now function.

In this volume the results of research by economists, international management experts, and political scientists have been brought together. Contributions to policy learning have been combined with studies relating to the broad social responsibilities of international firms, operating individually and in alliances. The University community is very grateful to all participants in the conference, and to the contributors to this conference volume, especially Professor Alan M. Rugman, Leslie Waters Chair in International Business, Kelley School of Business, Indiana University, USA.

We look forward, through this conference series, to providing an ongoing forum for informed discussion on emerging international trade and investment issues that will help shape the future of the world economy.

J. Colin Dodds, Ph.D.
President and Professor of
Finance
Saint Mary's University
Halifax, Canada

NA

Preface

Despite the temporary disruption to the process of multilateral trade liberalization at Seattle in December 1999, the work of the World Trade Organization continues. The election of a new US President presents an opportunity for the United States to reassert its commitment to multilateral trade and investment liberalization through a renewed Millennium Round of the WTO.

In this volume, we consider the principal items on the agenda for a new round of the WTO. We also embed these chapters in a careful integration of economic, political, cultural and legal factors. In particular, we consider the shape of the new round from the viewpoints of the contributions that need to be made by the key 'triad' members of the WTO, namely the United States, European Union and Japan.

Another attribute of this volume is the balanced focus upon foreign direct investment issues, as well as trade liberalization. For too long trade policymakers have been looking backwards at the need to reduce tariffs instead of forwards at the new measures needed to enhance access for foreign direct investment, which is the new form of international business. The Uruguay Round started to work on the new issues associated with foreign direct investment – intellectual property, services, competition policy and so on. These will remain as the backbone for a new Millennium Round. In addition, the need for environmental and labour/human rights agreements is discussed, although no contributors see these as core issues for the WTO.

Of particular importance is the new role of Non Governmental Organizations (NGOs) in their largely self-appointed role as participants in the WTO process. Several chapters examine the role and agenda of NGOs and add value to the analysis of their legitimacy in the WTO policy-making process.

The editor and others of the volume are delighted to acknowledge the sponsorship and dedicated assistance provided by Dr Colin Dodds, President, Saint Mary's University, where preliminary versions of their chapters were presented at a conference at Halifax, Nova Scotia, in September 2000.

Alan M. Rugman, Oxford
Gavin Boyd, Halifax

1. The World Trade Organization and the international political economy

Alan M. Rugman

The World Trade Organization (WTO) is in a crisis. This is due to a complex evolution of events in which the protests of its left-wing critics have diverted public and elite technical attention from the critical issues of interdependent trade and growth. These issues have emerged as international commerce has steadily expanded with major reductions of trade barriers, as negotiated in the Uruguay Round of multilateral interactions that concluded in the mid 1990s.

The present crisis at the WTO concerns the status and functions of the organization's secretariat, and the observance of its principles, norms and rules by member governments. The secretariat is an understaffed and over-worked technical bureaucracy, facilitating, often opportunistically, bargains by governments to reduce trade barriers. While these facilitating services are valued, the subjective preferences of governments are not to endow the WTO secretariat with substantial independent research and advocacy capabilities. Governments are committed in principle to non-discriminatory and recipro-cal reductions of their trade barriers, but tend to view their formal obligations in this regard as matters of expedience. The common trend is to press for their domestic protectionist interests with any available bargaining power. This results in hard and precise agreements, on the basis of which any subsequent disputes have to be settled through methods of adversarial legal-ism, combined with renewed bargaining leverage.

The crisis of the organization is primarily a consequence of increasing unilateralism – an intensification of the trend in which quasi protectionist interests have been rampant. With this trend the facilitating functions of the WTO secretariat have been weakened, and its dispute settlement mechanism has come under strain. Motivations for the unilateralism have derived from the domestic political interests of governments, affected in different ways by the costs and benefits of expanding international commerce. The push for unilateralism has been led by the United States and the European Union (EU), because of the vast size of their domestic economies and the absence of effective regional groups in the rest of the world.

The basic way to infringe the WTO's rules is to fail to accept the discipline of most-favoured nation (MFN), non-discriminatory treatment. If the United States allows one of its exporters to 'dump' a product in Europe, then the EU can get the European Commission to bring an 'antidumping' action, and, if successful, impose a tariff duty on the dumped imports. If Britain subsidizes an export to the United States, and a US firm complains to the US International Trade Commission, then it may recommend that a 'countervailing' duty be imposed to offset the margin of subsidy. Both the antidumping and countervailing duty actions are consistent with the WTO and the General Agreement on Tariffs and Trade's (GATT's) Uruguay Round Agreement of 1994.

The WTO-consistent 'retaliation' that a country can carry out, always in response to an infringement of its negotiated rights, is to re-impose tariffs or duties against the offending party's home country. Thus all the action is between governments. The WTO acts as a traffic cop, directing what are really domestic legal actions involving international players. Its only direct role is to hear appeals about failures to observe due process in the application of these trade laws. Here it can render a judgement, according to the timing of Table 1.1.

Table 1.1   Dispute settlement at the World Trade Organization

Time	WTO activity
60 days	WTO Report (for consultation)
9 months	WTO Panel
60 days	WTO Appellate Body
15 months	Implementation by countries
After 15 months	WTO sanctional retaliation

Source: Adapted by author from WTO website

INTERNATIONAL STRUCTURE OF THE WTO

The World Trade Organization, established on 1 January 1995, is the umbrella organization governing the international trading system. It oversees international trade agreements and provides the secretariat for GATT, based in Geneva. The GATT has undertaken eight 'rounds' of multilateral trade negotiations which have achieved major cuts in tariffs and, since the 1970s, some reductions in related non-tariff barriers to trade. The latest round, the Uruguay Round, lasted seven years, as its agenda broadened to include trade in services and intellectual property, and a revised system of dispute settlement mechanisms.

Contrary to popular belief, the WTO did not replace the GATT. An amended GATT remains as one of the legal pillars of the world's trade and, to a lesser extent, investment systems. The other pillars, set up in the Uruguay Round's Marrakesh agreement of 1994, include the General Agreement on Trade in Services (GATS) and the Agreement on Trade-Related Aspects of Intellectual Property Rights (TRIPs).

The members of the WTO now account for well over 90 per cent of the world's trade and virtually all of its investment; by 1998 the organization's membership had increased to 132, from the 76 founding members of 1995. Nearly all the developed, and most of the developing countries, have joined; a notable exception is the People's Republic of China, the entry of which was blocked by the United States throughout 1998 and 1999 on the grounds that its economy is not open enough and that intellectual property rights are not sufficiently protected.

The WTO's origins can be traced back to the Atlantic Charter of 1941, developed by then US President Franklin Roosevelt and British Prime Minister Winston Churchill. In order to counter US isolationism the principle of the Atlantic Charter was for an international trading system with equal access to trade for all nations. This was seen as a complement to an effective world political forum, the United Nations, established in 1946 with its permanent headquarters in New York City. The United States organized an international conference on trade and employment which resulted in the Havana Charter of 1948, in which it was proposed to establish the International Trade Organization (ITO). Twenty-three countries agreed to a set of tariff cuts and these were ratified by the GATT, which was set up as a transitory arrangement to be subsumed under the ITO. However, the ITO was never ratified and the GATT continued for 47 years, until the WTO finally emerged in the last stages of the Uruguay Round to take on the role originally designed for the ITO. The WTO now stands with the World Bank and the International Monetary Fund as the third leg of the global economic system.

A successful institution such as the WTO has many parents. The first public call for a world trade organization to be established was a proposal by the Canadian Government in early 1990, which was itself strongly influenced by Dr Sylvia Ostry, Chair of the Centre for International Studies at the University of Toronto. The Canadian proposal built on the work of Professor John Jackson and others at an informal meeting in Geneva in 1989. It was then incorporated into the 'Dunkel Text' of 1991, which eventually became the final text of the Uruguay Round adopted at Marrakesh in April 1994. In approving the Uruguay Round on its 'fast track' system, the United States insisted on the name World Trade Organization, rather than the European

Community's preference for Multinational Trade Organization. So the Canadian proposal literally gave the WTO its name.

BASIC PRINCIPLES OF THE WTO

The WTO continues the key GATT principle of non-discrimination; that is, any barrier to trade should be applied equally to all member countries. It also keeps the MFN principle; that is, any liberalization measures, with some exceptions, should be granted to all members. To understand these principles, it helps to think of the WTO as a club with membership rules which require that all members receive the same treatment. If one member rescinds a trade concession, then other affected members can retaliate by withdrawing their reciprocal concessions, or receive compensation to equivalent commercial effect. If trade disputes arise, they can be settled by the WTO's unified dispute settlement mechanism, which can ensure timely compliance, in contrast to the basically voluntary procedures of the GATT. Decisions made by a WTO dispute panel cannot be blocked by the disputant party, as was possible under the GATT. Panel findings can be subject to review by an Appellate Body of the WTO. In addition, the publication of trade policy reviews and the activities of the Trade Policy Review Body (which regularly monitors the trade policies of member countries) complement the WTO's dispute settlement activities by significantly enhancing transparency.

There are four important exceptions to the key GATT principle of non-discrimination.

- Developed countries can give tariff preference to developing countries.
- Countries entering into regional free trade agreements do not need to extend the preferences negotiated in this context on an MFN basis.
- A country can invoke temporary 'safeguard' protection to one of its industries suffering serious injury due to a surge of imports.
- Temporary quantitative restrictions can be invoked by a country with serious balance of payment problems.

In the latter two cases, these measures are temporary exceptions to the member's commitment to the GATT, and a public investigation has to be undertaken to allow for limited relief from GATT obligations.

Another important principle of the WTO, which significantly improves on the GATT, is the 'single undertaking'. WTO members must accept all of the obligations of the GATT, GATS, TRIPs and any other corollary agreements. This ends the 'free ride' of some developing countries which under the old GATT could receive the benefits of some trade concessions without having to join in and undertake their full obligations. Most developed countries in North America and Western Europe were already making the single undertaking and the WTO meant few new obligations.

UNRESOLVED ISSUES AT THE WTO

The major tensions in the WTO relate to the issues of agriculture, trade in services and trade-related investment measures. None of these issues was included in the GATT's original mandate, which dealt with trade in goods. There are committees looking at these issues and their reports were the basis for the proposed Seattle Round of the WTO.

Agriculture is a sector which most governments subsidize, and it was badly neglected in the GATT. One technical advance (undertaken largely at the Organization for Economic Cooperation and Development (OECD)) which helps to increase the transparency of subsidies is the calculation of producers' subsidy equivalents. As a result, in the Uruguay Round some progress was made towards the future reduction of the most egregious agricultural subsidies through a process of 'tariffication'; that is, the translation of existing subsidies and other barriers to trade into tariff equivalents. Thus regulations and codes to keep agriculture prices artificially high, such as marketing boards in Canada, had to be replaced by tariffs. Some of the milk tariffs in Canada were put at over 200 per cent. Much work remains to be done in future rounds to liberalize agricultural trade.

Today, services account for 70 per cent of employment and value added in advanced industrialized countries, and also for at least half the world's trade and investment. The Uruguay Round started to address issues of trade in services with the establishment of GATS. Trade-Related Investment Measures (TRIMs) were also considered, and a substantive agreement prohibiting a number of investment requirements affecting cross-border trade in goods was reached. For example, the TRIMs agreement restricted the imposition of export requirements on foreign investors. Future negotiations at the WTO (following the last Uruguay Round of the GATT) will need to develop a deeper and more comprehensive set of rules for multinational investment than the TRIMs agreement. These may well be based upon the model of North American Free Trade Agreement (NAFTA), using the national treatment principle as the basic logic. National treatment states that foreign investors should not be discriminated against, but that they should receive the same treatment as domestic firms in the application of domestic laws.

The WTO Seattle Round could have built upon a multilateral agreement on investment which was partially negotiated by the Paris-based OECD over the 1995–1998 period. Investment issues are still being discussed at the WTO, in the context of the Working Group on the Relationship between Trade and Investment which was established and given a two-year mandate at the 1996 ministerial meeting in Singapore. Another important working group established during the same meeting is still examining the interaction between trade and competition policy.

The GATT has moved forward over the last 51 years to the extent that today's new constitution for international trade, as embodied in the WTO, includes an even fuller agenda of policy issues than was envisaged by its pioneering founders. These issues include:

- further reduction of tariffs
- a set of rules for multinational investment and competition policy
- the development of increased linkages between trade and issues of social policy, such as the environment and labour policy.

The hurdles in the way of achieving these three sets of objectives are lower for tariff cuts, higher for investment and highest of all for environmental and other social issues.

POLITICS OF THE WTO

The reality of the WTO is that it is a bargaining forum dominated by the United States and Western Europe. A related analysis of the WTO appears in Hoekman and Kostecki (1996). Japan, and other Asian nations, have been relatively unimportant in shaping the agenda of the WTO. For most of the 51 years of the GATT, the United States provided leadership in setting an agenda of trade liberalization, first by reducing tariffs on goods and, in the Uruguay Round, starting to address non-tariff barriers to trade and services. The major post-war supporters of the US-led drive for world trade liberalization have been the United Kingdom, and rich, smaller, trading nations such as Canada, Australia and New Zealand. A broader coalition of countries is needed for future success.

I do not see the WTO as a relevant forum for the redress of perceived global income inequalities across the North–South dimension. Its success has been in liberalizing trade in goods between the major 'triads' of North America, the EU and Japan. Indeed, parts of the GATT/WTO, such as the Multi-Fibre Agreement, have slowed the economic development of poorer southern countries, due to the protectionist nature of the rules of origin for textiles and apparel produced in Asia.

To this extent, the WTO embodies several asymmetric elements, on the one hand consistently moving towards trade liberalization, but on the other being unable to eliminate the quasi-protectionist policies in some sectors by many of its members. As the United States has provided leadership in the tariff-cutting measures of the GATT, so too has it yielded too much power to its domestic protectionist lobbies in establishing its negotiating positions. The result is a mixed bag of policies at the WTO, where country negotiators make 'concessions' of protected sectoral markets in return for market access in their partners, but where producers and consumers usually benefit (on efficiency grounds) from such concessions.

A MILLENNIUM ROUND AGENDA FOR THE WTO

While the left-wing anarchy and violence in Seattle in December 1999 has delayed the formal launch of a new round of the WTO, background research and preparation continues. The agenda is pretty much agreed and has been for several years. For example, former leading US trade policy bureaucrat, Geza Feketekuty, organized a conference in October 1996 at his Monterey Institute of International Studies to help develop the new agenda for US trade policy. This led to a set of 18 essays which covered all the topics for the Seattle Round of the WTO in December 1999. The Council on Foreign Relations sponsored and published Feketekuty and Stokes (1998), and it deserves credit for pushing the agenda beyond parochial American concerns towards the underlying analytical and policy issues confronting the WTO.

The general theme of virtually all the papers is support for a multilateral rules-based system at the WTO rather than a triad/regional power-based system. The current 'multitrack' strategy of the United States seeks to use bilateral, regional and multilateral trade negotiations simultaneously. Within this, much more attention is given to Japan and China, and even to NAFTA, than to US–Europe trade relations. To redress this balance, Preeg and Stokes, among others, advocate a Transatlantic Free Trade Agreement (TFTA).

Robert Lawrence is representative in arguing, at a new round of the WTO, for strong US support for a multilateral rules-based system, extending into the new areas of competition policy, investment and perhaps environment and labour standards. Yet in the last four years Congress has persisted in denying 'fast track' negotiating authority to the President for any trade deals, including a new WTO round, while aggressive US bilateral policy with Japan, China and other countries appears to be the new norm. If books like this can turn the tide in Congress back towards support for the United States as a leader in multilateral trade and investment liberalization, then the world will benefit.

Most less developed countries are also in favour of a new WTO Round. The trade ministers of four Caribbean economies endorsed the Seattle Round.

Yet some academics still criticize the GATT/WTO. For example, Khan (1999) has published a set of technical economic papers dealing with aspects of structural adjustment in Pakistan. The ten papers are linked together by two rather thin introductory and concluding sections which talk critically about World Bank and IMF affecting development in Pakistan. The author, a macroeconomist, attempts to analyse the distinction between 'neo-liberalism' and 'alternative critiques' with little appreciation of political science considerations such as complex institutional responsiveness and its links to the business decisions behind inbound foreign direct investment (FDI). Instead of narrow economic-based research it would be more useful for development economists to get out of their offices and actually talk to some managers. Then they would find out that the real barriers to FDI in countries like Pakistan are domestic, political and bureaucratic problems, not a perceived failure of neo-liberalism. Framing the conditions for inward FDI is a precondition for consideration of the distributional aspects of structural adjustment, including impacts on the poor, gender, health, the environment and food security. Pakistan continues to experience huge development problems, not due to World Bank failures, but due to poor internal government policies which have increased political risk and reduced the incentive for inward FDI.

The major structural change at the new WTO, as compared to GATT, is the increased use of trade law and litigation for dispute settlement. The overworked, small, WTO secretariat is now having to deal with over a dozen dispute settlement cases a year, together with all of the lengthy appeal processes. Previously, the old GATT secretariat only dealt with 2–3 cases a year. Due to this complex judicial process, trade lawyers from North America and Western Europe are now more important than politicians and business people in determining trade policy at the WTO.

As an emerging stream of dispute settlement decisions develops, the WTO is taking on a different shape. Instead of multinational trade liberalization and non-discrimination, the new trade picture looks like one of a series of bilateral trade disputes. We will now look at three major US–EU disputes.

THE EU AND UNITED STATES TRADE WARS

Bananas: the Strategic Issues

The authority of the WTO and its dispute settlement body was threatened in 1999 by the banana war between the United States and the EU. Such trade law cases are brought to the WTO by the European Commission, which is the executive body of the EU. Chiquita Brands (formerly the United Fruit Company) and Dole successfully lobbied the US government to take the EU's banana regime to the courts of the WTO. Bananas produced by US companies in Central and South America can be up to 60 per cent cheaper than those produced in the Caribbean, but have faced tariffs, quotas and distribution barriers in Europe. The EU's banana regime gives preferential treatment to bananas originating from ex-colonies belonging to the Lomé Convention and to EU producers. Caribbean producers are guaranteed a market for their products at a much higher price than would be the case in an open market. The WTO has ruled against the EU twice but the EU has been reluctant to comply fully, choosing instead to modify its regulations and to let the WTO re-examine the case (WTO, 1997, 1998, 1999).

The dispute is about free access to the EU banana market. Restrictions on US imports practically guarantee a market for Caribbean bananas. However, the US fruit multinational enterprises (MNEs), together with Del Monte, form an oligopoly that controls 66 per cent of the world's supply of bananas. Moreover, US domestic production of bananas accounts for less than 0.02 per cent of the world total. Mostly produced in Hawaii and Puerto Rico, US-grown bananas are destined for domestic consumption. The United States is clearly fighting the battle for US-based MNEs whose production sites are located in South and Central America.

Chiquita Brands has a long and controversial history in Latin America and has experienced problems drawing the lines of its involvement with national governance. When countries like Honduras and Guatemala faced civil unrest, the US government sent its navy to protect the company's interests. Similarly, in 1954, The United Fruit Company was involved in the United States' decision to overthrow the left-wing government of Guatemala (*The Economist*, Dec. 20, 1997; Adams, 1999). More recently, Chiquita Brands, through its chairman, contributed more than $1 million to the Democratic Party. It also contributed heavily to the Republican Party, assuring itself allies in the US government.

Bananas: the Legal Issue

The EC's banana regime had created trade tensions for decades before it was disputed under the GATT and eventually the WTO/GATT proceedings resulted in the First and Second Banana Panels. These rulings and diplomatic tensions pressured the EU to change the banana regime, but never to the extent that it could satisfy all the parties involved. The United States could not act until the Marrakesh Agreement of 1994 was agreed, as this established the GATS, which opened an appeal to the WTO on bananas.

On 5 February 1996, the United States and four Latin American countries requested consultations with the EU. It was the beginning of a long dispute resolution process under the WTO, involving 40 member countries. The complainants argued that the EU's preferential treatment regime towards African, Caribbean and Pacific (ACP) countries was inconsistent with the GATT 1994, the Agreement on Import Licensing Procedures, the Agreement on Agriculture, the GATS and the TRIMs Agreement.

In 1993, as a result of the single market measures, the EU had adopted Council Regulation 404/93 to replace a previous system in which all countries, with the exception of ACP countries, faced a 20 per cent *ad valorem*. The new regulation imposed tariffs and quotas for non ACP importers. This preferential system dated back to 1975 when the First Lomé Convention (previously called the Yaoundé Convention) was signed. The convention is a trade and aid agreement and constitutes one of the largest development programmes of the EC. In 1989, the EC and 68 ACP countries signed the Fourth Lomé Convention, which, like its predecessors, contained a Banana Protocol. The Banana Protocol stated that 'no ACP State shall be placed, as regards access to its traditional markets and its advantages on those markets, in a less favourable situation than in the past or at present'. In December 1994, a waiver was granted allowing the EU to forgo its obligations under GATT 'as required by the relevant provisions of the Fourth Lomé Convention' until 29 February 2000.

The United States and its Latin American partners disputed the legality of the new regulation and the interpretation of the Lomé waiver. Their distribution system had allocated licensed rights to import and effectively guaranteed these rights to a handful of domestic distributors, such as Fyffes from Britain.

Europe is acting to protect one of its most important international development programmes but is also protecting the interests of domestic distributors through its licensing system. The system provides income to EU farmers and keeps quota rents in the EU. However, the net effect of the licensing system in the EU is uncertain and possibly negative. Not only are consumers faced with high prices, but their administrations are burdened with a costly bureaucratic process.

The EU amended its banana regime as a result of the first and second panel findings but never fully complied. This prompted the United States to impose sanctions of $191.4m on nine products, including lithographs (UK), batteries (UK), bath preparations (UK), handbags (France and Italy) and coffee and tea makers (Germany). At one stage Britain was targeted (as a key interest in the EU) and the Scottish cashmere industry was threatened. When Prime Minister Blair supported President Clinton in the Kosovo conflict with Serbia in spring 1999, the cashmere industry was promptly dropped from the US list.

Beef: the Strategic Issues

A dispute between the United States and the European Union over hormone-treated beef turned into a trade war when the EU failed to comply with the findings of the WTO's dispute settlement body. In 1996, the EU consolidated a series of regulations that prohibited the use of six hormones for growth promotion purposes, claiming that these were hazardous to human health. Two panels found against the EU. But, to date, no changes have been made to its regulations. EU citizens support the European Parliament in what appears to be a health and safety regulation.

Six hormones are under dispute: three natural (oestradiol-17β, testosterone and progesterone) and three synthetic (zeranol, trenbolone and MGA); these mimic the natural hormones. They can be used to influence growth and gestation of cattle. Scientists agree that very large intakes of these hormones are carcinogenic; however, there is no conclusive proof that the small levels administered under WHO/FAO international standards pose any serious threat to human health. Scientists disagree on the effects of prolonged exposure to small doses. The lack of information available at this time and the level of scientific uncertainty allow the EU to defend its policy under the precautionary principle.

Whether the EU is motivated by health and safety concerns or is attempting to disguise a trade barrier is not clear. The EU common agricultural policy is a well known subsidy to farmers but it has not been challenged as a trade barrier; this makes other agricultural practices more vulnerable to actions. Prior to the EU beef regulation, there was a beef surplus in the EU that was discussed during proceedings to ban hormones beginning in the early 1980s. Yet there has been no significant change in total imports of beef products to the EU since the 1970s. Instead, imports shifted from hormone-treated beef to hormone-free beef. A large decline in US exports to the EU is mainly attributed to the country's reliance on growth promoting substances. Ninety per cent of US beef is hormone treated.

Beef: the Legal Issues

Proceedings under the WTO were subject to controversy. The first panel found that the EU had not followed a proper risk assessment and that it must change its regulations and allow imports of hormone-treated beef. While the first and second panels found for the United States, the integrity of the first panel was called into question by the second panel. The good faith of the panel was questioned because testimony by scientists was intentionally misquoted and misinterpreted by the panel. The second panel also overturned the finding that human error and negligence should not be considered when assessing risk. It allowed the EU a period of grace to investigate further the effects of beef hormones on human health.

The EU produced a study of beef products that showed that US regulations on the use of hormones were frequently ignored by cattle ranchers. It also commented on the easy availability of these hormones. The EU did not change its regulations and the United States threatened to retaliate with $202 million in tariffs. The EU argued that the United States was inflating the damage caused by the ban. In July 1999, arbitration by the WTO set the amount of damage to the US cattle industry at $116.8 million.

Foreign Sales Corporations: the Strategic Issues

The United States has appealed against a 1999 decision by the WTO that its foreign sales corporations tax scheme is an illegal export subsidy. Foreign sales corporations are offshore subsidiaries of large US corporations, mostly located in tax havens such as the US Virgin Islands and the former British colony of Barbados. They carry out export transactions on behalf of their parent corporation. Fifteen per cent of a foreign sales corporation's profits are exempted from corporate income tax by the United States, adding up to US$2 billion in tax relief. The EU challenged this on the grounds that the tax scheme was directly tied to exports and was therefore an export subsidy that provided an unfair advantage to US corporations.

Boeing, General Motors, Eastman Kodak, Microsoft and Caterpillar are just a few US corporations to benefit from the scheme. US affiliates of foreign corporations, such as Daimler-Chrysler, can also claim tax relief. They set up a skeleton company in a tax haven to fill the requirements for a foreign sales corporation. There are 3600 corporations located in the US Virgin Islands and in Barbados with only a few dozen employees processing invoices.

Originally, for a foreign sales corporation to be able to claim tax exemptions on its profits, the goods had to be 50 per cent manufactured in the United States. This is still the case, but under a new clause in the Taxpayer Relief Act of 1997, software makers can ship master tapes overseas, make copies, and use their foreign sales corporations to receive a tax subsidy (Barlett and Steele, 1998). Movie makers already enjoyed these benefits. Ultimately, this clause creates jobs in overseas countries while increasing the net profit of US corporations.

Manufacturing industries are the largest sector benefiting from foreign sales corporations. Non-electrical machinery, chemicals, electrical machinery and transportation equipment accounted for a large part of total foreign sales corporations relief. Most industries, including manufacturing, must prove that goods funnelled through a foreign sales corporation have 50 per cent domestic content. Theoretically, this should increase the export performance and thus the international competitiveness of US-made goods. Domestic content should increase, at least to some degree, the amount of manufacturing in the US economy.

Critics of the scheme in the United States call it a corporate welfare system paid at the expense of taxpayers. Large MNEs reap most of the benefits. These are already well established exporters which would export anyway. It is argued that the tax relief puts US-based corporations, which have the largest stake in foreign sales corporations, on a better footing than international competitors. It targets particular industries and is therefore vulnerable to GATT/WTO sanctions which can affect subsidies not generally available to all industries.

Whether or not exports increase as a direct result of tax relief, Boeing is several million dollars better off every year than it would be without a foreign sales corporation. This money can be used to expand R&D, marketing or to undertake large capital investments. US companies are thereby better prepared to fight in the international arena, and to protect their own market from exports. The foreign sales corporations also provide an incentive for foreign companies to set up affiliates in the United States by decreasing the amount of corporate taxes that they would have had to pay otherwise.

Foreign Sales Corporations: the Legal Issues

In 1997 the EC held consultations with the United States regarding foreign sales corporations. Mutual agreement was not reached and the EC requested a WTO panel. In 1999, the panel decided that foreign sales corporations were an export subsidy directly related to export performance. Foreign sales corporations were found to be inconsistent with the obligations of the United States to the WTO, and the GATT's agreement on agriculture. The panel recommended that the United States withdraw the foreign sales corporation subsidies by 1 October 2000 (WTO, 1999).

The United States will appeal. If it loses the appeal, one alternative would be to withdraw the alleged subsidies from its key industries. Another option would be to keep the Domestic International Sales Corporation (DISC) scheme and accept EU retaliation, which could aggregate to as much as US$6 billion. This case will test the authority of the WTO and the consequences could be far reaching: the end of globalization and a new regionalism.

NGOs AND THE WTO

Globalization is at an end as there is no integrated world market. Instead, there are strong 'triad' blocks in which nation states still make the rules, imposing regulations such as environmental and health codes. The non-governmental organizations (NGOs) have challenged the MNEs as witnessed by the defeat of the Multilateral Agreement on Investment (MAI). The new agenda of NGOs and some governments is one of criticism of business and their perception of globalization. This is actually a false perception, but it has still led to major difficulties for the WTO and the other international institutions fostering trade liberalization and economic prosperity.

Internet Anarchy

Even before the Seattle WTO riots of December 1999, a widely reported example of the organizational capabilities of NGOs occurred on Friday 18 June 1999, when a mass demonstration disrupted the City of London. It was organized via an Internet site, J18, which coordinated the separate activities of groups of NGOs. The more radical of these received most of the media attention as the peaceful demonstration planned to coincide with the G7 Summit in Cologne turned into a full-scale riot. The major targets were two McDonald's restaurants, which were trashed, and the London International Financial Futures (and Options) Exchange, which was invaded.

According to press reports, a handful of young radical extremists organized much of the demonstration, which attracted more than 2000 people. A group called Reclaim the Streets (RTS) and a Cambridge chapter of People's Global Action (PGA) were prominent. These groups were able to promote the demonstration by using Internet sites to publish maps and details of London's financial institutions. On the day they provided leaders to incite groups to attack property and the police.

Radical groups such as these do not appear to differ in any marked manner from the student activist groups of the late 1960s, who organized sit-ins and demonstrations at leading universities from Berkeley to Columbia to LSE. If anything, the number of core activists appears to be far fewer. But today they can use Internet sites to gain worldwide attention. Previous generations of anarchists spread their ideas via the underground press and small circulation magazines and broadsheets; the current generation can tap into a potentially broader stream of support by using new technology.

One of the disadvantages of fast global communications via the Internet is that small activist groups can disseminate propaganda quickly and easily. The Internet has no quality control mechanism; junk sites and politically networked ones count equally with commercial and academic sites. There is no screening mechanism such as is provided by the mainstream media, where extremist views would find little space or airtime. The Internet taxes knowledge to subsidize anarchy. The anti-capitalist agenda is the same; only the communication medium has changed.

This street theatre was repeated, on a massive scale, in Seattle in early December 1999. The protectionist US labour unions were also present, wrongly seeing the WTO as an agent of free trade, leading to a coalition of labour, moderate and extreme NGOs. Unfortunately, the potentially legitimate concerns of labour and the moderate NGOs, such as OXFAM and WWF, are swamped by the extreme views of some NGOs and their supporters who seem to believe in anarchy and civil disobedience. This promotes a backlash against all NGOs and it serves to discredit their agendas. Until the more responsible NGOs either start to discipline their extreme members, or they disassociate themselves from street violence, the NGOs will not carry public opinion. In any case, the Seattle coalition has not been successfully put together in subsequent events, for example in demonstrations in London in May 2000 and in Washington DC against the role of the IMF and World Bank. On both occasions the more extreme NGOs received bad media coverage which concentrated on the confrontations with police and the damage to public monuments, such as Churchill's statue in Westminster, and not on the message of the NGOs. Indeed, the message seems to have been distorted to that of a simplistic anti-global capitalism rant rather than to any agenda of substance.

Ostry (forthcoming) has made a useful distinction between two groups of NGOs. The ones who engage in street theatre, she calls the 'mobilization NGOs'. These are really outsiders who criticize global capitalism and believe in the destruction of the major international institutions which promote free trade, such as the WTO, IMF and World Bank. Their agenda is protest and anarchy. These groups mobilize for specific events, such as the Seattle WTO meetings, or for protests at the annual meetings of the IMF. They include the PGA, the International Civil Society (ICS), N30 and the J18 group discussed earlier, which organized the June 1999 London protests.

Second, is a group of 'technical NGOs'. These are insiders, who will work with the international institutions in an attempt to improve the process and meet their essentially redistributive goals. Technical NGOs include OXFAM, WWF, the Third World Network and various environmental groups. Unfortunately, the WTO has not distinguished between these two groups. At Seattle some 600 NGOs were accredited, including the first group who use Internet anarchy. The technical NGOs have made the mistake of participating in major protest actions organized by the mobilization NGOs. It was felt that a coalition of all NGOs would have more impact. It did. It generated a negative backlash against the violence and extreme anarchistic behaviour of a few extremist NGOs, which now threatens the agenda of the technical NGOs. As an alternative, lessons can be learned from the successful NAFTA-generated cooperation of environmental NGOs with business and government in raising environmental standards and practices in Mexico (Rugman, Kirton and Soloway, 1999).

The Power of NGOs

The NGOs are new powerful actors on the stage of international business. From 1997 to 1998, they assumed a more effective role than before, which led to the defeat of the OECD's Multilateral Agreement on Investment (MAI). Canada's self-promoting Council of Canadians, chaired by economic nationalist Maude Barlow, was prominent in orchestrating the NGOs. In a clever campaign of misinformation and half truths, exhibited in the Clarke and Barlow propaganda booklet on the MAI (Clarke and Barlow 1997), the Council filled the websites of NGOs with anti-MAI hysteria which then influenced the media.

With the US and Canadian governments treating the MAI on a technical rather than political level, and ministers being poorly briefed by second-rate trade bureaucrats, there was little political will to counter the gross distortion offered by unelected and unaccountable NGOs. Business leaders were unwilling to speak out on the MAI's advantages, leaving its defence to a handful of industry association spokespeople. Finally, the academic world – with a few exceptions – had not researched the issue (this being especially true of economists who have no parallel theory of free trade to apply to liberalization of investment). Consequently, almost none were available or willing to debate the substantive issues of the MAI in public, while engaged in their full-time professional duties. The absence of informed government, business and academic commentary left the media open to the distorted propaganda of unrepresentative NGOs.

The NGOs' success in defeating the MAI built upon their less spectacular but consistent progress in capturing the environmental agenda of international organizations. The first notable success of environmental NGOs (entirely US and Canadian) occurred in the NAFTA when the first Clinton administration in 1993 made the mistake of inserting two side agreements, after NAFTA had been successfully negotiated over the 1990–1992 period by the Bush administration. These side agreements set up an environmental body, the Commission on Environmental Cooperation (CEC) in Montreal, and a labour standards body in Dallas.[1]

The UNCTAD Rio Earth Summit of 1993 was a jamboree for environmental NGOs, leading to an unbalanced agreement with sets of commitments

which the governments concerned were unable to meet. Despite these les-
sons, the Kyoto Summit in December 1997 resulted in standards for reduction
of greenhouse gas emissions that, again, most countries will not meet.
Ratification of the Kyoto protocol is unlikely, since the United States,
Canada, Japan and many other countries are unlikely to sign it – only the
EU appears to have the political will. In Canada's case, this is due to its
federal nature; the provinces have the power to control natural resources.
So Alberta, the largest energy-producing province, will need to agree to
implement Kyoto in order for the government of Canada to recognize the
treaty.

Analysis of the Role of NGOs

This brief description of recent events portrays a gulf between the self-
serving agendas of NGOs and the economic reality of global business. What
analysis can be used to explain this dichotomy? Two theories will be considered. First, there is a traditional division between the redistributional/equity
concerns of NGOs and the economic/efficiency drivers of business. Political
parties in the West have taken these dual concerns into account when formulating policies, allowing voters to decide which direction to follow. Recently,
this has not worked, since NGOs are operating outside democratic political
representation.

Second, complementary to the undemocratic nature of NGOs, especially
in their biased understanding of international trade and investment, is an
intellectual failure of academic theory. The twin basic paradigms of economics and politics are found wanting as explanations of today's global
economy and the nature of foreign direct investment. In economics, the
traditional efficiency-based neoclassical paradigm (with its associated theory
of comparative advantages and the overall country gains from free trade) is
unsuitable as an explanation of FDI. Despite the efforts of international
business writers over the last 30 years to develop a modern theory of the
multinational enterprise, most economists are unable to take on board this
literature on the reasons for FDI (Rugman, 1996). Meanwhile the GATT
and WTO have developed institutional frameworks to deal with the 'shallow' integration of tariff cuts, but have failed to deal with the 'deep'
integration of FDI.

The political science focus on the nation state is related to the out-of-date
economics paradigm of free trade. Despite minor modifications to nation
state paradigms, such as incorporating subnational units in decision making,
there is limited buy-in to the alternative International Political Economy
(IPE) viewpoint first popularized by Susan Strange (1988). Indeed, there is
another unfortunate parallel between economics and political science, in that

work on the role and power of the MNE has failed to change the out-of-date thinking of the majority of academics. This is despite abundant evidence of the relevance of MNEs to today's global economic and political systems. The NGOs have slipped into this vacuum with their simplistic view of MNEs as big, bad and ugly. Based on prejudice rather than evidence, NGO thinking is now more influential with governments in North America and Europe than the more scientific (and thereby more qualified) work of serious academic scholars working on MNEs (Ostry, 1997).

The issue here is one of process. There is an 'administrative heritage' of ideas. Today's journalists and other communicators are poorly trained in economics, politics and international business. Those few who have any training are usually victims of the paradigms of traditional economics and political science, which cannot explain FDI and the MNEs. Business school MBAs, who are now exposed to the new thinking on MNEs, are in business rather than the media. Professional intermediaries, such as management consultants, focus on their business or government clients rather than the media and their skills of confidential advice and in-house retraining make them poor advocates compared with the pessimistic and opinionated NGOs. Finally, the civil service is totally useless in dealing publicly with NGOs, since the role of bureaucrats is to support and influence ministers, not to enter the public forum. This institutional failure of academics, consultants and bureaucrats to prepare a credible case for the MAI and debate it publicly leaves the field open to NGOs.

Although the NGOs can be credited with the delay of the Seattle Round of the WTO, the real reason for its delay lies elsewhere. Even given the high profile activities of NGOs, the WTO would still probably have been started if one country had got its act together. That country was, of course, the United States. The real explanation for the delay of the WTO is the right of the US Congress to pass trade laws, and the corresponding lack of presidential power to negotiate international trade and investment treaties. The President's failure to obtain 'fast track' negotiating authority from Congress in his second term (for a free trade area of the Americas, but also for a future round of the WTO, and for an MAI) was the single most important reason for the WTO's delay. The NGOs then stepped into the vacuum and stole the agenda.

Trade and investment agreements have little hope of success without the full commitment of the United States to champion them. This is demonstrated by the WTO process. All countries are lobbied by various producer groups to protect certain sectors. The full participation of the United States is vital to broker an international agreement, as it is still the only country powerful enough to pull along other countries rife with internal dissent and sectional interests. Yet although President Clinton pushed through NAFTA in

1993, he was subsequently unable to assemble a coalition to follow any free trade and investment liberalization initiatives. The future of the WTO is undoubtedly linked to the success of the new US President to obtain fast track authority for a new round, and for him to provide leadership in moving the trade liberalization agenda forward once again.

CONCLUSIONS

The major triad-based trade disputes illustrate that the WTO is in trouble and it may well fail for three reasons:

First, it is a technical body, lacking in political power and even political understanding. It was successful for 51 years in dealing with a technical series of tariff cuts, but it is not equipped to deal with the new agenda of international trade and investment liberalization. Tariff cuts have allowed 'shallow' integration across many manufacturing sectors (but not in agriculture and textiles). Today's agenda, set by multinational enterprises engaging in foreign direct investment, is one of 'deep' integration. Here the issue is how to make domestic markets internationally contestable. This involves negotiating the role of government in society – a hopeless task for the WTO secretariat with its small staff of professionals in Geneva. The WTO is not designed to deal with non trade and investment issues such as environmental regulations, labour standards and human rights. These only come onto its agenda as indirect, technical matters in trade disputes. These 'big issues' are better handled in different international forums, for example human rights at the United Nations, labour standards at the International Labour Organization and environmental regulations at a new world environmental agency. But these issues are well beyond the capacity of the WTO to address, let alone resolve.

Second, the WTO may fail because its acute lack of political skill led it to make the dreadful mistake of giving standing to non-governmental organizations at the abortive Seattle Millennium Round of December 1999. For the WTO to succeed it must only work with governments, as it was designed to do. This is what the GATT did. The members of the GATT/WTO are nations, not firms, nor NGOs. Each country government negotiates on behalf of its businesses and NGOs. Throughout its existence the GATT has refused even to hear representations from business groups, MNEs or individuals. Now the WTO has given the NGOs a platform. So the NGOs can have two bites of the cherry; first they can lobby their home governments, then they can lobby the WTO (which is representing their governments again).

Multilateralism is being killed by the presence of NGOs at the WTO. The agent of multilateralism, the WTO, has always been a small, weak technocratic body. If it talks directly to NGOs, it cannot begin to function as a facilitator for governments to consider issues of deep integration. NGOs must be banished from such multilateral forums. They should be briefed by their home governments, just as the business sector is. Neither business groups nor other NGOs should be present at future meetings of the WTO. They should lobby their home governments and live with the results of government to government bargaining at the WTO.

Third, the catalyst for the ultimate failure of the WTO may, somewhat paradoxically, be a technical decision. The United States has lost a case to the EU involving export subsidies paid for many years by the US Domestic International Sales Corporation (DISC). The potential scale of retaliation by the EU against the United States runs into several billions of US dollars. In contrast, the 'wins' by the United States against the EU on the bananas and beef hormones cases were both under US$200 million. The vast scale of potential EU retaliation could cause a firestorm of protest in the US Congress and even lead to the withdrawal of the United States from the WTO. This could be achieved by a simple majority vote in the US Senate, based on the Dole Amendment of 1994. At that time, Senator Dole, as leader of the Senate majority Republican Party, convinced the Senate to pass and implement the GATT Marrakesh Agreement, subject to the ability of the Congress to revisit it in the future. One trigger for revisiting the Marrakesh Agreement (which established the WTO) is the loss of three US appeals at the WTO. This threshold has already been reached.

In the inward-looking presidential campaign of 2000, with major congressional elections also taking place, the United States was poised to turn its back on multilateralism and embrace economic isolation again. A trade war with the EU, over DISC sanctions, coupled with the ongoing US current account deficit with Japan (the other triad power) could open the doors for US protectionism to emerge. The US advocacy of free trade, and its advancement of national treatment for foreign investment, has always been fragile, with the executive branch office at odds with the more protectionist Congress. The approval of NAFTA in October 1993 by the first Clinton administration was the last case of 'first track' authority and, in retrospect, the end of US leadership in trade liberalization. The MAI failed at the OECD in Paris partly because of a lack of US commitment.

As the United States retreats from the global stage, the NGOs take its place. Many of these NGOs, especially the environmental ones, are US-based and funded. Most of the others are from Canada and Western Europe. They represent sectional interests in the rich countries. The NGOs' anti-business activities are fundamentally opposed to the economic interests of poorer countries. The NGOs, by reversing the benefits of multilateralism and free trade, are hindering the economic development of poorer Asian,

African and emerging countries. Their anti-business activities are profoundly illogical.

NGO activities, the possible withdrawal of the United States from the WTO, its lack of commitment to free trade, and the dissolution of the post-war consensus about the virtues of free trade will lead to the end of globalization. But globalization was a myth anyway. Economic and business activities have been organized in the triad/regions, as is demonstrated empirically in Rugman (2000), Chapters 6, 7 and 8.

NOTE

1. For discussion of the political process in the United States at the time of approval of NAFTA see Susan Liebler in Rugman (1994).

REFERENCES

Adams, David (1999), 'America's complex links with banana republics', *The Times*, 15 March.
Barlett, Donald L. and James B. Steele (1999), 'Special Report: Corporate Welfare', *Time.com*, 16 November.
Clarke, Tony and Maude Barlow (1997), *MAI: The Multilateral Agreement on Investment and the Threat to Canadian Sovereignty*, Toronto: Stoddart.
Feketekuty, Geza and Bruce Stokes (1998) (eds), *Trade Strategies for a New Era: Ensuring US Leadership in a Global Economy*, New York: Council on Foreign Relations.
Hoekman, Bernard and Michel Kostecki (1996), *The WTO in the International Political Economy*, Oxford: Oxford University Press.
Khan, Shahrukh Rafi (1999), *Do World Bank and IMF Policies Work?*, London: Macmillan.
Ostry, Sylvia (1997), *The Post-Cold War Trading System: Who's on First?*, Chicago and London: University of Chicago Press.
Ostry, Sylvia (forthcoming), 'The multilateral trading system', in Alan M. Rugman and Thomas Brewer (eds), *The Oxford Handbook of International Business*, Oxford: Oxford University Press.
Rugman, Alan M. (1996), *Multinational Enterprises and Trade Policy*, Cheltenham, UK and Brookfield, US: Edward Elgar.
Rugman, Alan M. (1999) (ed.), *Foreign Investment and NAFTA*, Columbia, S.C., University of South Carolina Press.
Rugman, Alan M. (2000), *The End of Globalization*, London: Random House. (Also to be published in 2001 by AMACON/McGraw Hill.)
Rugman, Alan M., John Kirton and Julie Soloway (1999), *Environmental Regulations and Corporate Strategy: A NAFTA Perspective*, Oxford: Oxford University Press.
Strange, Susan (1988), *States and Markets: An Introduction to International Political Economy*, London: Pinter.
World Trade Organization (1997), *European Communities – Regime for the Importa-*

tion, Sale and Distribution of Bananas – Complaint by Ecuador, Report of the Panel, WT/DS27/RW/ECU, 22 May 1997.

World Trade Organization (1998), *Focus*, October and November.

World Trade Organization (1999), *European Communities – Regime for the Importation, Sale and Distribution of Bananas – Recourse to Article 21.5 by Ecuador*, WT/DS27/RW/ECU, 12 April 1999.

F13 K33

2. Institutional development of the WTO

Gilbert Winham and Anna Lanoszka

---

1 THE WTO AS AN INTERNATIONAL ORGANIZATION

The World Trade Organization (WTO) came into existence on 1 January 1995. It was created as part of the results of the Uruguay Round of multilateral trade negotiations concluded on 15 December 1993, and adopted on 15 April 1994 by the ministers of 124 governments and the European Communities in a meeting held at Marrakesh, Morocco. The WTO is the first international organization of universal character to be created following the end of the Cold War, and it completed the third pillar of the post-war international economic architecture that was begun at Bretton Woods in 1944. Unlike the General Agreement on Tariffs and Trade (GATT), the WTO is invested with a legal personality and organizational presence arguably equivalent to the International Monetary Fund (IMF) or World Bank.

The WTO was adopted along with a series of far-reaching trade agreements covering, among other things, agriculture, services, trade rules, industrial tariffs and intellectual property. These agreements have the potential to strengthen substantially the rules-based nature of the trade regime.[1] The depth of the new regime, and its historical importance, can be found in a WTO clause described as a 'sleeper' by trade lawyer and negotiator Alan Wolff.[2] It reads: 'Each Member shall ensure the conformity of its laws, regulations and administrative procedures with its obligations as provided in the annexed Agreements.'[3] This clause, plus the depth of the annexed agreements, indicates how much nation states are substituting international policymaking for unilateral domestic policymaking in one of the most important relationships countries have with one another.

The WTO is an unusual international organization. Most international organizations, in the words of Harold Jacobson, are 'institutional structure(s) created by agreement among two or more sovereign states for the conduct of regular political interactions'.[4] They have specified procedures for making decisions in the name of the collectivity, and in large international organizations decisions are often made by limited membership councils that '...contravene the doctrine of sovereign equality'.[5] The WTO presents the appearance of an ordinary international organization, but according to the representative of one of its leading Member states, it is different from other such organizations. As stated by US Trade Representative Mickey Kantor: 'Some will liken [the WTO] to other international institutions. This is a contract organization, not a charter organization. It does not operate the way in which other international organizations have operated, neither by history nor by what we've agreed to under the Uruguay Round.'[6]

The purpose of this chapter is to examine the legal structure of the WTO, and to analyse the institution that has developed from that structure. Organizational tasks, decision-making processes, political relations between national players, and organization culture will be featured in this analysis. The chapter will conclude with an assessment of the contribution the WTO can make to problems of international cooperation in the international economy.

1.1   Nature of the WTO

The WTO is an incremental change from the previously existing GATT system. Whether it was needed or not was subject to negotiation, and, after the fact, how much change it represents from the GATT is subject to interpretation. Also subject to interpretation are the different aspects of the WTO system, particularly whether certain elements, such as dispute settlement, might have been achieved without creating a new formal international organization. As with negotiations generally, the parties to the Uruguay Round interpreted the WTO in a manner consistent with their positions during the negotiation.

The principal results of the Uruguay Round were a two-page Final Act[7] that incorporated the WTO Agreement,[8] which in turn contained an Annex 1 that included specific agreements related to goods, services and intellectual property,[9] and an Annex 2 which was a lengthy agreement on dispute settlement.[10] There were additionally two Annexes, a series of separate Ministerial decisions and declarations, and an understanding on financial services. Most of the subjects that are commonly associated with the Uruguay Round negotiation, ranging from agriculture and textiles, to services, anti-dumping rules and intellectual property, are contained in the various annexes included under, but separate from, the WTO Agreement.[11]

What is usually thought of as the 'WTO system' is contained in the agreements on the WTO and on dispute settlement. Both were negotiated concurrently in the Institutions Group under Chairman Julio Lecarte-Moro of Uruguay, and trade-offs were established across both areas. In the end the dispute settlement system was agreed to apply to all areas of the negotiation (itself a considerable concession by developing countries), which confirmed its inclusion as part of the architecture of the new trade system.

The most important aspects of the WTO system can be summarized by reference to six elements drawn from the WTO Agreement and four elements drawn from the dispute settlement understanding (DSU). First, the WTO Agreement provided explicitly for the establishment of a new organization.[12] In political terms this created a symbolic visibility and permanence for the international trade policy system that would not have occurred had the Uruguay Round results been promulgated simply as a series of agreements within the GATT context.[13] The symbolic value of creating a new institution was not lost on former GATT Director General Peter Sutherland, who characterized the WTO as the 'crowning achievement' of the Uruguay Round negotiation.[14]

Second, the WTO Agreement stated that the WTO should be the 'common institutional framework for the conduct of trade relations among its Members' relating to the Uruguay Round Agreements (Article II), and that it should '...facilitate the implementation, administration and operation...' of the agreements (Article III). These articles centralized and focused the responsibility for governance of the international trade system far more than that which occurred under the GATT. In comparison to the WTO, the GATT 'system' by the 1990s was rapidly becoming a pot-pourri of decentralized separate agreements, with different and sometimes inconsistent dispute settlement arrangements, and with differing country signatories.

Third, the Agreement provided the WTO with legal personality (Article VIII), which elevated the WTO in relation to the Bretton Woods organizations. In the jargon adopted during the Uruguay Round negotiation, this upgrading of the WTO over the GATT was claimed to promote greater 'coherence' of international economic policy, particularly because it raised the trade concern to the same international decision-making level as the monetary and development concerns.

Fourth, the WTO Agreement stated that acceptance of the Agreement '...shall apply to this Agreement and the Multilateral Trade Agreements annexed hereto'.[15] This provision incorporated the fundamental concept of 'single undertaking' that crystallized as a major negotiated commitment by all parties (especially developing countries) during the Uruguay Round. It meant that parties to the negotiation were not free to pick and choose among the various agreements under discussion, but were obliged to accept the agreements as a package deal. This commitment guaranteed that trade-offs would be made in arriving at final offers. Without this commitment, the Uruguay Round would have been moribund.

Fifth, as noted earlier, the Agreement provided for the implementation of the Uruguay Round agreements into domestic legislation.[16] Sixth, it provided for institutional structure and decision making procedures for the new organization. Regarding the first point, in Article IV there was a relatively uncontroversial creation of separate councils for the separate sections of the final agreement, which mainly provided for greater complexity of organizational structure to match the greater complexity of subject matter in the agreements. On the second, the WTO Agreement called for a continuation of the GATT practice of decision making by consensus, but it also explicitly allowed for voting in certain circumstances where consensus cannot be reached.[17] The voting provisions of the WTO Agreement were controversial, and US Congressmen among others claimed this represented a serious derogation of national sovereignty. The response was that the GATT had similar provisions for voting in the case of the '...contracting parties acting jointly...',[18] despite the fact that decisions were reached by consensus in practice. This dispute was one of perception, and was never reconciled during the implementation phase of the Uruguay Round agreements.

Turning to the Dispute Settlement Understanding (DSU), the first important provision deals with the adoption by the relevant body of the WTO (the Dispute Settlement Body (DSB)) of a report by a dispute settlement panel. In the GATT, the requirement for adoption was consensus, which meant a losing party to a panel decision could block a report from going forward. This arrangement was consistent with national sovereignty, and with a 'pragmatic' approach to international trade law that sees GATT law as an instrument of diplomacy.[19] The DSU reversed this principle by requiring that a report be adopted unless '...the DSB decides by consensus not to adopt the report'.[20] This means that '...dispute resolution decisions will be formally binding on WTO signatory states unless the winner of the case can be persuaded to vote to overrule its own victory'.[21] This represents a stunning shift from the 'pragmatic' conception of GATT/WTO law to a 'legalistic' conception, and it is probably the most far-reaching of the various changes introduced by the WTO system.

Second, the DSU established a standing Appellate Body within the WTO and provided for formal appeals from Panel cases under Article 17. The Appellate Body is a permanent commercial court consisting of seven members that will oversee dispute settlement arising in any of the various agreements under the WTO system. According to Article 17:6, the scope of appeal of the Appellate Body is to be '...limited to issues of law covered in the panel report and legal interpretations developed by the panel', but this standard will give the Body wide-ranging authority to apply agreements that in many cases are imprecise and leave a lot to subsequent interpretation.

The creation of the Appellate Body was a consequence of the increasing legalism of GATT/WTO dispute settlement practice. With the increased obligation to adopt and comply with Panel reports, governments became more concerned about the possibility that an individual Panel might produce an erroneous decision, leaving non-compliance as the only recourse to the aggrieved party. The Appellate Body was seen as a safeguard against legal error, as well as an opportunity to build case law that might further promote the development of a rules-based trade regime.

Third, the coverage of the DSU was a difficult problem in the Uruguay Round negotiation. At issue was whether the dispute settlement system would be 'integrated' and thus apply to all areas of the Uruguay Round accords, or whether a separate system would be constructed for disputes in goods, services and intellectual property. Developing countries maintained that an integrated system would allow for cross-retaliation, that is, for compensation for non-compliance with a Panel's report in one area (for example, intellectual property) to be awarded in another area (for example, textiles). Cross-retaliation would therefore allow developed countries to put increased pressure on developing countries in new trade areas by threatening to remove concessions on traditional goods where developing countries had a comparative advantage. This issue was resolved in favour of establishing an integrated system (Article 1), which will have a unifying effect on the overall WTO system and will eliminate the tendency to 'forum-shop', which occurs when multiple avenues to dispute settlement are available.

Fourth, the DSU included a provision in Article 23:2(a) that Members shall '...not make a determination to the effect that a violation [of WTO obligations by another Member] has occurred ... except through recourse to dispute settlement in accordance with the rules and procedures of this Understanding...'. This clause was the result of concerted efforts by the European Union and most other WTO Members to discipline the use of unilateral measures as represented by section 301 actions by the United States. The United States accepted this arrangement as part of a trade-off with the European Union reached at the time of the completion of the Draft Final Act in December 1993,[22] which saw the EU drop its historic objection to the automatic adoption of GATT panels and accept the equally long-standing US aspiration to strengthen the GATT dispute settlement system. In this trade-off the two superpowers in the Uruguay Round negotiation both accepted constraints on unilateral action in favour of a more effective system of multilateral agreement and compliance.

1.2 Organizational Behaviour of the WTO

The WTO is mainly a formally contracted body of rules backed up by a judicial system and a minimum of political structure. The GATT – which was essentially a contract between Parties – had provided for the possibility of joint action by the Parties, but in itemizing those actions, such as approvals of accessions or waivers of obligations, the General Agreement only made reference to the 'Contracting Parties'. By contrast, the WTO Agreement outlines specific functions to be taken by the WTO as a collective body.[23] These are: (i) to implement and administer the Uruguay Round agreements, (ii) to provide a forum for further negotiations, (iii) to administer dispute settlement, (iv) to administer the Trade Policy Review Mechanism (TPRM), and (v) to liaise with the IMF and World Bank. With the possible exception of the last item, these functions had accreted to the GATT on an informal and customary basis.

The principal structures created to carry out the functions of the WTO include a Ministerial Conference meeting every two years; a General Council, which can also meet as a DSB and a Trade Policy Review Body; and three councils in the areas of goods, services and intellectual property respectively. Sundry other organs are mandated in the WTO Agreement, such as the Committee on Trade and Development, and then additional bodies can be created by the Ministerial Conference as it deems necessary.

The WTO continued the customary practice of the GATT of decision making by consensus. Consensus is deemed to exist 'if no Member, present at the meeting when the decision is taken, formally objects to the proposed decision'.[24] Consensus is not unanimity, and it is clear that the legal definition – as well as past and current practice – allows for the possibility of cooperative behaviour even when Members disagree on the issues. Consistent with the requirement for consensus, the organs of the WTO are plenary and all Members are able to participate. The only bodies where plenary participation is not mandated are specialized organs, such as the Textiles Monitoring Board or plurilateral committees, or the organs associated with the dispute settlement process, such as Panels or the Appellate Body.

The WTO Agreement provides for a Secretariat, which in the GATT had developed on an informal and customary basis. The WTO Secretariat is arguably small in relation to the tasks it is expected to undertake, and it certainly is small in comparison to other international economic organizations. Blackhurst gives a figure of 513 for the number of WTO staff in 1996; comparable figures for the World Bank and the International Monetary Fund were 6781 and 2577 respectively.[25] Indeed, the WTO numbers were exceeded by some 15 organizations in Blackhurst's study, including the UN Industrial Development Organization (1758) and the World Intellectual Property Organization (630).

The capacity of the WTO is augmented by the vigorous involvement of the Geneva delegations of the WTO Members, which helps to explain the small size of the Secretariat. The WTO is usually described as a 'member-driven' organization, meaning that Members and not the Secretariat are mainly responsible for carrying out the functions of the organization. In the important routine tasks of the organization – including accession of new Members, initiation of disputes or complaints, interpretation of WTO rules, judgements on waivers of obligations, or working parties on free trade areas – action can only be taken by officials from Member governments. To cover this workload, there were in 1997 some 97 Members with representation in Geneva, with an average of about five professionals per delegation.[26] These officials, plus their back-up support in home capitals, will slightly exceed the manpower available in the WTO Secretariat.

The tasks involved in running the WTO are reflected in its organizational structure. In terms of formal organization, there are 19 committees (including one sub-committee), seven working parties or working groups, and a fluctuating number of working parties on accessions, all of which in principle are plenary bodies. In addition, there are organs with limited membership, including the Textiles Monitoring Body, plurilateral committees, dispute settlement panels and the Appellate Body. Exceptionally and additionally, multilateral trade negotiations create further structure and tasks, and during the Tokyo and Uruguay Rounds a parallel structure under a Trade Negotiations Committee was struck to service those negotiations. Finally, there is an informal and fluid structure of consultation groups designed to bring 'like-minded' Members together to discuss issues of common concern. The work associated with the organs listed above is conducted mainly by the Members' Geneva delegations, with the assistance of staff provided from the Secretariat. It goes without saying that the frequency of meetings within the WTO is large and growing, and countries with small delegations are pressed to monitor, let alone direct, the activities of the organization.

A summary of the activities of the WTO since its inception in January 1995 can be found in the organization's newsletter *WTO Focus*. These activities include: (i) Ministerial Conferences (including Seattle); (ii) dispute settlement procedures; (iii) accessions of new Members; (iv) trade policy review studies; (v) ongoing monitoring and implementation activities; and finally (vi) new negotiations. The first five activities are discussed later in this chapter. The latter activity is examined here.

An important task of the WTO is to promote trade negotiations. The WTO Agreement specifically mandates the organization to 'provide a forum for negotiation' on matters arising under the Uruguay Round agreements, and on further issues concerning the multilateral trade relations of Members.[27] This mandate is more precise than that which had existed in the GATT, which simply stated that the Contracting Parties 'may ... sponsor ... negotiations from time to time'.[28] However, GATT practice became regularized over time on the matter of negotiations, and those negotiations proved their value in terms of forwarding the agenda of trade liberalization. Hence, the WTO Agreement effectively codified GATT customary practice, and built negotiation of new issues into the organizational mission of the WTO.

The WTO lost no time in exercising its mandate to sponsor negotiations. In the services negotiation, the Uruguay Round had concluded without scheduled commitments in financial or telecommunications services. These became subjects of further negotiation after 1995, and by 1997 Director General Renato Ruggiero was able to announce landmark agreements in both areas.[29] The telecom agreement produced access commitments from 69 governments covering 90 per cent of global telecom revenues, while the financial services agreement included 56 scheduled offers from 70 countries (counting the EU as 15 countries). Most important, the United States dropped its reservations on the most favoured nation issue, and participated in both agreements.

There was yet another negotiation concluded in 1997 that was novel and not a continuation of the Uruguay Round. In March 1997, 40 governments concluded the WTO Ministerial Declaration on Trade in Information Technology Products (ITA) that reduced tariffs on computer and telecommunications equipment. This agreement was conducted very quickly and it is significant because, joined with the Telecom agreement, it covers trade equal to that of agriculture, automobiles and textiles combined. The former agreements represent the 'new economy' in terms of commerce between nations, and it is clear that commerce is more liberalized than the old economy.

Further negotiations were mandated in services and agriculture by the Uruguay Round Agreement, and are normally referred to as the 'built-in' agenda for new multilateral negotiations commencing in 2000. These negotiations got underway following the failure of the Seattle Ministerial Meeting to establish a more complete agenda, and are continuing into 2001. To sum up, it appears – despite the setback of Seattle – that the WTO has successfully carried out its mandate to sponsor new negotiations. Over time, it appears that negotiation has become less an exceptional part of the GATT/WTO regime and more part of the normal business of multilateral trade relations. The WTO is moving toward a regime of 'permanent negotiation', in which the organization begins to look more like a typical national legislature and less like the occasional diplomatic encounters of international relations.

2   MAIN ISSUES IN WTO DEVELOPMENT

2.1   Developing Countries and the Implementation of Uruguay Round Agreements

The WTO aspires to ensure a fair and non-discriminatory treatment of the international trade transactions that are taking place among its 140 member states.[30] The organization is five years old and a crucial task is to integrate all its Members, big and small alike, into the WTO global trade rules, particularly since a majority of developing countries continue to experience difficulties with their implementation. Clearly, it was not enough for the international community to fashion a substantive legal code in the context of the WTO. It should also ensure competent techniques for the implementation of this code and equal participation of all Members in a globalizing economy. There is an array of mechanisms designed to monitor the implementation of the WTO code. It is, however, up to the individual country to ensure its compliance with the WTO rules.

The WTO has a clear organizational structure with special Committees responsible for monitoring the implementation of obligations for different fields of trade. The obligations are meant to be realistic commitments since they take into account the level of development, and the particular circumstances, of the Member. Thus obligations, or the time required for their implementation, may differ according to whether the Member is a least-developed country, a developed country or a transition economy. Special transitional periods have been given depending on a country's level of development. Furthermore, the WTO code takes into account the sovereign interests of its members by permitting exemptions in the applications of measures, for example, for reasons of health, public morals and national security.[31] There are also a number of measures in the code that allow for the imposition of trade restrictions in an emergency, for example, to alleviate a balance-of-payments disequilibrium.[32]

The critical enforcement mechanism under the WTO is its centralized dispute settlement mechanism that works on a principle of compulsory adjudication and permits retaliatory measures against the violating country. There are, however, various consultation requirements to resolve disputes or to facilitate their avoidance. One of the new institutional developments that has emerged from the Uruguay Round of negotiations is the focus on securing implementation by Members of the WTO code through the Trade Policy Review Mechanism (TPRM). The TPRM has been set up to improve communication and to contribute to greater transparency among WTO Members.

The TPRM has been functioning since 1989.[33] It requires that each member produce a detailed survey of its domestic trade regime. Such a document serves as a basis for evaluating whether the country is in full compliance with the WTO rules. There are some disagreements, however, as to the question of whether the mechanism is a mere instrument of transparency, or is in fact a technique to ensure compliance with the WTO code. In addition to the TPRM, under the WTO code there are various notifications requirements of national trade measures and publication requirements for trade legislation and administrative decisions. Members must ensure that their laws, regulations and administrative procedures are in conformity with the obligations undertaken.[34] For developing countries the main task ahead is to transform their domestic trade regimes into effective instruments to promote economic progress and prosperity.

Despite the above institutional mechanisms in place many developing countries feel overwhelmed by the implementation process. They simply lack the financial and human resources to fulfil the complex requirements of their commitments. Developing countries also express concerns about the impact of the WTO rules on their economies given the fact that overall the implementation of the Uruguay Round agreements have not benefited them in the way they had expected. There are at least three main issues of concern for developing countries with respect to implementation of WTO agreements.

The first set of concerns relates to the new obligations and standards of protection required under the WTO agreements. These requirements no longer relate only to goods and corresponding border measures. The WTO expanded the scope of international trade rules by including under its mandate trade in services, intellectual property and issues of investment. Hence WTO obligations are quite demanding and often new from a developing country perspective. Developing countries must not only familiarize themselves with the new rules with respect to services and intellectual property but are also under obligation to liberalize those sectors of their economies that were traditionally under the control of the state. With respect to some of the agreements, most notably the Trade-Related Aspects of Intellectual Property Rights (TRIPs) Agreement, many developing countries are struggling to come to terms with the concept of a patent protection previously unknown to them. Consequently, many developing countries feel that they were not given sufficient time for the implementation of the WTO agreements.

Special and differential provisions for developing countries are included in some of the WTO agreements. They correspond to more flexible terms, longer transition periods and less demanding commitments. There are also special clauses, which say that developed countries are required to help developing countries with the implementation process.[35] However, after more than five years since the Uruguay Round agreements took effect, developing countries feel that these provisions are insufficient.

The second area of concern for developing countries has to do with enforcement of the WTO obligations on the domestic front. Several WTO agreements lay down certain general principles applicable to the enforcement procedures. The TRIPs agreement, for example, contains provisions on civil and administrative procedures and remedies, provisional measures, special requirements related to border measures and criminal procedures, which say that the procedures and remedies must be available so that right holders can effectively enforce their rights.[36] These requirements mean that developing countries have to introduce deep changes into their existing regulatory, judicial and administrative frameworks. Quite often they have to create completely new institutions, pass new laws, design procedures for their enforcement, and train experts that will be responsible for ensuring the speedy and lawful administration of all the relevant regulations. Developing countries worry about the high costs of establishing all the necessary institutional mechanisms to meet with WTO obligations effectively. Moreover, developing countries often lack expertise in designing the new WTO compatible laws and regulations.

Lastly, developing countries point out that the implementation of the Agreement on Textiles by the developed countries falls short of expectations. It is clear that the WTO must address the challenges associated with the implementation of its agreements in order to remain an effective organization and to maintain the credibility of the world trading system.

Considering the importance which WTO Members attach to implementation related issues and concerns, as reflected in the Geneva Ministerial Declaration and in numerous subsequent discussions in the General Council, WTO Members negotiated an understanding at the Special Session of the General Council on 15 December 2000. In the communication issued later that month WTO Members decided by consensus to take the appropriate steps to address implementation problems.[37] It was decided that the Committee on Agriculture would examine possible means of improving the effectiveness of the implementation of the Decision on Measures Concerning the Possible Negative Effects of the Reform Program on Least-Developed and Net Food-Importing Developing Countries. WTO Members also decided to work with the relevant international standard-setting organizations on the issue of the participation of developing countries in their work.[38]

The General Council's Decision also reaffirmed that WTO Members must put extra effort into addressing the outstanding implementation related issues and concerns, most importantly those relating to the implementation of the Agreement on Trade Related Aspects of Intellectual Property Rights[39] with a view to completing the process no later than the Fourth Session of the Ministerial Conference by the end of 2001.

2.2 Dispute Settlement

As noted by Richard Blackhurst, the WTO is not a 'best endeavors' organization; rather, it is 'the legal and institutional foundation of the multilateral trading system'.[40] Commonly, the WTO is described as a 'rules-based' system. Like the GATT before it, the WTO mainly comprises a set of rules designed to facilitate trade between member countries, and particularly to provide for non-discrimination in trading relations. In any system of rules, a mechanism for handling disputes is a natural and logical extension of that system. In the GATT, a dispute settlement system developed by customary practice; in the WTO, the system was mandated by international agreement in the form of the DSU, included in the Uruguay Round agreements. As noted earlier in this chapter, the DSU is a particularly powerful form of international dispute settlement.

Dispute settlement procedures have been heavily invoked in the WTO. As expected, developed countries have been the heaviest users of the DSU, but numerous cases have been brought by developing countries, including those against major trading countries. WTO statistics indicate that as of May 2000, some 193 complaints have been notified to the WTO since its inception on 1 January 1995.[41] This number represented 151 distinct trade issues; the difference occurs because more than one country can lodge a complaint against a given trade practice.

According to William Davey, former Director of the WTO Legal Division, approximately half of the complaints notified are settled or dropped in the consultation phase mandated by the DSU.[42] Consultation is an inherently political process that initially developed through customary practice in the GATT. There are likely to be demands to increase and improve the use of this mechanism – possibly through third-party mediation – in order to avoid the expense of formal WTO dispute settlement. Indeed, informal solutions can be pursued in the context of formal proceedings, for as Andrew Shoyer notes: '...the greater formality in the WTO dispute settlement system has not precluded Members from seeking and finding pragmatic solutions to procedural problems arising in dispute settlement'.[43]

WTO statistics cited above indicate that as of May 2000, 22 formal cases of dispute settlement were active, 34 were completed, and 32 were settled or inactive.[44] Of the completed cases, the next issue is implementation. This is a potential problem in WTO practice that reflects the risks assumed in moving to a legally binding dispute settlement procedure in international trade, as opposed to the more diplomatic and political system that existed previously in the GATT. In the WTO, countries cannot avoid the 'compulsory arbitration' aspects of dispute settlement, but the trade system is still composed of sovereign states, and there is no effective way – even through retaliatory sanctions – to oblige a powerful trading nation to implement an adverse Panel or Appellate Body decision that it is determined to ignore.

Davey has examined the WTO record on implementation. Of the 28 completed cases he reports, half were implemented or else required no implementation. Of the remaining 14 cases, the time limit for implementation had not expired on nine, but non-implementation was an issue in five cases. These cases included *Hormones* and *Bananas*,[45] two disputes that divided the United States and the European Union.

The conflict over these two cases has spotlighted the main weakness in the WTO dispute settlement system: non-implementation by major powers. Over time, the dispute settlement process is bound to touch upon the sensitive points in most countries' trade policies, and to cause painful if not unmanageable political problems for governments. When this occurs in weaker or more trade-dependent countries, trading partners can bring effective and often conclusive pressure to implement an adverse WTO Panel or Appellate Body Report. This is less true with major players, particularly the United States and the European Union. A further problem, discovered in the context of *Hormones* and *Bananas*, is that the language of the DSU is not clear where the dispute continues into the WTO consistency of implementation measures. The latter problem is a legal question, and will likely be resolved in time. However, the former problem will be a continuing concern for the WTO. If major powers are able to circumvent the obligation to implement adverse Panel decisions, the WTO dispute settlement will quickly lose the moral authority to secure implementation from any countries. Clearly, this would be a fatal blow to any rules-based regime.

Additional problems with dispute settlement have been identified especially by developing countries. One problem can be described as the burden of litigation. There has been a tendency for dispute cases to grow in legal complexity, which was already evident in the GATT, but which has sharply accelerated under the WTO. There are now more agreements to consider, and the prospect of appeal to the WTO Appellate Body has increased the importance of factual evidence and precise legal argument. The length of Panel and Appellate Body Reports has consequently escalated. The result is that the system has become extremely costly, both in terms of the time of trade officials needed to be devoted to dispute cases, and in terms of the monetary cost of engaging additional domestic or foreign counsel. These costs are hard to bear for poor countries, which would generally have small WTO delegations in Geneva. These costs also direct developing countries toward a defensive rather than an offensive posture in dispute settlement, and therefore reduce the market-opening possibilities that the dispute settlement system might hold for more affluent WTO Members.

A second problem is what some countries have called the 'politicization' of the dispute settlement system. An example would be the decision of the Appellate Body to accept *amicus curiae* briefs from environmental non-governmental organizations in the *Shrimp* case between the United States and a number of developing countries.[46] This action was taken to address criticisms that the WTO dispute settlement system is exclusive and undemocratic, but it undercuts the concept of the WTO as an organization having nation-states as Members. In attempting to increase democratization between developed country governments and their domestic constituents, the Appellate Body's action may have decreased democratization between developed and developing countries, and as well increased the burdens of legal defence for developing countries.

Despite these reservations, the judgement of Davey and most observers of the WTO is that the dispute settlement system is working well, and is indeed the cornerstone of the WTO system. In any system of rules, the judicial function is needed to interpret the rules and to apply the rules to specific cases, and the procedures of the DSU continue to serve the interests of the WTO Members. In the WTO, dispute settlement cannot alter the rights and obligations of Members, but the fact remains that some of the Uruguay Round agreements are not always clear, and some interpretation may be necessary to apply those agreements to actual cases. Therefore Panels and the Appellate Body will continue to walk a fine line in which criticism is inevitable, but outright condemnation is unlikely.

2.3   Pressures Surrounding the Seattle Ministerial Meeting

The WTO Agreement calls for a Ministerial meeting not less than every two years, and the Seattle meeting, held in December 1999, was the third Ministerial meeting since the commencement of the WTO on 1 January 1995. The Seattle meeting caused diplomatic divisions almost as soon as it was scheduled. All the major participating governments found it impossible to decide whether to start a new comprehensive round of multilateral negotiations or to confine negotiations to the so-called 'built in agenda' of agriculture and services mandated at the last Ministerial. Furthermore, the participants were unable to achieve a consensus on the agenda of the meeting that was to clarify the approach to and purpose of any future negotiations. In the months before the Seattle meeting it was slowly becoming clear that deep divisions existed between the main industrial players but, most importantly, that the fundamental divisions persisted between developed and developing countries. The meeting was unable to bridge these divisions and ended in stalemate. The large, well-organized demonstrations were not a direct cause of its failure although the odd coalition of protesters succeeded in bringing to a global media audience a wide range of strongly held views. However, it is essential that all concerned understand what really happened in Seattle and why, and learn the lessons of that experience.

As the Seattle Ministerial was approaching, developing countries, having been faced with the growing implementation problems, felt that their concerns were not being fully recognized. The reality was that many developing countries had not been able to meet the implementation deadlines. Consequently, the African, Caribbean and Pacific Group of States proposed the extension of transitional periods of the TRIPs, TRIMs and Custom Valuation Agreements.[47] These requests were resented by developed nations, particularly the US, which insisted on compliance with commitments on time and in full.[48] In addition, developing countries were becoming more vocal in stating how difficult it was to translate the special and differential provisions contained in the WTO agreements into meaningful results such as increased market access, particularly in agriculture and textiles. Some developing countries had taken more adamant positions. Brazil and India questioned whether further tariff liberalization was in the interest of developing countries unless the non-tariff barriers to trade like anti-dumping and countervailing duties imposed by developed countries were addressed, most notably in agricultural trade.[49]

Developing countries have repeatedly stated that their concerns have to be addressed in any future negotiations. Greater economic openness and interdependence among nations provide opportunities for poorer countries. But this is not without challenges. Developing countries[50] constitute the majority of the membership of the WTO and are expressing their concerns about the impact of the existing WTO agreements on their economies. Their demands centre on the following issues: adjusting implementation schedules, more influence in decision making, transforming special and differential treatment into tangible gains, duty-free and quota-free treatment of exports from the least developed countries and a moratorium on new forms of protectionism in the developed world. Consequently, developing countries want to participate in the agenda setting for any future multilateral trade negotiations. In preparation for Seattle these demands were ignored, leading to a breakdown of negotiations and a failure to reach a consensus over the purpose of the Seattle meeting.

The fact that developing countries felt ignored during the months leading to the Seattle Ministerial, however, might have had to do more with the unfavourable bureaucratic environment within the organization than mean intentions expressed by the major players. The preparatory work that should have addressed the above issues suffered from a lack of time because the Director General of the WTO assumed office only a couple of months before Seattle. His election was a result of a long and contentious bargaining over the choice of candidates. This prolonged electoral process reflected the divisions within the membership. It also translated to a significant delay in assuming the position by Mike Moore of New Zealand, who simply did not have a chance to assert leadership of the secretariat and direct preparatory work. This considerably reduced the progress, which was expected under normal circumstances. In addition, the four Deputy Directors, who play a significant role in the day-to-day work at the secretariat of the WTO, were not in place until a few weeks before convening the Ministerial.

The preparatory process was further hampered by the acrimonious relationship between the EU and the US. In particular, still fresh was the dispute over preferential treatment given to Caribbean banana growers that effectively restricted a US-owned company from selling its bananas in the EU.[51] This prolonged legal battle provided both major players with incentives to invoke almost all procedural devices possible under the WTO dispute settlement mechanism, as well as to propose some new legal options that were perhaps not even foreseen by the existing dispute settlement rules. Contentious and at times aggressive controversy between the two majors was further aggravated by disagreements over agricultural trade, genetically modified foods and use of hormone-treated beef.[52] As the preparatory work for Seattle was unfolding, the dialogue between the EU and the US degenerated into an exchange of accusations. In the end the atmosphere was hostile enough to prevent the two from reaching a consensus about the agenda of the Seattle meeting.

In many respects the Seattle meeting was politically premature. There was little substantive support and even less careful thought on which to build such a complex undertaking. In previous years, before the launch of a new round of negotiations the developed nations and the larger trading countries would have arrived at an agreement on a core set of issues and then tried to persuade the rest of the membership to adopt the agenda.

This time the Seattle meeting opened without consensus or even coordination between the EU, the US, Japan and India. In addition, the context of US domestic politics played a large part in this respect. The Clinton Administration did not have fast track authority effectively to negotiate new multilateral deals. The US position seemed unclear if not confused at times. The President's speech in Seattle, especially his remarks on sanctions for violation of labour standards, offended many delegations from developing countries.[53] While the President's comments were interpreted as mainly aimed at a domestic audience in an election year when the support of organized labour would be crucial, they aroused many suspicions among developing countries about the escalating demands for protectionism.

The document that finally arrived in Seattle to serve as an agenda consisted of two parts. The first was the so-called built-in agenda, mandated at the end of the Uruguay Round for further negotiations on liberalizing services and agriculture. The discussion on services achieved some progress before and during the Seattle Ministerial but still the disagreements persisted on what to include in the mandated negotiations. The developed countries pushed for air transport, and financial and professional services, while developing countries pressed for maritime transport, construction and tourism. In agriculture, however, the issues remained very contentious; the positions taken were in many instances diametrically opposed. The parties were far apart and there was little willingness to compromise.

The second part of the Seattle agenda included a list of new proposals on competition policy, electronic commerce, government procurement, investment, trade-related labour issues, environment, subsidies, intellectual property rights, changes to the DSU, extensions of transition periods for developing countries and even re-opening some of the WTO agreements. The EU advocated investment and competition policy as priorities while the US was insistent on electronic commerce and linking the trade issues with labour and environment. Developing countries aggressively opposed making any connection between trade, labour and environment. They feared that any legal provisions designed in this context would be abused by developed nations to cover their protectionist measures.

The overall structure of decision making at the WTO did not help to facilitate the preparatory work, or the meeting itself. The process had major deficiencies. It was developed under the GATT when the membership was so much smaller and where the process was dominated by the industrialized nations. As the membership grew under the WTO the management of the decision-making process was slowly becoming unworkable.

In Seattle, the Director General opted for 'The Green Room' scheme, under which the chair leads a meeting consisting of the developed countries and a number of developing countries constituting a group discussing any particular issue. The problem was that there were no clear criteria for admission into the Green Room and thus most of the membership felt marginalized. Even if sonic developing countries were present in the Green Room, they did not have a mandate to represent those that were omitted. Naturally, 135 countries that constituted the membership of the WTO in December 1999 could not constitute a manageable drafting committee and therefore there would have to be some smaller group charged with resolving key issues. Such a group, however, would have to satisfy the principles of transparency and representation. The question for the WTO membership on how to resolve this problem remains open.

3   CONCLUSION: CHINA, THE WTO AND THE RULE OF LAW

The most prominent issue currently on the WTO agenda is the accession of China. This is a very special case. China was one of the 23 original signatories of the GATT in 1947. After China's revolution in December 1949, General Chiang Kai-shek announced the establishment of the Chinese National Government on Taiwan. In 1950 the National Government sent a message to the GATT headquarters in Geneva withdrawing China from the GATT.[54] In 1965 Taiwan requested and was granted observer status at sessions of the Contracting Parties. In 1971, however, observer status was removed by the Contracting Parties[55] following a decision by the United Nations General Assembly that recognized the People's Republic as the only legitimate government of China.[56] In 1982, the People's Republic of China was granted observer status in the GATT and in June 1986, China requested 'resumption' of its GATT Contracting Party status, on the basis that the withdrawal notice sent by the Taiwanese Government was null and void. However, in its request for resumption China declared that it would be prepared to accept a non-retroactive approach to the negotiation of its rights and obligations resulting from resumption.[57]

It is worth remembering that from the first meeting in Punta del Este in 1986 China had been a full participant in the Uruguay Round and signed the Marrakesh Agreement Establishing the World Trade Organization on 15 April 1994 subject to ratification. Legally, in terms of becoming a WTO Member, this meant very little.

In March 1987, the Council established a Working Party on China's Status as a Contracting Party. The negotiations showed signs of good progress until June 1989, but they stalled for almost three years[58] following the Tiananmen Square massacre. The process was back on track in the spring of 1992 but it was not until seven years later a sure momentum was achieved. Politics, however, again played a detrimental role because in May 1999 China walked out of the advanced negotiations after the NATO forces damaged its embassy in Belgrade. About the same time Taiwan successfully finalized, in principle, its accession negotiations and reached an agreement with all the Members of its Working Party. However, the final protocol of its accession has not been drafted since the Chinese government has expressed concerns and disappointment at the prospect of finalizing the Taiwan accession negotiations ahead of China.[59] This led to mutual understanding between WTO Members and the government in Taiwan that its accession process would be put on hold until mainland China finalizes its negotiation.

At the time when a working party to examine China's status met for the first time in Geneva in October 1987, the Chinese reform programme, which began in the early 1980s, was already having a profound effect on the country's economy. From 1978, the value of China's trade increased from more than $20 billion to over $80 billion in 1987. China's trade has more than quadrupled in value since then. New figures for 1999 now show China as the world's 9th largest exporter and 10th largest importer. The value of China's merchandise exports in 1999 was $195.2 billion, while its imports totalled $180.7 billion. Chinese exports of services in 1999 totalled $23.7 billion. Imports totalled $24.5 billion, making China the 15th largest services exporter and 10th largest importer in the world.[60]

China's bid for WTO accession has involved negotiation of bilateral agreements with key WTO Members. These agreements will then be extended to all WTO Members upon accession. In November 1999 there was an important breakthrough in the Chinese accession process that produced a bilateral deal between the Chinese and US trade envoys, and in May 2000 the agreement with the EU was signed. However, even after signing these long-anticipated agreements China still has much negotiating to do before the rest of the Working Party members find a compromise that will allow it to assume full WTO membership.[61] As a former socialist state China must reform its foreign trade regime to address at least six issue areas that were particularly affected by the legacy of the state-run economy: removal of quantitative restrictions on exports and imports; national treatment for foreign investors; new industrial policy; agricultural subsidies; non-discriminatory market access of goods and services; and other issues like protection of intellectual property rights and recognition of international standards.[62] There is also a parallel problem of reforming an ineffective state sector that in 1996 provided employment for 110 million people.[63]

The goal of WTO Member states has been to secure greater access to the growing Chinese market. However, China's application to join the organization has aroused a number of concerns from both developing and developed Member states. Some of the issues raised have included how China's growth and accession will affect the world agricultural and merchandise markets; whether China's accession will further increase the US trade deficit; whether increased competition will result in lower real wages for skilled and unskilled workers; and how increased competition will affect the development prospects of other nations in South Asia who compete in similar markets to China.

The main problem, however, in negotiating a WTO accession protocol for China appears to be the very limited mandate for transparency in administrative and judicial processes, and consequent uncertainty that foreign investors and companies will be able to function according to the rule of law. The confusing historical condition of China's legal and administrative systems poses many questions about the implementation of all WTO obligations by China. Although the government of China has made enormous progress since reforms began in the late 1970s, the development of a modern legal and administrative system has been uneven and lengthy. Long-held traditions under authoritarian leaders have dictated the subordination of law to policy. Of equal importance, both traditional Chinese law and communist law reflect the primacy of collectivist norms that require that contracts and property rights be subjugated to political factors.[64] This reflects worries expressed by WTO Members that failure to address issues of due process and reform of legal institutions would lead to corrosive disputes within China, and ultimately within the WTO.[65]

In light of these conditions, the final rounds of accession negotiation have attempted to conclude a special Protocol of Accession for China, which would act as a vehicle to support the efforts of Chinese reformers to create a credible and equitable system of commercial and administrative law. This would entail minimum standards of due process, including provisions for notice of hearings, the right to appear with counsel in court, publication of the new commercial and investment regulations, introduction of standards of evidence, and an obligation for prompt legal and administrative decisions, accompanied by a discussion of the reasons behind the action and citations to Chinese or WTO law.

In addition, the protocol would build upon actions already taken by China to create a more effective court system through the creation of specialized courts to handle complex economic cases. While leaving exact details to the Chinese government, the protocol would mandate the establishment, within the existing People's Court framework, of a separate court system to deal with disputes over foreign trade and investment issues. These courts would serve two functions: create models for legal reform throughout the larger Chinese legal system and provide a foundation for a cadre of legal experts knowledgeable in WTO rules and procedures.

Over the past two decades that China has pursued WTO membership, the trading system has changed profoundly, bringing to the forefront regulatory issues – in services, investment and intellectual property – that call for highly sophisticated and efficient legal and administrative systems. Mandating administrative and legal reform in China will both protect existing WTO Members, and will keep China on the economic reform path and ensure the implementation of the concessions and offers it has made.

NOTES

1. Vernon has noted: 'These agreements, if taken at their face value, show promise of reshaping trade relationships throughout the world' (Vernon, 1995, p. 329).
2. Wolff (1995, p. 154).
3. Marrakesh Agreement Establishing the World Trade Organization, Article XVI:4.
4. Jacobson (1984, p. 8). Claude's definition is similar, but elevates collective decision making: '...international organization [is] an agreement of states to engage in regular consultation under set conditions and to establish machinery for the implementation of their joint decisions.' (Claude, 1964, p. 8).
5. Jacobson (1984), p. 89.
6. Hearing on the General Agreement on Tariffs and Trade (GATT) before the Committee on Commerce, Science, and Transportation, US Senate, 16 June 1994, p. 52.
7. Final Act Embodying the Results of the Uruguay Round of Multilateral Trade Negotiations, 15 April 1994.
8. Marrakesh Agreement Establishing the World Trade Organization, 15 April 1994.
9. Annex IA contains changes to the GATT and 12 separate agreements, ranging from agriculture to safeguards. Annex IB is the General Agreement on Trade in Services, and Annex IC is the Agreement on Trade-Related Aspects of Intellectual Property.
10. Understanding on Rules and Procedures Governing the Settlement of Disputes.
11. For a summary of the new institutional framework, see Preeg (1995).
12. WTO Agreement, Article 1 (Establishment of the Organization).
13. Jacobson notes: 'IGOs [International governmental organizations] are distinguished from the facilities of traditional diplomacy by their structure and permanence.' Jacobson (1984), fn. 4, 8.

14. Croome (1995, p. 272).
15. Article XIV (Acceptance, Entry into Force and Deposit).
16. See Article XIV, fn. 3.
17. See Articles IX (Decision-Making), X (Amendments) and XII (Accession).
18. GATT Article XXV (Joint Action by the Contracting Parties).
19. See Hudec (1970 pp. 615–65): 'The key to understanding the GATT legal system is to recognize that GATT's law has been designed and operated as an instrument of diplomacy'.
20. DSU, Article 16 (Adoption of Panel Reports).
21. Shell (1995, p. 849). It should be noted that once a Panel Report was adopted by the WTO, there was a further obligation spelled out in Article 21 for Members to comply with recommendations or ruling of the DSB in a reasonable period of time, understood as not more than 15 months. Sanctions in the form of 'mutually acceptable compensation' or withdrawal of concessions can be authorized in cases of non-compliance, in accordance with Article 22.
22. Croome (1995), fn. 13, 324.
23. Article III.
24. Footnote 1 to Article IX, WTO Agreement.
25. Blackhurst (1998).
26. Blackhurst (1998, p. 36).
27. Article III:2.
28. Article XXVIII.
29. WTO (1997a, p. 1) and (1997b, p. 1).
30. In December 2000, Oman became the most recent (140th) Member of the WTO.
31. See Article XX of the GATT 1994.
32. See Articles XXII, XXVIII, XIX, XXI of GATT 1994.
33. Recommendation 8 of the 1985 Leutwiler Report, in *Trade Policies for a Better Future: The 'Leutwiler Report', the GATT and the Uruguay Round*. Amsterdam, Nijhoff, 1987. And then for the final agreement on the TPRM see Annexe 3 of the Results of the Uruguay Round of Multilateral Trade Negotiations.
34. See Article XVI of the Agreement Establishing the WTO.
35. Article 67 of the TRIPs Agreement. Annex 1C of the Marrakesh Agreement Establishing the WTO.
36. Articles 42–49 of the TRIPs Agreement. Annex 1C of the Marrakesh Agreement Establishing the WTO.
37. See WTO document (WT/L/384) from 19 December 2000, 'Implementation – Related Issues and Concerns – General Council Decision of 15 December 2000'.
38. To help developing countries to comply with the WTO Agreements on Sanitary and Phytosanitary Measures and on Technical Barriers to Trade.
39. See WTO document (Job(99)/5868/Rev.1) on www.wto.org.
40. Blackhurst (1998, p. 32).
41. 'Overview of the State-of-play of WTO Disputes', WTO Informal Paper, 23 May 2000.
42. Davey (2000).
43. Shoyer (1998, p. 280).
44. 'Completed' means that Appellate Body or Panel Reports were adopted by the Dispute Settlement Body; and 'settled or inactive' refers to cases where the measure complained of was withdrawn, or the panel request was withdrawn, or the case was otherwise resolved.
45. *European Communities – Measures Affecting Meat and Meat Products (Hormones)*; and *European Communities – Regime for the Importation, Sale and Distribution of Bananas (Bananas)*.
46. *United States – Import Prohibition of Certain Shrimp and Shrimp Products (Shrimp)*.
47. 'Declaration on the Third WTO Ministerial Conference.' Adopted by APC Ministers of Trade in Brussels on 22 October 1999 (ACP/61/051/99), p. 3. TRIPs is the previously mentioned Agreement on Trade-Related Aspects of Intellectual Property Rights; TRIMs is

the Agreement on Trade-Related Investment Measures. See Annex 1A and Annex 1C of the Marrakesh Agreement Establishing the WTO.
48.   See 'American Goals in the Trading System', Testimony of Ambassador Susan Esserman, Deputy US Trade Representative, House Ways and Means Subcommittee on Trade, Washington, DC, 5 August 1999, pp. 3–4.
49.   'US, China Resume WTO Negotiations, Barshefsky Sees Time Crunch', *Inside US Trade*, Vol. 17, No. 36, 10 September 1999, pp. 1, 24–26.
50.   To keep things simple, from now on this chapter talks only about 'developing countries' encompassing the three main categories: developing, least-developed and transition economies.
51.   Sallas and Jackson (2000). Also see: 'EU Reacts to the Banana Dispute Reports' in *Inside US Trade*, 7 April 1999; and WTO documents: WT/DS/152/12; WT/DS27/49.
52.   'EU Blocks Hormone Retaliation at WTO with Arbitration Request', *Inside US Trade*, 4 June 1999.
53.   'The Seattle Fiasco', Editorial, *Journal of Commerce*, 7 December 1999.
54.   Tait and Li (1997, p.98).
55.   Jacobson and Oskenberg (1990, pp. 63–4).
56.   UN General Assembly Resolution 2758 – Restoration of the Lawful Rights of the People's Republic of China in the UN. Dated 26 October 1971.
57.   Rhodes and Jackson (1999, p. 500).
58.   From June 1989 to February 1992.
59.   *Globe and Mail*, 'Beijing, Taipei wage psychological warfare,' 16 August 1999.
60.   *International Trade Statistics 2000*. Published by the WTO, Geneva Switzerland, 2000.
61.   Tait and Li (1997, p. 99).
62.   Sachs and Woo (1997).
63.   Houben (1999, p. 6).
64.   See Zhang (2000, pp. 9–20).
65.   Compare Ostry (1998).

REFERENCES

Blackhurst, R. (1998), 'The capacity of the WTO to fulfill its mandate', in Anne O. Krueger (ed.), *The WTO as an International Organization*, Chicago: University of Chicago Press, pp. 31–58.

Claude, Inis L. Jr (1964), *Swords into Plowshares: The Problems and Progress of International Organizations* (3rd edn), New York: Random House.

Croome, John (1995), *Reshaping the World System: a History of the Uruguay Round*, Geneva: World Trade Organization.

Davey, William J. (2000), 'The WTO dispute settlement system', *Journal of International Economic Law*, Vol. 3, pp. 15–18.

Houben, Hiddo (1999), 'China's economic reforms and integration into the world trading system', *Journal of World Trade*, **33**(3), June.

Hudec, Robert E. (1970), 'The GATT legal system: a diplomat's jurisprudence', *Journal of World Trade*, Vol. 4, pp. 615–65.

Jacobson, Harold K. (1984), *Networks of Interdependence: International Organizations and the Global Political System* (2nd edn), New York: Knopf.

Jacobson, Harold K. and Michael Oskenberg (1990), *China's Participation in the IMF, The World Bank, and GATT: towards a Global Economic Order*, Ann Arbor: University of Michigan Press.

Ostry, Sylvia (1998), 'China and the WTO: the transparency issue', *UCLA Journal of International Law and Foreign Affairs*, Vol. 3, Summer.

Preeg, Ernest H. (1995), *Traders in a Brave New World: the Uruguay Round and the Future of the International Trading System*, Chicago: University of Chicago Press, pp. 207–10.

Rhodes, Sylvia A. and John H. Jackson (1999), 'United States law and China's accession process', *Journal of International Economic Law*, **2**(3), September.

Sachs, Jeffrey D. and Wing Thye Woo (1997), 'Understanding China's economic performance', NBER Working Paper 5935, Cambridge, Mass.

Shell, G. Richard (1995), 'Trade legalism and international relations theory: an analysis of the World Trade Organization', *Duke Law Journal*, **44**(5), 829–927.

Shoyer, Andrew W. (1998), 'The first three years of WTO dispute settlement: observations and suggestions', *Journal of International Law*, Vol. 1, pp. 277–302.

Tait, A. Neil and Kui-Wai Li (1997), 'Trade regimes and China's accession to the World Trade Organization', *Journal of World Trade*, **31**(3), June.

Vernon, Raymond (1995), 'The World Trade Organization: a new stage in international trade and development', *Harvard International Law Journal*, **36**(2), 329–40.

Wolff, Alan W. (1995), 'Comment', in Peter B. Kenen (ed.), *Managing the World Economy: Fifty Years after Bretton Woods*, Washington DC: Institute for International Economics.

WTO (1997a), 'WTO telecom talks produce landmark agreement', WTO *Focus*, No. 16, February.

WTO (1997b), 'WTO achieves landmark agreement on financial services', WTO *Focus*, No. 25, December.

Zhang, Wei-Wei (2000), *Transforming China*, Macmillan Press.

3. Agenda setting for a Millennial Round: challenges and opportunities

Julie Soloway[1] and Andrey Anishchenko[2]

1 INTRODUCTION

Writing on the topic of the 'Millennial Round Agenda' of the World Trade Organization (WTO) is a challenging task because a Millennial Round of multilateral negotiations has not, as yet, begun. Since the failed launch of the Millennial Round in 1999 at Seattle, and indeed before that time, a number of seemingly intractable issues have surfaced which have indefinitely stalled the progress of future trade negotiations. Only by understanding the reasons for the failure at Seattle can we examine any attempts at re-launching any future WTO negotiations.

The WTO is at a crossroads in its existence. The failure at Seattle to agree on an agenda to launch the new negotiating round represented the culmination of several issues that, until resolved, threaten to undermine the progress, and indeed the very existence, of the WTO. This chapter examines those issues with a view to bridging the divides that prevent future trade negotiations from taking place. The first part of this chapter examines the reasons for the failed launch of the Millennial Round at Seattle, and offers a number of recommendations for their resolution. The second part of this chapter examines the minimal progress that the WTO has made to date (primarily in the areas of agriculture and services) since Seattle. Finally, conclusions are made.

2 THE SEATTLE DEBACLE

The meeting of the world's trade ministers at Seattle from 30 November to 3 December 1999 was meant to begin a new round of trade negotiations under the WTO. In the end, the delegates went home empty-handed and the failed launch will forever be remembered for the resulting chaos and street theatre. When the conference collapsed, it was seen as the heralding of a revolution by civil society against the forces of globalization. Yet the real failure at Seattle occurred within the halls of the conference, as the result of three fundamental tensions, all of which must be resolved before a new round of trade negotiations can be successfully launched.

The first major issue concerned the developing world and the decision making structure of the WTO. Many developing countries felt that the WTO's decision making structure had failed to evolve with current political realities. The Seattle Ministerial operated on the assumption that the organization was a club of developed nations, as the General Agreement on Tariffs and Trade (GATT) had been for most of its existence. In the years leading up to Seattle, developing nations had developed a strong interest in trade negotiations, particularly with respect to the implementation of the Uruguay Round agreements in areas such as services and intellectual property, which they felt a new WTO Round should address. Many developing countries felt that the Ministerial was run as if the organization was still a club of developed nations, and consequently did not feel that they had the chance to raise their concerns adequately.

The second major issue was the fact that the United States was equally as concerned with the upcoming US election as the future of the WTO. US President Bill Clinton's open support of sanctions-backed environmental and labour standards, favoured by Democratic Party constituencies, offended the developing world and brought the negotiations over the future agenda to a standstill.

The third major issue concerned major differences between the United States and the European Union about the substantive issues subject to negotiation. The United States favoured a 'narrow but deep US agenda of new demands (especially on agriculture, with vigorous support from other exporters including Canada)... and a broad but shallow European agenda aimed, in part, at minimizing exposure of their agricultural subsidies'.[3] In particular, the United States was not prepared to compromise with other members on key issues such as antidumping, which protected US domestic business interests, and questions of international standards on competition and investment policies, which risked rejection in a Congress hostile to multilateralism.

2.1 The Demonstrations: The Source of the Failure?

Instead of being remembered for starting a new phase of negotiations, the conference will forever be associated with the pictures of 50,000 demonstrators taking over Seattle's downtown core, making the conference a logistical nightmare and embarrassing the American hosts.[4] The non-governmental organizations (NGOs) that organized the demonstrations claimed credit for preventing a new round of trade talks.[5] Dymond and Hart suggest that the protests in Seattle may have made some politicians and business leaders reluctant to publicly assert the need for a new round of trade negotiations.[6] Delegates were prevented from attending meetings and the meetings that were held were short-staffed. The conference slipped into 'crisis mode', with organizers launching meetings between select developed countries while Third World delegates were cast to the side.[7] Social events, where delegates are able to converse informally, and where small country representatives are able to spend time conversing with major players, were shut down, slowing progress and further alienating developing nations.

The protests further helped to turn the field of international trade negotiations, once the preserve of mandarins acting in relative obscurity, into an area of high politics. The media attention was unprecedented for a trade conference. Although the demonstrators may have been in some instances incoherent and disparate, representing everyone from environmentalists to labour groups to Tibetan nationalists, they did provide strong evidence of widespread dissatisfaction with the WTO.[8]

However, those who participated at the meeting, and many who have studied the matter since, have concluded that the conference was doomed to failure regardless of what was happening on the streets. While the demonstrations did wreak considerable havoc, the Seattle conference 'failed inside the hall and not outside on the streets'.[9] This suggests that in order to truly understand what happened at Seattle, one must look at what occurred within the conference, among the member states themselves.

2.2   Missed Opportunities for Compromise

Compromise is essential to the success of the WTO system. The structure of the WTO differs greatly from the other Bretton Woods institutions, the World Bank and the International Monetary Fund, where decisions are made based on weighted voting, under which wealthier member states have more influence than poorer member states.[10] Unlike those bodies, the WTO is a member-driven organization operating on a consensus rule.[11] Indeed, the legitimacy of the WTO as a regime depends on general consensus of the member states to the overall regime. Furthermore, the dynamics of WTO and GATT negotiations have always been such that agreements on various issues being negotiated at the same time are linked to each other. There are no small deals, just one 'final deal'.[12] Therefore, when compromise is lacking, trade negotiations become doomed to failure.

There was much missed opportunity for compromise on a range of issues at Seattle.[13] For example, developing countries' manufacturing sectors had expanded as a share of their total exports and one commentator suggests that they could have exchanged their high tariffs, or agreed to tariffication of remaining non-tariff barriers for tariff concessions by developed countries in this area.[14] There may have been some room for trade-off between US demands to have labour standards recognized in the WTO and developing countries' demands for concessions by developed countries in areas such as services, textiles and apparel. The United States on one side, with its advocacy for greater transparency in the WTO dispute settlement process, and Japan and the EU on the other side, with their advocacy of common rules for foreign direct investment, may have had some room for horse-trading. New commitments in different service sectors could have been traded off. Yet these opportunities were not seized.

2.3 Developing Countries and the WTO

In terms of how compromise was made, the WTO as it existed by the time of Seattle was a world away from the GATT for most of its history. For decades, finding compromises in the GATT essentially depended on a handful of leading countries. Only 23 countries signed the original GATT in 1947, compared to today's WTO membership of over 130.[15] Even as recently as the launching of the Uruguay Round in 1986, there were 85 contracting parties, but only about 40 or 50 of these played an effective part in terms of drafting proposals and participating in meetings.[16] Many small states ended up endorsing an agenda that was negotiated by others.[17]

Indeed, even these numbers do not adequately describe just how narrow the negotiating game was. The real power lay with the so-called Quad group of leading developed countries made up of the United States, the European Community, Japan and Canada.[18] This power was exercised through the so-called 'Green Room', where the chairperson of the conference and the Director General of the GATT worked mainly with the Quad to devise consensus documents.[19] Indeed, at least one scholar, Preeg, suggests that power was even more narrowly based. He writes that it was US–European leadership which dominated the previous eight negotiating rounds.[20] In any case, it is clear that GATT negotiations had long been an affair of developed nations.

By the time of Seattle, more members than ever insisted on playing an active role.[21] Besides the increased number of members, the nature of developing countries' participation in the system had changed. While some developing nations, such as India, had always been known to make their voice heard, additional developing nations now felt the need to get involved as well.

At least three factors effectively increased the perceived importance to developing nations of playing an active role in negotiations. One was their growing exposure to the global economy. During the 1960s and 1970s, developing nations tended to view the concept of free trade as contrary to their interests, and pursued more state-oriented development policies.[22] In the 1980s, many developing countries began unilaterally liberalizing their trade regimes.[23] Indeed, in the last two decades of the twentieth century, developing countries actually undertook much more substantial reform of their domestic policies than developed countries.[24] Applied tariffs were lowered and, in some cases, developing countries bound their tariff lines in the context of the Uruguay Agreement.[25] The overall use of non-tariff barriers decreased and government intervention in trade in general declined.[26] Instead of isolating themselves, these nations began to tie their development to an outward-oriented development strategy, based on participation in the global marketplace.[27] As a result, the share of these developing countries' GDP accounted for by trade rose dramatically. In 1989, the ratio of developed countries' total trade (merchandise exports plus imports) was 38.3 per cent of GDP.[28] By 1997, the figure was 44 per cent.[29] Merchandise exports of developing countries increased by 9.5 per cent and imports by 10.4 per cent, which was higher than the overall increases for the entire world.[30] As a result, developing countries were now, more than ever, affected by any changes to the global trading regime.

Another factor that made developing countries more interested in participating in trade negotiations was that they had learned that they had bargaining power. During the Uruguay Round, developing countries were able to negotiate the phasing out of the Multifiber Agreement, which had been an irritant for their clothing and textile exports, accounting for more than 20 per cent of their industrial exports.[31] Their participation in the Cairns Group was also critical in getting negotiations on agriculture into the Uruguay Round.[32] Later, during the Spring of 1999, developing countries learned how to 'flex their muscle' during the fight over who the next Director General of the WTO would be. While there were both developed and developing countries among the supporters of both Mike Moore of New Zealand and Dr. Supachai Panitchpakdi of Thailand, the general split was along economic development lines. The Clinton administration favoured Moore as it perceived, among other things, that he might be more sensitive to the wishes of labour and environmentalists.[33] Many developing countries, including Malaysia, India, Pakistan, Egypt, Uganda, Zimbabwe, Cameroon, Haiti and Cuba, felt that it was high time there was a Director General from a developing country.[34] The final result was that it was agreed that both candidates would serve consecutive three-year terms instead of either of them having a full six-year term. Many developing countries came away with the feeling that they had some new-found clout in the WTO's decision making.[35]

By far, however, the most important factor driving developing nations' participation was that the rules of the international trading system now had more direct effect on their policies and economies than ever before. Previously, as one Indian commerce minister has described it, developing countries used to 'free ride' in GATT negotiations.[36] They insulated themselves by taking advantage of the GATT's balance of payments and development exceptions to protect their nascent industries.[37] As a result, they were able to make only minimal commitments over access to their markets.[38] However, in the Uruguay Round of trade talks, developing countries participated for the first time as full-scale members of the GATT, rather than just observers.[39] Furthermore, the Uruguay Round Agreements were developed as a single package, so that any nation had to implement the entire package in order to enjoy the benefits of any single component of them.[40] Thus developing nations were now directly affected by the WTO Agreement.

However, developing nations were particularly concerned about the GATT rules post-Uruguay. This concern developed into the 'implementation' issue, which itself had as many as three different meanings.[41] The first meaning involved a perceived imbalance between what developed nations had given up at the Uruguay Round and what they had received in return. Developing countries agreed at Uruguay not only to reduce trade barriers, but also to reform their import licensing procedures, customs valuation systems, technical, sanitary and phytosanitary standards, and their intellectual property law.[42] In exchange, they achieved some concessions in agriculture, textiles and clothing. However, the developed countries were either slow in implementing their side of the bargain or, as it turned out, did not really agree to much in the first place.

This was particularly true with respect to the agreement on textiles and clothing, where developed nations agreed to remove the Multifiber Agreement-sanctioned quantitative restrictions on imports of textiles and clothing. In fact, 49 per cent of the imports involved did not have to be integrated into the new regime until January 2005.[43] By 1999, the United States had managed to integrate its clothing and textiles categories into the agreement in a way that eliminated only 1 per cent of its Multifiber Agreement Restrictions, the EU had eliminated 7 per cent and Canada 14 per cent.[44]

In the area of agriculture, the agreement was for importers to change non-tariff barriers into tariff barriers.[45] However, developed countries reduced their levels of protection on a smaller percentage of agricultural imports than industrial imports, and tariffs on agricultural products remained higher than those on industrial products.[46] There was also evidence of some 'cheating'. The US tariffication of agricultural products has resulted in tariffs that were more than three-quarters of the tariff equivalent of the non-tariff barriers that country had in the late 1980s and early 1990s.[47] In the EU, tariffication resulted in tariffs that are two-thirds higher than the non-tariff barriers Europe had ten years ago.[48] Japan has announced a tariff on rice of $3.05 per kilogram, a rate estimated to be a 1000 per cent tariff, but some have estimated that Japan's non-tariff barriers in the area were actually equivalent to a tariff of approximately 650 per cent.[49] Furthermore, although the Uruguay Agreement involved cuts in domestic producer subsidies and such subsidies have indeed fallen by more than a third in advanced industrialized countries, about two-thirds of that reduction is due to a rise in international prices.[50]

There was also concern over the Agreement on Subsidies and Countervailing Duties. It seemed to allow the developed world to claim that subsidies normally used by developing nations, involving assistance to export industries, were actionable.[51] On the other hand, subsidies normally used by developed nations, involving broader assistance to businesses, were considered non-actionable.[52]

Even beyond the actual texts of the agreements, there was concern that developed nations had violated the spirit of their commitments, and of trade liberalization in general, through antidumping and dispute settlement procedures. In 1997, there were 94 per cent more antidumping cases initiated than in 1987.[53] Although the use of antidumping measures by developing countries has risen significantly, half of the actions brought in 1997 were by the United States, EU, Canada, Australia and New Zealand.[54] European cases against textile imports from India and Pakistan, among others, led some to feel that the Multifiber Agreement was essentially useless.[55] The US initiated a case against salmon imports from Chile, which threatened that country's ability to diversify its export industries from a traditional reliance on the copper industry.[56] Other US cases against crude oil imports from Venezuela and Mexico threatened exports on which those nations' national budgets largely relied.[57] India also argued that developed countries were using the WTO's dispute settlement mechanism to attack legitimate policies pursued by developing nations.[58] Many developing countries, because of their small size and a lack of resources, were not adequately equipped to deal with the WTO's dispute settlement process.[59]

A second meaning of 'implementation' was that developing countries were having structural difficulties, in terms of the setting up of the institutions and the training of officials necessary for implementing Uruguay Round commitments.[60] For example, on the matter of customs evaluation processes, many developing countries prepared needs assessments asking for help in training officials in new procedures, issuing new documentation, and the adoption of new software.[61] With respect to sanitary and phytosanitary measures, assessments were prepared requesting assistance in establishing appropriate legislation, the appropriate test laboratories and inspection services, as well as asking for the general dissemination of information with regard to standards that would help them conform with the Agreement.[62]

Yet a third meaning of 'implementation' involved the re-opening of existing agreements. India, with the support of other developing nations, proposed changes to the agreements on subsidies, antidumping and sanitary issues.[63] On top of this, there was lingering resentment over the fact that developed nations had been able to achieve sectoral agreements in areas where they have comparative advantages, such as services through the General Agreement on Trade in Services (GATS) and intellectual property through the Trade-Related Intellectual Property (TRIPs) Agreement. During the GATS negotiations, nations such as Brazil and India resisted the agreement, arguing that services were a matter for domestic regulation,[64] and no doubt were still unhappy with it. Under the TRIPs Agreement, which essentially requires the adoption of Western patent law, UNCTAD studies have found that developing countries will face significant costs in implementing reforms needed to their legal systems and the training of personnel.[65] Many developing nations felt that they had signed agreements they should not have, in order to be able to gain the perceived benefits they received in areas such as agriculture and the Multifiber Agreement.

With all these interests in mind, developing nations' new-found enthusiasm for participation was clear even before the Seattle meeting started. Pre-conference submissions for negotiation came from Costa Rica, Cuba, the Dominican Republic, Honduras, Jamaica, Indonesia, Malaysia, Mexico, Kenya, Tanzania, Zimbabwe and Zambia, either as individual nations or in groups.[66] Overall, more than 135 official submissions were made for consideration and the amount of negotiating issues reached 15.[67] Developing countries did not come to Seattle simply to observe.

The Africans were particularly well organized. As far back as April 1998 at a meeting of Organization for African Unity/African Economic Community trade ministers in Harare, Zimbabwe, it was decided to coordinate efforts in the formation of an agenda for WTO negotiations.[68] African nations used the Geneva staff of the OAU/AEC to help them develop their negotiating positions for the upcoming Ministerial. African trade ministers caucused in Harare again in September 1999.[69] There was also an OAU and UNCTAD-sponsored workshop in Pretoria in July 1999 and the UNCTAD organized sub-regional workshops for senior advisors to trade ministers in Abuja, Nigeria; Cape Town, South Africa; Harare, Zimbabwe; and Libreville, Gabon.[70] African ministers contributed heavily to general negotiations among WTO members in Geneva between September and November 1999 on the language and details of the Declaration that was intended to be adopted at the Seattle Ministerial.[71] Finally, during the Seattle conference itself there were four meetings between African delegates, two at the ministerial and two at the senior officials' level.[72] As Luke writes: '…for the first time ever in multilateral trade negotiations, Africa was fully prepared to articulate its demands'.[73]

Developing nations thus came to Seattle with concerns about complex issues, many proposals, and a great deal of preparation. The challenge was for the organizers of the Seattle conference to take account of this new force at the WTO. In this, they failed.

2.4   US Politics and the Seattle Ministerial

The internal failure to take account of the presence of the developing nations was compounded by the fact that the United States government let its domestic politics intervene in the conference in a way that threatened both developed and developing countries' interests. On the issues of labour and environmental standards, antidumping, and even competition and investment policy, the Clinton administration refused to risk its political capital by compromising. These positions contributed directly and significantly to the failure at Seattle.

The Americans were on the eve of a critical election year, the first without an incumbent president running for re-election since 1988. Clinton's support was solidly behind Vice-President Al Gore, whom polls suggested was in for a tough race. It was critical to secure the Democratic Party's traditional base, of which labour and environmentalists were important components. Indeed, labour was a particularly important constituency, which the Clinton administration had risked alienating by having supported the North American Free Trade Agreement (NAFTA) and Chinese accession to the WTO.[74] It was important that these constituencies were not offended.

Added to this was the fact that there were no apparent political payoffs coming from other domestic sources that would have supported trade liberalization. Traditionally, the business community had fulfilled this role. During the Uruguay Round in the 1980s, American CEOs devoted much of their time to lobbying for the cause.[75] But this time, it seemed that the US business community had exhausted much of its energy and resources on the issue of Chinese accession to the WTO.[76] As well, the US Trade Representative's office had spent much of its resources on the China matter, which it might have spent cultivating business support for a new round.[77] In any case, as one WTO ambassador stated: 'For services and TRIPS you had powerful constituencies in 1986. There was not such a clear impulse for a round in 1999.'[78] For an administration as politically conscious as Clinton's, proceeding on trade liberalization without tangible domestic support would have been foolhardy.

Finally, there was the fact that Congress had generally become hostile to further trade liberalization. Clinton even faced challenges from House Democratic Party leader Dick Gephart, known as a friend of labour and protectionist on trade matters.[79] Recently, the Congress had prevented the extension of the North American free trade regime to Chile. More importantly, Congress had defeated the granting of fast-track authority, which would have allowed for expeditious Congressional consideration of trade agreements.[80] This means that any trade agreement that comes up for ratification will be subject to amendments by various legislators seeking to protect their constituents. US trade reforms were inhibited as American negotiators became reluctant to negotiate agreements that would involve significant changes in US policy or infringe on US sovereignty.[81]

The link between this domestic US political situation and damage done to the Seattle Ministerial was most evident when President Clinton himself decided to speak out on the issue of labour and environmental standards. In an interview with the *Seattle Post-Intelligencer* published on the Wednesday of the conference, the President stated:

> What we ought to do first of all is to adopt the United States' position on having a working group [that] should develop these core labour standards, and then they ought to be a part of every trade agreement, and ultimately I would favour a system in which sanctions would come for violating any provision of a trade agreement.[82]

For anyone aware of the history of the Clinton administration's trade policy, this was a clear repetition of what had previously occurred with NAFTA. The US labour movement whose support Clinton coveted had been concerned during the NAFTA debate about Ross Perot's 'giant sucking sound', the flight of jobs from the US to Mexico with its perceived lower wages and less stringent regulations. During his original campaign for president in 1992, Clinton promised that if elected he would negotiate side agreements to the NAFTA on the issues of labour and environment.[83] By August 1993, he had reached such agreements with the NAFTA partners, which called on the parties to, among other things, enforce their own standards in these areas effectively and for certain dispute settlement regimes.[84]

There was now the apparent threat of an even larger sucking sound pulling jobs from the US to all over the world. Although Washington had already supported a dialogue between the WTO, the International Labour Organization and others on coordinating their work, the American Federation of Labor and Congress of Industrial Organizations (AFL-CIO) wanted a more direct approach.[85] Environmentalists in the United States, as well as elsewhere, had been upset by WTO panel and Appellate Body rulings which had appeared to go against environmental interests and pushed for a refinement of GATT rules in this regard.[86] Clinton's suggestion of WTO-enforced standards on labour and environment, with the power of sanction behind them, addressed the concerns of US NGOs. It also applied a tried and true method of securing domestic support for trade liberalization in the WTO context.

But whereas with NAFTA the United States was dealing with only one less-developed country, Mexico, it was now dealing with the entire Third World. Developing countries had been resisting linking labour with WTO negotiations since the WTO Ministerial at Singapore in 1996.[87] In general, they preferred to discuss labour issues at the International Labour Organization, which lacks the enforcement capacity of the WTO.[88] Although developing nations had finally agreed to discuss labour at the WTO, they did so only under narrow conditions. On 1 November 1999, a month before the Seattle Ministerial, the United States proposed a Working Party on Trade and Labour, limited to simply studying matters such as trade and its relationship with employment, social protections and labour standards, and the presence of forced child labour in industries engaged in international trade.[89] The United States made clear that this did not encompass actual negotiations, much less discussion of sanctions against violators of labour standards. The labour discussions that got under way at Seattle were within this framework.[90] Clinton's public statement seemed to change the rules by explicitly advocating the eventual use of sanctions.

Others in the developed world may well have had sympathy with Clinton's position, but they seemed to understand that his approach would be too provocative. The Europeans wanted to see the adoption of international labour standards, but through incentives, not sanctions.[91] They wanted to deal with the environmental issue by having the relationship between the WTO's rules and multilateral environmental accords and eco-labelling schemes clarified.[92]

Developing nations were concerned with President Clinton's interview because it seemed that the labour standards involved in determining whether sanctions would be applied would be on developed nations' terms. The issues of interest to Third World members on this matter, such as the rights of migrant workers, were likely not to be addressed.[93] Indeed, the idea that the WTO would ever be able to apply sanctions against the United States or another developed nation for failure to live up to standards on the migrant worker issue seemed far-fetched. Thus, any labour standards imposed would involve developing countries having to meet much higher standards than currently exist.

Developing countries also tended to fear that if they gave in at all on this matter, they may have ended up making concessions without getting any tangible returns. For example, it was not clear that agreeing to a Working Group on Trade and Labour would, by itself, lead American unions and NGOs to support trade liberalization.[94]

Similar concerns arose from the idea of the WTO being able to sanction nations based on failure to live up to certain environmental standards. The fact that developed nations are ahead of developing nations in the area of environmental protection suggests that the latter would have had to raise their standards or risk losing access to markets. As with labour standards, the true motivation seemed to be one of protectionism.[95]

In a narrow sense, Clinton's statement had the direct effect of derailing progress on the labour issue. He undermined the credibility of his own diplomats, who had insisted that sanctions were not on the table.[96] The talks that were proceeding on the matter, and which were apparently making some progress, ended.[97]

But on a wider scale, Clinton's statement to the *Post-Intelligencer* was key to derailing the entire Ministerial. One Southeast Asian diplomat later stated that 'the worst possible thing at Seattle was President Clinton's statement. It hardened the resolve of a lot of developing countries to resist.'[98] Preeg writes that Clinton's statement 'led to a bitter, emotional reaction by developing country ministers, and the Seattle conference, already heading for an impasse, was effectively over'.[99] Alexandroff states that 'Clinton's tilt to domestic interests in the face of growing complexity in reaching consensus in the WTO heightened the view that his administration had essentially abandoned the goal of further trade liberalization.'[100] Odell writes of other nations being 'infuriated' by Clinton's statement and that 'virtually everyone concluded that Clinton's top priority was not reaching agreement but helping Vice President Gore and the Democratic Party in the coming elections'.[101]

2.5   The Substantive Issues

The damage to the Seattle conference was also evident on a number of substantive issues. In the context of antidumping laws, giving in to other countries' calls for reform risked offending the US steel industry, and by extension American steel workers, who wanted to maintain the current regime in that area.[102] During the Uruguay Round, the steel industry had demanded a broad antidumping regime in exchange for supporting the Uruguay Agreement.[103] Furthermore, the fact that Congress had refused to grant fast-track negotiating authority would have made it difficult to get reforms of antidumping through Congress.[104] Clinton knew that even if he were to risk his own political support by achieving a deal, congressmen from industrial states would likely work hard to block it or amend it. Antidumping was included within the domain of the Working Group on Implementation, and privately the Americans had said that they were willing to 'consider' the matter, as long as it did not mean re-opening the Uruguay Agreement.[105] However, when it came time to bargain, Washington did not seem to concede very much. The parties were so far from reaching an agreement, despite the fact that 'implementation' in general was discussed in the Green Room, that no significant discussion was held there on antidumping.[106]

The US position obviously disappointed developing nations, for whom the antidumping issue was an important part of 'implementation'. However, the US position on antidumping also offended the Europeans and the Japanese. Although the European steel industry itself hid behind antidumping regimes, especially in light of new steel imports from the former Soviet Union, they were themselves the victims of US antidumping actions.[107] Brussels had also hoped to use concessions on antidumping as a trade-off in negotiations with developing nations.[108] Therefore, the Europeans were willing to engage on the issue. The Japanese, who were major exporters to the United States, had their own interest in reforming antidumping. At one point during the negotiations, President Clinton made a middle-of-the-night phone call to Prime Minister Obuchi of Japan, asking him to drop antidumping negotiations, only to be told by the prime minister that this was not a bilateral US–Japanese issue.[109] The Americans were failing to charm virtually all of their negotiating partners. The antidumping issue demonstrated that American politics was instrumental, not only in clashes between the developed and developing nations at Seattle, but also in clashes between developed nations themselves.

Both the Europeans and the Japanese came to Seattle with broad agendas, and had support from others for doing so. Besides antidumping, the EU wanted to add foreign direct investment, competition policy and new rules on services to the agenda at Seattle.[110] The Japanese also wanted to talk about antidumping and investment and competition, while also promoting talks on electronic commerce.[111] For the Europeans and the Japanese, the addition of these issues was critical to their success in the negotiations. European negotiators claimed that if they could advance these issues, they could more successfully convince their constituents at home to accept concessions on agriculture.[112] The Japanese no doubt had similar ideas. With regard to the prospect of the Americans setting the agenda, Japan's Ministry of International Trade and Industry said that a narrow approach would be 'too selfish' and not viable.[113]

The United States made things difficult for the Europeans and the Japanese by resisting talks on these issues. The US was firmly opposed to adding competition and little progress was made on the matter at Seattle.[114] Barshefsky proposed adding investment to the agenda midway through the next round of trade talks, instead of agreeing to discuss it at Seattle.[115] Of all the other issues, some progress appeared to have been made only on services, for which a section of the final declaration was virtually finished.[116]

Officially, the United States claimed that its desire to keep the talks narrow was for the good of the negotiations. As one US official put it: 'Our concern, frankly, is that if you put everything into the round, nothing will come out of the round.'[117] This was indeed a factor that had to be considered, given how crowded the agenda was becoming. In fact, US concerns over these issues may well have had very honest dimensions to them. However, political concerns played at least a partial role in the Americans' resistance on at least two of these issues, competition and investment.

Competition policy is most directly affected by politics through its antithesis to antidumping measures. Competition policy serves to increase competition, while antidumping measures essentially work to lessen it. As Barutciski writes:

From a competition policy perspective (concerned as it is with the level of competition in a market rather than the welfare of individual competitors) antidumping laws are perverse and often operate to the detriment of the country imposing the measures.[118]

In fact, nations such as Mexico, Japan and Korea, supportive of putting competition on the agenda, saw it as a way to constrain the use of antidumping and safeguard measures.[119] As long as the use of such measures was in keeping with domestic US economic interests, it was not politically desirable for the US to agree to an international agreement on competition.

There was also no support for putting competition policy on the agenda from those in the United States who may have had an interest in doing so. At one time, US multinational corporations had supported the idea of using the GATT to break up local cartels in Japan.[120] Some had even supported somehow using domestic US anti-trust law to pry open foreign markets.[121] But now, according to one US official at Geneva, multinationals that enjoy dominant positions in developing nations fear that international competition policy could lead to the setting up of domestic competition agencies that would take action against them.[122] For whatever reason, US firms opposed allowing the WTO to go beyond simply studying the subject.[123]

There was also concern in the United States about sovereignty on the competition matter. Fox cites sovereignty as a concern the Americans had when, in 1948, they rejected a draft of the Havana Charter that would have forbidden certain 'business practices affecting international trade which restrain competition, limit access to markets, or foster monopolistic control...'[124] At the time of Seattle, the US Department of Justice was reluctant to have the WTO meddling in what it saw as a law enforcement matter.[125] This would be consistent with traditional US resistance to being constrained by international standards on almost any matter. It is likely that a Congress dominated by the right wing would be reluctant to agree to the globalization of competition law.

Political concerns could not have been absent from the US thinking on investment policy either. Global civil resistance had helped destroy the OECD's Multilateral Agreement on Investment.[126] Odell describes the MAI as having 'provoked more widespread public outrage than any international economic deal in a decade'.[127] This may be one issue on which the Seattle protesters had a tangential effect, reminding negotiators of the power that NGOs had previously demonstrated in killing an investment deal.

2.6 Lessons of Seattle

The failure at Seattle demonstrated some underlying problems, both in how negotiations are organized within the organization and how members approach them from a political standpoint. Structural changes ensuring a more democratic approach to negotiations and greater planning and coordination ahead of major meetings must be sought. The substantive failure of agreement both among developed nations and between developed and developing nations demonstrates the need for a spirit of understanding on all sides with regard to sensitive issues. This may include looking to cooperation in forums outside of the WTO, such as the International Labour Organization. On issues such as investment and competition, success in the future may be a matter of patience, whereby global regimes in these areas may eventually be necessitated by the globalization of the economy. Finally, the failure demonstrates the need for national leaders to cultivate domestic constituencies that would favour trade liberalization, so that their negotiators are not left without a mandate to achieve success at trade talks.

Some of the changes that should be made seem rather obvious in the wake of the controversies at the Ministerial. The Green Room should give way to more inclusive forms of governance. It served a valuable purpose throughout most of the GATT's history, but an organization with a membership as broad as the WTO, with the important mandate that the WTO has in the era of trade liberalization, cannot afford even the appearance of elitism.

To compensate for the loss of the Green Room's coordinating function in negotiations, a number of reforms could be implemented. For example, a WTO executive board should be created.[128] It could be chaired by the Director General and have a rotating membership in which balance would always be sought between states from the developed and developing worlds and states from different continents. Or it could be formed out of the WTO Secretariat. In either case, this board would have to function within the consensus-based structure of the WTO.[129] Therefore, it would not be a trade version of the United Nations Security Council in that it would not have any authority in and of itself. With that one major constraint, there are various roles that such a board can play. It could form and circulate proposed compromise texts on outstanding WTO issues, which could serve as bases for negotiation among the larger WTO membership, with the understanding that the membership would be free to reject them outright. The circulation of these texts should begin as much as six months before any negotiating deadline to give members as much time as possible to bridge their differences.[130] The board could also appoint chairs for WTO meetings from within the WTO Secretariat. This would help prevent the disaster that occurred at Seattle, when US Trade Representative Barshefsky took it upon herself to chair the Ministerial and offended many of its participants, who felt she did not act fairly.[131]

The Seattle failure also suggests that WTO ministerial meetings should not be hampered by any artificial time constraints, as Seattle was. It is understandable that trade ministers are busy, but it is worth asking what in their schedules could possibly take priority over such meetings. Given the current size of the active membership, the only way to allow work to proceed in a democratic fashion is to give individual working groups the time necessary to fulfil their tasks. Hopefully, with the aid of the preparation that a new executive board could provide, the time periods involved would not be unduly long.

The lessons and implications from each of the substantive failures that occurred at Seattle warrant further investigation. However, some thoughts are worth noting. The biggest controversies at Seattle, that is sanctions-backed labour and environmental standards, represent a problem that will resurface in future trade talks. As trade liberalization proceeds, the WTO must find a means to better negotiate the trade and domestic regulation interface.

With respect to the issues on which the Americans proved intransigent, such as antidumping, competition policy and investment policy, the lesson was that governments should not enter into trade negotiations without having cultivated constituencies at home in whose interest it is to liberalize trade. There will always be opposition to any initiative that touches domestic interests, whether it be due to the dismantling of antidumping regimes or the implementation of new global regulations.

Finally, Seattle demonstrated that member states should not try to achieve all their trade goals in a single set of negotiations. As one European diplomat reflected after Seattle, 'we tried to do too much too fast'.[132] As it stands, negotiations become cluttered and, in the end, very little is accomplished. The difficulty is that the current system, where everything tends to be done at once, allows for trade-offs between various interests. Overcoming this can be done by setting priorities with constituencies at home[133] and thus gaining a sense of which issues are truly worth pushing with trading partners. The success of this approach will depend on the politics of each individual country, but it should at least be attempted.

3 POST-SEATTLE ATTEMPTS AT TRADE NEGOTIATIONS

3.1 Agriculture

The Agreement on Agriculture negotiated during the Uruguay Round included a commitment to commence discussions on agriculture by the end of 1999. The Seattle Ministerial failed to come to an agreement on the agenda for these talks, but discussions have nonetheless proceeded. Progress with regard to agriculture has been limited to agreement on the general structure of the negotiating process rather than agreement on substance. Members have agreed to a time-frame for the tabling of negotiating proposals, allowing for submissions up to March 2001. However, the challenge remains bridging the gap between agricultural protectionists, such as the Japanese and the Europeans, and those pushing for further liberalization of trade in agriculture, such as the Americans and members of the Cairns Group.

In March of 2000, member states agreed to allow for the tabling of negotiating proposals by the end of 2000, and the tabling of further or more detailed proposals leading up to March of 2001. At that time, members are scheduled to meet to undertake a stock-taking exercise. By June of 2000, 45 governments, comprising a third of the WTO's membership, had already submitted proposals and these were examined at a second negotiating session held that month. Further sessions took place during 2000 along with an additional meeting likely to take place prior to March 2001.

Among the issues at stake in the area of agriculture are export subsidies, import quotas and market access, domestic agricultural subsidies and food security for developing countries.[134] The Japanese government has suggested that the first phase of work should concentrate on implementing Uruguay Round commitments, rather than the undertaking of new obligations.[135] The Japanese can be expected to resist any further liberalization of agricultural trade, using tariff rate quotas (TRQs) to keep market access as restrictive as possible, while also resisting reforms to increase the transparency of the TRQ system.[136] A sole hope for progress may be for other members to make concessions in other sectors, important to the Japanese, contingent on Tokyo being more conciliatory on the agricultural front.[137]

The Japanese will have an ally in the Europeans. While the Europeans admit that liberalization in this area would serve their export interests, they caution that the process will take time.[138] Brussels can be expected to push for the retention of low TRQs, whereby agricultural imports enter at no or low tariffs up to an assigned limit, after which high tariff rates begin to apply.[139] The Europeans will also likely resist further reductions in export subsidy levels, and changes to the 'blue box' system whereby direct payments to farmers are exempted from domestic support reduction commitments.[140] Finally, they will push, against opposition from the United States, to re-open the agreement on the Application of Sanitary and Phyto-Sanitary Measures to deal with consumers' and environmentalists' acceptance of biotechnology.[141]

No doubt, in order to dilute any final agreement on agriculture, the Japanese, the Europeans and their allies have urged a broadening of the considerations involved in agricultural negotiations. In March 2000, delegates of the EU, Japan and Slovenia insisted that negotiations take into account the multifunctional role of agriculture and that issues such as rural development, food safety and animal welfare be borne in mind. Japan and

Norway stressed that negotiations must allow for the co-existence of different agricultural systems. The Europeans have also argued that all export competition measures, not just export subsidies, be brought into the negotiations and be treated on an equal basis.[142]

The United States will continue to stand on the other side of the issue. The Americans have called for an 'ambitious' target of expanding market access.[143] They have the necessary domestic consensus to push for the elimination of all export subsidies.[144] They will also push for stronger rules with regard to state trading enterprises, such as the Canada Wheat Board and the New Zealand Dairy Board.[145] Because of low commodity prices and their effect on domestic producers, the Americans may have to rethink their opposition to the blue box exemptions, but there could still be some friction with the Europeans over the issue.[146] Finally, the Americans will likely push for agreement on a standard method of establishing TRQs, thus assuring greater compliance with agreements in this area.[147]

Although disagreements may arise over areas such as state trading enterprises, the Americans will likely find allies for the cause of liberalization among the Cairns Group. This group, consisting of Australia, Argentina, Brazil, Canada, Chile, Colombia, Fiji, Indonesia, Malaysia, New Zealand, Paraguay, the Philippines, South Africa, Thailand and Uruguay, can be counted on to push for greater market access in the agricultural sector. Specifically, they will push for an increase in the no/low tariff levels of TRQs, for a reduction in bound tariffs, and for a tightening of the list of allowable subsidies.[148]

The Central and Eastern Europeans, as relatively new players in the process, will be focused on the compatibility of their agricultural and trade policies with the rules of the WTO and with the EU's Common Agricultural Policy.[149] The matter is complicated for Central and Eastern European members that are EU members, because raising their tariff levels to conform with the EU's external tariff will put them in violation of WTO rules.[150] These states will thus have a great interest in how WTO negotiations come out on tariff issues.

3.2 Services

Members agreed to further negotiations on the liberalization of services five years after the entry into force of the General Agreement on Trade in Services (GATS) and periodically thereafter.[151] In keeping with this commitment, new negotiations were launched in 2000. However, as in agriculture, what has occurred so far has been a pre-negotiations phase. Negotiating proposals were to be submitted by the end of 2000, with a deadline for the technical phase of negotiations of March 2001. Substantive negotiations were scheduled to begin in the Spring of 2001.

Work in 2000 concentrated on rule-making in areas such as safeguards and domestic regulation.[152] Agreement was reached on an organizational roadmap for negotiations leading up to March 2001. In the first half of the year, members carried out a review of existing Most Favoured Nation (MFN) exemptions in the area to see whether the conditions that had created a need for these exemptions continued to exist.[153] Discussions on air transport were scheduled to take place in Autumn 2000.

Both the Americans and the Europeans have presented proposals for services negotiations, with clear differences between them. While the US proposal calls for negotiations to conclude in three years, by 2002, the EU proposal does not stipulate a time for concluding negotiations or tabling offers. The US and EU proposals also place different emphasis on the negotiating methodologies that should be used to achieve further market opening. The US proposal favours alternatives to the traditional request–offer approach and calls for a deadline of the 2001 mid-term review for agreeing on the methodology for negotiations. The Europeans would supplement the request–offer method as necessary. The Americans have also criticized the Europeans for not endorsing alternative methodologies such as model schedules and cluster approaches. (A model schedule approach works out a template for a given sector that lays out the priority obligations that countries should undertake to achieve market access. The cluster approach brings together a series of activities covered in different parts of the schedules developed under the GATS to formulate business pursuits in actual markets.[154])

The next set of negotiations on services are likely to focus on expanding the coverage of specific commitments and improving multilateral rules.[155] The Americans propose that, during the negotiations, countries should not apply any new trade-restrictive practices to improve their negotiating position and that GATS commitments generally come to encompass more sectors and become more transparent. A great deal of interest in liberalizing the financial sector exists in the US, Europe and Japan. Furthermore, there is a great deal of room to improve existing commitments, either by extending them into the financial sector or by reducing limitations that governments currently have in place. A number of small developing nations have already undertaken unilateral commitments in the telecommunications sector in order to attract foreign investment.

4   CONCLUSIONS

While the demonstrators at Seattle stole the show, the Ministerial failed for a number of other reasons. The set-up of the conference did not take account of the proliferation of interested members, namely the developing countries.

Time constraints forced organizers to revert to the Green Room, not allowing the more democratic working group sessions to fulfil their tasks. To add to this, the Americans came to the meeting constrained by their domestic political situation, unprepared to compromise on key issues such as antidumping, competition policy and investment policy. President Clinton felt the need to allay domestic constituencies which upset the developing world by raising the prospect of global labour and environmental standards backed by sanctions. Yet in the end, the meeting will not have been in vain if the lessons from its failure are heeded and the opportunity is seized to make necessary changes. The structure of the WTO must become more democratic and better equipped to deal with its enlarged and diversified base. Greater sensitivity must dictate the approach to issues such as labour and environmental regulatory standards in the developing world. Finally, member governments must work to mobilize domestic constituencies that would support trade liberalization and to ensure that they enter trade negotiations with a clear sense of their priorities.

NOTES

1. S.J.D. (University of Toronto). Dr. Soloway practises international trade and competition law in Toronto with Davies Ward Phillips & Vineberg LLP. We are grateful to the helpful comments of John Kirton and Alan Rugman and the financial support of the SSHRC project 'Strengthening Canada's Environmental Community through International Regime Reform', University of Toronto, [www.envireform.utoronto.ca].
2. Year III, LL.B. Program, Faculty of Law and MA in International Relations (candidate), University of Toronto.
3. Dymond and Hart (2000, pp. 21–2).
4. Laidlaw (2000, p. A21).
5. Schott (2000, p. 11).
6. Dymond and Hart (2000, p. 32).
7. Laidlaw (2000, p. A21).
8. See also Graham (2000).
9. Dymond and Hart (2000, p. 32).
10. Jackson (2000, p. 6).
11. Alexandroff (2000, p. 108).
12. Odell (2000, p. 8).
13. Odell (2000, pp. 9–10).
14. Odell (2000, p. 9).
15. Trebilcock and Howse (1999, p. 21).
16. Odell (2000, p. 6).
17. Odell (2000, p. 6).
18. Schott (1994, p. 7).
19. Alexandroff (2000, p. 108).
20. Preeg (2000, p. 183).
21. Alexandroff (2000, p. 108).
22. Preeg (2000, p. 184).
23. Krueger (1999, p. 2).
24. Schott (2000, p. 20).

25. Michalopoulos (1999, p. 8).
26. Michalopoulos (1999, p. 8).
27. Krueger (1999, p. 2).
28. Michalopoulos (1999, p. 5).
29. Michalopoulos (1999, p. 6).
30. Michalopoulos (1999, p. 5).
31. Finger and Schuler (1999, p. 32).
32. Krueger (1999, p. 1).
33. Odell (2000, p. 14).
34. Odell (2000, p. 14).
35. Odell (2000, p. 28).
36. Preeg (2000, p. 184).
37. Odell (2000, pp. 6–7).
38. Preeg (2000, p. 184).
39. Krueger (1999, p. 1).
40. Odell (2000, p. 7).
41. Odell (2000, p. 16).
42. Finger and Schuler (1999, p. 1).
43. Finger and Schuler (1999, p. 32).
44. Finger and Schuler (1999, p. 33).
45. Finger and Schuler (1999, p. 6).
46. Finger and Schuler (1999, p. 6).
47. Hoekman and Anderson (1999, p. 1).
48. Hoekman and Anderson (1999, p. 3).
49. Finger and Schuler (1999, p. 35).
50. Hoekman and Anderson (1999, p. 4).
51. Odell (2000, p. 16).
52. Odell (2000).
53. Horlick (2000, p. 180).
54. Horlick (2000, p. 180).
55. Horlick (2000, p. 181).
56. Horlick (2000).
57. Horlick (2000).
58. Odell (2000, p. 16).
59. Krueger (1999, p. 13).
60. Odell (2000, p. 16).
61. Michalopoulos (1999, p. 41).
62. Michalopoulos (1999).
63. Odell (2000, p. 16).
64. Sauve (2000, p. 85).
65. Finger and Schuler (1999, p. 21).
66. Odell (2000, p. 7).
67. Odell (2000, p. 7).
68. Luke (2000, p. 40).
69. Odell (2000, p. 7).
70. Luke (2000, p. 40).
71. Luke (2000, p. 41).
72. Luke (2000, p. 41).
73. Luke (2000, p. 41).
74. Alexandroff (2000, p. 109).
75. Odell (2000, p. 5).
76. Odell (2000, p. 27).
77. Odell (2000, p. 27).
78. Odell (2000, p. 5).
79. Gephart had opposed the NAFTA and Most Favoured Nation status for China.
80. Schott (2000, p. 23).

81.   Schott (2000, p. 11).
82.   Alexandroff (2000, p. 109).
83.   Robert (2000, p. 42).
84.   de Mestral (1998, pp. 175 and 179).
85.   Odell (2000, p. 18).
86.   Esty (2000, p. 177).
87.   Odell (2000, p. 17).
88.   Odell (2000, p. 17).
89.   Odell (2000, p. 19).
90.   Alexandroff (2000, p. 109).
91.   Odell (2000, p. 16).
92.   Odell (2000, p. 16).
93.   Salazar-Xirinachs (2000, p. 381).
94.   Salazar-Xirinachs (2000, p. 382).
95.   See Rugman *et al.* (1999).
96.   Odell (2000, p. 23).
97.   Alexandroff (2000, p. 109).
98.   Odell (2000, p. 23).
99.   Preeg (2000, p. 185).
100.   Alexandroff (2000, p. 109).
101.   Odell (2000, p. 23).
102.   Horlick (2000, p. 182).
103.   Odell (2000, p. 18).
104.   Schott (2000, p. 19).
105.   Horlick (2000, p. 182).
106.   Horlick (2000, p. 182).
107.   Horlick (2000, p. 181).
108.   Horlick (2000, p. 182).
109.   Horlick (2000, p. 183).
110.   Odell (2000, pp. 4 and 16).
111.   Odell (2000, pp. 4 and 17).
112.   Odell (2000, p. 5).
113.   Odell (2000, p. 17).
114.   Odell (2000, pp. 4 and 26).
115.   Odell (2000, p. 20).
116.   Odell (2000, p. 25).
117.   Odell (2000, p. 21).
118.   Barutciski (1999, p. 12).
119.   Odell (2000, p. 4).
120.   Odell (2000, p. 6).
121.   Fox (1999, p. 668).
122.   Odell (2000, p. 6).
123.   Odell (2000, p. 6).
124.   Fox (1999, p. 666).
125.   Odell (2000, p. 4).
126.   See Graham (2000) and Soloway (2000).
127.   Odell (2000, p. 4).
128.   Odell (2000, p. 29).
129.   Odell (2000, p. 29).
130.   Odell (2000, p. 29).
131.   Odell (2000, p. 29).
132.   Odell (2000, p. 27).
133.   Odell (2000, p. 27).
134.   Kerr (2000, p. 125).
135.   *Inside US Trade*.
136.   Kerr (2000, p. 128).

137. Ibid.
138. Josling (2000, p. 55).
139. Kerr (2000, p. 126).
140. Kerr (2000, p. 126).
141. Kerr (2000, pp. 126–7).
142. *Inside US Trade.*
143. Josling (2000, p. 55).
144. Kerr (2000, p. 127).
145. Kerr (2000, p. 127).
146. Kerr (2000, p. 127).
147. Kerr (2000, p. 127).
148. Kerr (2000, pp. 128–9).
149. Kerr (2000, p. 129).
150. Kerr (2000, p. 129).
151. Hoekman and Anderson (2000, 1999, p. 31).
152. *Inside US Trade.*
153. *Inside US Trade 2.*
154. *Inside US Trade*, **18** (29) – July 21, 2000.
155. Hoekman and Anderson (1999, p. 42).

REFERENCES

Alexandroff, Alan S. (2000), 'Guerrilla theatre and the uncivil society', *Policy Options*, January/February, pp. 106–10.
Barutciski, Milos (1999), 'The two solitudes: trade and competition policy', Presented to the World Trade Organization Symposium on Trade and Competition Policy, April.
Dymond, William A. and Michael M. Hart (2000), 'Post-modern trade policy: reflections on the challenges to multilateral trade negotiations after Seattle', *Journal of World Trade*, **3**(1), June, pp. 21–38.
Esty, Daniel C. (2000), 'An environmental perspective on Seattle', *Journal of International Economic Law*, **3**(1), March, pp. 176–8.
Finger, J. Michael and Philip Schuler (1999), 'Implementation of Uruguay Round commitments: the development challenge', supported by *The Global and Regional Trust Fund Component of the Bank/Netherlands Partnership Programme.*
Fox, Eleanor M. (1999), 'Competition law and the Millennium Round', *Journal of International Economic Law*, **3**(4), December, pp. 665–79.
Graham, Edward (2000), *Fighting the Wrong Enemy: Antiglobal Activists and Multinational Enterprises*, Washington DC: Institute for International Economics.
Hoekman, Bernard and Kym Anderson (1999), 'Developing country agriculture and the new trade agenda', Presented at the American Economic Association Annual Meeting, New York, January.
Horlick, Gary (2000), 'Antidumping at the Seattle Ministerial: with tear gas in my eyes', *Journal of International Economic Law*, **3**(1), March, pp. 178–83.
Inside US Trade, Inside Washington Publishers, Washington DC, various issues, year 2000.
Jackson, John H. (2000), 'International economic law in times that are interesting', *Journal of International Economic Law*, **3**(14).
Josling, Timothy (2000), 'The agricultural negotiations: an overflowing agenda', *Federal Reserve Bank of St Louis Review*, **82**(4), July/August, pp. 53–72.

Kerr, William A. (2000), 'The next step will be harder – issues for the new round of agricultural negotiations at the World Trade Organization', *Journal of World Trade*, **34**(1), pp. 123–40.

Krueger, Anne O. (1999), *The Developing Countries and the Next Round of Multilateral Trade Negotiations*, Washington: The World Bank.

Laidlaw, Stuart (2000), 'Seattle set new agenda on trade', *The Toronto Star*, 27 November, p. A21.

Luke, David F. (2000), 'OAU/AEC Member States, the Seattle preparatory process and Seattle', *Journal of World Trade*, June, **3,4**(3), pp. 39–46.

Maestral, A.L.C. de (1998), 'The significance of the NAFTA side agreements on environmental and labour cooperation', *Arizona Journal of International and Comparative Law*, **15**(1).

Maryse, Robert (2000), *Negotiating NAFTA: Explaining the Outcomes in Culture, Textiles, Autos, and Pharmaceuticals*, Toronto: University of Toronto Press.

Michalopoulos, Constantine (1999), 'Trade Policy and Market Access Issues for Developing Countries. Implications for the Millennium Round', Washington: The World Bank.

Odell, John S. (2000), 'The Seattle impasse and its implications for the World Trade Organization', Prepared for a conference on The Political Economy of International Trade Law held to honour Professor Robert Hudec, September.

Ostry, Sylvia (1999), 'The future of the World Trade Organization', *Brookings Trade Forum*.

Preeg, Ernst H. (2000), 'The south rises in Seattle', *Journal of International Economic Law*, **3**(1), March, pp. 183–5.

Press Briefing (1999), US Trade Representative Charlene Barshefsky *et al*. 2 December 1999 at http://usinfo.state.gov/topical/econ/wto99/pp1202a.htm.

Rugman, Alan, John Kirton and Julie Soloway (1999), *Environmental Regulations and Corporate Strategy: A NAFTA Perspective*, Oxford, UK: Oxford University Press.

Salazar-Xirinachs, Jose M. (2000), 'The trade–labour nexus: developing countries' perspectives', *Journal of International Economic Law*, **3**(2), June, pp. 377–85.

Sauve, Pierre (2000), 'Developing countries and the GATS 2000 Round', *Journal of World Trade*, **34**(2), June, pp. 85–92.

Schott, Jeffrey J. (2000), 'Toward WTO 2000: a Seattle odyssey', *Review*, **82**(4), July/August, pp. 11–30.

Schott, Jeffrey J. (1994), *The Uruguay Round: An Assessment*, Washington, DC: Institute for International Economics.

Soloway, Julie A. (2000), 'Environmental regulation as expropriation: the case of NAFTA's chapter 11', *Canadian Business Law Journal*, Vol. 33.

Trebilcock, Michael (2000), 'Mostly smoke and mirrors: NGOs and the WTO', Paper written for US Library of Congress and New York University Law School, 10 March.

Trebilcock, Michael and Robert Howse (1999), *The Regulation of International Trade*, 2nd edn, London: Routledge.

4. Corporations and structural linkages in world commerce

John B. Davis and Joseph P. Daniels

The Millennium Round of multilateral negotiations under the auspices of the World Trade Organization (WTO) confronts international trade and investment issues that are more complex and intractable than those in past rounds on account of increasing structural and policy interdependencies between the industrialized nations. Negotiators will have to think not only in terms of trade and investment between separate nations but also in terms of a system of production that operates across nations. In previous rounds, liberalizing international trade dominated the agendas. But international trade and investment have become more highly interlinked in the last decade, so that it has become difficult to consider trade liberalization apart from capital flows. At the same time, the issue of liberalizing international financial flows has been complicated by the massive expansion in the 1990s of portfolio capital flows and by financial crises in Asia and elsewhere.

This chapter consequently examines international trade and investment linkages in terms of long-term structural change, tying this to corporate strategies responding to and underlying this change. Our principal subject is the theory of international production and the emerging system of international production, and we comment on policy initiatives regarding trade and investment generated by increased recognition of their interlinked character.

International production has been investigated within at least six branches of theory: international capital movements, trade, location, industrial organization, innovation, and the firm (Cantwell *et al.*, 1986). Various theories of international production investigate different questions posed in theoretical branches they draw upon, some taking macroeconomic and others microeconomic perspectives. The theory of international capital movements and foreign direct investment (FDI), especially where it bears on balance of payments and exchange rate effects, has mainly a macroeconomic focus, whereas the theory of the transnational corporation (TNC) is more microeconomic. Both subjects, however, concern closely related matters, and accordingly understanding important issues in international production generally requires an eclectic approach, as argued by Dunning (1977, 1981,

1988). Our focus is restricted to economics and international business, and does cover social and cultural issues.

1   CHAPTER OUTLINE

First we describe a number of key structural developments, to portray general trends in globalization.[1] These structural developments concern: the relation of world FDI flows to world trade flows; the dominance of Triad trade and FDI flows in the world economy; the importance of mergers and acquisitions (M&As) in world FDI; and the geographical and sectoral distribution of FDI and cross-border M&A. We conclude this section with a discussion of the relationship between trade and investment as substitutes and/or complements.

Next we turn to TNCs as a principal vehicle of globalization processes, and explain how the strategies of major firms in the world economy are shaped by their need to operate in foreign locations. The current state of trade negotiations has given added importance to international firms expanding through FDI. We then emphasize that firm search and deliberation costs, as transaction costs, are particularly important to TNCs, and argue that TNCs become 'embedded' in host social and business networks as they establish foreign affiliates. This 'embeddedness' helps to account for the structural changes and developments described earlier, particularly the concentration of FDI in the Triad, where business networks are generally highly developed. To illustrate the implications of this for the relationship between trade and investment, we return to the topic of trade and investment as substitutes or complements, and discuss three cases showing how firms' FDI affects exports and imports.

Finally, we discuss economic policy toward FDI and TNCs, particularly in connection with recent unsuccessful efforts to establish the Multilateral Agreement on Investment (MAI). We first consider debate about the national loyalties of TNCs and the impact of liberalized capital flows. We then distinguish between short-term and long-term investment flows, and argue that liberalization of the latter can be in the interest of host countries as TNCs become embedded in them. We then discuss the difference between national competitiveness and the competitiveness of a nation's firms, and make a general case for an international agreement at least along the lines of the MAI. This section closes with an argument in favour of a collection of piecemeal changes that taken together will accomplish much of what was intended by the MAI, and will also create an agenda for more comprehensive reform.

2   EVIDENCE OF STRUCTURAL CHANGE

The collapse of the Bretton Woods system ushered in a new era of globalization, with capital market liberalization beginning in the mid-1970s in the United States and Canada. The process continued, though unevenly, throughout the remainder of the twentieth century as other developed nations began removing and reducing capital barriers in the 1980s (Williamson and Mahar, 1998). Many developing countries followed suit, although it was a forward–reverse–forward process for some. The risks and rewards became clear as the century came to a close. Long-term capital flows were concentrated in the developed nations, increasing their global production capacity and providing access to lucrative consumer markets. Developing and emerging nations gained jobs created by FDI, but also suffered extreme financial crises created by hot-money or portfolio flows.

Meanwhile the growth of global trade gradually declined, while foreign direct investment increased. At the same time, different stages of the production processes moved to different world locations, in a 'disintegration' of production as a means to greater global integration (Feenstra, 1998). In this section we focus on developments in trade and capital markets over the last decade. We present the stylized facts only, relating these patterns to strategies and theories of transnationals in the following section.

2.1   World FDI Flows Relative to World Trade Flows

In spite of declining transportation costs and advances in telecommunications technology, the rate of growth in world exports has decreased during the last thirty years. As shown in Table 4.1, five-year growth rates in world exports have declined from a high of 24 per cent in the early 1970s to single digit gains in the 1990s. The long-delayed conclusion to the Uruguay Round of

Table 4.1   Periodic growth of world FDI and exports

	FDI inflows	FDI outflows	World exports
1971–1975	19.8	17.3	24
1976–1980	18.5	17.4	18.1
1981–1985	2.1	2.4	–0.56
1986–1990	31.5	34.6	14.5
1991–1995	11.3	9.2	8.3
1996–1998	25.6	22.8	2.2

Source: UNCTAD *Handbook of Statistics* (2000).

trade negotiations, the loss of Presidential fast-track authority in the United States, recent WTO skirmishes, and the lack of G7 leadership suggests that further gains in world trade are more likely to come from regional and bilateral agreements than from multilateral pacts.

Capital flows have expanded over this same period in a climate of liberalization and gradual harmonization of national tax policies and accounting rules. FDI rates of growth now significantly surpass trade flow rates of growth. As illustrated in Table 4.1, the change begins after the worldwide recession and the Latin American debt crises of the early 1980s. Further gains in economic liberalization are likely to stem from the expansion of international production fuelled by high rates of FDI as opposed to increased multilateral trade liberalization.

2.2   Triad Trade and FDI Flows

Figure 4.1 illustrates Triad and rest-of-world (ROW) shares of world exports. During the last thirty years, the Triad has consistently contributed 60 to 70 per cent of total world exports. Figure 4.2 shows inward FDI flows for the Triad and the ROW for the last thirty years. Though the average inward FDI flow to the Triad is 60 to 70 per cent of the total, these inflows demonstrate a fair amount of variability, perhaps reflecting the Latin American debt crises of the 1980s and the financial crises of the late 1990s, and reveal a short-lived

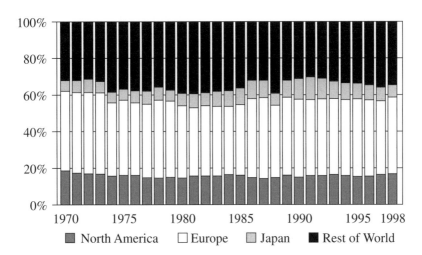

Source: UNCTAD *Handbook of Statistics* (2000).

Figure 4.1   World exports: Triad proportion of total

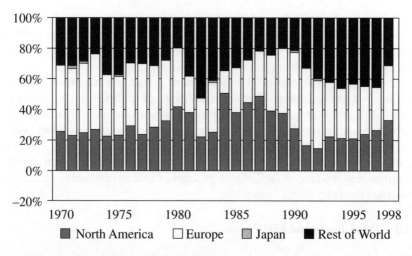

Source: UNCTAD *Handbook of Statistics* (2000).

Figure 4.2   Inward FDI flows: Triad proportion of total

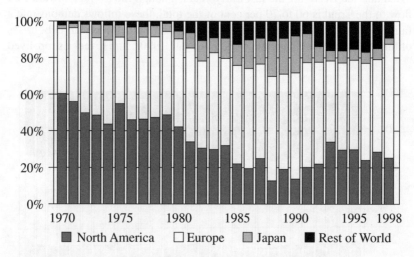

Source: UNCTAD *Handbook of Statistics* (2000).

Figure 4.3   Outward FDI flows: Triad proportion of total

interest in global capacity diversification in developing economies. Of particular interest is the small fraction of FDI inflows to Japan, indicating the relatively closed nature of its economy.

The Triad's share of FDI outflows, shown in Figure 4.3, also demonstrates greater variability than their export share, with decreases occurring in the early 1980s and mid-1990s. The thirty-year average of the Triad, however, remains above 90 per cent. The general or overall decline in the Triad's share may reflect efforts of developing economies to integrate globally and to increase worldwide capacity and market share.

In general, then, the Triad's dominance of trade flows is reproduced in its dominance of FDI flows, as the Triad is the principal source and host of FDI flows.

2.3   FDI M&A

Cross-border mergers and acquisitions accounted for most FDI flows in the late 1990s. More favourable tax conditions, relaxation of regulations and labour laws, and a changing shareholder culture spurred dramatic increases in cross-border M&A activity. From 1996 to 1999, as shown in Figure 4.4, M&A inflows to the Organisation for Economic Cooperation and Development (OECD) nations increased over 280 per cent to US$718 billion, while M&A outflows from the OECD nations increased over 200 per cent to US$767 billion. In 1999 alone, cross-border M&A inflows and outflows increased approximately 50 per cent.

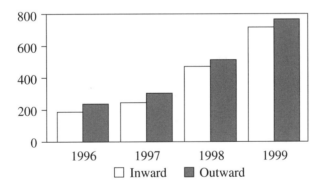

Source: United Nations 1999 *World Investment Report*.

Figure 4.4   OECD international M&A ($US billions)

As shown in Figure 4.5, the majority of M&A deals were concentrated in the Triad. According to OECD data, in 1999 European companies led in M&A deals. In the same year, the United Kingdom completed more acquisitions than any other nation, accounting for 30 per cent of global M&A value

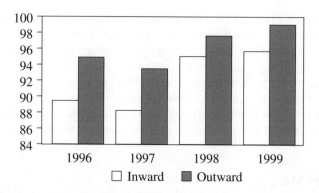

Source: United Nations 1999 *World Investment Report*.

Figure 4.5   International M&A in OECD countries: Triad share of total

(Wessel, 2000), while the United States continued to attract more M&A purchasers than any other nation, capturing over 35 per cent of the value of global M&A purchases.

2.4   Geographical and Sectoral Distribution of FDI Flows and Cross-Border M&A

The recent shift in FDI flows and M&A to the Triad nations relative to the rest of the world is illustrated in greater detail in Tables 4.2 and 4.3 below, which provide the geographical distribution of FDI inflows and cross-border mergers and acquisitions. We chose not to combine these two measures (that

Table 4.2   Geographical distribution of FDI inflows (percentage of total inflows)

	1993	1994	1995	1996	1997	1998
Developed nations	61.0	57.7	63.4	58.8	58.9	71.5
European Union	35.0	30.6	35.1	30.4	27.2	35.7
Other European nations	0.9	2.7	1.8	1.8	1.9	1.2
North America	22.0	21.0	20.7	23.9	26.0	32.6
Other developed	3.1	3.4	5.7	2.8	3.8	2.0
Developing nations	35.9	39.9	32.3	37.7	37.2	25.8
Transitional nations	3.1	2.3	4.3	3.5	4.0	2.7

Source: United Nations 1999 *World Investment Report*.

Table 4.3   *Geographical distribution of cross-border M&As, by seller (percentage of total)*

	1993	1994	1995	1996	1997	1998
Developed nations	60.3	65.8	71.0	67.9	68.4	85.9
European Union	31.9	29.7	31.5	27.9	39.1	40.6
Other European nations	0.4	1.3	0.6	1.8	1.4	1.5
North America	24.8	32.0	31.2	29.6	22.6	39.8
Other developed	3.2	2.7	7.6	8.5	5.4	4.0
Developing nations	30.0	31.1	22.2	30.4	28.0	12.4
Transitional nations	9.8	2.5	6.8	1.5	2.9	1.6

Source: United Nations 1999 *World Investment Report.*

is to express M&A as a percentage of FDI flows, as is often done), as M&A may be financed by means other than foreign direct investment, thereby overstating the importance of M&A as a percentage of FDI. Nonetheless, the data illustrate a significant increase in FDI inflows in the developed nations, and in the Triad in particular, at the expense of developing nations. As in the previous section, the increase in FDI corresponds with the dramatic increase in M&A activity in the developed nations.

Table 4.2 indicates that the developed countries increased their share of world FDI inflows by an additional 13 per cent and their share of world cross-border M&A by an additional 17 per cent at the expense of developing and

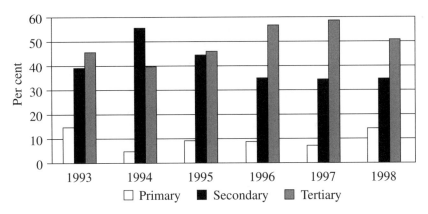

Source: author's estimates.

Figure 4.6   *Cross-border M&A by sector (percentage of total)*

transitional nations. This trend is best understood in light of the sectoral distribution of M&A deals. Figure 4.6 illustrates the distribution of cross-border M&A by primary, secondary, and tertiary sectors. The growing importance of tertiary M&A reflects, in particular, recent deals in banking, finance, and related services conducted almost exclusively among the developed nations.

2.5   The Relationship Between Foreign Direct Investment and Trade Flows

Further international economic integration is likely to result from increases in international production capacity due to larger capital flows rather than the expansion of world exports resulting from the reduction of trade barriers. What might this imply about the relationship between capital flows and trade flows? Not too long ago, business economists believed global expansion occurred along two relatively independent routes: through trade or through foreign direct investment. Global strategies were simple in that a firm could expand internationally by exporting goods and services or by FDI and producing abroad. Recent theoretical and empirical research, however, suggests that the relationship between trade and FDI is more complex, and that trade and foreign direct investment complement each other. FDI may spur greater amounts of trade and trade may spur greater amounts of FDI.

Fantagné and Pajot (1997) provide estimates of the impact of bilateral FDI flows and FDI stocks on bilateral trade flows, controlling for such things as market distance, income levels, and market sizes. Their evidence suggests that Japan's exports to the United States are 149 per cent higher than they would have been in lieu of bilateral FDI flows, while US exports to Japan are 86 per cent higher than they would have been without the bilateral FDI flows. FDI flows between Japan and the United States contribute to a bilateral trade deficit for the United States, as a greater amount of exports to the United States are generated than exports to Japan.[2] In contrast, the bilateral FDI relationships between Canada, the United States, and the United Kingdom generate approximately equal amounts of imports and exports, and do not accordingly explain trade imbalances between the countries.[3] This shows that FDI flows may either complement or substitute for trade flows, depending, presumably, on the nature and purposes of the FDI. Below in Section 3, in connection with our discussion of firm strategies, we consider three types of cases in which FDI has specific implications for trade flows.

3 UNDERSTANDING THE EVIDENCE IN TERMS OF THE STRATEGIES OF TNCs

In this section we seek to explain the structural relationships underlying the data on trade and investment in terms of the strategies of major firms in the international economy. According to the 1999 *World Investment Report* (United Nations Conference on Trade and Investment, 1999), though TNCs include over 500,000 foreign affiliates established by some 60,000 parent companies, a relatively small number of such firms have dominated international production since 1990, with the list of the top 100 firms virtually unchanged since then, of which 90 per cent are from Triad countries. While the growth of the largest TNCs does not tell the whole story about the globalization of production, their operations are central to it. They dominate world markets for oil, minerals and agricultural products, and play a leading role in the globalization of manufacturing production and services. They also create production and distribution networks in both Triad and non-Triad nations in which small and medium-sized enterprises (SMEs) operate.

3.1 Change in the Relationship between Trade and Investment

The data above regarding the growth rates of trade and FDI over the period 1985–1999 provide evidence of a change in the relationship between trade and investment in the world economy. Our understanding of this development is that uncertain prospects for future trade negotiations have provided an important stimulus for higher levels of FDI. Until the Uruguay Round, liberalization of international trade through the General Agreement on Tariffs and Trade (GATT) and the WTO principally targeted the reduction of tariff barriers. But the success of these earlier negotiations created incentives for countries to increase their reliance on non-tariff trade barriers as their principal means of protection. Moreover, because non-tariff barriers are quantitatively and qualitatively more complex than tariffs, multilateral negotiations for their reduction have been, and are likely to continue to be, less successful than negotiations over reductions in more traditional barriers. The protracted nature of the Uruguay Round, which took up non-tariff barriers, and the largely failed 1999 ministerial talks in Seattle seem to bear this out. Thus, both because countries may rely more heavily on non-tariff barriers, and because progress in reducing such barriers is likely to be slow, firms now have good reason to look upon foreign investment as a key means of continuing expansion.

There may have been a period in the heyday of earlier GATT negotiations when many believed that international economic integration would soon produce a world in which markets for goods, services, and factors of production were perfectly integrated. It has now become apparent that the traditional paradigm of a world economy divided into nation states and segmented markets will not be replaced by a borderless world in the foreseeable future (cf. Helliwell, 1998). Trade flows will continue to encounter numerous obstacles, some created by national policies (tariffs and quotas, regulations, national standards, competition policies, and government procurement); some by differences in culture, language, and custom; some by geography (affecting transportation and communication); some by collusive practices of national firms; and others by first entrant advantages (economies of scale, learning by doing, control of distribution systems, privileged access to inputs, and customer loyalties). All of these give rise to imperfect competition, market segmentation, and international price and cost differences. But firms that engage in FDI can take advantage of the opportunities of such segmentation and thus arguably the dramatic growth in FDI since the mid-1980s reflects the decision (and the ability) of TNCs to exploit foreign profit opportunities and locational advantages not available through export strategies alone.

This conclusion may be understood in terms of two of the leading theories. First, it recalls Hymer's emphasis on structural market imperfections and market power approach (Hymer, 1976), more in regard to the advantages these create for firms than regarding the removal of conflict between them. But an emphasis on market segmentation also demonstrates the importance of transactions costs, since firms encountering obstacles to trade that invest abroad presumably regard transactions costs as greater than the costs of relocation and organizing production through direct managerial control. Obstacles to trade, whether created or natural, cause transaction costs which may be internalized through FDI. We agree with Buckley (Buckley, 1990, p. 658) that 'the internalisation and market power explanations ... should not be viewed as mutually exclusive or competing theories but should be combined to give a full and rich explanation of the growth of multinational firms.'

At the same time, we believe there are advantages in using the transactions cost framework to account for both the concentration of world FDI in the Triad (Section 2.2 above) and also the high degree of M&A in world FDI (Section 2.3 above). The Hymer framework, with its focus on imperfect competition, would lead us to expect developing countries to be an especially important destination for FDI, since their markets tend to be less competitive than those in developed countries. But the evidence indicates that developing countries have received a relatively small share of FDI since the mid-1980s. Further, if developing countries were an important destination for FDI, we would expect a higher share of FDI to be greenfield investment, both because of fewer opportunities in developing countries for M&A and because of greater opportunities for investments targeting unexploited resources. But the evidence indicates that greenfield investment, though still important, has been relatively unimportant in world FDI since the mid-1980s. Thus in the section that follows we rely on a transactions cost framework to explain both the concentration of FDI in the Triad countries and the importance of M&A in total world FDI. We use this framework in terms of search and deliberation costs taken as a general form of transactions costs.

3.2 Search and Deliberation Costs as Transactions Costs

Another way of understanding the obstacles to trade described above is in terms of cross-border information discontinuities that create significant search and deliberation problems for TNCs (Rangan and Lawrence, 1999, ch. 4). Within countries, information flows tend to be smoother and more homogeneous on account of shared market regulations and culture. Across borders, information flows tend to be irregular and interrupted, so that there may be significant interpretation problems, as different systems of regulation and culture come into contact. In general, search problems arise when firms seek to identify potential customers and suppliers as exchange partners. The costs of search increase not only as potential exchange partners become more physically dispersed, but also because across the international economy culture, language, and custom are different. In general, deliberation problems arise in connection with firms' assessments of the reliability and trustworthiness of potential exchange partners. The costs of deliberation rise as it becomes more difficult to reverse past decisions, implying that minimizing deliberation costs calls for stable relationships with exchange partners. Clearly domestic markets typically involve both lower search and deliberation costs for firms. We explain this by saying that domestic markets involve lower costs because firms are embedded (Granovetter, 1985) in established social, cultural, and business networks that help them identify and evaluate those with whom they do business. The lesson this implies is that success in international business similarly depends upon firms becoming embedded in social, cultural, and business networks in foreign locations that reduce search and deliberation costs. We use this insight to emphasize the importance to TNCs of internalizing search and deliberation costs as a general form of transactions costs through cross-border M&A, FDI, and strategic alliances.

The modern theory of the internationalization of markets in the literature on international production (see Buckley and Casson, 1976) draws on Coase's (1937) original contribution establishing transactions cost analysis. One important emphasis in this literature is on intangible assets such as technology that are particularly costly to exchange in arm's-length transactions, and are consequently important candidates for transactions costs internalization. In the international economy, TNCs thus internalize their acquisitions of technology through investment in foreign research and development (R&D) facilities, particularly through M&A with foreign firms that already possess desirable tacit capabilities that have been organizationally embedded in those firms through collective learning processes. There is a spectrum of such possible arrangements (cf. Kay, 1983). At one end are joint ventures and decentralized TNCs in which internal markets regulated by transfer prices have replaced external markets (Rugman, 1981). At the other end of the spectrum are globally integrated multinationals with foreign affiliates in production and distribution in which control over all divisions and operations is centralized and hierarchical (Williamson, 1975).

Acquisitions of technology, of course, account for only one category of exchange partners for TNCs. Putting aside the transformation of business through technological change, firms also have relationships with suppliers, subcontractors, distributors, labour and management personnel, consultants, and financial institutions in carrying out routine operations. All of these relationships are likely to differ in important respects in foreign country locations as compared to home country locations. The 'foreign-ness' of these relationships, however, is much the same as relationships aimed at technology acquisition. Just as many important technologies involve intangible assets and are embedded in firms through collective learning processes, so the relationships with most exchange partners, domestic or foreign, presuppose tacit understandings and expectations that guide these relationships and get embedded over an extended period of time.

When firms operate in their home locations, they often take these tacit features of exchange for granted. In foreign locations, however, they become sharply aware of the role that tacit understandings and expectations play between business partners. TNCs, we suggest, are firms that have learned how to identify the implicit features of exchange relationships in foreign countries, and then form relationships with suppliers, subcontractors, distributors, and so on. In doing so, they internalize transactions costs involved in operating supply and distribution chains outside of their home countries, where those transactions costs might be labelled *business and economic network* transactions costs, and are closely associated with search and deliberation costs of doing business there. As Rugman puts it (Rugman, 2000, pp. 215ff), TNCs serve as 'flagship firms' by operating at the hub of a business network or cluster. Long-term contracts are established with four basic kinds of partners – key suppliers, key customers, key competitors, and the non-business infrastructure – and the whole constitutes a relatively settled business system that internalizes an entire structure of transactions costs, not just transactions costs on a partner-by-partner basis.

The behaviour of US TNCs in manufacturing is illustrative. Although in 1990 the top 50 US TNCs accounted for nearly 40 per cent of US manufacturing exports, exports were not a large share of these firms' overall foreign sales, which were carried out by these firms' foreign affiliates (*Fortune*, 1991,

p. 59). In general (see Rangan and Lawrence, 1999, pp. 34ff), US TNCs appear to ship about half of all their exports on an intrafirm basis to their affiliates abroad. Moreover, a very significant share of these exports are inputs awaiting further value-added rather than finished products ready for sale. Some might suppose from this that these US firms have thus simply located production facilities in other countries, and carry out manufacturing operations there with home produced inputs. In fact, however, US input content in sales by foreign affiliates in developed economics is typically low, now amounting to about 10 per cent or less (Rangan and Lawrence, 1999, p. 65).[4] Thus, US TNCs rely on their developed country foreign affiliates – not home exports – for foreign sales, and focus on intrafirm exports of inputs to those affiliates, but then rely primarily upon local sourcing of inputs in generating products for final sale. We believe this illustrates the embeddedness of TNCs, especially in developed economies in which the pervasiveness of search and deliberation costs requires that firms internalize transactions costs on a systemic, wide-ranging basis.

The point stands out more clearly when we compare the practices of US TNCs in developing countries. While these firms rely on their foreign affiliates and less and less on home exports for their foreign sales, when we consider intrafirm exports of inputs to those affiliates, it turns out that TNCs depend less on local sourcing in developing countries. Thus, US input content in 1982 for a selection of developing economies ranges between 15 and 50 per cent (Rangan and Lawrence, 1999, p. 83). In our view, this reflects the lesser extent to which developing economies have established complex social and economic networks into which US TNCs must insert themselves in order to internalize search and deliberation transaction costs and carry out profitable transactions. Clearly business and economic networks exist in such economies. However, their number and variety of possible exchange partners do not compare with networks in developed economies. Thus we suppose that search and deliberation costs are lower in these economies, so that the expansion of TNCs into these economies reflects less the need to internalize such costs and perhaps more the pursuit of market power advantages *à la* Hymer. It should be noted, nonetheless, that the general pattern since 1982 is rising local content in US TNC foreign affiliate production. This suggests that the development of those economies, plus possibly technological spillover effects on local business networks (see below), is slowly creating a business environment for TNCs in developing economies guided by the same factors as those in developed ones.

We would not want to suggest by the analysis above, however, that the social and economic frameworks into which TNCs enter are static in nature and unaffected by this entry. A long literature dating from the earliest studies of TNCs has examined the transformative effects these firms have on local economies. Consider the case of technology transfer. Dunning (1958) pioneered this work in his study of the operations of British affiliates of US TNCs as compared to their British-owned counterparts. The former were generally more successful than the latter, and Dunning argued that this was due to the capacity of TNCs to transfer often intangible assets (technology, marketing, managerial skills) to their affiliates. Moreover, after a time the British firms were able to catch up with the US affiliates, demonstrating the spillover character of the original transfers.

One way that this spillover may occur is through transformation of TNC–supplier and TNC–distributor relationships. Seeking low-cost input supplies and efficient distribution networks, TNCs transfer organizational methods and technologies to their business partners, who then re-employ these methods and technologies in their business relationships with domestic firms. The latter then change their methods of organization and technologies, and so on. Thus FDI has interrelated transformative effects on host countries' technology levels and systems of business organization. Not surprisingly, developing countries have sought to take advantage of this by imposing local content requirements on TNCs (now generally banned by the WTO under the Agreement on Trade-Related Measures or TRIMs). Other 'downstream' spillovers include local human capital development (Borenszstein *et al.*, 1994). Finally, a recent OECD study (2000, p. 25) emphasizes the transformative effects of TNC activity in terms of the self-perpetuating nature of FDI. Not only do competing TNCs tend to follow one another into foreign locations, but they are also likely to induce local investments in supply chains and other business service providers. This is important for understanding the emerging role for SMEs operating in conjunction with TNCs in developed countries.

How, then, do these conclusions relate to the structural trends presented in Section 2 above? What stands out is the concentration of trade and investment in the Triad, the importance of M&A, and (to a lesser extent) the rising importance of tertiary production in FDI activity. Based on the discussion above, our argument regarding these trends is two-sided. First, though the obstacles to FDI as contrasted with domestic investment place a special burden on TNCs to overcome cost disadvantages in entering foreign locations, that burden may be eased through exploitation of search and deliberation transaction cost savings when these firms succeed in embedding themselves in foreign business and economic networks. We thus conclude that because these networks are more highly developed in the Triad, the *opportunities* for expansion there are greater. Second, once embedded in these networks, our analysis suggests that there is considerable promise of *profitable returns* on TNC investments, because highly developed business networks offer firms the flexibility to regularly adjust their commitments with exchange partners, which should be to their advantage. We believe the level of M&A FDI in the

Triad particularly reflects this. The embeddedness/transactions cost framework, then, takes us a considerable way toward understanding firm strategies responding to and underlying recent structural changes in the world economy.

3.3   Firm Strategies Producing FDI and Trade Flow Linkages

With our conclusions about TNC strategies developed above, we return to the topic of whether trade and investment are substitutes and/or complements, and describe three cases in which firm investment decisions have implications for countries' exports and imports. The importance of the topic lies in how countries assess the costs and benefits of liberalizing capital flows when the effects include changes in their trade accounts. In our view, one obstacle to successful international negotiations over capital flows liberalization is uncertainty regarding whether higher FDI creates trade deficits. The case has been made more frequently for capital-exporting countries, but it has also been made for capital-importing countries. Here we do not provide a comprehensive analysis of the subject, but rather suggest by our three cases that the effects of FDI on trade depend upon the purposes for which FDI is carried out. Trade and investment may thus be substitutes and/or complements for one another according to the circumstances involved, and we may accordingly rule out the impact of FDI on countries' trade balances as a policy concern.

First, consider perhaps the simplest type of relationship between FDI and trade. A firm moves production from a home location to a foreign location, and replaces its home exports with foreign affiliate sales. The home country trade account may be more or less unaffected, if some home input suppliers now export to the new foreign location, and prior imports of inputs to the home location now fall. The host country may lose exports if it was an input supplier to the original location of production in the home country, and see some added input imports, but may also gain exports if the new plant employs new technologies that make it possible to add capacity to export. Thus the overall effects depend on the character of the original investment, and there does not appear to be a general relationship between FDI and trade.

Second, consider the case of a developed country firm that moves labour-intensive production to a foreign location, and then imports the output for final assembly at home. Since final output is now cheaper, the export capability of the firm is enhanced. The home country may thus increase its imports and also its exports. At the same time, the country to which the labour-intensive production was relocated now has higher exports. But if, as is not unlikely, it purchases the now relatively cheaper output of the home country firm, then its imports rise as well. Thus the ultimate impact on trade of FDI again depends upon the kind of FDI and the circumstances involved.

Third, consider the trade effects of using FDI to outsource stages of the production process in pursuit of cost advantages in foreign locations (Feenstra, 1998; Davis and Daniels, 2000). Though attention is often focused on the stages of production that leave a home country, equally important for understanding the trade effects of FDI are those stages of production that it retains. When a country retains stages of the production process in which it lacks comparative advantage, the possible comparative advantage it possesses in other stages may be concealed by a focus on whether the final product is cost competitive. Conversely, when a country relocates stages of production in which it is not cost competitive, say, simple assembly in developed countries, then those remaining stages in which it is especially cost competitive, say, marketing and design stages, become a more obvious source of export earnings. In these circumstances, imports rise when the output of foreign assembly operations is brought back to the home country to produce the final product, but exports may also rise if firms exploit the foreign marketability of business services in which they have comparative advantage. The increasing importance of tertiary cross-border M&A may reflect this re-positioning of firms in developed countries in the higher value-added stages of the production process. Thus again, the ultimate impact on trade of FDI depends on the character of the investment.

3.4 Policy Toward FDI and TNCs

TNCs have been characterized as firms that have shed their home-nation identities and operate essentially as stateless entities (Ohmae, 1990). This has led to a concern that TNCs will locate operations wherever in the world they are able to minimize costs, making it increasingly difficult for nations to tax TNCs, thus resulting in a shifting of tax burden from capital to labour (Rodrik, 1997). The implication of these views and arguments is that further liberalization of regulations on capital flows and entry of foreign firms into domestic markets and on FDI, such as was involved in the efforts within the OECD to develop an MAI, is undesirable (see, for example, Braunstein and Epstein, 1999).[5] On the other side of the debate, Swank (1999) has argued that international capital mobility and the internationalization of capital markets need not jeopardize the institutions of the welfare state, since democratic institutions that facilitate collective representation of interests may structure governmental responses to TNC strategies. Relatedly, others have argued that the development of new forms of corporate governance as promoted by a variety of NGOs can also help accommodate the international economy to significant social and environmental needs (for example, Nadkarni, 1999).

To sort out this debate, we first emphasize the difference between FDI and portfolio investment, then discuss the difference between national competitiveness and the competitiveness of a nation's firms, and finally close with an argument in favour of the ultimate objectives of the MAI. Our argument is that because FDI has a stabilizing influence on national economies, and because the competitiveness of nations is enhanced by inward FDI flows, careful liberalization of long-term capital flows, such as was intended by the MAI, is desirable. However, the venue and form of such an agreement remain an issue.

3.5 FDI versus Portfolio Investment

It is important to emphasize the economic difference between portfolio and FDI flows. Portfolio flows as a non-ownership, liquid form of investment, are easily reversible, whereas FDI as a relatively illiquid, ownership form of investment typically involves long-term commitment. Significant portfolio inflows can, and often do, overwhelm a nation with an inefficient or under-developed system of financial intermediaries, and the allocation of this new source of liquidity may often be economically unsound. Worse, as learned in the 1994–95 Mexican and 1997 East Asian financial crises, when portfolio flows slow or reverse, the system of intermediaries then often becomes illiquid and a financial crisis may ensue (see Chang and Velasco, 1998). In the case of Mexico and the rest of the western hemisphere's emerging economies, portfolio flows increased relative to FDI from 1990 to 1994. Following the crisis that began in December 1994, the outflow of portfolio capital resulted in a 112 per cent decline and overall negative net portfolio flows for the region. When portfolio flows reverse in one nation, they often trigger a crisis in the entire region, as seen in the cases of Mexico and Thailand. Empirical work by Glick and Rose (1998) indicates that currency crises affect 'clusters' of nations, working through established trade channels. Hence, over-reliance on portfolio capital can be destabilizing for individual countries and entire regions.

In contrast, FDI appears to be a stabilizing factor. When TNCs establish foreign affiliates or enter into strategic alliances, they seek long-term commitments. Search costs are reduced, because participation in host country networks transfers information within the network regarding customers and suppliers that is not available to firms engaged in arm's-length trade. Deliberation costs are reduced, when long-term relationships reduce the need to regularly evaluate potential exchange partners. Thus one would not expect TNCs to enter and exit foreign countries with high degrees of frequency. Indeed, as it is more difficult to enter into foreign business and market networks than in home countries, exit from established facilities and operations seems less likely in foreign locations. Against the argument that tax costs create footloose TNCs, it seems that tax costs are a relatively minor element in decision-making regarding the location of production. FDI and

TNCs, then, appear to have a stabilizing influence on the economies in which they locate, bringing income and employment to those economies.

3.6 National Competitiveness versus a Nation's Firms' Competitiveness

Despite arguments that TNCs have dissociated themselves from their national origins, many still believe that national economic strength is linked to the success of a country's TNCs. Thus whether or not these firms are internationally competitive is an important measure of whether nations are competitive in the world economy. But there are good reasons to think this emphasis on a nation's firms is misplaced. Reich (1990) asks us to consider the positive impact that foreign firms have on a country's employment and income when they locate production or distribution subsidiaries in that country. Of course the opposite impact occurs when foreign firms leave a country, but Reich thinks that seeing exit as an inevitable consequence of entry misconceives the nature of FDI. Firms invest in foreign markets because they perceive advantages to doing so: skilled workforces, good distribution networks, developed supply chains, access to finance, and so on. A country that invests in education, research, training, and infrastructure, then, can expect to continually attract FDI, enabling it to maintain high levels of employment and income. If we add the benefits of technology spillovers discussed above, we might imagine a virtuous spiral of growth and investment, whereby domestic investment and FDI continually reinforce one another.

Reich's argument is mostly pitched at a macroeconomic level. Our argument emphasizes the factors affecting firms' decision-making regarding where they wish to locate their subsidiaries and develop strategic alliances. In virtue of the importance of business and economic networks in a foreign venture, firms will generally be reluctant to abandon commitments to an interlocked complex of exchange partners, both because of the original cost of building up that set of commitments and because of the anticipated cost of having to re-establish similar commitments elsewhere. Seen in this light, Reich's recommendation that nations pay less attention to who owns firms and more attention to creating the economic conditions in which all firms will prosper, is tantamount to a call for governments to help bear the cost of setting up such networks. In effect, Reich recommends that governments socialize search and deliberation costs for firms (foreign and domestic) through public goods expenditures, in order to help create national and regional business networks that rival those elsewhere.[6]

One important implication of this is that FDI appears to have a greater stabilizing influence on national economies than some of its stronger proponents have supposed. Indeed, FDI may be argued to move more inertly than even domestic long-term investment flows, since domestic firms inherit a variety of home country advantages that enable them to move across different national business networks, providing them with consistently lower search and deliberation costs than foreign firms have in those same networks. To be competitive, then, foreign firms need to be more successful than domestic firms in internalizing search and deliberation costs, and consequently they need to be more committed to building up their involvement in the networks in which they participate. TNCs, then, should be quite reluctant to exit from foreign locations in which they set up operations, and when they do find this their best course of action, it is likely that there are deeper causes at root having to do more with national economic policies than the liberalization of long-term capital flows.

3.7 The MAI

There is currently no comprehensive set of international rules on FDI or the operations of TNCs comparable to the international rules for trade embodied in the WTO, and progress in multilateral negotiations on the subject has been modest at best. Issues relating to host country policies toward FDI and TNCs were first raised in GATT discussions in 1981, and by the time of the WTO Uruguay Round a limited set of trade-related investment measures (TRIMs) principally concerning local content restrictions had been agreed upon. Somewhat more success in the Uruguay Round came about in connection with trade-related intellectual property policies (TRIPs), perhaps because developing countries were prepared to encourage technology transfers from developed countries. However, the perception of many in the industrial countries was that further progress in liberalizing capital flows was unlikely to occur within the WTO on account of the different interests of developed and developing countries (Graham, 1996). Accordingly, in 1994 an effort began to work out an agreement on investment within the OECD, where it was believed there was greater commonality of interest. The collapse of negotiations over the MAI in late 1998 thus generated considerable pessimism not only about progress in liberalizing capital flows, but also in terms of where efforts ought to be initiated. All now seem to agree that limited negotiations hold the only prospect. Two proposals have been advanced for returning to the WTO as the proper venue for such negotiations, and relying on the WTO's 'built-in' agenda to avoid the need for authorizing any new initiatives.

Moran (1998) has argued for restricting the agenda to performance requirements and investment incentives within the context of the existing TRIMs agreement. The former are of particular concern to developed countries and the latter are of particular concern to developing countries. Thus in principle there is potential for an agreement with reciprocal concessions. But it is by no means clear that the two sets of countries will be able to bargain as blocs. For example, developed countries include federal and non-federal forms of government. The former, particularly the United States, have insisted that they cannot compel subfederal governments (states) to restrict investment incentives. In addition, a number of developing countries appear unwilling to compromise on performance requirements.

Sauvé and Wilkie (2000) have argued that a restricted agenda can be pursued through the WTO General Agreement on Trade in Services (GATS) by applying national treatment in services. They contend that the current GATS agreement is quite limited in scope, and that most countries' laws and policies that are inconsistent with national treatment are to be found in service industries covered by GATS (cf. Rugman and Gestrin, 1994). Graham (2000) argues in favour of this initiative on the grounds that the chief application of the proposal would be to developed countries, between which it might be more realistic to seek agreements on the matter, and there appears to be a very considerable business constituency interested in services liberalization.

We favour progress on both these fronts, but think it is also possible to extend piecemeal reform in venues additional to the WTO. In his diagnosis of the Asian financial crisis, Eichengreen (1999) argues for a reform of international financial intermediary and corporate practices that would increase banking and corporate transparency and disclosure through enhanced accounting and auditing standards, establish capital requirements for foreign lending in line with risk, and generate new expectations regarding corporate governance. But Eichengreen does not suggest that the International Monetary Fund or any other single international organization take on responsibility for all these changes. Rather, he believes a collection of *private-sector* bodies with appropriate expertise already exists, including: the International Accounting Standards Committee (IASC), the International Organization of Supreme Audit Institutions (INTOSAI), Committee J of the International Bar Association (regarding bankruptcy laws), the International Corporate Governance Network (ICGN), the International Organization of Securities Commissions (IOSCO), and the Basle Committee on Banking Supervision (also cf. Daniels, 2000a, p. 127).

Reform in the international financial architecture generated by these groups and organizations would not in itself constitute a liberalization of international investment. But such reform would most likely create a more stable international climate for investment. On the one hand, such reform would ease information asymmetries that impede FDI. On the other hand, to the extent that national currencies were more stable as a result of such reforms, investment risk would be reduced. Thus, if only modest gains are now expected from negotiations over investment carried on in multilateral organizations such as the WTO, these potential improvements in international financial architecture may by comparison be important. There is a further reason to emphasize this avenue. Since the groups and organizations above are private-sector bodies, their deliberations and decisions are unlikely to cause the sort of conflict that has been associated with the WTO. Moreover, should these groups and organizations be subject to public scrutiny, it is still arguable that their recommendations would not be controversial.

SUMMARY

In this chapter we present a collection of stylized facts regarding structural changes and developments in the world economy in connection with trade, FDI, M&A, and their distribution across the Triad and the ROW, and then provide an explanation of TNC strategies responding to and underlying these trends that emphasizes the transactions costs savings available to TNCs that become embedded in host economies. In our view, this picture provides good grounds for supposing that FDI and trade are substitutes and complements, and thus that the impact of FDI on trade balances should not be a primary policy concern. In the concluding section, then, we discuss policy toward FDI, and argue that the embeddedness of TNCs makes FDI a stabilizing factor in national economies. Despite this positive case, progress in liberalizing international capital flows has not been significant. We favour a set of piecemeal reforms, including changes in international financial architecture that stem from private-sector bodies.

NOTES

1. Globalization should be understood in terms of the interdependence of trade and investment *within as well as between* regions (Rugman, 2000).
2. This relationship between FDI and trade in the case of Japan and the United States may be transient, since Japan appears to be moving from a bank-based system of corporate governance to a more securities-based system – a change which would have implications for Japanese FDI and trade (see Ozawa, 2000).
3. However, the FDI relationship between the United Kingdom and Canada results in slightly lower trade flows than would have occurred without FDI taking place.
4. The exceptions are Canada and Japan. Nor is the US case unreflective of the behaviour of non-US TNCs, with foreign content in sales by their US affiliates also in the neighbourhood of 10 per cent.
5. Note that the issues often raised in connection with FDI to developing countries of labour exploitation and environmental dumping are not relevant to the MAI, which was an agreement being negotiated between developed countries.
6. Here we see one of the important dimensions of Rugman's (2000) characterization of globalization as a process of regionalization.

REFERENCES

Bhagwati, J. and V. Dehejia (1994), 'Freer trade and wages of the unskilled – is Marx striking again?', in J. Bhagwati and M. Kosters (eds), *Trade and Wages: Leveling Wages Down?*, Washington: American Enterprise Institute, pp. 36–75.

Borenszstein, E., J. De Gregorio and J. Lee (1994), *How Does Foreign Direct Investment Affect Economic Growth?*, Washington: International Monetary Fund Working Paper WP/94/110.

Braunstein, E. and G. Epstein (1999), 'Creating international credit rules and the Multilateral Agreement on Investment: what are the alternatives?', in J. Michie and J.G. Smith (eds), *Global Instability. The Political Economy of World Governance*, London: Routledge, pp. 113–33.

Buckley, P. (1990), 'Problems and developments in the core theory of international business', *Journal of International Business Studies*, **21** (4), pp. 657–65.

Buckley, P. and M. Casson (1976), *The Future of the Multinational Enterprise*, London: Macmillan.

Cantwell, J., T. Corley and J. Dunning (1986), 'An exploration of some historical antecedents to the modern theory of international production', in G. Jones and P. Hertner (eds), *Multinationals: Theory and History*, Farnborough: Gower.

Chang, R. and A. Velasco (1998), 'The Asian liquidity crisis', *Federal Reserve Bank of Atlanta Working Paper*, no. 98–11.

Coase, R. (1937), 'The nature of the firm', *Economica*, **4** (4).

Daniels, J. (2000a), 'Global capital flows: maximising benefits, minimising risks', in Karl Kaiser, John Kirton and Joseph Daniels (eds), *Shaping a New International Financial System: Challenges of Governance in a Globalizing World*, Aldershot: Ashgate, pp. 113–33.

Daniels, J. (2000b), 'The United States and global capital markets', in T. Brewer and G. Boyd (eds), *Globalizing America: The USA in World Integration*, Cheltenham, UK and Lymc, US: Edward Elgar, pp. 154–72.

Davis, J. and J. Daniels (2000), 'US corporations in globalization', in S. Cohen and G. Boyd (eds), *Corporate Governance and Globalization: Long Range Planning Issues*, Cheltenham, UK and Lyme, US: Edward Elgar, pp. 190–215.

Dunning, J. (1958), *American Investment in British Manufacturing Industry*, London: Allen & Unwin.

Dunning, J. (1977), 'Trade, location of economic activity, and the MNE: a search for an eclectic approach', in B. Ohlin, P.-O. Hesselborn, and P.M. Wijkman (eds), *The International Allocation of Economic Activity*, London: Macmillan.

Dunning, J. (1981), *International Production of Multinational Enterprises*, London: Allen & Unwin.

Dunning, J. (1988), 'The eclectic paradigm of international production: an update and a reply to its critics', *Journal of International Business Studies*, **19** (1).

Eichengreen, B. (1999), *Toward a New International Financial Architecture: A Practical Post-Asia Agenda*, Washington: Institute for International Economics.

Fantagné, L. and M. Pajot (1997), 'How Foreign Direct Investment affects international trade and competitiveness: an empirical assessment', *CEPII Working Papers*, November, no. 97-03.

Feenstra, R. (1998), 'Integration of trade and disintegration of production in the global economy', *Journal of Economic Perspectives*, **12** (4), pp. 31–50.

Fortune (1991), 'Top 50 U.S. Exporters', Summer–Spring.

Glick, R. and A. Rose (1998), 'How do currency crises spread?', *Federal Reserve Bank of San Francisco Economic Letter*, no. 98-25.

Graham, E. (1996), *Global Corporations and National Governments*, Washington, DC: Institute for International Economics.

Graham, E. (2000), *Fighting the Wrong Enemy: Antiglobal Activists and Multinational Enterprises*, Washington: Institute for International Economics.

Granovetter, M. (1985), 'Economic action and social structure', *American Journal of Sociology*, **91** (November), pp. 481–510.

Helliwell, J. (1998), *How Much Do National Borders Matter?*, Washington, DC: Brookings.

Hymer, S. (1976), *The International Operations of National Firms*, Cambridge, MA: MIT Press.

Kay, N. (1983), 'Review article: multinational enterprise', *Scottish Journal of Political Economy*, **30** (3).

Moran, T. (1998), *Foreign Direct Investment and Development: The New Policy Agenda for Developing Countries and Economies in Transition*, Washington: Institute for International Economics.

Nadkarni, A. (1999), 'World Trade Liberalisation: national autonomy and global regulation', in J. Michie and J.G. Smith (eds), *Global Instability. The Political Economy of World Governance*, London: Routledge, pp. 134–50.

OECD (2000), 'Recent trends in Foreign Direct Investment', *Financial Market Trends*, **76** (June), pp. 23–41.

Ohmae, K. (1990), *Borderless World: Power and Strategy in the Interlinked Economy*, New York: Harper.

Ozawa, T. (2000), 'Japanese firms in deepening integration: evolving corporate governance', in S. Cohen and G. Boyd (eds), *Corporate Governance and Globalization: Long Range Planning Issues*, Cheltenham, UK and Lyme, US: Edward Elgar, pp. 216–44.

Rangan, S. and R. Lawrence (1999), *A Prism on Globalization: Corporate Responses to the Dollar*, Washington, DC: Brookings.

Reich, R. (1990), 'Who is us?', *Harvard Business Review*, January–February, pp. 53–64.

Rodrik, D. (1997), *Has Globalization Gone Too Far?*, Washington, DC: Institute for International Economics.

Rugman, A. (1981), *Inside the Multinationals: The Economics of Internal Markets*, London: Croom Helm.

Rugman, A. (2000), 'From globalisation to regionalism: the Foreign Direct Investment dimension of international finance', in K. Kaiser, J. Kirton, and J. Daniels (eds), *Shaping a New International Financial System: Challenges of Governance in a Globalizing World*, Aldershot: Ashgate, pp. 143–57.

Rugman, A. and M. Gestrin (1994), 'NAFTA's treatment of foreign investment', in A. Rugman (ed.), *Foreign Investment and NAFTA*, Columbia, SC: University of South Carolina Press.

Sauvé, P. and C. Wilkie (2000), 'Investment liberalization in GATS', in P. Sauvé and R. Stern (eds), *GATS 2000: New Directions in Services Trade Liberalization*, Washington: Brookings.

Swank, D. (1999), 'Global capital, democracy, and the welfare state: why political institutions are so important in shaping the domestic response to internationalization', Working Paper 1.66, Center for International Studies, Harvard University, University of California Center for German and European Studies.

United Nations Conference on Trade and Development (1999), *World Investment Report 1999*, New York and Geneva: United Nations.

United Nations Conference on Trade and Development (2000), *Handbook of Statistics*, New York and Geneva: United Nations.

Wessel, David (2000), 'Cross-border mergers soared last year', *Wall Street Journal*, 19 July, p. A18.

Williamson, J. and M. Mahar (1998), 'A survey of financial liberalization', *Essays in International Finance*, no. 211, Princeton: International Financial Section, Department of Economics, Princeton University.

Williamson, O. (1975), *Markets and Hierarchies: Analysis and Antitrust Implications*, New York: Free Press.

(US, EU, Japan)

F13 L80 L60

5. Triad policy and interdependencies in the WTO

Gavin Boyd

On trade and investment issues the USA, the European Union, and Japan interact at a level of global dominance in the multilateral pattern of the World Trade Organization (WTO). This is a pattern in which Atlantic relations are the most active, on the basis of cultural affinities and high levels of structural interdependence, and are for the most part managed separately from US–Japan relations: the European Union and Japan interact distantly, thus in effect allowing the USA much scope for initiative. In this regard the USA has strong incentives to assert its interests as it has to cope with very large current account deficits.

Associated with the overall configuration of Triad interactions are diverse asymmetries of policy interdependence, attributable to nationally very distinctive problems of advanced political development, diverging structural profiles, and differing orientations toward, as well as capacities for, competitive or cooperative management of foreign economic policies. The interactions are not becoming sufficiently productive to sustain a system of collective management, primarily because of the problems of advanced political development, which for diverse reasons are tending to become more intractable as the largely ungoverned processes of globalization pose structural and distributional issues. The structural and policy interdependencies in the global political economy set requirements for building comprehensive systems of collective management, but the highly constructive political entrepreneurship that is clearly needed is not being provided.

The problems of advanced political development cause macromanagement deficiencies, which tend to become more serious because of losses of economic sovereignty: exchange rate interventions that might assist trade policy objectives have become less feasible because of the internationalization of financial markets, and firms have become more focused on the expansion of their international production and trading operations. Weaknesses in political institutions become all the more serious, meanwhile, as strains in the globalization processes activate more competitive and conflictual rather than cooperative representations of interests, hindering consensus formation aligned with the public interest. The USA's macromanagement problems assume prominence in this context because strongly pluralistic policy processes hinder effective engagement with a complex conjunction of structural issues that affect much of the world economy. Foreign production by US firms greatly exceeds domestic production for export, while strong import-drawing effects result from internal demand kept high by the attraction of international investment and by high levels of speculative asset appreciation. Openness to low-cost imports, meanwhile, is necessary for inflation control. Hence large current account deficits persist.

Macromanagement problems in the European Union contribute substantially to the continuation of growth levels below that of the USA, but without serious external imbalances. Rather large flows of investment to the USA, as a higher growth area, however, have important implications for the financing of European firms; in prospect are structural problems which could lead to major problems in foreign economic relations.

Japan's macromanagement problems are exceptional because they have severely affected the national financial system, without disrupting large accumulations of surpluses in foreign trade that have been sources of strain in relations with the USA and the European Union. Economic recovery through increased export-led growth is becoming possible, but with much dependence on the US market because of financial strains in industrializing East Asian states and slow growth in Europe. The financing of growth is affected by drifts of investment to the USA, but these are less significant than those from Europe to the United States, yet ensure a potential for leverage to counter US pressures for more balanced trade.

Triadic structural profiles exhibit much complexity, and are significant in contexts of issues in structural interdependence that obligate trade policy responses, as well as adaptations in foreign direct investment policies. Much of the complexity in the pattern results from sharp contrasts between the USA and Japan. The USA is a dynamic, resource-rich system of intensely individualistic managerial capitalism operating with a high degree of independence from a liberally oriented national administration very receptive to corporate interest representation; large high-technology sectors maintain considerable competitive advantages over European and Japanese industries. Japan is a dynamic, resource-poor system of cooperative managerial capitalism operating in close collaboration with a mercantilist national administration distinguished by relational functionally oriented technocratic interaction with the corporate level; capacities for applied frontier technology rather than for fundamental research are sources of competitive advantages, that is together with the benefits of intercorporate solidarity.

European Union structural profiles show considerable dysfunctional diversity, despite continuing regional market integration and monetary integration.

At the centre of the pattern is Germany, ranking high because of size and level of industrial development, as well as because of strong economic links with most of the less developed and smaller member states. The German system of cooperative managerial capitalism is less dynamic than Japan's, in part because of weaker relational ties with the national administration's technocrats, and sustains competitive advantages mainly in mature technology sectors. This structural profile and the larger Union structural profile tend to ensure considerable balance in the overall current account, but, as noted, with unfavourable shifts in Atlantic structural interdependencies.

Triadic foreign economic policies differ in coherence and functional significance. The strongly liberal US policy orientation makes for coherence but this is qualified by the effectiveness of protectionist pressures from sectors losing international competitiveness; antidumping measures result, and these indirectly advantage US firms sourcing products from abroad. The functional consequences of the liberal orientation are evident principally in the development of industrial capacity at foreign locations, in response to multiple incentives, on a scale that substantially alters trade patterns. In Japanese foreign economic policy mercantilism imparts greater coherence, with more functional results. The European Union's external trade policy derives considerable coherence from the European Commission's aggregating endeavours, but member states implement their own structural policies. The Union current account is not adversely affected by the ratio of foreign production to exports from Europe, or by the relatively low import-drawing effects of internal demand, but the structural challenges of outward investment, as a form of capital flight, are not being addressed. Shifts in degrees of European corporate control over Atlantic trade are in prospect.

INTERACTING DYNAMICS: POLICY AND STRUCTURAL LEVELS

Triadic interactions over issues of trade in goods and services, and over related investment matters, are bargaining processes with elements of policy learning and degrees of informal accountability. Exchanges between policy communities are very active in Atlantic relations, but very much on an adversarial basis, and there is more adversarial behaviour in the smaller-scale interactions between the USA and Japan. Capabilities for leverage in the Triadic bargaining, meanwhile, are altered by the structural effects of, and spreads of gains from, transnational production and trade.

In the Triadic bargaining the USA has superior leverage, because of the size of its economy and its import-drawing strength, and because the European Union and Japan, while relating distantly to each other, have become increasingly dependent on access to the US market. Domestically based growth in Europe is slack, and Japan's financial difficulties together with those of industrializing East Asian states have made the promotion of exports to the USA all the more important.

The USA, because of its large current account deficits, has strong incentives to demand increased access to the European and Japanese markets. The retaliatory capacity of the European Union, however, is increasing as its economic links with East European states in line for membership are expanding, and as the establishment of the European Monetary Union gives some impetus to growth. An intensification of strains in Atlantic relations seen to have been caused by the USA moreover could trigger shifts by European and other investors from US to Euro securities. In the relationship with Japan there is a similar and more important reason for restraint, as there are large Japanese holdings of US government and corporate securities.

Because of the European Union's bargaining capacity only moderate increases in its already substantial market openness would be likely in response to strong US leverage. The structural interdependence moreover could be expected to continue to evolve more through the expanding operations of US firms producing in Europe.[1] Such operations are encouraged by the weaknesses of Union firms, the importance of a strong European presence for the development of global strategies, the opportunities for intercorporate collaboration somewhat outside the effective scope of US anti-trust policy, and the tax advantages associated with multinational production, as well as the potentials for securing favourable treatment by host governments.

The most substantial processes of structural change in Atlantic relations have been continuing on the basis of US corporate choices for transnational production which have become stronger over the past decade; Japanese competition has weakened and market integration has progressed in Europe; the European Union's relatively low level of protection has been reduced, but only after protracted negotiations which could well be followed by more protracted bargaining over smaller reductions of trade barriers.

The US corporate incentives to produce in Europe constitute a potent rationale, in the context of a larger rationale relating to the advantages of multinationality in the rivalry for world market shares.[2] In Europe, moreover, Japanese competition is a less significant challenge for US firms than it is at home. European trade and investment policies have discriminated rather severely against Japan, and Japanese firms, unlike the US corporate presence, have little scope for representation of their interests in Brussels.

In the main processes of Atlantic structural change, US firms operating in Europe are acquiring more control over US exports to the Union and are tending to gain more control over European exports to the USA. This is possible mainly because of intercorporate links within the US presence in

Europe, but also because European corporate involvement in the USA is fragmented: the various British, German, Dutch, French and other European firms have few significant links on the basis of their European identities.[3] The fragmentation reflects the diversity of European systems of corporate governance and the ties of many European firms with their national governments. In the overall contrasts between Atlantic corporate presences, moreover, the entrepreneurial thrust of US firms in Europe is generally superior, and operates with technological advantages as well as greater financial resources.[4]

In US–Japan relations structural change and its trade consequences are evolving with much less US corporate control. Japanese firms, linked relationally with each other and with their national administration, have a highly integrated presence in the USA which is not matched by a significant US counterpart in Japan, and have much control over the bilateral trade, in which large favourable balances are maintained.[5] US interactions with Japan, while pressing for greater market access, also press for increased openness to US foreign direct investment, but the public emphasis is on the need for change in Japanese levels of effective protection that will allow increases in US exports.

The contrasting patterns of corporate involvement in Atlantic and in the Pacific contexts have implications for the incentives motivating political action on trade issues by US firms. For the enterprises constituting the US presence in Europe, consultative exchanges with the European Commission and with major European host governments are evidently as important as, if not more important than, lobbying activities at home on Atlantic trade issues.[6] In this context there is an interest in discouraging tendencies toward abrasive behaviour in US trade diplomacy that could cause unfavourable European reactions. European firms in the USA have similar interests in encouraging restrained Union management of trade disputes with the USA, but the lack of cohesion between the British, German, French and other European corporate groups in the USA limits their potentials for political action. Japanese firms operating in the USA appear to have a greater capacity to represent their interests to US policymakers, because of the scale of their operations and the efforts of American states to attract their investment. In Japan, however, the US presence is disadvantaged by its small size and the extent to which the Japanese political economy operates as a closed system.

For Triad governments, imperatives to increase gains from external trade, in the intensifying competition for world market shares, necessitate concerns with enhancing benefits from inward and outward direct investment, in which intrafirm trade becomes larger than arm's-length commerce. Structural policies thus become more closely linked with trade policies, altering the significance of interactions over market openness. In multilateral trade negotiations there is a rationale for interactions to liberalize foreign direct investment policies, but the possible collective good that may be seen may not be persuasive for governments striving to enhance national competitiveness through structural policies.

In international trade negotiations the USA is the main source of pressure for the removal of structural impediments to commerce, including not only state aids to industry but also liberal competition policies and non-market-based systems of corporate governance. European and Japanese resistance can be countered by US leverage in what are recognized to be trade negotiations. The US advocacy, however, is under constraints, because of domestic opposition to large outflows of direct investment, and because of the effects of foreign production/export ratios on the current account.

Foreign production/export ratios have become complex for the industrialized states, and especially for the USA, because of increasing vertical specialization, in which products move across borders several times in sequences of manufacturing, with intranetwork as well as intrafirm transfer pricing. Trade liberalization, to the extent that it facilitates increased vertical specialization as well as the shipment of intermediate goods outside such specialization, assists the expansion of foreign production, and in the US case is likely to be more significant in that respect than in its contribution to export expansion. For Japanese firms trade liberalization has similar significance, but their expansion of foreign production is more of a process of systemic development, without negative current account consequences. The smaller-scale foreign production by European Union enterprises has even less current account significance.

Altogether, the intersections of analytical perspectives necessitated by causal processes in Triad trade policies reflect the tightening of linkages between those policies and entire policy mixes, including structural policies, and contrasts in governmental capacities to manage those linkages. Issues for policymakers regarding the spread of gains from involvement in the world economy become more critical as globalization continues, and capacities to cope with these issues depend very much on potentials for alignment between structural policies and corporate strategies. The entire pattern of Triad trade policy interactions meanwhile obligates assessments in the light of public goods imperatives; these demand recognition because globalization entails the internationalization of market failure problems, and problems of government failure.

TRANSNATIONAL AND NATIONAL POLICY NETWORKS

Continuing trade policy interactions can have system building potential, if perceptions of actual shared gains lead to recognition of opportunities for further benefits through cooperation. The system building potential of collabo-ration between policymakers can have positive significance for transnational policy networks, depending on the scope for interactive policy learning in the common interest, and for building trust and goodwill. In this regard the influence of economic advice to governments is usually noted with reference to the proposition that all states will benefit from the growth effects of general trade liberalization.[7] When structural profiles and competition policy issues are con-sidered, however, possibilities for the development of systems of alliance capitalism demand attention.

In *Atlantic relations* strong cultural ties and large communication flows, together with widely recognized imperatives to cooperate in all policy areas, have aided the development of transnational communities of experts, com-prising academics and specialists at policy oriented research institutes. There are intensive professional exchanges, at conferences in Europe and the USA, resulting often in shared assessments of trends and issues in Atlantic struc-tural linkages. Flows of economic advice to governments originate in these communities, and receive some publicity in the more sophisticated media, such as the *Financial Times* (London). A prominent theme in the professional economic advice is the importance of economic openness for growth and employment, but there are qualifying themes related to mercantilist incen-tives and the interests of ruling parties or coalitions in meeting the demands of major interest groups.

The economic advice does not activate in-depth exchanges between US and European policymakers. These, especially in the USA, are under intense pressures to attend to constituency demands, and those in Europe are very much immersed in conferencing and intergovernmental exchanges related to the activities of the European Commission and the Council of Ministers.[8] The scale of the lobbying that demands responses is very great in the USA, and this is all the more significant because of aggregating problems resulting from the organizational weaknesses of the major political parties and the fragmented pattern of corporate interest representation.[9] On the European side the lobbying, directed mainly at the European Commission, imposes severe strains on its capacity to deal with intra-Union affairs.[10]

In the European Union corporate interest groups make up a pattern even more fragmented than that in the USA, and no significant transatlantic links between the two are emerging, although US firms in Europe have become very active in Union business associations.[11] British firms in the USA constitute the largest European direct investment position but are becoming localized, tend-ing to give more attention to their US operations than to those in Europe, thus becoming more immersed individually in the assortment of US business asso-ciations. German enterprises in the USA, constituting a somewhat strategically more significant presence in medium and higher technology manufacturing, retain substantial home country ties, but appear to have few relational links with other European groups of firms in the United States. At home the parent companies of these firms, and other German corporations, represented in Germany's strong peak economic associations, are well placed to represent their interests to the European Commission. German companies stand to benefit more than their Union rivals from any liberalization of Atlantic commerce, and have grounds for confidence that solidarity in their intercorporate system will continue to restrain import penetration as well as incoming foreign direct investment.[12]

In the fragmented Union pattern of corporate interest representation the links of national groups with their governments strongly influence the trade policy preferences of those administrations, articulated at the Council of Ministers level and in interactions with the European Commission. The national business groups, while also lobbying and straining the aggregating capacities of the Commission, evidently tend to make it more responsive to the demands of member governments. At the same time, however, the Commission appears to be receptive to the views of large Union firms with research capabilities that enable them to relate effectively to its technocratic functions, which have a regulatory orientation.[13]

The Commission and the US administration have sponsored discussions between European and US corporate elites on ways of facilitating increases in Atlantic commerce. These began in the mid-1990s, and resulted in significant proposals for regulatory improvements, but the intended effects on trust and goodwill were offset by strains caused by trade disputes in which each side sought to use the World Trade Organization's dispute settlement mechanism against the other. One of the main consequences of the trade conflicts has been increased awareness, in the USA and Europe, of each side's use of direct and indirect subsidies to assist exporters, and reliance on adversarial methods of managing trade policy issues. For participants in US trade policy discussions the adversarial methods have seemed appropriate because of perceived European reluctance to reduce structural impediments to free trade, especially aids to industry.[14] The perspectives of European trade policy groups, however, appear to have been dominated by concerns about vulnerabilities to market penetration resulting from inferior competitiveness.

US–Japan relations have evolved with very little scope for the development of transnational policy networks. Japanese policy communities have included much fewer and smaller independent research institutes than those in the USA, and have been operating very much under the influence of representatives from strong peak corporate associations, expressing interests and concerns aggregated on a scale much larger than that possible in the USA. Relational interactions between the Japanese corporate associations and the economic ministries in their national administration, moreover, have sustained a tradition of partnering for export-led growth, and absorption in this partnering, within a cultural context resistant to foreign penetration, has limited interest in possibilities for building trust and understanding with US and European business groups.[15] Organizational weaknesses in the US groups have tended to prevent substantial initiatives for cooperation, partly because of the demands of intensely active lobbying in the US policy process, but also because of beliefs that the solidarity in the Japanese political economy virtually obligates US corporate reliance on strong leverage against Japan at the policy level.

The Asia Pacific Economic Cooperation forum has provided occasions for exchanges between US and Japanese policy communities. Potentials for productive interaction, however, have been severely limited by US opposition to the formation of an East Asian economic association in which Japan would be the leading member, and by US pressures on Japan for economic policy changes during the East Asian financial crises in the late 1990s.[16] For Japanese policy communities, it must be stressed, those crises have entailed increased dependence on the US market for renewed export-led growth, but have also required strong resolve to counter US pressures for the reduction of Japanese structural impediments to trade.

Since the disruption of the Ministerial Meeting of the World Trade Organization in Seattle by anarchist groups in late 1999, European and Japanese trade policy communities have had to recognize the problems which such groups can cause in the management of US foreign economic relations, especially by dramatizing labour union opposition to import penetration. The larger problem which has been evident, moreover, has been the constraint on US trade policy resulting from the importance of low-cost imports for low inflation in the USA.[17] The labour union opposition, however, has become a major obstacle to the adoption of initiatives for freer trade with Latin America, and with East Asian countries, as well as with Europe. For European trade policy networks this state of affairs has become a significant contrast with the situation of their Union as a vast regional integration scheme that is expanding without significant internal difficulties.

TRIAD MACROMANAGEMENT

The major industrialized states in the Triad pattern interact over issues of market openness while responding with varying degrees of effectiveness to the challenges of globalization. Losses of economic sovereignty are experienced, notably as interventions in money markets have little effect on exchange rates, as the transnational production operations of firms alter national economic structures and the linkages between them, as shifting flows of portfolio investment affect the financing of industry and commerce, as speculative activities inflate asset prices, and as attempts at monetary tightening for inflation control are frustrated by the expanding operations of securities firms.

The losses of economic sovereignty hinder efforts to enhance structural competitiveness – efforts motivated by desires to increase national gains from foreign commerce. Japan, however, as a rather highly integrated political economy, experiences much smaller losses of economic sovereignty than the USA: Japan's system of alliance capitalism, operating with large favourable current account balances, with a financial system informally protected against speculative attacks, a pattern of transnational production linked in functional balance with the domestic economy, is recovering from a collapse of inflated asset prices, but has to cope with outflows of investment to the USA in search of higher yields. Of the major European states, Germany has degrees of economic sovereignty comparable with Japan's, due to efficiencies in a substantially integrated political economy which is less involved in transnational production but which has not experienced destabilizing asset inflation. As in Japan, however, growth is affected by outflows of investment to the USA.[18]

The United States, with a liberal political tradition, has experienced considerable erosion of economic sovereignty. The vast operations of US financial institutions in global markets have pushed to low levels the significance of the resources available to US monetary authorities for interventions to alter exchange rates.[19] The transnational production operations by US firms, very large in relation to the outward orientation of manufacturing activity at home, have weakened potentials for a structural policy capability, in a context in which the import-drawing effects of internal demand have been very strong. This internal demand has been high because of prolonged fiscal expansion and very substantial speculative inflation of stock prices, coupled with extensive credit expansion through the very active securities sector – a process that has weakened the monetary transmission mechanism.

The differing losses of economic sovereignty in the Triad have had trade policy effects in contexts in which there have been problems of governance. In the USA the most serious problem has been dysfunctional pluralism, aggravating institutional weaknesses and tending to perpetuate the political culture's intense individualism. In the European Union individualistic cultures hinder French and Italian institutional development, and tend to have a similar effect in Britain. Japan's communitarian culture is conducive to institutional development, but its solidarity building potential, similar to Germany's, has been flawed by failures to establish strong regulatory structures: much high-risk speculation has been destabilizing, indicating the inadequacy of self-governing practices in the financial sector.

The USA's dysfunctional pluralism has entailed neglect of its large trade deficits, and this neglect has been prolonged because current account difficulties which could have caused currency depreciation have been avoided by inflows of investment attracted by high growth.[20] The challenge of currency depreciation which would otherwise have forced a decisive response has in effect been postponed, in circumstances which are making it more serious. Potentially destabilizing speculation, contributing substantially to the high growth, could suddenly reduce it drastically, after having increased its import-drawing effects, in which foreign sourcing by US firms has been an important factor. This has led to a situation in which the magnitude of the policy imperatives demanding attention has motivated issue avoidance in the legislature and the administration, because of the political difficulties likely to be encountered. The issue avoidance tends to be obscured from public view by displays of zeal for fair trade and for the reduction of foreign structural impediments to such commerce.[21] These displays can be politically rewarding for executive figures and legislators. Aggregating the preferences of lobbyists, however, can be difficult, and this can increase the incentives for issue avoidance.

As Atlantic trade is roughly balanced the main imperatives for deficit reduction are evident in relations with Japan, China, and developing countries. Pressures to restrict imports from these trading partners come principally from US labour unions. The interests of the US firms seeking to penetrate the Chinese market, or sourcing from it and from developing countries, conflict with the union demands, and meeting those demands would go against requirements to hold down inflation by allowing continued imports of low-cost consumer products. Meanwhile the orientations of US manufacturing firms toward foreign production for the service of the Chinese and other developing markets – which can facilitate sourcing from the host countries – limits US export expansion, but politically cannot be subject to review without encountering corporate opposition. Corporate and union support for trade policy activism directed against Japan, however, is forthcoming; yet such leverage is subject to a major investment constraint, as Japanese holders of large volumes of US government debt could choose to diversify on a scale that could have severe consequences for the international role of the dollar, while reducing other flows of investment that offset the US balance of payments deficits.[22]

The European Union's problems of governance and losses of economic sovereignty do not prevent maintenance of roughly balanced external trade, but hinder engagement with structural issues posed by lagging competitiveness, slow growth, and high unemployment, as well as by investment outflows. Failures to engage with the structural issues – because of difficulties of consensus building – suggest that in the longer term there could be increasing pressures to protect the single market, pending improvements in the efficiencies of Union firms. Meanwhile broad defensive support for a policy that will maintain the external balance is a major source of resistance to US Atlantic trade liberalization proposals. Germany is the principal state standing to benefit from such proposals, but they represent challenges for the less industrialized Union members, as well as for France, Britain, and Italy.[23] Problems of governance in these states may well increase because of the effects of slow growth and high unemployment on domestic political balances and investment outflows: a protectionist trend in external trade policy could thus become more probable.

Japan's problems of governance, more manageable because of greater economic sovereignty, are not causing change in its established export-led growth strategy. The nation's acute resource deficiencies which are at the basis of this strategy have not changed, and the strategy has become all the more important because of the intensifying competition between international firms for world market shares, as well as the need to recover from the recession of the 1990s. Dependence on the US market has increased because of the financial crises in industrializing East Asia, but this dependence may decrease as growth resumes in South Korea, Malaysia, and Thailand, and as the European Union absorbs new members, while benefiting from the establishment of its monetary union. China, moreover, after entry into the World Trade Organization, will become a more important trading partner. Very high levels of corporate debt threaten the export-led growth strategy, however, and the costs of extensive restructuring are slowing economic recovery. Resistance to market opening pressures from the USA is thus evidently seen to be necessary, to facilitate orderly domestic management of the restructuring. A weakening of intercorporate solidarity makes this restructuring difficult, but a vital role assumed by the banking system is tending to ensure rather comprehensive adjustment, under strong direction by the Ministry of Finance.[24]

TRADE POLICY INTERACTIONS

In the Triad pattern the USA has superior scope for initiative to promote post Uruguay Round liberalization of trade in goods and services, and more liberal treatment of foreign direct investment, on a preferential or multilateral basis. The European Union's decisional problems and weak competitiveness tend to obligate a reactive and defensive policy style, with consensus formation dependent to a considerable extent on widening recognition of Union interests in response to US pressures. Japan, because of relative political isolation and heavy dependence on the US market, has to manage trade policy under exceptional constraints, but subject to these can operate without serious decisional problems, and with some capacity for leverage that can be threatened by its investors holding large volumes of US government debt.

The US administration is challenged by urgent imperatives to reduce its large trade deficits without restricting cheap imports of primary products and low technology manufactures, and without provoking protectionist measures by trading partners that could limit export expansion while increasing the incentives for US firms to produce abroad. Executive and legislative calculations in this context have to reckon with the disruptive capabilities of diverse protest groups, aligned generally with opposition to trade liberalization by labour unions in sectors experiencing deep import penetration and movements of industrial capacity to foreign locations. Options for regional trade liberalization, through Southern extensions of the North American Free Trade Agreement (NAFTA), tend to be excluded from planning because of the prospect of vigorous domestic protests and of requirements to enter into large numbers of special arrangements with legislators whose approval would be needed for any preferential trade agreement extending into Latin America.[25]

The potential for protests gives legislators incentives to make appropriate displays of zeal while avoiding responsibility for trade policy and setting demands for possible approval of negotiated agreements. Requirements for effective leadership by the executive on trade policy issues have become stronger, because of the range of sensitive sectors and communities and of likely legislative demands. Because of the uncertainties, executive leadership may be attempted experimentally, incrementally, and disjointedly, responding to immediate incentives to restrict imports from trade surplus states, but also to bring imports of low-cost primary products and manufactures more under the control of US firms sourcing from developing countries, through the use of antidumping measures against arm's-length exports of such items.[26] The system of administered protection through which antidumping policy is implemented is biased in favour of domestic producers, and this bias can be increased.

Japan would be vulnerable to import restraints designed to reduce its surpluses in bilateral trade. Displays of aggressive unilateralism in this bilateral relationship could be politically rewarding because of long-standing antipathies toward Japan, and because of increases in unfavourable US business and labour attitudes to the World Trade Organization since the late 1990s. Beliefs that the bilateral commerce should be balanced appear to have much influence on popular US views of the relationship, despite strong consumer demand for Japanese products. Caution would have to be observed in applying the import restraints, however, because of the danger of provoking reactions by Japanese investors, especially if the Euro were becoming a stronger currency, and if speculative asset appreciation in the USA was being slowed by prominent failures in the financial sector.

For coalition building in Triad economic relations the USA, it must be stressed, has extremely important interests in seeking Japanese goodwill. The

European Union's bargaining strength, enhanced by the addition of new members and by the apparent consolidation of political will behind its monetary union, is likely to be felt in further strains over Atlantic trade issues. In all the linkages associated with trade policy, as noted, the interests of Japanese investors in diversifying into Euro securities have to be considered. For the assertion of US influence within the World Trade Organization, moreover, Japanese cooperation with diplomacy directed at industrializing East Asian states can be helpful, especially because of the prospect of increased flows of Japanese direct investment into these states, with increased Japanese official aid.[27] All these considerations about Japanese goodwill receive little media treatment and have little impact on public attitudes, but they may well be given attention at the executive level.

Executive idiosyncratic preferences and views may at times dominate the management of US trade policy interactions, under the pressures to bring the current account into balance while meeting corporate and labour expectations. In the context of labour union dissatisfactions and uncertainties in stock markets, there is a clear danger of executive choice for ventures in aggressive unilateralism that would display effective zeal to induce cooperation by unfair trading partners.

Because of the urgency of the USA's trade deficit problem, it must be reiterated, Japanese and European decision makers probably see advantages in waiting upon events, especially to discern how US trade policy processes are evolving, and to estimate how US initiatives may in effect contribute to reactive assertions of interests, as a basis for assertive responses. The European Union's decisional problems, as basic sources of preferences for a delaying strategy, could well be increased by US inclinations toward aggressive unilateralism. A delaying strategy, meanwhile, could seem all the more appropriate in Japan.

To cope with reactive European and Japanese tendencies the strong US interest in improving the trade balance could be given expression in ambitious proposals for managed trade. This option is extremely important, because of the gravity of the current account deficits, the potential for short-term results, and the advantage of moving a major area of trade management out of the WTO system. An important form of managed trade, in effect over the past decade, is Japan's observance of an expired agreement for 'voluntary' restraint on exports of automobiles to the USA: this is observed to avoid provoking US countermeasures, but there would be no formal basis for a US complaint to the WTO if the original export quota were exceeded.

Managed trade, relying on explicit or tacit methods, could be seen as an attractive option for the USA if broad corporate support could be enlisted. Informal Japanese commitments to reduce automobile exports to the USA could be sought in exchange for more favourable treatment of Japanese direct investment in the USA, especially in the automobile industry. Managed trade in semiconductors with Japan has yielded results that could assist planning for further agreements in this and other sectors.[28] This relationship is more open to ventures in managed trade than the relationship with the European Union, because of the precedents that have been set, Japan's greater dependence on the US market, and the probability that any managed trade proposals directed at the European Union would provoke strong reactions, in part because individual members of the Union would have to be principal suppliers. The large size of the US corporate presence in the Union would obligate much care in designing proposals for managed Atlantic trade, and it would no doubt be very difficult to set terms that would promise a surplus for the USA. For the Union, as noted, substantial increases in exports to the USA are needed to supplement the impetus given to growth by the European Monetary Union.

Managed trade, it is argued, distorts market forces. The venture in semiconductor trade with Japan, however, through direct and indirect structural effects, can be considered to have contributed to improved efficiencies in international market forces. A more balanced and more dynamic trading relationship appears to have resulted. The functional logic in this context may well have much less political significance for the key US decision makers than the prospect of improvements in the current account, but the way in which the managed trade is put into effect could afterwards appear to validate its claimed economic rationale.[29]

TRADE IN MANUFACTURES

Triad trade in manufactures, facilitated by liberalization measures adopted in the Uruguay Round Agreements, has been altered by the East Asian financial crises of the late 1990s. In the years immediately before those crises high-volume commerce between the European Union and the USA ($270 billion in 1996) was increasing much slower than total US trade, and very much slower than US trade with East Asia, but European shipments of manufactured goods to the USA were more than double US exports of such products to the European Union.[30] The East Asian crises made the Atlantic commerce more significant for each side, while the imbalance in trade in manufactures continued, reflecting the import-drawing effects of strong internal demand in the USA.

Trends in Triad commerce have reflected differences in sectoral and structural competitiveness, with implications for interests receiving expression in trade policies, but have tended to conceal the structural significance of transnational production patterns and their related trade effects. The most prominent trend until the East Asian financial crises was Japan's highly competitive specialization in iron and steel, shipbuilding, motor vehicles, and electrical machinery, as well as non-electrical machinery.[31] Germany, France and Britain were becoming less competitively specialized in a narrow range of medium technology sectors, while Japan's manufacturing output had become more than double Germany's. The USA's share of total OECD manufacturing production was showing a decline of competitive specialization in medium technology sectors but it continued to lead in some high technology industries, including especially aircraft, where however the European Airbus consortium was becoming a challenge.[32]

In Atlantic trade a US deficit of about $23 billion in manufactures, despite Europe's lagging competitiveness, has reflected the market power of strong European oligopolistic retailing firms, advantaged by potent bargaining relations with national manufacturing enterprises;[33] also evident, however, has been the service of the European Union market by US firms producing in the Union, while importing from their parent companies at transfer prices. Informal ties between Union governments and national firms, including the retailers, have been hindrances to penetration of the Union market by outside enterprises, while delaying complete integration of the single market.

The USA thus has a major interest in pressing for substantially increased openness in European retailing, and can stress the potential benefits for Europe in terms of living costs and employment.[34] The increased openness in retailing that could be hoped for would be of great importance for US corporations producing in the Union, but considerable higher volume exporting of manufactures from the USA to Europe could be expected, as well as larger scale shipments of inputs from the USA to the firms producing in the Union. On the European side, however, resistance to US requests for more open retailing has to be expected, because of the influence that the major Union retailing firms appear to have gained on the policies of their administrations, as well as because of broadly shared anxieties about the superior competitiveness of US enterprises. While the entry barriers maintained by the European retailers remain high, the incentives for US corporations to produce in the Union for its market will continue to be strong, thus making improvement in the manufacturing trade deficit difficult.

The Japanese retailing system is a further structural impediment to commerce which the USA is well positioned to target on grounds of welfare and efficiency, as well as for the purpose of bringing external trade in balance. The main US sectoral deficit in this relationship, however, is in manufactures (about $70 billion in 1997), principally in automobiles, and the scale of this imbalance, as noted, indicates that there is a rationale for US efforts to seek managed trade while facilitating increased Japanese production of automobiles in the USA. Over the longer term the managed trade endeavour could be broadened to include industrializing East Asian states that have been linked increasingly with Japan through trade, direct investment, and official aid. Higher volume Japanese exports of automobiles to these states, and larger scale Japanese imports of consumer goods (in other categories) could be linked with greater US exports of machinery to those states.[35]

The managed trade option has to be identified as a highly significant choice for the USA because its trade deficit is becoming unsustainable, and because the need for a solution has been increased by the danger of a financial crisis in the USA (caused by losses of investor confidence) and by the emerging role of the Euro in the global monetary system. This is opening up opportunities for diversification that may reduce the flows of investment to the USA that have been aiding management of its current account deficits. The possibility of abrupt major shifts in the exchange rate has to be recognized.

The way is open for the USA to justify a regional managed trade arrangement as a structural imperative designed to avert a financial crisis and provide a structural basis for subsequent liberalization with a sustainable balance. This choice could well be acceptable to US interest groups and policymakers aware of the dangers of the trade deficit and of the difficulties of overcoming foreign structural impediments to trade through resolute diplomacy within or outside the World Trade Organization. Recognition of the gravity of the US trade problem and its implications for the world economy could induce Japanese and European cooperation.

A preferential trade arrangement with Japan and industrializing East Asian states could be made WTO compatible not only as a remedy for the now very serious US deficit but also as a means of assisting faster recoveries in the industrializing East Asian states affected by the financial crises of the 1990s. Understandings about regional trade liberalization that were reached in the Asia Pacific Economic Cooperation forum before those crises could be maintained, for later implementation. Under the Uruguay Agreements states remain free to act unilaterally on trade matters affecting their vital interests, and it is clear that a number of them may adopt such actions in concert.[36] Voluntary Export Restraints are not allowed, but it can be argued that tacit observance of such restraints is not actionable under the Uruguay Agreements and that collaborative direct investment arrangements can legitimately include specific understandings regarding related trade flows that affect vital interests.

Options regarding managed trade also have to be considered regarding China. The USA has been the main source of pressure on the Chinese Communist government to allow wide scope for market forces, so as to qualify for entry into the World Trade Organization, so a shift toward managed trade in this relationship could be considered inconsistent. The US trade deficit with China, however, has become very large (about \$50 billion in 1997) – growing at more than double the increases in US exports to that regime – in circumstances that have indicated the effects of large structural impediments sheltering the Chinese market. The gravity of the overall US trade deficit problem, as noted, would justify a resort to managed trade in this relationship, so as to induce structural changes that would allow the development of a viable balance of market forces at a later stage. An initial move by the USA to restrain imports from China would be justified in view of the scope for unilateral trade restrictions allowed under the Uruguay Agreements, and would be acceptable to US labour unions in sectors affected by Chinese exports. As in the Japanese case, however, the US endeavour would have to offer a new form of cooperation: the most appropriate arrangement could be a set of import restrictions that would be phased out as Chinese imports of US machinery and transport equipment increased.[37]

The USA's resorts to managed trade in East Asia need not strain Atlantic relations. The European Union is affected by structural impediments to trade in Japan and China, and would be vulnerable to the adverse effects of a US financial crisis. The large subject of structural impediments to Atlantic commerce, moreover, could be opened up for constructive engagement in conjunction with Triad interactions relating to Pacific trade. This could open the way for more effective collective management of the world trading system, on the basis of understandings about the development of the structural basis for international commerce. Dialogue in quest for such understandings would have to recognize the increasing volumes of intrafirm, intra-alliance and intranetwork trade, notably in intermediate products associated with expanding vertical specialization.[38]

TRADE IN SERVICES

Triad interactions on trade in services are dominated by the USA as the most extensive and most competitive provider, with a surplus of about $80 billion in 1997. Increased liberalization of services trade is promoted by the USA, especially in Atlantic relations, and increases in services exports (roughly 10 per cent yearly during the 1990s) have partly offset rises in the deficits on trade in goods. Roughly 35 per cent of US exports of private services go to Europe, and in this trade the US surplus accounts for about a third of the total surplus on services trade.

The development of Atlantic trade in services is facilitated by cultural ties and is given impetus by high volume cross investment as well as trade in goods but there are numerous hindrances to increased market openness on each side. The very large US corporate presence in European financial sectors gives the European Union a strong interest in pressing for US liberalization that would allow substantial increases in the small European presence in US financial sectors, but for the USA reciprocity is difficult to grant.[39] The extensive operations of US airlines between European Union members necessitates Union concern about the absence of corresponding traffic rights for European airlines in the USA, but in this area of services trade the Union also encounters obstacles to reciprocity.[40] In the finance and air transport sectors US firms have superior competitive advantages, based on large resources and the greater international spread of their operations; accordingly further superior gains from the present pattern of European activities are expected. In telecommunications US firms have superior competitive advantages as well, based on strengths in their large home market and on advanced technology. These advantages are increasing, as European enterprises seeking to become more active internationally have to make greater use of services provided by the US firms.

For the European Union US endeavours to liberalize trade in services express interests in increasing the asymmetries in market penetration that ensure substantial favourable balances for American financial, airline, and telecommunications enterprises. The most important European concern is in the air transport sector, which has special significance for the Airbus consortium, and which is vulnerable to divisive strategies that have been used by US airlines. The asymmetries in the financial sector have complex implications for European interests because of the special position of Britain as the Union's main area of financial activity and as a potential member of the European Monetary Union. Britain's financial interests are strongly oriented toward expansion of its extensive links with the US sector, for which there is scope through networks and alliances that are more open to cooperation with British institutions than to other European enterprises.[41]

For the USA the favourable overall trend in market penetration evidently warrants only moderate efforts to promote Atlantic services trade liberalization, in view of the dimensions of the reciprocity issues and the sensitivities of these for European interests and governments. Hence it seems that priority can be given to bargaining for the reduction of European structural impediments to commerce, especially those in retail sectors. The complex imbalances in Atlantic goods and services trade are sources of strain that tend to make negotiations adversarial, but that clearly set requirements for constructive interactions that will build trust and goodwill. These requirements, as noted, have become all the more significant because of the importance of Atlantic cooperation for reduction of the USA's trade deficits.

Services trade liberalization in the Pacific is promoted by the USA with major advantages because of the great importance of its market for East Asian exporters of manufactures, the superior degrees of multinationality enjoyed by its principal service providers, the weakened roles of East Asian institutions since the area's financial crises, and the relatively moderate scale of service sector links between East Asia and Europe. Regional market penetration by US financial institutions has grown considerably because of opportunities provided by the financial crises (including biases in IMF conditionality) and because of decreases in Japanese commerce with industrializing East Asian states. The absence of significant ties between Japan and those states enables the USA to exert strong bargaining leverage in separate bilateral interactions.

The urgent requirement for more balanced trade in goods evidently has to assume highest priority in US Pacific trade policy, perhaps even at the cost of restraint in exploiting the scope for expansion in the regional market for services. This consideration may well have special significance for Japan, as a US endeavour to set up a managed trade arrangement oriented towards more structural balance and subsequently freer market forces could be acceptable without reductions of economic sovereignty in the area of services trade, except with some concessions in retailing. Solidarity in the Japanese political economy, it must be stressed, motivates strong emphasis on the retention of economic sovereignty, and in certain respects that can be increased by managed trade, in so far as the administration has to exert more control over the operations of national firms.

STRUCTURAL CHANGE

Corporate operations within the present pattern of Triad policy mixes are changing national economic structures and the linkages between them in ways that pose especially difficult issues for the USA. These issues are not confined to the trade policy area, and demand responses across several areas, with European and Japanese cooperation. This has to be said because of the gravity of the issues, the USA's scope for initiative, and the tendencies of European and Japanese decision makers to wait upon events, in view of the uncertainties to be reckoned with regarding the USA's management of its interdependencies.

The structural change projections that are necessary, especially for the guidance of US policy, have to start with recognition that Triad firms, more or less in national clusters, are engaging in transnational production and acquiring the advantages of multinationality on differing scales, at different speeds, while the growth and employment effects in home and host countries are exhibiting contrasts, with diverse macromanagement challenges. The overall trend is oligopolistic, with high growth in the USA, as the base for leading transnational enterprises, drawing much passive international investment and importing high volume, low cost consumer products from less developed areas. In this process US transnational enterprises are tending to assume more control over the nation's exports and imports, through expanding intrafirm, intra-alliance and intranetwork commerce. The principal competitors are Japanese firms, which, however, have much less scope for operations in Europe, and which, because of their nation's economic difficulties, have incentives to seek alliances with US enterprises, notably in high technology sectors.

In the USA the investment-drawing effects, together with high levels of speculative asset appreciation contributing to those effects, weaken potentials for restraint on internal demand through monetary tightening, while tending to prevent currency depreciation that would reduce the import-drawing effects of strong internal demand. This exceptional state of affairs reflects the great size of the US economy, but also the limited economic sovereignty of the US administration; what is virtually unprecedented, however, is the importance of low-cost imports of consumer goods and primary products for continued growth with low inflation while internal demand remains strong on account of the investment inflows and the speculative asset appreciation.

Highly constructive dialogue about fundamentals has thus become imperative in the internal dimension of US policy making and in interactions with the USA's major trading partners. Because of the gravity of the issues there can be an understandable preference for limiting the participants to the Triad, rather than seeking a wider ranging involvement in a larger forum. A sound Triad plan for adjustment and progress toward balanced structural interdependence could then prepare the way for more orderly and more productive management of relations with developing countries. Domestically, meanwhile, the gravity of the issues will necessitate focus on the linkages between trade, foreign direct investment, and monetary and financial policies.

The engagement with fundamentals will have to recognize the significance of recent vast increases in trade in financial assets. International trade in stocks and bonds has become a huge component of the financial flows that determine Triad current accounts and exchange rates. The operations of US investors dominate these financial flows, and proceed mainly on the basis of superior capacities to draw investment from low growth foreign areas into higher yielding opportunities, especially in the speculation-driven growth of the home economy. This trade in financial assets is profitable in part because of reduced tax exposure,[42] and it assumes extensive structural significance because of its effects on the funding of industry and of trade in goods and in the general area of services. A major consequence of the flow of financial assets is that the downward pressure of a trade deficit (in goods and services) on an exchange rate is offset by upward pressures associated with trade in financial assets: but, as noted, this process can be disrupted by a crisis that sharply reduces speculation-driven growth in the economy that has been drawing foreign investment.

Monetary tightening to reduce speculation-driven growth in the USA, through effects on the trade in financial assets, can tend to cause currency depreciation and thus lower the trade deficit. This expected consequence, however, may not result because the expansion of credit through speculation, together with the investment inflows, may more than counteract the monetary tightening, while that monetary tightening meanwhile attracts stronger investment inflows.

Questions about the high volume trade in financial assets, then, it must be stressed, demand attention in Triad dialogue on fundamentals affecting trade in goods and services. The linkages here indicate that comprehensive cooperation management of trade policies will require interactions broader in scope than those that have to be conducted within the World Trade Organization. The issues have great importance for the stability and interdependent growth of the US economy, and for the European Union and Japan, but the USA is in an exceptional position, at the centre of the trade in financial assets. Japan and Germany (prominent as the largest member of the European Union) have capabilities for control over the involvement over their institutions in the trade in financial assets, but US financial corporations operate very independently, because of the liberal orientation of national policy which is sustained in a large measure by the preferences of major institutions in this sector.[43]

The increasingly extensive trade in financial assets exerts pressure on the structural foundations of trade in goods and services, principally by aiding the funding of large firms that demonstrate high short-term returns, while contributing to the financing of overall growth in the USA, although this is somewhat lowered by outward direct investment into foreign production operations. The outward drift of investment from the European Union as a low growth area, which tends to increase as its financial markets become more international, is a major factor perpetuating the overall pattern, and is a source of pressures for change in Germany's financial system. The similar outward drift of investment from Japan, however, may be brought more under national control if an export-led economic recovery is achieved.

The Triad pattern, it must be stressed, is vulnerable to disruption by a financial crisis in the USA, resulting from unsustainable speculative asset appreciation. It is also vulnerable to risky speculation in the trade in financial assets across the Triad that may be related to the asset appreciation in the USA. Critical assessment is needed of the extent to which stable balanced growth in the Triad is made possible by the trade in financial assets.

The commonly expressed rationale for free trade in goods and services is that this will lead to service of the open markets by the most efficient producers, whose specializations will contribute to overall growth. This has always raised questions about the emergence of international oligopoly power, and thus about the possibilities for forming a global competition policy authority, in view of the permissive attitudes of governments toward the international operations of their firms. The extraordinary expansion of trade in financial assets now obligates comprehensively critical analysis of the free trade rationale. The flow of financial assets contributes to oligopolistic trends in the markets for goods and services by rewarding the firms gaining large market shares. Yet another effect is to divert investment into rent seeking rather than productive activity, in part because of the scope for tax avoidance.

In the dialogue on fundamentals, then, problems of reform in world financial markets demand attention. This has to be stated with reference to estimates of the sustainability of the USA's current account deficits. Some of the estimates in recent years have been deficient in that there have been no references to the possibilities for use of diversifying strategies by investors able to shift out of US financial assets into Euro securities. Small shifts could trigger attempts at market manipulation by large international investors, thus causing widespread impressions of acute uncertainty that could generate herd behaviour, aggravated by indicators of a US financial crisis. In evaluating the significance of the sustainability estimates, moreover, the possibility of investment-drawing recoveries in East Asia, beyond the short term, has to be considered. Such recoveries would provide occasions for financial market manipulation that could affect the sustainability of speculation-driven growth in the USA.[44]

INSTITUTIONAL ISSUES

The Triad dialogue on fundamentals, because it would have to deal with problems in international financial markets, could benefit from involvement by the International Monetary Fund as an international institution with well developed capabilities for surveillance of the trade in financial assets and also the trends in real economies affected by that trade. The Fund's potential for a constructive role, however, would be more significant if the European Union were given representation in that organization as a single unit, with voting strength corresponding to its size.[45] This representation could ensure that the Fund's substantial research capabilities would be used with considerable objectivity in the assessment of issues of order and stability in world finance. The European Union clearly has a strong interest in pressing for appropriate change in the Fund, and for a focus of its assessments on the US balance of payments problem. This, moreover, is an interest with which Japan can identify, as a state highly vulnerable to the effects of a US financial crisis.

Since the East Asian financial crises the Fund has been given a special responsibility for detecting signs of instability in emerging markets. This function has evidenced, in part, the interests of the USA as the state whose financial institutions have been most active in Third World areas, and whose influence has been felt in the Fund's conditionality during the East Asian crises. That conditionality required borrowing states, including especially South Korea, to open their markets to foreign firms, despite indications that market manipulation by large US investors had contributed to and had aggravated the crises. The Fund, however, has since honoured its larger surveillance obligations by issuing warnings about requirements for monetary tightening in the USA to avoid a financial crisis that could result in sharp currency depreciation.[46]

Fund studies, while avoiding politically sensitive issues, have for several years drawn attention to the problems of instability in world financial markets, and, indirectly, to the interests of larger investors in manipulating those markets, and to the degrees to which those markets have become divorced from the real economies which they should be serving. Specifically, some of the Fund's studies have understandably emphasized that the problems of international financial stability have to be approached comprehensively, because of the vast scale of operations in securities markets – the trade in financial assets that has severely reduced monetary sovereignty while opening the way for rent seeking on a global scale, with high risks. Very high volume use of derivatives in this trade, it has been made clear, while avoiding regulatory and tax exposure, greatly increases the opaqueness of financial markets, and raises difficult questions about the significance of the far smaller official balance of payments figures.[47] The main guides for interpretation of those figures are statistics for trade in goods, of which, in the US case, about 70 per cent is accounted for by transfer prices.

The problems about the reliability of official balance of payments figures do not invalidate judgements of the gravity of the US balance of payments deficits. The extraordinary scale of trade in financial assets, however, is increasing much faster than payments related to trade in goods and services, and foreign direct investment. The capacity of the International Monetary Fund to provide substantially independent assessments of the issues for major interdependent real economies can be stressed with reference to this trend and its implications for the future growth of gains from non-financial trade. Fund studies have been explicit about the risks for financial institutions and about the unreliability of balance of payments estimates, while indicating that balance of payments deficits, however difficult to assess, do provide opportunities for risky speculation that can reach very high volumes.[48]

For the necessary Triad dialogue on fundamentals the Fund may be able to contribute to a consensus on imperatives to work for effective regulation of trade in financial assets, and effective taxation of this commerce. The Federal Reserve's statements on international financial markets appear to have been influenced by political factors obligating reticence, and the European Central Bank seems to have had little freedom so far to address the subject of financial market stability. Some challenging observations on this problem by the Fund could evoke significant inputs into the development of a Triad consensus by the Federal Reserve and the European Central Bank. Other significant inputs could follow from the Japanese monetary authorities.

A *market friendly* approach to international financial regulation has been taken by the Basle Committee on Banking Supervision since the 1980s. The realism of this approach has been open to question because its reliance on the prudential motivations of managements of financial institutions has been challenged by streams of academic literature drawing attention to risk-taking propensities in world financial markets and to the significance of large volumes of credit available for speculation.[49] Distinctive problems of market failure in international finance have become evident: informational failure, due to the opaqueness of market processes; herd behaviour triggered by manipulative operations intended to cause volatility; and, as noted, the large scale diversion of investment into rent seeking rather than productive activity. The persistence of these problems of market failure has reflected problems of government failure.

The operation of international financial markets in a way that funded growth in less developed countries, for reasonable returns, on a stable basis, and that facilitated increasing specializations in these and more industrialized states, in a balanced pattern, without manipulations to exploit volatility, would be a global public good. A Triad dialogue on fundamentals motivated by immediate concerns with unsustainable trade imbalances and unsustainable speculative asset appreciation should be conducted with constant reference to the global public good of an orderly international financial system serving real economies with equity.

In positive political economy perspectives a Triad dialogue on fundamentals can be thought of simply as an exercise in which interests in increasing gains from trade can be adjusted and reconciled through bargaining without regard for public goods. Such perspectives have to be challenged because of the diversity of complex reciprocal asymmetric interdependencies within and between national economic structures that are becoming more extensive as globalization continues. These interdependencies indicate requirements for governance dedicated to the public interest. In globalization each nation's common good assumes international dimensions. The articulation of industry group, sectoral, and community expectations and demands can be seen to contribute to aggregations of concerns shaping foreign economic policy, but, in opposition to agency concepts of democracy, it must be affirmed that the basic requirement is highly dedicated management of each national policy mix. Competitive value-free marketing of policies by contenders for office tends to cause bias and failure in macromanagement. In a complex industrial society vast numbers of citizens focused on their diverse specializations are not willing or able to devote energies to political activity, but depend on the government to serve the common good and have few resources to monitor its performance. The need for highly dedicated macromanagement is therefore clear, and becomes greater as professional specializations multiply and extend across national borders with the expansion of multinational corporations. The necessary high principled macromanagement has to be inspired by concepts of extended accountability to numerous enterprises and communities at home and abroad whose interests are not and realistically cannot be substantially articulated.

DIALOGUE POTENTIALS

The level of motivation that is clearly imperative in Triad dialogue deserves emphasis because the discussions of fundamentals could develop as preludes to negotiations guided by interests in securing hard, precise agreements. Such negotiating styles were evident in the conclusion of the Uruguay Agreements and of the North America Free Trade Area Agreement.[50] The principal dialogue requirement is dedicated policy learning, and this can be obstructed by approaches to interaction that have been influenced by adversarial legalism and by the dynamics of agency style government.

Hard and precise agreements were sought by the principal negotiators who reached understandings on the establishment of the World Trade Organization.[51] The motivations were to set out very specific terms for reductions of trade barriers that would reduce uncertainties for firms and governments and that would indicate clearly how disputes would be settled. In part the precision reflected unwillingness to allow the Secretariat of the World Trade Organization scope to develop independent research and surveillance capabilities, but there were also concerns to *avoid* precision that would restrict freedoms for unilateral action in defence of vital interests.

Quests for hard and precise agreements are commonly contrasted with quests for soft agreements with implicit understandings emphasizing goodwill and readiness to cooperate in coping with uncertainties. Arm's-length and low-trust interactions are associated with hard and precise agreements, while relational high-trust interactions generate soft agreements.[52] For policy learning, what is significant is the potential for sharing and developing knowledge through exchanges dedicated to the building of high-trust relational ties, expressed in agreements that can be described as 'soft' but that manifest strong commitments to integrative cooperation. Shared comprehension of the problems of efficiency and failure in goods, services, and financial asset markets has to be sought in Triad dialogue. In an arm's-length and low-trust context information is distributed strategically, and interest in new knowledge tends to be limited to its utility for bargaining. Absorption in the details of actual or intended progress toward hard and precise agreements, moreover, limits interest in new knowledge that does not have immediate strategic utility.

The focus of a Triad dialogue on fundamentals will have to be on the functional and political linkages between policies bearing on the interdependencies that are being shaped through the markets for goods, services, and financial assets. With this focus the management of policies regarding trade in goods and services will have to be studied with reference to structural changes effected by firms operating in diverse policy environments. The collective learning in this area, meanwhile, will have to develop in conjunction with learning about the significance about trade in financial assets for real economies.

A rationale for structural policy cooperation in support of trade policy cooperation for the balanced interdependent growth of real economies could emerge from the Triad dialogue. This rationale could emphasize the sponsorship of concerted innovative entrepreneurship, through which dynamic complementarities would multiply, within and between Triad economies. Issues regarding market openness and exchanges of concessions concerning trade liberalization would then be seen as problems calling basically for collaborative structural policies. These policies, meanwhile, would incorporate knowledge gained interactively at technocratic levels through intensive consultations with firms. Research on technology-based entrepreneurial collaboration by firms exploring potential complementarities has indicated that technocratic knowledge for the consultative orchestration of such corporate innovations, *as a public good*, could well be oriented toward the promotion of productive complementarities in the Triad. The trade policy significance of this could thus be greater as collaborating firms drew more on advances in frontier technology.[53]

In the service of structural policy cooperation the Triad dialogue could also yield a comprehensive rationale for engagement with issues in the trade in financial assets. This would be an even more demanding exercise, and a more urgent one. The problem of speculation to cause and exploit volatility, using opportunities for the avoidance of regulatory exposure, would have to be taken up with strong resolve, to motivate firm and comprehensive regulatory cooperation in the Triad, with pressure on financial sector communities to secure their collaboration, in part to curb tax evasion. A highly important process in the dialogue, of necessity, would be complete study of the movement of portfolio investment from Europe and Japan to the USA: requirements for greater funding of economic growth in Europe and Japan would have to be recognized. In this context, moreover, the weakening of monetary transmission mechanisms by the growth of securities sectors would also have to be recognized, that is as a problem to be overcome through collaborative recoveries of monetary sovereignty. These could then cope with the growing problem of tax evasion through trade in financial assets. That is a problem which will evidently become more acute for the European Union as the difficulties of reviving Union growth are made more formidable by high unemployment, heavy taxation, shifts to transnational production, and the drift of passive investment to higher growth areas.[54] The introduction of the necessary tax mechanisms, however, could well proceed with controls that would induce reorientations of passive investment flows in line with the developmental needs of the countries of origin.

DIALOGUE AND NEGOTIATIONS

The Triad dialogue on fundamentals could introduce a new spirit of integrative cooperation into interactions within the World Trade Organization on the promotion of general increases in economic openness. To the extent that goodwill and trust were developing within the Triad, indicating prospects for increasing interdependent growth, developing and transition countries could be attracted toward more active commercial cooperation with the industrialized states. Aggressive bargaining within the Triad, however, in quests for hard and precise agreements on further trade liberalization, would no doubt lead to very protracted negotiations, especially because of European and Japanese interests in delaying final decisions until improved bargaining advantages had been gained. Developing and transition countries, meanwhile, would have incentives to delay also, and to respond defensively to pressures from the Triad states.

If integrative Triad cooperation were to develop this could make possible institutional development of the World Trade Organization. US–European domination of the WTO, with considerable Japanese cooperation, has ensured its continuity as a bargaining forum, but with deficiencies due to competing efforts to use the organization for conflict resolution while virtually preventing it from acquiring independent monitoring and advocacy functions. A governing structure with weighed voting proportional to size and economic development would clearly be a major institutional advance, and it would be appropriate if leadership for this could be provided by the European Union, which would have the largest voting share. In the absence of a suitable governing structure the World Trade Organization may well become a bargaining forum based less and less on rules and understandings affirmed at the conclusion of the Uruguay negotiations. This seems probable because of signs of rising protectionist demands in the USA and Europe related to agitation about the costs of globalization.[55] Slower growth in the USA, predicted because of the unsustainability of speculative asset appreciation, can be expected to increase public concerns about the costs of import penetration while the trade deficits remain high. The continuation of weak growth in Europe, meanwhile, with slow increases in exports to the USA, will no doubt tend to encourage demands for emphasis on regionally based economic development, pending attainment of improved overall competitiveness. Upsurges in demands for protection in both the USA and Europe, moreover, may be evident as export-led growth resumes in Japan.

Further enlargement of the European Union, to be expected because of the attraction of its market, will make regionally based growth more feasible. On this account, and because of improved bargaining strength in Atlantic relations, less importance may be attached to involvement in the World Trade Organization. For most member governments in the Union the potentials of the larger regional market will probably tend to be more significant than opportunities in the rest of the world that might be increased through participation in multilateral trade negotiations. Those opportunities are emphasized in the European Commission's efforts to manage external trade relations, but the Commission is under pressure to be more responsive to the concerns of member states.

The prospect of more difficult bargaining in the World Trade Organization, with less respect for proclaimed principles, norms, and rules, together with the urgent requirement to reduce trade deficits, may increase the importance of regional initiatives in US foreign economic relations, particularly if the enlargement of the European Union causes it to become more assertive for the advancement of its interests. Endeavours by Latin American states to form a large regional economic community could encourage renewed US efforts to negotiate Southern extensions of the North America Free Trade Area. The record of Latin American attempts at regional economic cooperation is not impressive, but there is wide scope for the expansion of US trade and investment links with this region. The prospect of resistance from US labour unions could be discouraging, but their cooperation could be sought through the sponsorship of broadly representative union–corporate conferences on structural issues.

US interest in regional cooperation may also be expressed in the Atlantic context, perhaps in part because of conflicted relations with the European Union in the World Trade Organization. In a Triad dialogue on fundamentals the Atlantic exchanges could be expected to be very active, but in the absence of such a dialogue the clear rationale for seeking Atlantic regional cooperation would be persuasive if hopes for productive interaction in the World

Trade Organization were diminishing. Increased Atlantic cooperation would complement US quests for freer commerce with Latin America, and could be seen as an advance toward restructuring the World Trade Organization, so as to give it what could be seen as high-level guidance in the service of general trade liberalization.

The prospect of more conflicted and less productive interactions within the World Trade Organization, it can be argued, makes the launching of a Triad dialogue on fundamentals more necessary. The absence of such a dialogue, in conditions of high asymmetric and inadequately managed structural interdependence, is the result of failures in institutional development for collective governance. Institutional development can be conceptualized as a response to multiple articulations of interests that do not aggregate spontaneously. In a public goods perspective, however, institutional development has to be thought of not with agency concepts of governance but with understandings of the responsibilities of governments for high principled knowledge-intensive action in the service of the common good, with constructive guidance of the interests that have to be aggregated, and with understandings that the aggregation of interests through bargaining in the course of agency type governance involves democratic deficits, as weaker articulations of interests are often numerous but ineffective.

NOTES

1. The US direct investment position in Europe on a historical cost basis was $581,791 million in 1999 – $161,527 million in manufacturing and $237,659 million in finance, the remainder including services and petroleum – *Survey of Current Business*, US Department of Commerce, **80** (7), July 2000, 67.
2. On this rivalry see Rangan and Lawrence (1999).
3. The development of intercorporate links within the US presence in Europe tends to be given impetus by their political cooperation to represent their interests in Brussels. See Coen (1999).
4. On the global significance of US international firms see *World Investment Report 1997*, United Nations Conference on Trade and Development.
5. For a study of the origins of this control see Encarnation (1992).
6. See Coen (1999): sales by the US firms in Europe are far greater than US exports to Europe. Sales of US non-bank majority owned affiliates in Europe in 1996 totalled $573,270 million – *Survey of Current Business*, US Department of Commerce, **78** (9), September 1998, 62.
7. See for example symposium on Multilateral Trade Negotiations, *Federal Reserve Bank of St. Louis Review*, **82** (4), July/August 2000.
8. See Wallace (1999).
9. On the scale of the lobbying in the USA see Coen (1999). See also Deardorff and Stern (1998).
10. The Commission also has to contend with increasing pressures from member governments, notably on trade issues: see Meunier and Nicolaidis (1999).
11. See Coen (1999).
12. See references to Germany in Cohen and Boyd (2000).

13. See Bennett (1999).
14. See Tyson (1992).
15. The solidarity in the Japanese system is reflected in Encarnation (1992).
16. For several years before the East Asian crises the USA had been opposed to the formation of an East Asian economic association. See Leong (1999).
17. See Rich and Rissmiller (2000).
18. On the USA's importance in international capital markets see IMF (1998).
19. See IMF (1998) and Schwartz (2000).
20. See Rich and Rissmiller (2000). On the magnitude of the trade deficit problem see Mann (1999). On the consequences of pluralism see Deardorff and Stern (1998).
21. See Destler in Deardorff and Stern (1998).
22. See Sobol (1998).
23. See observations on competitiveness in Wolff (2000).
24. See Corbett (2000) and Bayoumi and Collyns (1999).
25. See Destler and Balint (1999).
26. On the sourcing by US firms see Kotabe (1996).
27. On Japan's regional role see references to Japan in Rugman and Boyd (1999).
28. See Macher, *et al.* (1998).
29. See Macher, *et al.* (1998).
30. See Slater (1999) and Wolff (2000).
31. See Wolff (2000).
32. See Wolff (2000).
33. See Dobson and Waterson (1999) and Matthews and Pickering (2000). See also observations on market openness in *European Economy: 1999 Broad Economic Policy Guidelines*, European Commission, Brussels, European Commission, no. 68.
34. See Dobson and Waterson (1999).
35. See comments on Japan's regional ties in Rugman and Boyd (1999).
36. See Deardorff (1997).
37. The trade in manufactures is highly imbalanced. See figures in Slater (1999).
38. On vertical integration see Feenstra (1998).
39. On the disparities in size between the direct investment positions in finance see *Survey of Current Business*, US Department of Commerce, July 1998.
40. See Warren and Findlay (1998).
41. The main concentration of US direct investment is in Britain. See *Survey of Current Business*, US Department of Commerce, July 1998.
42. See Tanzi (1999) and Alworth (1999). See also references to US trade in financial assets in Mann (1999).
43. See Henning (1994, chapter 6) and Coleman (1996).
44. See IMF (1998).
45. See comments on the IMF in Henning and Padoan (2000).
46. See International Monetary Fund (1999), section on consultation with the USA.
47. See observations by Folkerts-Landau and Garber (1997).
48. See IMF (1998).
49. See *Oxford Review of Economic Policy*, **15** (3), 1999 – symposium on Financial Instability.
50. See Abbott (2000).
51. See Abbott (2000).
52. Some soft agreements, however, can result from arm's-length and low-trust interactions. See Kahler (2000).
53. The widening range of advances in frontier research makes intercorporate exchanges of tacit knowledge all the more important for the identification of potentials for entrepreneurial collaboration. On the increasing significance of such cooperation see Dunning (1997).
54. European direct investment in the USA rose substantially during the first half of 2000 – *Financial Times*, 30 August 2000.
55. See Destler and Balint (1999) and *Federal Reserve Bank of St. Louis Review*, cited **82** (4), July/August 2000.

REFERENCES

Abbott, Frederick M. (2000), 'NAFTA and the legalization of world politics: a case study', *International Organization*, **54**(3), Summer, 519–48.

Alworth, Julian S. (1999), 'Taxation, financial innovation, and integrated financial markets: some implications for tax coordination in the European Union', in Assaf Razin and Efraim Sadka (eds) *The Economics of Globalization*, Cambridge: Cambridge University Press, chapter 9.

Bayoumi, Tamim and Charles Collyns (eds) (1999), *Post-bubble Blues: How Japan responded to Asset Price Collapse*, Washington: International Monetary Fund.

Bennett, Robert J. (1999), 'Business routes of influence in Brussels: exploring the choice of direct representation', *Political Studies*, **47**(2), June, 240–57.

Coen, David (1999), 'The impact of US lobbying practice on the European–Government relationship', *California Management Review*, **41**(4), Summer, 27–44.

Cohen, Stephen S. and Gavin Boyd (eds) (2000), *Corporate Governance and Globalization*, Cheltenham, UK and Northampton, MA, USA: Edward Elgar.

Coleman, William D. (1996), *Financial Services, Globalization, and Domestic Policy Change*, New York: St Martin's Press.

Corbett, Jenny (2000), 'Japan's banking crisis in international perspective', in Masahiko Aoki and Gary R. Saxonhouse (eds), *Finance, Governance, and Competitiveness in Japan*, Oxford: Oxford University Press, pp. 139–76.

Deardorff, Alan V. (1997), 'An economist's overview of the World Trade Organization', in *The Emerging WTO System and Perspectives from East Asia*, Joint US–Korea Academic Studies, Vol. 7, pp. 11–36.

Deardorff, Alan V. and Robert M. Stern (eds) (1998), *Constituent Interests and US Trade Policies*, Ann Arbor: University of Michigan Press.

Destler, I.M. (1998), 'Congress, constituencies and US trade policy', in Deardorff and Stern (1998).

Destler, I.M. and Peter J. Balint (1999), *The New Politics of American Trade: Trade, Labor and the Environment*, Washington DC: Institute for International Economics.

Dobson, Paul and Michel Waterson (1999), 'Retailer power: recent developments and policy implications', *Economic Policy*, **28**, April, 135–50.

Dunning, John D. (1997), *Alliance Capitalism and Global Business*, London: Routledge.

Encarnation, Denis (1992), *Rivals beyond Trade*, Cornell University Press.

Feenstra, Robert C. (1998), 'The integration of trade and the disintegration of production in the global economy', *Journal of Economic Perspectives*, **12**(4), Autumn, 31–50.

Folkerts-Landau, David and Peter M. Garber (1997), 'Derivative Markets and Financial System Soundness', in Charles Enoch and John H. Green (eds) *Banking Soundness and Monetary Policy*, Washington DC: International Monetary Fund, chapter 13.

Henning, C. Randall (1994), *Currencies and Politics in the United States, Germany and Japan*, Washington DC: Institute for International Economics.

Henning, C. Randall and Pier Carlo Padoan (2000), *Transatlantic Perspectives on the Euro*, Washington DC: Brookings Institution.

IMF (1998), *International Capital Markets*, Washington DC: International Monetary Fund.

IMF (1999), *Annual Report 1999*, Washington DC: International Monetary Fund.

Kahler, Miles (2000), 'Legalization as strategy: the Asia Pacific case', *International Organization*, **54**(3), Summer, 549–72.

Kotabe, Masaaki (1996), 'Global sourcing strategy in the Pacific: American and Japanese international companies', in Gavin Boyd (ed.) *Structural Competitiveness in the Pacific*, Cheltenham, UK and Northampton, MA, USA: Edward Elgar.

Leong, Stephen (1999), 'The East Asian economic caucus', in Bjorn Hettne, Andras Inotai and Osvaldo Sunkel (eds) *The New Regionalism and the Future of Security and Development*, New York: St Martin's Press.

Macher, Jeffrey T., David C. Mowery and David A. Hodges (1998), 'Reversal of fortune? The recovery of the US semiconductor industry', *California Management Review*, **41**(1), Autumn, 107–36.

Mann, Catherine L. (1999), *Is the US Trade Deficit Sustainable?*, Washington DC: Institute for International Economics.

Matthews, Duncan and John F. Pickering (2000), 'Business strategy and evolving rules in the single European market', in Richard A. Higgott, Geoffrey R.D. Underhill and Andreas Bieler (eds) *Non-state Actors and Authority in the Global System*, London: Routledge.

Meunier, Sophie and Kalypso Nicolaides (1999), 'Who speaks for Europe? The delegation of trade authority in the EU', *Journal of Common Market Studies*, **37**(3), September, 477–501.

Rangan, S. and R. Lawrence (1999), *A Prism on Globalization: Corporate Responses to the Dollar*, Washington DC: Brookings Institution.

Rich, Robert W. and Donald Rissmiller (2000), 'Understanding the recent behaviour of US inflation', *Current Issues in Economics and Finance*, Federal Reserve Bank of New York, **6**(8), July.

Rugman, Alan M. and Gavin Boyd (eds) (1999), *Deepening Integration in the Pacific Economies*, Cheltenham, UK and Northampton, MA, USA: Edward Elgar.

Schwartz, Anna J. (2000), *The Rise and Fall of Foreign Exchange Intervention*, National Bureau of Economic Research Working Paper 7751, June.

Slater, Courtenay M. (1999), *Foreign Trade of the United States*, Washington DC: Bernan Press.

Sobol, Dorothy Meadow (1998), 'Foreign ownership of US treasury securities: what the data show and do not show', *Current Issues in Economics and Finance*, Federal Reserve Bank of New York, **4**(5), May.

Tanzi, Vito (1999), 'Is there a need for a World Tax Organization?', in Assaf Razin and Efraim Sadka (eds) *The Economics of Globalization*, Cambridge: Cambridge University Press, chapter 8.

Tyson, Laura D'Andrea (1992), *Who's Bashing Whom? Trade Conflict in High Technology Industries*, Washington DC: Institute for International Economics.

Wallace, William (1999), 'The sharing of sovereignty: the European paradox', *Political Studies*, **47**(3), Special Issue, 503–21.

Warren, Tony and Christopher Findlay (1998), 'Competition policy and international trade in air transport and telecommunications services', *The World Economy*, **21**(4), June, 445–56.

Wolff, Edward N. (2000), 'Specialization and productivity performance in low-, medium- and high-tech manufacturing industries', in Alan Heston and Robert E. Lipsey (eds) *International and Interarea Comparisons of Income, Output, and Prices*, Chicago: University of Chicago Press, pp. 419–52.

F13 F21
F14 L16

6. The USA in the WTO

Thomas L. Brewer and Stephen Young

ABSTRACT

The industry structure of the US economy and the international strategies of firms are key elements of the political economy of US trade policymaking. A principal feature of the US economy is the increasing dominance of the services sector and the declining importance of the agricultural, mining and manufacturing sectors. A principal feature of firms' strategies is their increased reliance on international ownership and movement of factors of production through foreign direct investment (FDI). These structural and strategic tendencies, furthermore, interact and thus shape the policy agenda and the central tendencies of US policy. This chapter analyses these structural and strategic trends and their relationships to US policies concerning three types of World Trade Organization (WTO) issues: meta-institutional issues, sector-specific agreements, and dispute settlement cases. The analysis emphasizes the importance of the General Agreement on Trade in Services (GATS), including its provisions concerning FDI.

INTRODUCTION

United States policies on WTO-related issues are shaped by a combination of economic and political conditions. The economic conditions of particular importance include: (1) the structure of the US economy, in which services have become relatively more important; and (2) the international business strategies of firms, which have come to rely more on foreign direct investment, relative to cross-border trade. Both of these changes have significantly altered the economic interests that business groups promote in the policymaking process, and they also therefore affect the agenda and other key features of the politics of specific issues. The structural and strategic changes affect a broad range of variables in the policymaking process and the substance of policies. The theme of the chapter, therefore, is that an understanding of US policy on WTO-related issues requires an understanding of these two related and interacting features of the economic context of US policymaking; the political economy of services issues differs from the political economy of other sectors, and the political economy of foreign direct investment differs from the political economy of cross-border trade.

Investors' and Traders' Interests – and the Policy Agenda

There are both similarities and differences in the interests of foreign direct investors and traders. Most obviously, because foreign direct investors are also traders (about one-third of US imports and exports of goods are intrafirm transactions), there are some identical interests between investors and traders. However, the interests associated with FDI are generally broader and deeper than the interests associated with trade. Directly related FDI interests extend across a wider range of policy areas: host government restrictions on FDI-related foreign exchange transactions such as profit and dividend remittances; competition policy restrictions on mergers and acquisitions; home and host country transfer pricing and other tax policies; host government restrictions on the nationalities of executives and boards of directors; the international transfers of technical personnel; restrictions on international transfers of technology; host country protection of intellectual property rights (IPRs). Because the interests of international direct investors thus extend more broadly than do those of international traders across many issue areas in both home and foreign countries, the political agenda of FDI is more encompassing than the agenda of trade.

At the same time, the interests of direct investors penetrate more deeply into the 'domestic' politics of foreign countries than do the interests of traders. This difference between FDI and trade is a key element in the notion of 'deep integration'. The difference is also reflected in the much greater complexity and significance of the non-discrimination principle of 'national treatment' – that is, the principle that a government should not discriminate against a foreign-made product (in the case of trade) or a foreign-owned corporation (in the case of direct investment). In the US, for instance, the issues involved in not discriminating against Toyotas that are imported into the US from Japan are relatively simple as compared with the issues involved in not discriminating against Toyota of the United States, a foreign-owned US corporation. The political agenda created by the latter is not only more extensive in terms of the types of issues that are raised, it is also more sensitive in the 'domestic' political system. In that sense, the FDI political agenda is deeper as well as broader than the trade agenda.

Types of WTO-Related Policies

In order to facilitate understanding US policies, it is useful to classify WTO issues into three types: (a) meta-institutional issues such as the launching of new WTO negotiating rounds, major expansion of the scope of issues addressed or other transformations of WTO institutional arrangements – issues that are addressed at WTO ministerial-level meetings and in US legislative processes; (b) meso-level issues concerning particular economic sectors and/ or types of barriers to trade – issues that are about individual WTO agreements such as the agriculture agreement, the services agreement (GATS) or the anti-dumping agreement; and (c) micro-level issues that emerge in dispute cases and that typically concern specific US products, firms and industries in bilateral US relations with a specific foreign country. Of course, there are also often implications for issues in categories (a) and/or (b) as a result of the resolution of dispute cases. Although these three categories in this simple typology are therefore neither entirely exclusive nor exhaustive, they are nevertheless analytically useful for identifying tendencies in US policymaking on WTO-related issues.

The chapter discusses US policies on WTO-related issues in terms of these three issue categories, and it also presents data on the structure of the US economy and the international strategies and operations of firms. The analysis is cast in terms of the recent and prospective evolution of economic and political conditions and policies – particularly during the 1990s and early 2000s. The chapter was being completed shortly after the US congressional and presidential elections of 2000, and it briefly considers the prospect for the evolution of policies from 2001. This chapter complements others in the book, including in particular those by Brenton, 2001; and by Pedler (Chapter 7) on EU policies.

For further information on the evolution of US trade policy and politics, see especially Baldwin and Magee, 2000; Destler, 1995, 2000; Destler and Balint, 1999. Discussions of the WTO system and its agenda can be found in Brookings, 1998, 1999; Deardorff and Stern, 1998; Graham, 1996, 2000; Hoekman and Kostecki, 1995; Jackson, 1997; Schott, 1998; Trebilcock and Howse, 1999; Woolcock, 1998. For the texts of the Uruguay Round agreements, see WTO, 1995; for the institutional and legal backgrounds to the Uruguay agreements, see GATT, 1994. An extensive collection of trade and investment studies of policies, politics, economics and institutions is available in Brewer, 1999. Analyses of WTO agreements and disputes are available in Brewer and Young (1998; 1999; 2000; 2001).

The next section of the chapter analyses the interests at stake in US policymaking: first, in terms of the industry structure of the US economy, with an emphasis on the services industries, as opposed to manufacturing, agriculture and mining; second, in terms of the strategic modes of international business, with an emphasis on foreign direct investment as opposed to trade; and third, in terms of the economic geography of the patterns of US trade and FDI.

ECONOMIC CONTEXT

The Structure of the US Economy: The Importance of Services

Table 6.1 reveals changes in the sectoral structure of the US economy over the four-decade period from the late 1950s to the late 1990s. The decreasing shares of GDP of agriculture, mining and manufacturing, and concomitantly the increasing share of services, are clear. The share of GDP in services increased from slightly less than half to nearly two-thirds. By 1998, agriculture, forestry and fishing altogether contributed only 1.4 per cent of GDP –

Table 6.1   Structure of the US economy: GDP by industry sector (per cent)

Industry sector	1959	1977	1987	1998
Agri., forestry, fishing	4.0	2.7	1.9	1.4
Mining	2.5	2.7	1.9	1.2
Manufacturing	27.7	22.8	18.7	16.4
Services [total]	48.1	51.7	58.9	64.7
Construction	na	na	na	na
Transport, utilities	8.9	8.8	9.0	8.7
Wholesale trade	7.0	7.0	6.5	7.0
Retail trade	9.8	9.4	9.2	8.9
Fin., insur., real estate	12.9	13.9	17.5	19.1
Other services	9.5	12.6	16.7	21.0
Government	12.9	14.4	13.9	12.6

Note: The data are based on the 1987 Standard Industrial Classification (SIC) scheme, except that it has been reorganized as follows: In the original source, the 'services' category includes only those indicated as 'other services' here, and in the original source there is no 'services-total' category, which has been computed for this presentation by the author. The subcategories in this table are listed as separate categories (not 'services') in the original source. In this table, therefore, 'other services' include: business, health, legal, educational, social, lodging, amusement, auto, and other types of services not included elsewhere. The 'services-total' category corresponds to 'private services-producing industries' in the addenda of the source table.

Source: Adapted by the author from US, *Survey of Current Business*, **80**(6) (June 2000): p. 29, Table E.

down from 4.0 per cent in 1959. In terms of employment, those sectors included only 2.5 per cent of the people engaged in production in the economy (Table 6.2), and in terms of their share of earnings they decreased by 4.2 per cent over the four-decade period. Manufacturing's share of GDP, meanwhile, had decreased from 27.7 per cent of GDP in 1959 to 16.4 per cent in 1998. Mining, which had never been a major sector except in some regions of the country, declined from 2.5 to 1.2 per cent of GDP.

These changes in the sectoral structure of the economy are reflected in the structure of international economic transactions, not only in cross-border trade, but also in direct investment. Further, the shifts are evident in imports and inward FDI, as well as exports and outward FDI. As both a producer-exporter of services and as a consumer-importer of services, the US has been experiencing a shift in the relative importance of the services sector as compared with other sectors of the economy (see Table 6.3). Although cross-border services trade remained less than goods trade in 1999, the rate of increase in

Table 6.2   Structure of the US economy: persons engaged in production by industry sector (per cent, 1998)

Industry sector	1998
Agri., forestry, fishing	2.5
Mining	0.5
Manufacturing	14.5
Services [total]	[68.2]
Construction	5.8
Transport, utilities	5.1
Wholesale trade	5.3
Retail trade	15.7
Fin., insur., real estate	5.8
Other services	30.3
Government	14.3
Number-millions	130.0

Note: The data are based on the 1987 Standard Industrial Classification (SIC) scheme, except that it has been reorganized as follows: In the original source, the 'services' category includes only those indicated as 'other services' here, and in the original source there is no 'services-total' category, which has been computed for this presentation by the author. The subcategories in this table are listed as separate categories (not 'services') in the original source. In this table, therefore, 'other services' include: business, health, legal, educational, social, lodging, amusement, auto, and other types of services not included elsewhere.

Source: Adapted by the author from US, *Survey of Current Business*, Dec. 1999: p. 91, Table 6.8C.

Table 6.3   *Changes in types of US and foreign firms' strategies and operations: types of international business transactions ($ billions)*

	1979	1989	1999	Ratio: 1999/1979*
(a) Exports and outward FDI				
Goods trade	184.4	362.1	684.4	3.7
Services trade	39.7	127.1	271.9	6.8
Royalties, lic.	6.2	13.8	36.5	5.9
FDI income	38.2	62.0	118.8	3.1
FDI flows	25.2	43.4	150.9	6.0
FDI stocks**	207.8***	381.8	1132.6	5.5
(b) Imports and inward FDI				
Goods trade	212.0	477.4	1030.0	4.9
Services trade	36.7	102.5	191.3	5.2
Royalties, lic.	6.2	13.8	36.5	5.9
FDI income	38.2	62.0	118.8	13.1
FDI flows	3.7	68.3	275.5	74.5
FDI stocks**	124.7***	368.9	986.7	7.9

Notes:
*   The ratios are computed on the basis of current dollar values. The relative sizes of the ratios across types of economic transactions are comparable because they all implicitly include the same inflation rates. However, their absolute values should not be used to interpret changes for each individual type of transaction.
**   Basis: historical cost.
***   1982.

Source: US, *Survey of Current Business*, 1979, 1989, 1999 issues.

services was much higher for services than for goods during the two decades from the late 1970s to the late 1990s.

The increasing importance of services in the US economy is related to the increasing importance of both outward and inward foreign direct investment (Table 6.3). FDI is a more common strategic mode – relative to cross-border trade – in services than in other sectors. Changes in the sectoral composition of the economy and international economic relations interact with changes in firms' strategies. FDI tends to be more commonly used than trade as a strategic alternative in services industries, as compared with their relative importance as strategic modes in other sectors. This tendency is one of the reasons for the increasing importance of FDI in US international economic relations: as services become more important, FDI becomes more important. The next section presents data on this strategic shift and considers the implications for US policy on WTO issues.

The Strategy of Firms: The Importance of FDI

In Table 6.4, which contains data on services sales abroad by US-based firms and sales in the US by foreign-based firms, the greater importance of FDI, versus cross-border trade, is evident. The ratio of foreign affiliates' sales to cross-border sales is greater than 1.0 for both sales in the US and sales abroad. The sectoral composition of both inward and outward FDI flows in services industries and other industries is indicated in Table 6.5 for 1999. FDI outflows in the services sector exceeded FDI outflows in manufacturing by nearly 100 per cent. Services FDI inflows also exceeded manufacturing FDI inflows, though only by a small amount.

Table 6.4　*International sales of services: direct investment and cross-border trade ($ billions, 1997)*

Mode of supply	Sales abroad by US-based firms	Sales in US by foreign-based firms
Direct Investment (DI)	258.3	205.5
Cross Border (CB)	240.4	152.4
Ratio of DI/CB	1.07	1.35

Note:　The first years in which foreign sales from direct investment projects exceeded foreign sales from cross-border transactions were 1996 for US-based firms' sales abroad and 1989 for foreign-based firms' sales in the US.

Source:　US, *Survey of Current Business*, **79** (10) (October 1999): p. 48, Table A.

The Regional Patterns of US Trade and FDI

Whether indicated by trade or by FDI, the basic regional patterns in US international economic relations are similar (see Table 6.6). In terms of exports and outward FDI and in terms of imports and inward FDI, the relative importance of Europe is apparent, as is the importance of Canada and Mexico. Canada, in fact, was more important than Japan in 1999 in three of the four categories reported in Table 6.6; only in inward FDI into the US did Japan exceed Canada in their relative importance to the US. The importance of

Table 6.5   FDI by industry sector ($ billions, 1999)

Industry sector	Outward FDI	Inward FDI
Petroleum	99.9	55.9
Manufacturing	318.1	391.0
Food and kindred products	36.1	16.7
Chemicals	82.8	103.5
Primary and fabricated metals	18.8	21.8
Industrial machinery and equipment	37.8	76.6
Electronic and other electric equipment	38.4	
Transportation equipment	36.0	
Other manufacturing	68.1	172.4
Services – total	624.7	425.2
Wholesale trade	80.1	108.9
Fin., ins., real estate	475.9	258.7
Other services	68.7	57.6
Total	1132.6	986.7

Note: Historical cost basis.

Source: US, *Survey of Current Business.*

Mexico is also evident: only in terms of imports in the US is Japan more important than Mexico; otherwise, in terms of exports and in terms of outward FDI from the US, Mexico is more important to the US economy than is Japan. On the other hand, in terms of imports and inward FDI, flows into the US from Japan exceeded those from Mexico.

Outside the 'triad' and outside NAFTA, US economic relations with other countries in the western hemisphere are substantial – as of course is oil trade, in particular, with OPEC countries in the Middle East and other regions of the world.

US POLICIES

The roles of the structural, strategic and geographic features of the economic context of US policymaking are evident across the three types of US policies on WTO-related issues mentioned above in the introduction – namely (a) meta-institutional issues, (b) meso-level issues, and (c) micro-level issues in dispute cases.

Table 6.6   US trade and FDI by geographical area ($ billions, 1999)

(a)   Exports and outward FDI

	Exports of goods and services*	Outward FDI – net outflows	Outward FDI stock (historical cost)
Canada	209.9	14.3	111.7
Latin America and Caribbean	254.3	19.5	223.2
Mexico	108.3	5.4	34.3
Western Europe	259.8	70.9	581.8
EU	148.9	58.2	
Other W. Europe	110.9	12.7	
Eastern Europe	12.2	1.2	
Asia, Africa, Middle East	244.7	21.5	212.1
Japan	88.0	10.6	47.8

(b)   Imports and inward FDI

	Imports of goods and services*	Inward FDI – net inflows	Inward FDI stock (historical cost)
Canada	187.8	12.2	79.7
Latin America and Caribbean	202.2	9.5	44.6
Mexico	120.6	1.1	3.6
Western Europe	293.3	233.6	
EU	236.5	228.1	685.8
Other W. Europe	56.8	5.5	
Eastern Europe	14.5	1.4	
Asia, Africa, Middle East	355.6		176.5
Japan	148.0	9.5	148.9

Note: * Trade data include non-factor services (such as transportation) but exclude factor services (such as income or payments on direct investments).

Source: US, *Survey of Current Business*, **80** (7) (July 2000): pp. 88–9, Table 1.

Meta-Institutional Issues: The Coverage of Services and FDI

The US pushed for many years – before, during and after the Uruguay Round negotiations – to have liberalization in services on the agenda. One result of these efforts was the General Agreement on Trade in Services (GATS), which entered into force with the WTO on 1 January 1995 and which was subsequently expanded to include additional telecommunications services and financial services (Brewer and Young, 1998, 2000, 2001; Dobson and Jacquet, 1998; Mann, 2000). The scope of the coverage of services in the GATS is extensive in the types of transactions that it includes – at least in principle. In Table 6.7, this is evident in both dimensions of the table – that is, the form of market access (whether through cross-border trade, FDI or the movement of people) and the types of barriers (whether at the international border or internal within the country). The contrast of the relatively broad coverage of FDI in services versus the quite limited coverage in manufactured goods is also evident in Table 6.7; in manufactured goods, only Trade Related Investment Measures (TRIMs), such as domestic content requirements, are covered.

Table 6.7   Comparison of coverage of types of transactions in GATT and GATS

	Form of market access					
	Cross-border trade		FDI		Movement of people	
Type of barrier	GATT	GATS	GATT	GATS	GATT	GATS
Border barriers for foreigners	Yes	Yes	Only TRIMs	Yes	No	No
Internal barriers for foreigners	Yes	Yes	No	Yes	No	Yes
Barriers for both foreigners and nationals	No	Yes	No	Yes	No	Yes

Note: Yes = covered; No = not covered.

Industry Sector Issues: Specific Commitments in the GATS

The commitments made in the GATS to liberalize market access and national treatment vary across industry sectors as well as across modes of supply. In Table 6.8 the exceptions of the US, the EU and Japan are indicated – first in panel (a) in their 'horizontal' exceptions across all service industry sectors, and then in panel (b) in their exceptions in particular sectors. The complexity

Table 6.8   *GATS specific commitments by US, EU and Japan*

	Limitations	
	Market access	National treatment
(a) Horizontal exceptions across industries		
US		
Cross-border supply	Subsidies	Taxes
Consumption abroad	Subsidies	Taxes
Commercial presence	No exceptions	Real estate
Presence of natural persons	Unbound except temporary stay	Subsidies incl. R&D
	Subsidies	Unbound
Presence of natural persons	EU: unbound except temporary stay	EU: subsidies
		EU: subsidies
		EU: unbound except temporary stay
Japan		
Cross-border supply	No exceptions	No exceptions
Consumption abroad	No exceptions	No exceptions
Commercial presence	No exceptions	Unbound for R&D subsidies
Presence of natural persons	Unbound except for temporary stay	Unbound except for temporary stay
		Unbound for R&D subsidies

(b)   Exceptions for basic telecommunications

US

*Subsectors a–g***

Cross-border supply	No exceptions	No exceptions
Consumption abroad	No exceptions	No exceptions
Commercial presence	Radio licences	Attachment
Presence of natural persons	Unbound except temporary stay	Unbound except temporary stay

EU

All subsectors

Exceptions to horizontal cross-border supply	MGs: FIN* EU: No exceptions	MGs: F EU: No exceptions
Consumption abroad	EU: No exceptions MGs: P, GR	EU: No exceptions MGs: No exceptions
Commercial presence	EU: No exceptions MGs: GR, P, F	EU: No exceptions MGs: No exceptions
Presence of natural persons	EU: Unbound except temporary stay	EU: Unbound except temporary stay

Subsectors a–g^i

Cross-border supply	EU: No exceptions MGs: E, IRL, P, GR	EU: No exceptions
Consumption abroad	No exceptions	No exceptions

Table 6.8 continued

	Limitations	
	Market access	National treatment
Commercial presence	EU: No exceptions MGs: E, IRL, P, GR	No exceptions
Presence of natural persons	Unbound except temporary stay	Unbound except temporary stay
Subsector: Other (o)		
Cross-border supply	EU: No exceptions MGs: IRL	No exceptions
Consumption abroad	No exceptions	No exceptions
Commercial presence	EU: No exceptions MGs: IRL, P	No exceptions
Presence of natural persons	Unbound except temporary stay	Unbound except temporary stay
Japan		
Subsectors a–d		
Cross-border supply	No exceptions	No exceptions
Consumption abroad	No exceptions	No exceptions
Commercial presence	Limits on foreign capital participation in NTT & KDD	Board members & auditors of NTT & KDD
Presence of natural persons	Unbound except temporary stay	Unbound except temporary stay

Notes:

*Abbreviations of EU Member Governments (MGs):

E   = Spain
F   = Finland
GR = Greece
IRL = Ireland
P   = Portugal

**Subsectors are as follows:

a.   Voice telephone services
b.   Packet-switched data transmission services
c.   Circuit-switched data transmission services
d.   Telex services
e.   Telegraph services
f.   Facsimile services
g.   Private leased circuit services
h.   Electronic mail
i.   Voice mail
j.   On-line information and database retrieval
k.   Electronic data interchange (EDI)
l.   Enhanced/value-added facsimile services including store and forward, store and retrieve
m. Code and protocol conversion
n.   On-line information and/or data processing (including transaction process)
o.   Other

Sources:

(a)   Compiled by the author from GATT, *Uruguay Round of Multilateral Trade Negotiations*, Vol. 28 (Geneva: GATT, 1995).
(b)   Compiled by the author from WTO, GATS, specific commitments, documents, website, 15 April 1999 (GATS/SC/31/Suppl. 3, 11 April 1997).

Table 6.9 *GATS specific commitments by EU members*

Signatories	Cross-border supply	Consumption abroad	Commercial presence	Presence of natural persons	Subtotal
(a) *Basic telecommunications – exceptions*					
Austria	0	0	0	0	0
Belgium	1	0	0	0	1
Denmark	0	0	0	0	0
Finland	0	0	2	0	2
France	0	0	1	0	1
Germany	0	0	0	0	0
Greece	2	0	2	0	4
Ireland	3	0	2	0	5
Italy	0	0	0	0	0
Luxembourg	0	0	0	0	0
Netherlands	0	0	0	0	0
Portugal	3	0	3	0	6
Spain	1	0	1	0	2
Sweden	0	0	0	0	0
UK	0	0	0	0	0
Totals	**10**	**0**	**11**	**0**	**21**
(b) *Financial services agreement/banking and other financial services (excluding insurance)*					
Austria	0	0	4	0	4
Belgium	1	0	1	0	2
Denmark	0	0	1	0	1

Country					Totals
Finland	0	1	3	0	4
France	0	0	0	1	1
Germany	0	1	0	0	1
Greece	0	1	2	1	4
Ireland	1	0	3	0	4
Italy	1	0	6	1	8
Luxembourg	0	0	0	0	0
Netherlands	0	0	0	0	0
Portugal	0	0	2	0	2
Spain	0	0	1	0	1
Sweden	0	0	3	0	3
UK	0	0	1	1	2
Totals	**3**	**3**	**27**	**4**	**37**

Notes: Illustrative excerpts of exceptions to GATS:

Telecommunications – exception for all modes of supply for market access and national treatment – by Finland: 'The general horizontal requirements [of the EU] for legal entities in GATS/SC/33 shall not apply to the telecommunications sector.'

Banking – exception for xxx mode of supply for market access – by Denmark: 'Financial institutions may engage in foreign exchange only through subsidiaries incorporated in Denmark.'

Banking – exception for commercial presence for national treatment – by Sweden: 'A founder of a banking company must be a natural person resident in the European Economic Area.'

Insurance – exception for cross-border mode of supply for market access – by Denmark: 'Compulsory air transport insurance can be underwritten only by firms established in the Community.'

Insurance – exception for commercial presence mode of supply for national treatment – by Finland: 'The managing director, at least one auditor and at least half of the promoters and members of the board of directors and the supervisory board of an insurance company shall have their place of residence in the European Economic Area, unless the Ministry of Social Affairs and Health has granted an exemption.'

Sources:
(a) Computed by the author from WTO, GATS, specific commitments documents, website, 15 April 1999.
(b) Computed by the author from WTO website, 15 April 1999.

of the structure of the GATS arises in part from the combination of a 'positive list' approach to the sectors covered, according to which governments have listed those sectors that they do want included, versus the negative list approach to the modes covered within each sector, according to which governments have listed exceptions by mode to their market access and national treatment liberalization commitments within each industry sector. Furthermore, some of the exceptions are specified 'horizontally' across all sectors (panel (a) in Table 6.8), while others are specified for individual sectors (panel (b)). In general, compared with other governments the US has included a relatively large number of sectors in its positive list and a relatively small number of exceptions in its negative list; in that sense, the US has indicated a relatively liberalized schedule of specific commitments in the GATS; this of course is not surprising since the US tends to be relatively competitive in service industries and consequently wants other countries to adopt more liberalized policies on investment and trade in services. At the same time, the US remains quite uncompetitive and hence protectionist in some services sectors, for instance maritime transport services; as a result, in that industry the US has refused even to negotiate a maritime services agreement that could be integrated into the larger GATS.

For US-based service providers who wish for more access to foreign markets through trade and/or investment, of course, the key issues concern the specific commitments made by other governments in their GATS schedules. The array of barriers to trade and investment in EU countries, in particular, that they face is complicated by the fact that there are two levels of commitments and exceptions to them made by the EU countries. For each of the 15 member governments of the EU has been given an opportunity to register its own individual exceptions to the schedule of commitments made by the EU Commission in the negotiations with other WTO members. Thus, although the EU may have a 'common commercial policy' in manufactured goods, it surely does not have one in services. Instead, it has a patchwork of policies comprising a combination of EU-level commitments and national-level exceptions to those commitments. The details for portions of the telecommunications and financial services industries are displayed in Table 6.9.

In Table 6.9, the relatively large numbers of exceptions lodged by Portugal, for instance, in telecommunications are evident in the row subtotals of panel (a), and similarly the relatively large numbers of exceptions lodged by Italy in financial services are evident in panel (b). At the other extreme, as a reflection of its tendency to have open, liberal policies, the Netherlands is the only EU member that did not register exceptions in either of the two sectors represented in the table. In terms of strategic modes, as represented by the columns of Table 6.9, there is a tendency for more exceptions to be placed on foreign direct investment (represented by the 'commercial presence' column) than on other modes; this tendency is particularly strong in the case of financial services. Foreign direct investment in services is thus a particularly sensitive mode within the political economies of prospective foreign markets of competitive multinational firms based in the US. This sensitivity is a reflection not only of the perception of the relatively weak competitive positions of the foreign firms, but also the fact that the privatization programmes in these industries are still evolving in many countries.

In the services sector, therefore, US-based firms still face many barriers to trade and FDI, and the US government continues to put liberalization in many (though certainly not all) services industries high on its list of negotiating priorities. Partly because of the many remaining gaps in the GATS, as represented by industry sectors not listed in countries' schedules of commitments and as represented by their modal exceptions to their commitments, the incidence of disputes concerning the GATS has been relatively small thus far. This is likely to change, however, when the commitments of developing countries are phased in, starting in 2005, after an initial delay to allow them time to develop appropriate new policies. In contrast, disputes on other WTO matters have been relatively frequent, as discussed in the next section.

Dispute Settlement Cases

During the initial five-year period of the existence of the WTO from 1995 to 1999, there were 183 WTO official requests for consultation in the dispute settlement process.[1] The US was often a complainant or a respondent in those cases. In panel (a) of Table 6.10 it is apparent that the US was a complainant in nearly one-third of the cases but a respondent in only one-fifth of the cases. The basic pattern of being a complainant more often than a respondent was evident in four of the five years. Another pattern evident in the table (in panel (b)) is that most cases involved GATT and thus goods, including agricultural goods; 18 of the 56 cases in which the US was a complainant and 8 of the 38 cases in which the US was a respondent concerned agriculture, food or fishing. These relatively small sectors of the US economy thereby contribute disproportionately to US trade conflicts, whether as complainant or as respondent. This tendency is not surprising, however, given the relatively protectionist policies of other countries faced by US firms, for instance in grains, and at the same time the relatively protectionist US policies faced by foreign firms, for instance in sugar.

Though developing countries have been more active in the WTO dispute settlement process – as both complainants and respondents – they were involved in only a minority of cases in which the US was on either side. In total, as panel (c) of Table 6.10 indicates, nearly one-half of the US cases involved EU countries as adversaries (whether collectively *qua* the EU, or

Table 6.10   US involvement in WTO disputes, 1995–1999

(a) *Cases per year*

Year	US as complainant		US as respondent		Total WTO cases
	N	%	N	%	
1995	5	20	4	16	25
1996	15	39	8	21	38
1997	17	33	6	20	51
1998	10	24	8	15	41
1999	9	32	10	36	28
Total	56	31	38	21	183

(b) *WTO agreements at issue in US cases*

Agreements	US as complainant	US as respondent
GATT	27	23
TRIMs	6	0
GATS	3	0
TRIPs	10	2
Other	10	13
Total	56	38

(c) *Countries involved in cases with US*

Countries	US as complainant against other countries	US as respondent against other countries
EU	28*	16
Japan	5	4
Canada	3	3
Mexico	1	3
Others	19	12
Total	56	38

Notes:
* Includes cases against individual member governments of the EU, such as five essentially identical cases concerning taxes as export subsidies, as well as cases against the EU as an entity. The latter include five cases concerning the EU's banana import regime and three cases concerning computer local area network systems.

These and other tables reflecting patterns and trends in all WTO dispute cases are available at www.wtodisputes.com, which is maintained by Thomas L. Brewer and Stephen Young.

Sources: WTO website, Disputes, State of Play, www.wto.org, 6 September 2000; and USTR; website, WTO, Disputes, www.ustr.gov, 14 September 2000.

individually). See Brenton, forthcoming; and Pedler (Chapter 7 in this volume) for further analysis of EU-related issues in the WTO. Many of these US–EU cases, as well as the cases between the US and Japan, have attracted much attention in the press as well as policy specialists in the public and private sectors. The individual cases, with their WTO case numbers and summaries of the issue and outcomes, are presented in Table 6.11. At the time of writing, many of the cases were still pending at some stage in the WTO dispute settlement process, and therefore their outcomes were not yet known.

The outcomes of individual cases are of course of great interest to government officials as well as the executives of the firms and industries directly involved in them. Hence, 'scorecards' that register the 'winners' and 'losers' are kept for instance by the US government, and the results as of 13 September 2000, according to the US government, are presented in Table 6.12. Several patterns and relationships in that table are particularly interesting. One is that the US was a winner as a complainant about as often in relative terms as it was a loser as a respondent – 24 per cent and 23 per cent of the time, respectively. Hence, there was a tendency towards a kind of symmetry at least during the first five years: the odds of winning as a complainant were about the same as the odds of losing as a respondent. As a corollary, the US had lost in only 5 per cent of the cases as a complainant and won in only 3 per cent of the cases as a respondent. In short, complainants are more likely to win (respondents more likely to lose) no matter which role the US and its adversaries had in the particular disputes. The US, like other members of the WTO, clearly tends to take disputes to the WTO when it has a strong case.

As part of the research undertaken by the authors, interviews were undertaken with a range of interest groups in the US in order to obtain detailed insights into the mechanisms surrounding case selection. The aim was to establish the relative importance of market opening or commercial criteria as compared with, say, political influences on the choice of cases; and linked to this, US government strategy (through the office of the United States Trade Representative (USTR)) towards the dispute settlement process in the WTO.

Comments from USTR officials stressed that there was no formal process of ranking cases by importance in terms of commercial criteria, and that economic factors were not necessarily paramount in the selection of cases. One observation was that the system was 'surprisingly random'; while another suggestion was that although the USTR did try to think strategically, this was difficult because of the 'noise' in the system. The consequence was that the WTO dispute settlement route was used because the USTR did not believe that they could succeed in any other way. Accepting these points, a variety of explanations were posited for the US selection of WTO cases:

- The commercial significance of the case.

Table 6.11   *US cases involving EU and Japan (WTO case numbers, issues,*
            outcomes as of 6 September 2000)

(a)   US–EU cases

US as complainant

---

13 – Grain duties.

16 (and 27, 152, 158, 165) – Banana import regime. Decided against EU.
Retaliation by US authorized and implemented.

26 – Beef hormones. Decided against EU. Retaliation by US authorized.

37 – Patents (Portugal). No decision; mutually agreed solution notified.

62 (and 67, 68) – Computer LAN equipment classification. Decided against
EU.

80 – Telephone directory licensing (Belgium).

82 (and 83, 86, 115) – IPR, copyrights in Denmark, Sweden, Ireland. No
decision; mutually agreed solutions notified.

104 – Cheese export subsidies.

124 (and 125) – Motion picture and television IPRs in Greece.

127–131 – Export tax subsidies.

172 (and 173) – Flight management system subsidies.

174 – Geographical indications in agricultural and food products.

US as respondent

---

38 (and 176) – Cuba sanctions (Helms-Burton). Panel's authority lapsed after
EU–US resolution.

39 – Tariff increases as retaliation in beef hormones case. No decision; US
withdrew measures.

63 – Anti-dumping, urea from former GDR.

85 (and 151) – Rules of origin. No decision; mutually agreed solution notified.

88 – Burma sanctions. Panel's authority lapsed. US Court case overturned
law.

100 – Poultry imports.

108 – Tax export subsidies (FSCs). Decided against US. Change in law being
implemented.

Table 6.11   continued

(a)   US–EU cases

US as respondent

118 – Harbour tax.

136 – Anti-dumping Act of 1916. Decided against US.

138 – Countervailing duty.

152 – Sections 301–310 of Trade Act of 1974. Decided in favour of US.

160 – Copyright Act. Decided, in part, against US. Change being implemented.

165 – Retaliation in bananas case. Decided against US.

166 – Wheat gluten imports. Decided, in part, against US.

(b)   US–Japan cases

US as complainant

11 – Taxes on alcohol. Decided against Japan. Changes were implemented.

28 – Sound recordings copyrights. No decision, but mutually agreed solution notified.

44 – Film distribution and sale [Fuji-Kodak]. Decided in favour of Japan. No change in policies.

45 – Distribution services (Large-Scale Retail Store Law). Consultations are continuing.

76 – Agricultural imports. Decided against Japan. Testing and quarantine methods changed.

US as respondent

6 – Auto import surtax. No decision, but mutually agreed solution notified.

95 – Burma sanctions. Panel's authority lapsed. US Court case overturned law.

162 – Anti-Dumping Act of 1916. Decided against US. Implementation of changes is pending.

184 – Anti-dumping in steel. Panel has been established.

Source: WTO website, Disputes, State of Play, updated on 6 September 2000, www.wto.org.

Table 6.12   Outcome or other status of dispute cases involving US (as of 13 September 2000)

	US as complainant		US as respondent	
Outcome	N	%	N	%
Won	13	24	1	3
Resolved without formal ruling	13	24	11	28
Lost	3	5	9	23
Not completed, withdrawn	24	44	17	43
Merged with other cases	2	4	2	1
Total	55	100	40	100

Source: Computed from USTR, Web Site, 'Snapshot of US Cases Involving the United States', 14 September 2000 www.ustr.gov

- The strength of the case; that is, was it winnable? The need to achieve victories (and more especially to avoid defeats) is undoubtedly important given hostile attitudes in the US Congress.
- Cases brought by companies or industries, sometimes backed by strong political support. Examples include the high fructose corn syrup anti-dumping case against Mexico which had strong political backing across the American corn belt. The dispute case against the EU's regime for the importation of bananas is also in this category (this is discussed further in a later section of this chapter).
- Retaliatory cases. A classic example concerns the Foreign Sales Corporations tax provisions case, which was brought by the EU against the United States. The US retaliated by taking out petitions against a number of EU countries individually, alleging that various income tax measures constituted export subsidies.
- Collaborative cases. Illustrations include cases against discriminatory tax regimes on imported spirits in Japan, Korea and Chile, where the US had the support of other complainants such as the EU.
- 'Demonstration' cases. There have been a number of instances where the objective of the case was to generate a demonstration effect. This was important in the so-called 'mail-box' TRIPs cases against India and Pakistan, and again in respect of India's import quotas on over 27,000 agricultural and industrial product tariffs lines, which were maintained under the BOP exceptions of GATT.
- Cases designed to establish case law. This relates to the demonstration effect noted above. In this respect the Indonesian autos case was help-

ful in addressing a wide range of issues. The complaint against Japan, concerning that country's copyright regime for sound recordings, was the first case under the TRIPs agreement.

Some explanations were also suggested for the small number of cases in certain areas where barriers undoubtedly exist. The TRIMs agreement is a case in point. When US multinationals have invested in the market, it could well be in their interest to support the maintenance of TRIMs. If such major US companies had the support of US unions, it would be difficult for the USTR to propose a case. Anti-dumping falls into this category, since the US, formerly a major user of anti-dumping legislation against Japan and other Asian producers, has brought no cases to the WTO. In part this was explained by the fact that the US economy had enjoyed a lengthy period of domestic and export growth. But another explanation may concern the fact that the US did not wish to encourage the reciprocal use of dumping provisions by, for instance, developing countries.

Timing is an issue too. For both TRIMs and TRIPs, for example, there were phase-out periods written into the Uruguay Round agreements for developing countries. The major disputes may emerge at the end of the phase-out period if countries either haven't complied with their obligations or seek to extend the transition period. Finally, there have been few cases relating to the GATS largely because there are many exceptions to the rules in its present early stage of development.

While of course very tentative, the results suggest that about half the cases brought by the US have been 'political' or more strictly 'non-economic'. Because of this, about the same proportion have limited economic significance in terms of their contribution to the wider market opening objectives of the WTO. Notwithstanding this, in general there are grounds for cautious optimism in respect of progress towards market liberalization through the WTO, and, therefore, in support of further globalization.

Finally, it should be noted that many disputes are resolved relatively easily and quickly once they are taken to the WTO for consultation; such cases as the US–EU banana and beef hormones cases, which have dominated the news because of the intensity and duration and public salience of the WTO dispute resolution processes involved in them, are not representative of the disposition of disputes. In fact, the US has often relatively easily obtained agreement from other members to change their policies, and it has often changed its own policies relatively quietly in response to complaints by other countries.

FUTURE EVOLUTION OF US POLICY

The institutional scope and procedures of the WTO, the details of many of its industry-specific agreements, and the outcomes of many of its dispute cases – all of these features of the multilateral trade-investment regime reflect US interests and policy preferences. The evolution of the regime from the GATT to the WTO as a result of the Uruguay Round negotiations – and subsequent agreements as well – have been shaped to a significant degree by US influence. The expansion of the regime to include services, albeit with an incomplete and complex patchwork of multi-tiered commitments and exceptions to them, represents an important accomplishment of many years of negotiations by US administrations. Furthermore, although the outcomes of disputes have almost inevitably been a mixture of victories and defeats for particular US industries, the process has functioned more effectively than its precursor in the GATT and in that respect served US interests as well.

The central issue about the future of the US in the WTO is more about the changing domestic politics and its effects on the agenda of so-called 'new' issues, such as labour and the environment. The election results of 2000 suggest that there will be much partisan controversy and Presidential-Congressional conflict over US–WTO policy issues. Those issues will play out against a backdrop of a combination of increases in the economic significance of international services and foreign direct investment.

In the World Trade Organization the USA is generally an advocate of increased multilateral trade liberalization, and is advantaged by strong bargaining power. Increases in imports, however, are contributing to large trade deficits (Mann, 2000). Greater access to foreign markets has to be sought, with increased reciprocal openness to exports from trading partners in exchange for their concessions on market entry. There are uncertainties about the degrees of access that would have to be granted, however, as well as about the length of prospective multilateral trade negotiations. These uncertainties influence the strategies of US international firms.

Complex structural interdependencies with many asymmetries thus affect estimates of what may be achieved through trade policy activism in the multilateral context. Such estimates, moreover, have to take into account issues concerning the institutional development of the World Trade Organization. The established US foreign economic policy orientation favours continuation of the WTO as a 'member driven' institution in which very modest functions are assigned to its Secretariat and there are no firm formal rules about voting rights.

Regional options may thus command more attention in US trade policy if possibilities are seen for export expansion. These options may appear to be more significant as the European Union enlarges with the admission of East

European countries. The main area of opportunity for the USA is Latin America, and it will clearly remain important while slow recoveries are made in Japan and industrializing East Asian countries from the financial crises of the late 1990s. A challenge to be overcome is domestic opposition in the USA.

NOTE

1. There are several bases for computing quantitative patterns, trends and other features of the dispute cases brought to the WTO. The most direct way is to use the simple number of cases, as such a tabulation is commonly understood, and that is the practice used here. Cases can also be grouped into 'matters' on the basis of a common set of complaints brought by different countries against a single country. For further information on counting issues, see the annex of Brewer and Young, 1999; and also Petersmann, 1997; and Shoyer, 1998.

REFERENCES

Baldwin, Robert E. and Christopher S. Magee (2000), *Congressional Trade Votes: From NAFTA to Fast-Track Defeat*, Washington, DC: Institute for International Economics.

Brenton, Paul (forthcoming), 'The EU in World Trade', in Thomas L. Brewer, Paul Brenton and Gavin Boyd (eds), *Globalizing Europe*, Cheltenham, UK and Northampton, MA, USA: Edward Elgar.

Brewer, Thomas L. (ed.) (1999), *Trade and Investment Policy*, 2 volumes, Cheltenham, UK and Northampton, MA, USA: Edward Elgar.

Brewer, Thomas L. and Stephen Young (1998), 'Investment issues at the World Trade Organization: the architecture of rules and the settlement of disputes', *Journal of International Economic Law*, **1**, 457–70.

Brewer, Thomas L. and Stephen Young (1999), 'Developing countries and disputes at the WTO', *Journal of World Trade*, **33** (5), 169–82.

Brewer, Thomas L. and Stephen Young (2000), *The Multilateral Investment System and Multinational Enterprises*, updated paperback edition, Oxford: Oxford University Press.

Brewer, Thomas L. and Stephen Young (2001), 'The multilateral regime for FDI: institutions and their implications for business strategy', in Alan M. Rugman and Thomas L. Brewer (eds), *Oxford Handbook of International Business*, Oxford: Oxford University Press.

Brookings Trade Forum, 1998 and 1999, Washington DC: Brookings Institution.

Deardorf, Alan and Robert Stern (eds) (1998), *Constituent Interests and US Trade Policies*, Ann Arbor: University of Michigan Press.

Destler, I.M. (1995), *American Trade Politics*, Third Edition, Washington, DC: Institute for International Economics.

Destler, I.M., and Peter J. Balint (1999), *The New Politics of American Trade: Trade, Labor, and the Environment*, Washington, DC: Institute for International Economics.

Dobson, Wendy and Pierre Jacquet (1998), *Financial Services Liberalization in the WTO*, Washington, DC: Institute for International Economics.

General Agreement on Tariffs and Trade [GATT] (1994), *Guide to GATT Law and Practice*, 6th edn, Geneva: GATT.

Graham, Edward M. (1996), *Global Corporations and National Governments*, Washington, DC: Institute for International Economics.

Graham, Edward M. (2000), *Fighting the Wrong Enemy*, Washington, DC: Institute for International Economics.

Hoekman, Bernard M. and Michael M. Kostecki (1995), *The Political Economy of the World Trading System*, Oxford: Oxford University Press.

Jackson, John H. (1997), *The World Trade System*, Cambridge, Mass.: MIT.

Mann, Catherine (2000), *Is the US Trade Deficit Sustainable?*, Washington DC: Institute for International Economics.

Petersmann, E.-U. (1997), *The GATT/WTO Dispute Settlement System*, London: Kluwer Law International.

Schott, Jeffrey J. (ed.) (1998), *Launching New Global Trade Talks: An Action Agenda*, Washington, DC: Institute for International Economics.

Shoyer, Andrew W. (1998), 'The first three years of WTO dispute settlement: observations and suggestions', *Journal of International Economic Law*, **1**, 277–302.

Trebilcock, Michael J. and Robert Howse (1999), *The Regulation of International Trade*, Second Edition, London and New York: Routledge.

United States, Department of Commerce, *Survey of Current Business*, various issues.

Woolcock, Stephen (1998), 'The multilateral trading system into the new millennium', in Brian Hocking and Steven McGuire (eds), *Trade Politics*, London and New York: Routledge, Chapter 1.

WTO (1995), *The Results of the Uruguay Round of Multilateral Trade Negotiations: The Legal Texts*, Geneva: WTO.

L80 F13 F41
L90 F14
Q17 F23

7.   The EU in the WTO

Robin H. Pedler

In the international political economy the European Union (EU), as a large single market with a system of collective management, is comparable with the USA, with which it has strong cultural affinities and substantial structural interdependencies. The Union is enlarging, through the absorption of new members in its immediate environment, and these are attracted by its opportunities as an extensive area in which the transaction costs and risks of foreign trade have been virtually eliminated. In multilateral trade negotiations under the World Trade Organization (WTO) the Union has strong bargaining capabilities, and since the late 1990s these have become more significant because of the decline of the Japanese economy.

The Union has a common external commercial policy, shaped through interactions between member governments and between them and the European Commission. Most of these governments are coalitions (the UK is an exception) and in four of the largest member states – France, Germany, Italy and the UK – power is held by Socialist parties. Only in France, however, are there traditional 'left' policies that may fuel protectionism. In the other three countries the ruling parties define themselves as 'centre-left', committed to the 'third way'. UK Premier Tony Blair allies himself on important issues with the right-wing premier of the next largest country, Jose Maria Aznar of Spain. Their alliance was a driving force behind the Lisbon summit of March 2000 at which the 15 member governments committed themselves to promote growth and employment through deregulation in goods and labour markets. The EU has a recent history of weak growth and low job creation (see Tables 7.1 and 7.2).

Some member states are growing fast (Ireland, Sweden, Finland) and some are enjoying historically low unemployment (Netherlands, Ireland and the UK). The EU growth average is dragged down by the weak performance of two large countries – Germany and Italy. Perhaps the most remarkable conundrum in seeking to match the effects of Socialist policies and regulation with growth and employment is provided by Sweden. The minority government is Socialist and the country is highly taxed and regulated. Nevertheless the economy is growing strongly and has been ranked by the International

Table 7.1   Employment in the EU

Economic Growth	Unemployment	
Faster than Japan, slower than US	EU – finally reducing:	8.5%*
Small 'fringe' countries growing	Japan – growing:	4.7%*
fastest	US – record low:	4.1%*
	* *May 2000*	
Employment creation: annual jobs growth	EU Social policy	
EU	0.6%	Social security costs
Japan	1.0%	Excessive regulation?
US	2.2%	Working time directive extended
		Atypical work

Source: European Commission, May 2000

Table 7.2   EU growth league

Country	Forecast % increase in real GDP, 2000
Ireland	7.5
Finland	4.9
Netherlands	4.1
Greece	3.9
Spain	3.8
Germany	2.8
Italy	2.7
UK	3.3
Euroland average	**3.4**

Source: European Commission, April 2000

Data Corporation World Times Index as 'The world's leading information technology nation', the first to displace the USA from that position.

Green parties belong to governing coalitions in Germany, France and Belgium, and support the minority Social Democratic government in Sweden. The most notable Green politician is Joscka Fischer, the German foreign minister, who has a major role in trade policy. The Greens have 48 of the 626 seats in the European Parliament and are thus represented among the lead members who guide the passage of legislation; they are active on trade and environment issues and categorically reject Genetically Modified Organisms (GMOs).

EU INSTITUTIONS

On trade with the outside world the EU members have complementary and diverging interests which they endeavour to aggregate for the management of a common external commercial policy. The principal interactions are between member governments, in the Council of Ministers, responding to trade policy initiatives from the European Commission, which implements the Council's decisions. The third player in this central policy process is the European Parliament, whose members are directly elected from member countries to sit on the basis of political affinities rather than national identities. Increasing degrees of participation in the central policy process have been given to the Parliament under the 1986 Single European Act, the 1991 Treaty of Maastricht, and the 1998 Treaty of Amsterdam, and on trade issues it has considerable influence.

Under pressures to achieve results that will be functional and broadly representative, the Council's decision processes have shifted from a unanimity rule to a system of Qualified Majority Voting in which outcomes depend on the dynamics of coalition formation, influenced understandably by the differing degrees to which member countries are involved in trade with the rest of the world. On Atlantic trade issues, which are especially prominent, differences within the Council are noted by the USA, which threatens or applies countermeasures selectively. In EU–US disputes over banana trade Denmark and the Netherlands have been spared US sanctions because in June 1998 they opposed a Council decision that was unacceptable to the USA.

The European Court of Justice (ECJ) can have a role in the management of trade policy on the basis of a responsibility for determining whether the Council, the Commission, and the Parliament are acting legally under the founding and amended Treaties. It has a Court of the First Instance that hears cases brought by commercial interests, for instance in antidumping cases.

The activities of the Council tend to be dominated by France and Germany, working in an informal coalition that is occasionally under strain, notably because of French interest in maintaining a high level of agricultural protection for the Union, and in retaining voting power comparable with Germany's, despite that country's larger population.[1] Motivations for the Franco-German cooperation derived in the 1950s from shared security interests and from trade complementarities, which have since been altered by shifts in comparative advantages, as Germany has become more com-

petitive in manufactures while France has remained competitive in
agricultural products.

GLOBAL AND REGIONAL TRADING INTERESTS

Globally the Union is one of the two largest traders, exporting more than the
USA but importing less (see Table 7.3). In international investment it ranks
after the USA, but in recent years investment sourced in the EU has expanded
at a faster rate.

*Table 7.3   Leading importers and exporters in world merchandise trade
(excluding intra-EU trade), 1999*

Exporters	Value ($ billion)	Share (%)	Importers	Value ($ billion)	Share (%)
EU (15)	798.6	18.9	USA	1059.9	23.6
USA	695.0	16.4	EU (15)	851.2	18.9

Source: *WTO Focus*, March–April 2000[2]

WTO rules allow countries to make preferential or free trade agreements
only as steps on the road to a customs union, 'effectively' covering all areas
of trade (some EU agreements exclude or severely limit agriculture) and
when the agreement does not diminish access by other WTO members. The
EU has a series of agreements, some of which give rise to complaints from
other WTO members.

The oldest is the Lomé Convention, dating from 1971, which gives preferential access to the EU market for some 70 developing countries, mostly
former colonies of France, the UK, the Netherlands and Portugal, in Africa,
the Caribbean and the Pacific – known collectively as the ACP countries. The
convention is renegotiated every five years; it provides aid and market
stabilization measures which its members seek to preserve. The current agreement, signed in June 2000, pledges cooperation in international forums, in
services trade, competition policy, the protection of intellectual property,
standards and certification, sanitary and phyto-sanitary measures, trade and
the environment, trade and labour standards, and consumer protection.[3]

The ACP countries, however, are not considered eligible for a customs
union with the EU, and there are periodic complaints from other tropical
countries under the WTO disputes system. To cope with this problem the
current agreement places the EU's commitments in the context of its efforts

to improve its trade regime for all least-developed countries. This is additional to and is intended to reinforce a 'permanent waiver' by the other countries, recognizing the Lomé concessions as an exception.

Politically, Lomé indicates the extent to which several EU members are influenced by sympathy, perhaps also by linguistic and sporting ties, with their former colonies. The sympathy is reflected in popular opinion, the media, and the activities of non-government organizations (NGOs), which are far more likely to be moved by distress in a less developed former colony.

The EU also has formal agreements with Mercosur and Mexico. In the development of commercial ties with Latin America, however, the EU has been much less active than the USA, in part because of geographic factors but also because of intra-Union differences related to the expected gains from such involvement. The weaknesses of regional economic integration projects in Latin America have been further factors. In this vast region, moreover, the USA has had wide scope for initiatives to establish preferential trade arrangements that would extend the North America Free Trade Agreement (NAFTA) southwards.[4]

The orientations of the economic policies of the 15 EU members are primarily intraregional. In 1999 60.6 per cent of their exports and 59.4 per cent of their imports were within the single market. These proportions are expected to rise as the European Monetary Union becomes established, as cross-border mergers and acquisitions continue, and as the region's financial markets become more closely linked.[5] In the spread of gains from intraregional commerce the industrialized Northern members, notably Germany and France, benefit more than the less industrialized Southern members, and are more significant as areas of technological progress. The contrasts are related to differences in trade with the rest of the world: Germany is the most active exporter of manufactured products, and this trade helps to finance the development of the Union's most active centres of innovation.

In the Union's immediate environment, Iceland, Liechtenstein and Norway trade freely with the EU as members of the European Economic Area, established in 1993, and Switzerland has similar access under a series of bilateral treaties. In Central and Eastern Europe, Bulgaria, the Czech Republic, Estonia, Hungary, Latvia, Luthuania, Poland, Romania, Slovakia and Slovenia are prospective entrants of the Union, under agreements that are of keen interest to Union firms. These countries are growing faster than the present members, and offer markets for manufactures. As the EU reduces protection against their exports, however, there can be strains in the relationships. Antidumping actions have been taken against steel from the Czech Republic. When these countries join the EU, they will of course come within the Common Commercial Policy. Under Article XXIV–6 of the GATT agreement, the EU will then have to make compensating trade concessions to WTO members whose exports suffer from the change.

Association Agreements

There is another group of neighbouring countries, most of which are not expected to join the EU. They are indeed not eligible under the Treaties that establish the EU, as they are not 'European' (Cyprus and Malta are the exceptions). These are mainly around the Mediterranean. They have association agreements, giving preferential access to the EU for a range of their goods. The EU has declared its intention to establish a 'Mediterranean Free Trade Zone'.

COUNTRIES THAT HAVE ASSOCIATION AGREEMENTS WITH THE EU

Algeria, Cyprus,* Egypt, Israel, Lebanon, Malta,* Morocco, Tunisia

* These two countries have been accepted to open EU accession negotiations

---

The various republics of ex-Yugoslavia may be expected to secure accession agreements and in most cases to move towards membership (except Slovenia, already formally a candidate).

Customs Union

Turkey has recently signed a Customs Union with the EU. Turkey has also been accepted as an applicant for membership.

Partnership and Cooperation

The EU has 'Partnership and Cooperation' agreements with the Russian Federation, Belorussia and the Ukraine. It is the declared strategic intent that these should develop into free trade agreements.

THE EU TRADE POLICY PROCESS

Since the ratification of the Amsterdam Treaty in 1998, the EU has seen progress towards a Common Foreign and Security Policy, but achievement still seems distant. In fact, an important aspect of foreign policy, the Common Commercial Policy, has been pursued jointly and the Commission has negotiated in the GATT/WTO on behalf of the member states since the signing of the original Treaty of Rome in 1957, and in the past decade and a half this has become increasingly effective. It is founded on Articles 131 and 133 of the Treaty.[6]

ARTICLE 131

By establishing a customs union between themselves, Member States aim to contribute, in the common interest, to the harmonious development of world trade, the progressive abolition of restrictions on international trade and the lowering of customs barriers.

ARTICLE 133

1. The common commercial policy shall be based on uniform principles, particularly in regard to changes in tariff rates, the conclusion of tariff and trade agreements, the achievement of uniformity in measures of liberalization, export policy and measures to protect trade such as those to be taken in the event of dumping or subsidies.

2. The Commission shall submit proposals to the Council for implementing the common commercial policy.

3. Where agreements with one or more States or international organizations need to be negotiated, the Commission shall make recommendations to the Council, which shall authorize the Commission to open the necessary negotiations.

The Commission shall conduct these negotiations in consultation with a committee appointed by the Council to assist the Commission in this task and within the framework of such directives as the Council may issue to it.

4. In exercising the powers conferred upon it by this Article, the Council shall act by a qualified majority.

The Commission's negotiations on behalf of the member states are mandated by the General Affairs Council.[7] This council meets monthly and involves the foreign ministers of the 15 member states. When, however, it comes to discuss trade issues, they generally yield their seats to their colleagues, the national trade ministers.

The politics of the EU are of course very clear in the debates and votes of the General Affairs Council. Some member states are traditionally more protectionist than others. In analysing the political forces at work in the EU, it is quite usual to find a 'North/South split' in the positions of member states. This emerges on trade issues, when there is an informal, but not unshakable, free-trading alliance between 'Northern' member states – Germany, the Netherlands, UK, Ireland, Denmark, Sweden and Finland – while the 'Southern' alliance trends to be more protectionist – France, Spain, Italy, Greece and to a lesser extent Portugal. The problem about this split is that the system of Qualified Majority Voting effectively means that, in order to resolve disagreements around the Council table, one must muster a two-thirds majority. A great deal of persuasion and political compromise is therefore necessary. Senior civil servants from each trade ministry form the '133 Committee'. They develop the negotiating mandate to be approved by the Council and, once negotiations are under way, provide detailed follow-up. They meet weekly on a Friday.

The division of responsibilities and authority in the four stages of the development of trade policy are illustrated in Table 7.4 by Meunier and Nicolaidis.[8] The 133 Committee reports directly and frequently to the European Commission. The Commission negotiates on behalf of the member states, acting in its 'representative' role. It is also very conscious of its duty, as 'Guardian of the Treaty',[9] to preserve its sole right to negotiate under Article 133.

MINI CASE STUDY: GERMANY–US TELECOMMUNICATIONS AGREEMENT

In 1993, Germany concluded a bi-lateral agreement on telecommunications with the USA. This provoked a sharp letter from the Trade Commissioner, Sir Leon Brittan. Germany acknowledged the Commission's rights as negotiator and modified its position accordingly.

It is important for business to bear this in mind. Large companies that have good contacts with one member state government may be tempted to seek support in commercial cases 'via their usual channels'. This may be a correct approach, but only if the member state in question is seen as a member of the General Affairs Council. To get a decision, the foreign (or trade) minister will have to build a 'qualified majority' amongst his or her colleagues and take into account their politics and priorities. Any tendency to act bi-laterally will be reined in by the Commission, supported if necessary by the ECJ.

Table 7.4   Stages in development of EU trade policy

	Authorization (Flexibility of mandate)	Representation (Autonomy)	Ratification (Authority)	Enforcement
Exclusive Competence (i.e. in GATT under Article 133)	133 Committee Council Qualified Majority	Commission (On-going informal consultation)	Council – Qualified Majority (But informal veto by large member states)	Commission (Exclusively)
Mixed Competence (i.e. EC Association agreements – Articles 133 and 235)	133 Committee Council Unanimity + member states	As above	Council Unanimity + ratification by member state parliaments	Commission (With delegated ability and in consultation)

163

The Commission: Responsibility for Commercial and External Economic Policies

'The Commission' has its responsibilities under Article 133, but it is up to the President of the Commission to decide who should exercise them. Romano Prodi, who became President in mid-1999 and then allocated tasks amongst his 19 colleagues in a newly appointed Commission, assigned responsibility for trade to Pascal Lamy, a French Socialist. On agricultural trade matters, he was accompanied by Frans Fischler, the Austrian Christian Democrat.

'New Areas' and the Growth of Trade in Services

The Uruguay Round agreement extended the rules of multilateral trade, including the 'Most Favoured Nation' principle, to cover Agriculture, Trade Related Investment Measures (TRIMs), Trade in Intellectual Property (TRIPs) and Trade in Services.

The new areas are all-important, partly because of the progress that has been made in the reduction of traditional restrictions on trade in goods via tariffs and quotas. The extension is also important because of the growth of trade in services. World trade as a whole is growing at 8 per cent per annum, impressively faster than the average growth of GDP, and 2.5 times the most optimistic rate projected for the growth of EU economies. Within this, however, trade in services is growing twice as fast as trade in goods. This mirrors the economies of the most developed nations and means that debates and disputes about trade in services are likely to increase. The responsibility for this area within the EU is, however, somewhat unclear and is likely to evolve over time.

Trade in Services: Divided Responsibilities in the EU

The Commission's sole responsibility for negotiating trade in goods is clear and vigorously enforced. In the important and rapidly growing area of trade in services the position is less clear. Following the ratification of the Uruguay Round accord by the EU, the Commission sought an 'advisory opinion' from the ECJ on responsibility for the 'new areas'.[10] The Commission believed that the court would 'confirm' its sole responsibility to negotiate in these areas. It was, however, opposed by eight of the then 12 member states: Denmark, France, Germany, Greece, Netherlands, Portugal, Spain and the UK. The ECJ ruling was a compromise, dividing responsibility between the Commission and the member states (ECJ Opinion I/94, 15 November 1994: I – 123). Meunier and Nicolaidis attribute the member states' reluctance to accord new powers to the Commission to a combination of economic interests (protectionist desire to limit competitive access to some service sectors) and principle. They describe the state of mind that had been engendered as annoyance at the way in which the Commission had reached an agreement with the United States to remove the remaining obstacles concerning agricultural trade in the 'Blair House accord' in December 1992. Indeed, the member states, led by France, refused to endorse all the details of that accord. Their mood was summed up by the exchange between the French Premier, Alain Juppé and the then Trade Commissioner. 'You want to know whether we trust you, Mr. Brittan? Well, we do not trust you. Your role is to be the servant of the council.'[11]

Following the ECJ ruling, the question of responsibility for negotiation in the 'new areas' was again addressed at the Inter-Governmental Conference that led up to the Treaty of Amsterdam in 1997. At Amsterdam, it was agreed that the sole and shared responsibilities found by the ECJ in its 1994 opinion would continue, but that the member states might, by unanimity, allot further areas to the Commission to negotiate as they saw fit.

In practice, when services are being negotiated in the WTO context, the Commission and representatives of the member states are all present. By convention, however, only the Commission speaks on behalf of the EU.

Within the Commission, there is further a split responsibility for external aspects of transport policy. In a dispute over the negotiation of landing rights, one of the most 'tradable services', the Commission is represented, in its argument with some of the member states, by the Commissioner for Transport – Loyola de Palacio.

Market Opening

An example of offensive trade policy is the market opening measures applied against third countries by both the United States and, more recently but increasingly, the EU. Congress in the United States passed Act 301 and strengthened its application in 'Super 301'. These acts require the President to implement retaliatory measures against countries that are identified as restricting US trade, and which fail to reform rapidly when given notice. For the EU, in February 1996, the Commission published its own 'Market Access Strategy' (COM (96) 53). While less prescriptive and draconian than the American bill, it argues for the same methodology: identify where barriers are keeping EU traders out of promising markets and then use a range of market opening mechanisms. Market opening will usually begin as a bilateral negotiation. It is important that it should not stop there, or there is a risk that powerful countries, able to deploy the full range of trade instruments, may create a series of preferential relations for themselves, damaging the principle of 'Most Favoured Nation'. This has, indeed, been the criticism levelled by the EU against America's use (or threat) of 301 procedures against Japan. It alleged that these might lead to US imports being favoured at the expense of those from other countries.

THE EUROPEAN PARLIAMENT'S ROLE IN TRADE POLICY[12]

Most trade instruments are implemented under the 'Consultation Procedure', which means that Parliament must give an opinion, but has limited powers of amendment. Parliament has a significant role in policy formation and should not be ignored. For example, one may take two of the current 'high profile' trade disputes: hormone treated beef and bananas. The beef issue was first raised in the Parliament in the mid-1980s and Parliament effectively required the Commission and Council to ban hormone treated beef. It was able to achieve this by 'moral force', even though it had no formal, legal right to propose policy. On bananas, Parliament remains committed to the need to protect 'poor' Caribbean growers and will probably seek to curb any tendency on the part of the Commission or the Council to pursue more 'liberal' solutions.

Agreements with other countries that have 'institutional, budgetary or legislative implications' fall under Article 300 – the Assent Procedure, which is quite different. It means that Parliament may reject the agreement by an absolute majority. A recent case was the vigorous debate, lasting several months, which preceded parliamentary acceptance of the Customs Union with Turkey.

The European Parliament Committee responsible for trade matters is number 8 – External Economic Relations, Chairman, Carlos Westendorf, a Spanish Socialist.

INSTRUMENTS OF TRADE POLICY

Tariffs

These are by far the most common means of affecting the flow of goods between countries or areas. They are usually levied as a percentage of the landed price of the goods in the importing country, but may also take the form of a fixed amount or a levy on a weight or volume basis.

Quotas

These are quantitative restrictions such as 'so many automobiles per year'. They may or may not be combined with tariff variations, for example the EU

Banana trade regime, which allows the import of a given quantity at a reduced tariff, with the level of duty multiplied by about four in respect of
imports that exceed the limit.

Non-tariff Barriers

Apart from quotas, these may take the form of standards, labelling requirements or environmental compliance measures. Trade restrictions that are
claimed necessary to protect health and hygiene may also be non-tariff barriers, but are treated separately.

Antidumping and Safeguard Measures

The multilateral system does permit countries to restrict imports when their
industry is suffering damage, but only in certain circumstances and subject to
strict controls. Antidumping measures are supposed to prevent exporters from
attacking foreign markets with predatory pricing. They are founded on the
principle that one may not sell in a foreign market at a lower price than in the
domestic market. This sounds simple, but in real life can be extremely complex, for example because of variations in specification and notions of 'price'
including marketing costs. The EU is one of the main users of antidumping
measures within the WTO.

The report that the Commission delivered to the European Parliament on
11 July 2000 includes analysis of the antidumping cases opened, resolved
and terminated over a five-year period. The most striking conclusion that
emerges, as the Commission itself comments, is 'the large number of new
initiations in comparison with the previous year; in 1998, the Commission
initiated 29 new investigations while in 1999, new initiations reached 86'.

Safeguard Clauses

Safeguard clauses allow a country to impose restrictions similar to antidumping
if an industry is badly affected by imports, even though these are not 'dumped'.
They may, however, only be imposed for a limited period, to allow the
industry concerned to restructure.

Grey Areas

As the world trade system becomes increasingly effective, it is more and
more difficult for countries to impose restrictions that will not be successfully
challenged. Where domestic politics do force countries to impose restrictions, these are increasingly 'voluntary'. Examples of such 'voluntary' regimes

are the agreements concluded in the 1980s and 1990s between the Japanese motor manufacturers and the United States and the EU respectively to restrict their exports.

There is a striking difference between the ability of each of the two largest trading blocs to reach this relatively 'peaceful' solution of a major trade issue with Japan and their apparent readiness to go further and move into the dispute procedure on matters that bring the two of them into conflict. Terutomo Ozawa (author of Chapter 8) comments: 'There is something special about Japan and Japanese policy-making. I believe it is in line with Japanese-style diplomacy, which avoids confrontation and seeks compromise. Japanese society as a whole is not as litigious as the US or EU.' Specifically in the case of the EU–Japan VRA on automobiles, his findings are confirmed by the work of Tomofumi Watanabe.[13]

One worldwide 'voluntary' agreement, the Multi Fibre Agreement, has recently been incorporated into the system as the textiles code, a step, so liberal traders believe, towards getting rid of it.

Rules of Origin

As soon as there is a differential trade regime, preferential or restrictive, legally enforced or 'voluntary' questions of rules of origin arise. In the case of a modern car, whose components are delivered for final assembly from hundreds of sub-manufacturers, often in different countries, what determines its nationality? This issue nearly destroyed the agreement on Japanese cars, because of the fierce argument (now apparently resolved) about the products of 'transplant' factories.

Administrative Measures

Even more widespread than voluntary agreements, and far more difficult to identify and control, is the use of administrative measures. These may be brutally simple, such as leaving a container full of perishable merchandise in the direct heat of the sun during lengthy administrative checks, or more subtle, for example the French decision that all imports of VCRs would have to be cleared through the one small, inland customs post at Poitiers.

EU MANAGEMENT OF ATLANTIC RELATIONS

The basis of formal transatlantic relations is that all countries concerned are members of the WTO. They must therefore either apply 'Most Favoured Nation' or, if they seek closer relations with any other country, submit to the

MINI CASE STUDY: JAPAN–EU VEHICLE IMPORT AGREEMENT

Prior to 1992, all the member countries of the EU imposed quotas on the import of Japanese vehicles, ranging from the very restrictive, (Italy) to the fairly liberal (Portugal). With the abolition of internal frontiers, it would no longer be possible to enforce national quotas, so a new solution had to be found. This took the form of an agreement between the EU, represented by the Commission, and the Japanese Ministry of Trade and Industry, that Japanese manufacturers would limit themselves to a 12 per cent share of the EU market in 1991, rising to 16 per cent in 1999, after which it was assumed that quantitative restrictions would fall away. Such 'voluntary' agreements can work well. In this case, as the Secretary General of the European Motor Manufacturers' Association commented:

> The pact has no legal base; it is not a legal agreement, it is an understanding about the progressive full opening of the biggest automobile market in the world. The fact that it has no legal base is probably the best reason why it will be respected; it is in the interest of both parties to make it work.

Events seemed to justify M. Lepeu's confidence. When the EU car market was hit by recession in 1992/93, the Japanese agreed to a proportional decrease in their exports, to respect their agreed market share.

Arrangements in the motor sector have continued without apparent upset since the planned end of the VRA in 1999. It seems that there is now an informal agreement that visible exports will remain at the agreed market share, while European manufacturers will cease their efforts to limit the volume of vehicles produced for the market in 'transplant' factories in France, the Netherlands and the UK.

WTO rules on free trade areas or seek a waiver. Facing each other across the North Atlantic are the world's two largest economic players: the EU and the United States. Each of them is surrounding itself with preferential or free trade areas. Perhaps not surprisingly, the two large players are locked in a series of high profile and expensive trade disputes. If these are not resolved by clear respect for the WTO's dispute mechanism, it will put a severe strain on that system.

In 1998, there was a proposal from the then EU Trade Commissioner, Sir Leon Brittan, to expand and deepen relations by the creation of an 'Atlantic Free Trade Area'. He was unable, however, to secure a mandate from the General Affairs Council to negotiate his project. It was particularly opposed by France, which rallied the support of other member states, an indication of the political forces at work in setting trade policy. In 2000, there has been a proposal in the other direction, which, however, would apply only to one member state of the EU. United States Republican Senator Gramm suggested that the UK join NAFTA. He attracted little political support on either side of the Atlantic.

Both the large players are reaching across the Atlantic, wherever trade rules permit, to seek market openings for their businesses or advantages for third countries with which they have links. The USA has concluded 'open skies' agreements with Belgium, Germany, Luxembourg and the Netherlands to give increased access to its airlines. It is negotiating very hard for a similar agreement with the UK. The Commission has complained publicly and loudly at the Council's refusal to mandate it to negotiate air traffic rights across the Atlantic on behalf of the EU as a whole and has opened a case before the ECJ to challenge the agreements that four member states have concluded.

The EU, as noted, has favourable trade agreements with Mercosur (Argentina, Brazil, Paraguay and Uruguay) and with Mexico, even though Mexico is a member of NAFTA. Under the Lomé system described above, the EU has favourable trading arrangements by treaty with some 15 countries spread through the Caribbean and Central America. It is indeed the determination of the EU to preserve their favourable status in the banana market that has engendered that transatlantic dispute. Many EU countries also trade actively with Cuba and the EU mounted a strong campaign against 'Helms/Burton' that stayed the US President's hand in applying punitive elements of the bill. The French system that includes in its territory 'Départements d'Outremer' means that four islands on the west side of the Atlantic are legally in Europe: St Pierre, Miquelon, Martinique and Guadeloupe.

Competition Policy

This is not yet formally a part of the WTO system (though had the Millennium Round taken off, there was a proposal that it should be). It is an area of policy that affects business on each side of the Atlantic. Competition authority officials from each side consult regularly, seeking consistent application of their rules and may indeed assist each other in certain cases. The EU[14] and the United States have strong but different policies, but one detail of application on which they agree is that their 'domestic' policies affect 'foreign' companies that do substantial business in their jurisdiction. Thus the merger of Boeing with McDonnell Douglas was taken unilaterally by the Commission to be considered under its merger approval procedure. An open case that raises further interesting issues of varying merger policies is that of the proposed acquisition of a US telecoms company by Deutsche Telecom. Senator Hollings sought support in Congress to block this move on the grounds that Deutsche Telecom was owned 49 per cent by the German government. EU policy does not discriminate against state-owned companies, though it does require them to act in a competitive manner.

Summit Meetings

Regular EU–US summits are organized every six months. They are attended by the President of the US, the head of the government that holds the six-month rotating Presidency of the EU, the President of the European Commission and a series of senior officials, often including the trade negotiators from each side. While discussions at these meetings are not limited to trade issues, significant existing or potential disputes are addressed. A recent success at the summit of May 2000 was the so-called 'Safe Harbor Agreement' (spelt that way on both sides of the Atlantic).[15] This agreement defuses a dispute that was building up over the application of the EU directive restricting the transmission of personal data, seen by American companies as restrictive enough to be anti-competitive. Summits may also be valuable for their role in setting agendas and in forewarning of impending disputes. In May 2000, for example, there were wide-ranging discussions of contentious issues in the Defence and Aeronautical industries.

Business-to-Business Relations: TABD

Formal relations across the Atlantic have their parallel in organized business-to-business contacts, designed to remove practical barriers to trade. Collectively, these are known as the Trans-Atlantic Business Dialogue (TABD). The initiative was launched at a high level event in Seville in 1996, attended not only by heads of governments and senior trade negotiators, but also by the CEOs of many corporations from both sides of the Atlantic. TABD is organized into 27 Committees, each specialized in one area of trade. Committee Chairs rotate between European and US members. Key areas for improving and facilitating trade are:

- Mutual recognition agreements (MRA): this has already produced an agreement on auto spare parts and in 2000 has been broadened to include services (insurance, engineers, architects).
- Early warning (of problems that may arise): work is progressing on the precautionary principle, biotechnology, the animal testing ban for cosmetics, recreational marine and refrigerants.
- Regulatory cooperation: 'to reduce trade frictions and facilitate business'.

Unfortunately, TABD excludes deliberately and by design trade in agricultural commodities, which is exactly where many of the transatlantic trade disputes arise.

TABD has been rated a success over its first five years and the process has been followed in the development of transatlantic Environment, Consumer and Labour dialogues. In the autumn of 2000, however, MRA and regulatory cooperation appear threatened by the reluctance of United States regulatory agencies to accept the findings of their European counterparts. (The situation is complicated, since in many areas the responsible regulators are national rather than EU bodies.)

TRANSATLANTIC TRADE WARS

The EU and United States are both using the WTO dispute settlement procedure to challenge aspects of each other's trade policies. Thomas Brewer shows in Chapter 6 that in the five-year period 1995–99 the United States brought 28 dispute cases in which the EU was respondent, while the EU brought 16 in which the US was respondent. In most cases, findings have been accepted, but in three open cases, either the finding has not been accepted or amending measures have been judged inadequate and war has escalated to involve trade sanctions.

The Banana War

The seeds of the banana war were sown in 1945. During World War II, the population of Europe had been totally deprived of bananas by the U-boat blockade. Unfortunately, the traditional pre-war suppliers, plantations in Central America, were in the Dollar zone and European governments were desperately short of dollars. The UK and France therefore launched banana growing schemes in Sterling and Franc zone territories in the Caribbean and Africa. Growing bananas in these areas was clearly much more expensive than in Central America, since most of the Caribbean islands with suitable climates are effectively the crests of volcanoes. This did not matter when the world was divided into currency zones and GATT had yet to be established (1948).

The EU's banana position became more complicated with the accession of Mediterranean member states in the 1980s. Greece and Portugal grow some bananas, while Spain in its Canary Islands is a major producer. Thus the EU now had about 25 per cent of its consumption grown within the EU. Once again, however, costs of production were much higher than in Central America (see Table 7.5).

Table 7.5   Banana production efficiency

	Total production cost*
Latin America	0.200 ecu/kg
Caribbean**	0.460
Canary Islands	0.520
Martinique and Guadeloupe	0.550

Notes:
*   Includes cost of storage, transport and export taxes
** Dominica, Grenada, St Lucia, St Vincent and Jamaica

Source: Brent Borrell, Centre for International Economics 1992

The Caribbean and African sources and the EU's own banana growers are capable of producing about half of the bananas the EU consumes. At least half must therefore be imported from what are still known as the 'dollar' growing countries. Given the cost structures, however, if the EU and Caribbean growers are to continue to thrive, they have to be protected.

The Internal Market Drives Reform

Prior to 1992, the necessary protection for EU and ACP growers was afforded by national quota systems. These not only imposed border restrictions but also limited the circulation of bananas within the EU. The determination to create the Internal Market meant that those barriers had to disappear and be replaced by a common external system. The Dollar producers believed that the solution would be 'free trade' or at the worst a common external tariff that would permit them to benefit from their lower production costs to seize control of the market. In preparation, they 'loaded' bananas into those parts of the EU market that were accessible in 1990–92 to create a strong position. They were aided in this by the fall of the Berlin wall (1989). Once again the banana was the symbolic fruit of peace and freedom and those 17 million Germans who had been citizens were each consuming 30 kg annually (EU average 10.5 kg). The EU solution was to unify its internal market but to continue to apportion sourcing by tariff quotas under its Common Commercial Policy. This was enforced by a complicated system of licensing (see Table 7.6).

Table 7.6   The banana trade regime: Regulation (EEC) 404/93

	Tonnes '000
CAP banana regime	750
Imports	
ACP countries	
'Historic quantities' enter tariff free	858
Dollar bananas	
Favourable tariff quota (75 ecu/tonne)	2200
Total	3808

All regulated by a complicated A, B, C licensing system, to ensure that bananas from each source get into each national market.

In international trade terms, the EU faced conflicting treaty obligations. Its own policies, expressed in the Lomé Convention, meant it was bound to give preference to the ACP suppliers. On the other hand, it faced a series of challenges under GATT/WTO. Two GATT dispute panels, resulting from cases brought by Central American countries, found against the EU's restrictive regime, but under that system the EU was entitled to reject the findings and did so.

The establishment of the WTO changed the situation in two ways. Contracting parties undertook to accept panel findings under the dispute settlement mechanism and the trade system was extended to cover services.

The United States could not be a party to the complaints under GATT, as it does not export bananas to the EU. (The claim that it does nevertheless grow 6000 tonnes of bananas in Hawaii produced one of the few real laughs in a WTO dispute panel.) The main aggrieved parties, however, are the United States companies Chiquita and Dole and they certainly provide services, transporting the Dollar bananas to Europe in their ships.

The United States, jointly with Ecuador, the largest Central American producer, began a complaint procedure in the WTO in 1996. This went to finding and then to appeal, so that in September 1997 the EU regime was adjudged to be incompatible with WTO rules. The EU undertook to modify its practices and in June 1998 produced a new regime. This was not adjudged, however, to have gone far enough and first the United States and then Ecuador were given the right to impose trade sanctions. The United States has already done so, as Table 7.7 shows.

Table 7.7   Bananas – 1999/2000: the battle develops

April 1999	US receives WTO clearance for 'hit list' worth $191 m. (Had requested $520 m.)
November 1999	EU proposes 'two-tier tariff quota regime' as a 'transitional arrangement to tariff-only'.
April 2000	Ecuador receives WTO clearance for 'hit list' worth $201.5 m. May apply it to services.
May 2000	Congress directs 'carousel tariffs'.
October 2000	Council agrees to propose an eventual 'tariff only' system, with an interim period of six years to be administered on a 'first come first served' basis.

Nine Central American exporters reject the EU's plan of tariffication with licences to 'first come first served'. 'They will develop their proposal.'

If the EU and the United States, the two largest members of the WTO, cannot resolve this long-running dispute, it will put the dispute resolution procedure, indeed the whole system, under severe strain. Perhaps with this in mind, in October 2000 the EU Council adopted a new proposal that it hopes will defuse the issue. The eventual objective is a 'tariff only system'. It is expected, however, to take six years to reach this point. In the meantime, it proposes a 'first come first served' system. Initial reactions from the USA and from Central American producers have been negative.[16] Chiquita for its part continues to press the United States government to hold out for a settlement that will guarantee the company a substantial share of the market. Chiquita's president, Carl Lindner, is a vigorous lobbyist who has added political weight to his arguments by contributing an amount estimated by *Time* magazine at $5.5 million to political candidates, both Democratic and Republican.[17] For this reason, Chiquita seeks to insist on a 'reference period' of 1990–92, when it was achieving maximum volumes. 'Reference period' is increasingly the battleground in this dispute, just as in others 'rules of origin' becomes key. As the trade lawyer of one of Chiquita's competitors put it to the author: 'Basically no one wants free trade, because they fear a collapse of the price of bananas in the EU. Therefore they would like a quota system to continue. They just want a bigger share of the quota.'

Hormone Treated Beef

The origins of this trade dispute lie in Northern Italy in the early 1980s. Consumers there became convinced that male infants had been adversely affected by eating baby food containing excessive quantities of growth-promoting hormones. The issue was raised in the European Parliament by Italian members and taken up vigorously and generally, so the Parliament demanded that the Commission act to make a proposal to ban the use of such hormones. (The Commission may have been more willing to listen to their demands, in that the effective use of hormones is said to increase the efficiency of beef production by 15 per cent and the debate took place at a time when the Common Agricultural Policy had produced a 'beef mountain'.)

In any case the use of hormones within the EU was prohibited in 1985. EU producers then complained that they were facing unfair competition from imports, since the substances were permitted in other countries. The ban was therefore extended to imports in 1987 and has been the subject of transatlantic trade disputes ever since.

To a large extent, the dispute is a classic case of an attempt to apply extraterritoriality. The EU insists that foreign beef might be imported if it were accompanied by a certificate that the animal had never been subject to hormone treatment. This the United States refuses to supply, partly on the grounds that it has no system of keeping track of animals throughout their life. (The EU, for its part, sees Helms/Burton as an attempt by the United States to apply its extra-territoriality.)

The United States lodged a number of complaints under GATT and then in 1996 under the WTO. The WTO found, in April 1997, that the EU had failed to furnish a properly conducted risk assessment on which to base the import ban. The EU was given 15 months to prepare such an assessment and claimed to have done so. The assessment has so far satisfied neither the United States nor the disputes panel.

In July 1999, the United States was authorized to apply trade sanctions of $117 million and is doing so. The total sanctions to which the EU is subject from these two disputes is therefore $408 million from the US (already applied) and $202 million from Ecuador (threatened).

The United States feels that in this case it is on strong ground, if the rules of the Sanitary and Phytosantiary (SPS) agreement are applied, since its own Food and Drugs Administration finds no fault in the hormones, when properly used. There is an FAO code governing their use, to which the United States declares it conforms. European consumers, however, remain strongly opposed to the concept and they will almost certainly be supported by massive majority votes in the European Parliament, should there be a proposal that hormone treated beef be re-admitted.

In the Autumn of 2000, it appears that both sides are prepared to work on a practical settlement that will result in a doubling of the quantity of high-quality US beef that is admitted to the EU under a special quota system, while adjourning the arguments on principle. A spokesman of the US National Cattlemens' Beef Association is quoted as saying: 'There is a renewed realization that it isn't in our best long-term interests to continue to relatiate.'[18]

Foreign Sales Corporations

The EU brought a complaint in the WTO against the United States practice, dating from 1967, of permitting American companies with substantial export sales to reduce the tax payable on revenues from those sales by channelling them through a 'Foreign Sales Corporation', a subsidiary incorporated in an offshore 'haven'. The dispute panel agreed that this amounted to an export subsidy and was not compatible with WTO rules. The EU then applied to impose sanctions and has the right to impose $4 billion worth, effective 1 October 2000. Imposition was, however, delayed and during October the United States administration brokered a bi-partisan deal in Congress to amend the system.[19] While approval for the package was voted in the Senate, the House had not managed to do so ahead of the election dissolution, so the question remains open. It is said that, if passed, this would be the first occasion on which the United States has amended legislation to meet the requirements of the WTO. The EU, not satisfied, threatened to impose sanctions amounting to $3 billion, but only after hearing the WTO dispute panel's assessment of the new US law.

THE EU AND ASIA

In May 2000, Pascal Lamy, on behalf of the EU, concluded negotiations with China that satisfied the member states meeting in Council and hence enabled the EU to support China's accession to the WTO. The key issues that Lamy reported he had brought to a successful conclusion were: market access for insurance companies and for mobile-telephone manufacturers; phased reduction on tariffs for car imports; and reduction in the 'red tape' involved in setting up car manufacturing ventures – Commission press release, 22 May 2000.

The EU also intends to reach a favourable trade agreement with the countries that make up ASEAN, but this project is at an early stage.

THE INTERNAL MARKET AND THE COMMON AGRICULTURAL POLICY

The Internal Market programme of 1987–92 was the lasting achievement of Jacques Delors, then President of the European Commission. He was ably supported in the work by Lord Arthur Cockfield, then senior UK Commissioner. Their objective was to complete the work of the Treaty of Rome, creating a truly frontier-free Europe and ensuring the free movement of goods, services, persons and capital. They were successful in that nearly all the measures included in the programme were implemented and in many areas the four freedoms have been much enhanced. Some areas, however, were deemed too sensitive even to attempt to liberalize, and in others implementation and compliance are patchy. As they pursued their programme, doubts were expressed in the United States as to whether they were creating a 'fortress Europe', where internal free movement would be accompanied by increased protection at the borders. In general, this fear has not been realized in respect of manufactured goods. The average tariff imposed by the EU on manufactured imports in 1999 was 4.2 per cent and trending downwards – WTO Review of EU Trade Policy 12, 14 July 2000.[20] High barriers, however, remain for textiles and clothing and there are still some areas of disagreement on trade in services. The Common Agricultural Policy (CAP), while it does also ensure internal free movement, does indeed involve entrenched protection on the borders and leads to many trade disputes.

Free Movement of Goods

Physically, free movement of goods has been largely achieved. Trucks no longer have to stop at each frontier within the EU, so there is no reason why the journey from Birmingham, England to Milan should take any longer than a journey of similar distance in the USA.[21] (One of the justifications of the whole programme was that, before the Internal Market, it used to take nearly four times as long as the journey between Birmingham, Alabama and Chicago.)

Many other restrictions on the free movement of goods have also disappeared. National quotas in some areas, notably passenger cars, were converted into an interim European quota, to disappear in 2000, allowing free import of Japanese and Korean vehicles. Thanks partly to the Internal Market programme and partly to a series of ECJ decisions, restrictions based on composition, recipe or labelling requirements have also gone. In most areas, the Internal Market has harmonized standards.

There are some remaining exceptions: there is the issue of indirect taxation. The Single Market was supposed not only to ensure the free movement of goods, but also to reduce the amount and complexity of paperwork associated with that movement. Lord Cockfield's original proposals included the approximation of indirect taxes, to avoid distortions. The member states, however, were jealous of their taxing powers, so VAT was not harmonized. This has resulted in an 'interim' system of VAT accounting, which has considerably increased the administrative burden on businesses that sell across borders. This is a clear example of the political tensions that arise between institutions. The Commission may be expected to seek to extend its 'competence' (legal right to act) into new areas, but certain areas are vigorously protected by the member states as 'off-limits'. One such area is any move by the Commission that threatens their absolute control over tax levels in their own jurisdictions.

Free Movement of Services

A huge area of activity (11 per cent of EU gross product) opened up to cross-border competition by the Internal Market programme was public procurement. Any works contract worth over 5 million euros now has to be published in the *Official Journal* (*OJ*) and is open to bidding from anywhere in the EU. The limit for supplies contracts is reduced to 0.4 million euros. Some contractors, though, complain that the bidding procedures are so long and complex as to discourage them. Others, however, have found that, by studying the *OJ*, they can discover and successfully bid on contracts in their own country about which they would never have known. While contracting is, at least in theory, now open, defence procurement, another major area for contractors, has been up to now a strictly national concern. There are, however, proposals for member states to cooperate much more closely in areas of defence, particularly procurement. Given the enormous value of military hardware sold across borders and especially across the Atlantic, this is potentially a large trade issue.

There are other service areas in which the Internal Market has penetrated progressively. The significance for international trade and investment is that, not only does the EU market thus become more efficient and competitive, but also the privatization of state monopolies creates many opportunities for cross-border acquisitions. This part of the process has seen both American utility companies investing in Europe and privatized European utilities investing abroad, seeking growth and also some escape from the regulatory regimes that have accompanied privatization (see Table 7.8).

Telecoms
Liberalization of fixed line telephony was achieved in 1998 and resulted in rapid and substantial reductions in the cost of long distance calls. Most

Table 7.8   Large cross-border mergers in and by privatized utility companies, 1998–99

Target	Acquirer	Value ($000)
AirTouch (US)	Vodaphone (UK)	65 902
CWC Consumer (UK)	NTL (US)	12 984
Energy Group (UK)	Texas Utilities Co. (US)	10 947
Qwest (US)	KPN (NL)	8 300
TeleDenmark (Dk)	Ameritech (US)	3 160
Wessex Water (UK)	Enron Corp (US)	2 227
ComTel	NTL (Japan)	908
More Group (UK)	Clear Channel Communications (US)	776

Source: *Acquisitions Monthly* and *Financial Times* review

member states have also privatized their former monopolies, unleashing a wave of mergers and acquisitions.

Air travel
A 'Freedom of the Skies Directive' became effective in 1997. Results can be seen in the arrival of a number of low-cost operators (Virgin Express and others). The European Commission is using Competition Law to attack and limit subsidies to inefficient state airlines. Nevertheless, the cost of air travel around Europe remains higher than in America. Bi-lateral negotiations continue between the United States and individual member states to secure 'open skies' agreements. These are however perceived by many in Europe as being heavily weighted in favour of the United States, as they do not confer 'freedom of American skies' on airlines based in countries that subscribe to them.

Energy
Depending on the business, a reliable and economic supply of energy may be the most important input. Electricity supply was liberalized by a Directive in 1997 and gas supply in 1998. While monopolies continue to operate in some member states, notably France, there has once again been a rapid move to privatization and cross-border mergers.

Financial services
There are still some barriers to the free movement of financial services, especially in the areas of life insurance and pensions.

Cross-frontier broadcasting

The original Directive of 1989 was seen by its authors as part of the Internal Market programme, ensuring that TV and radio broadcasts could circulate freely. As adopted, however, it included quotas that seek to ensure substantial European content ('a majority'). This provision was strongly promoted and supported by France. It is seen as hostile by others, especially American providers of programme content. The Directive contains the provision that it should be reviewed every five years. The reviews provide the opportunity to challenge the content restrictions that have so far been retained and also for various interest groups to lobby for restrictions on the advertising that may be carried (for example advertising for tobacco and spirit drinks, now banned throughout Europe, and advertising directed at children, up to now permitted but likely to come under renewed attack).

Agriculture after the Uruguay Round – and the CAP

The most controversial new area brought under WTO rules in the Uruguay Round was agriculture. Most countries have special systems to improve the lot of their farmers, which may include subsidies, special prices and border protection. The Organization for Economic Cooperation and Development (OECD) reviews the agricultural protection effect of its members' policies annually. Its June 2000 review notes that, in general, protection is increasing, the level in 1999 being substantially higher than what now appears to have been a low point in 1997. The OECD ranks countries by the percentage of their farmers' incomes for which protective measures are responsible. 'Protective measures' are much broader than direct subsidies, since 'two-thirds of the aid is provided by market price support, the most trade distorting'.[22]

It is clear from Table 7.9 that the EU affords substantial support. It is well up the list, though far from the highest. This study also shows that the United States, while its aggregate is lower than the EU, also offers substantial support. Indeed Europeans were disagreeably surprised to note that, even after the passage of the FAIR act in 1996, which had apparently established American farming on a 'commercial' basis, very substantial subsidies were paid in 1998/99, both as domestic support measures and to subsidize exports. Under the Marrakesh Agreement that ended the Uruguay Round in 1995 negotiations on agricultural trade were to reopen in 2000. EU–US relations are for the moment on a relatively calm basis under a bi-lateral agreement to apply a 'peace clause'. This implies that they will not attack fundamental elements of each other's agricultural policies. It, however, expires in 2003.

EU pro-farmer measures are grouped together in the Common Agricultural Policy (CAP). This is not monolithic, but consists of a series of regimes (e.g. 'dairy products regime', 'sheep-meat regime') which offer farmers a guaran-

*Table 7.9   OECD member countries: agricultural support as a percentage
of farmers' income, 1999*

Japan		
Norway		
Switzerland		

In all the above countries, support accounts for more than 65% of income.

EU	49%	(1997 – 38%)
USA	24%	(1997 – 14%)
Australia	6%	
New Zealand	2%	

Source: OECD (2000)

teed price (intervention price), independent of world market conditions. Since there are few crops for which EU farmers have a differential advantage, intervention price tends to be above world market price. This implies that cheaper imports must be excluded, in order to sustain the price guaranteed to farmers, and that if the policy produces a surplus, exports will have to be subsidized (see Figure 7.1).

Prior to 1995, the CAP's external protection requirement was met by variable levies, to bridge the gap between prices outside and inside the EU. Under the Marrakesh accord all countries agreed to convert external protection into tariffs, which in turn were to be steadily reduced. The starting level of EU tariffs was generally high, though not as high as that of countries where imports had been effectively prohibited, as with rice in Japan.

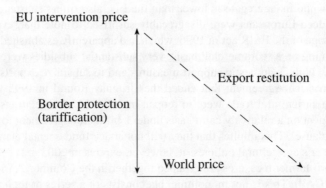

Figure 7.1   The need for border protection created under the CAP

Export subsidies proved a harder nut to crack. Under the GATT/WTO system all export subsidies are in principle prohibited but countries generally agreed that it would be unduly disruptive to apply this immediately to agriculture. Subsidies have been steadily reduced over a six-year period, in order to bring agriculture closer to the system, but they have far from disappeared.[23] These measures are important to business as well as to farmers, since the food industry is the largest in the EU and is a very significant exporter. Clearly, it is buying its raw materials at EU prices, whether they are locally grown or imported. When it exports it must have a subsidy (or restitution) to compete on world markets. This practice has, however, been challenged by other countries, notably the United States.

CAP reform

The CAP was substantially reformed at the Berlin summit of 1999. It was foreseen that intervention prices in the grain and beef regimes would be progressively reduced over six years, which will bring them closer to world prices and reduce tensions. The Commission has promoted a series of studies that may pave the way to a substantial 'mid-term' reform of the CAP in 2002–3 (see Table 7.10).

The EU has submitted a position paper and has stated that a comprehensive Round is not a pre-requisite for progress on agriculture. The EU's paper posits that 'the Round must recognise what agriculture means to the EU'. Four supporting documents therefore lay out the following issues in detail:

1. Quality, with particular relation to labelling requirements and regional appellations.
2. 'Blue box' – which seeks to validate the direct aids to farmers that are an essential part of the 'Agenda 2000' reforms.
3. Animal welfare – proposes that compensation measures arising from promotion of animal welfare should be accepted as in a 'green box'.
4. Export competition – the EU, while recognizing that it does subsidize exports, seeks to be proactive in comparing this practice directly with the practices of other contracting parties, for example Food Aid and State Trading. Commissioner Fischler went so far as to attend a meeting of the Cairns Group in October 2000 and lay out the position vigorously.

ENLARGEMENT

When the 14 countries now negotiating join the EU, they will add another 169 million inhabitants to the economic area (see Table 7.11).

Table 7.10   Reform of the Common Agricultural Policy as agreed in 'Agenda 2000'

Treaty base	CAP reforms to implement 'Agenda 2000'
Art 32–38	
Commission	• Phased cuts in support prices for cereals (15%) and beef (20%)
Commissioner: Hans Fischler (A)	• Milk quotas will continue until 2006, increased by 1.5%
	• Olive oil regime will be capped with an amount per producer state
Director General: José Manuel Silva Rodriguez (E)	• No reform to sugar or sheepmeat regimes
	• Farmers will be compensated for resultant loss of income by 'direct payments'. There will be some national discretion
Other DG's in the area: External trade, Food industry, Consumer protection, Food safety	Results will be: • EU budget cost is frozen • Probably an improvement for next WTO round

They will be joining a single internal market and applying its rules. This may have curious effects when the EU is required, under Article XXIV of the GATT, to grant compensation to third countries. Examples of such effects are the 'abatamento' that resulted from Spanish accession, giving US producers the right to export a million tonnes of corn to the EU tariff-free. There was a similar concession to US rice producers when Sweden joined, giving them a tariff-free concession of 10,000 tonnes. Since, however, they are effectively quotas, these concessions entail all the problems of quota allocation and quota rents. (Indeed, the US was unable to exercise its rights to the rice concession for two years because its producers were unable to agree with the administration a system of licence allocation.) Once the tariff-free goods are inside the EU they are not restricted to the market of the country that 'benefits' but may circulate freely.

CIVIL SOCIETY: NGO CAMPAIGNS IN THE EU

As the European Commission was preparing for what it hoped would be a new world trade round during 1999, it took great pains to consult 'civil

Table 7.11   EU-existing and accession states

	Population*	GDP index**	NATO member?
Existing 15 member states			
Germany	82	108	Y
France	59	99	Y
Italy	57	100	Y
UK	59	102	Y
Spain	39	82	Y
Netherlands	16	113	Y
Belgium	10	111	Y
Greece	11	67	Y
Portugal	10	76	Y
Sweden	9	102	N
Austria	8	112	N
Denmark	5	118	Y
Finland	5	100	N
Ireland	4	112	N
Luxembourg	0.4	184	Y
TOTAL	374	100	
Applicant countries			
Cyprus	1	79	N
Slovenia	2	68	N
Czech Rep.	10	60	1999
Malta	0.4	52***	N
Hungary	10	48	1999
Slovakia	5	46	N
Poland	39	39	1999
Turkey	62	32	Y
Estonia	2	36	N
Lithuania	4	30	N
Romania	23	29	N
Latvia	3	27	N
Bulgaria	8	23	N
Total	169	40	

Notes:

*   Population rounded to nearest million
**   1999 GDP/capita indexed at PPS – source Eurostat (Applicants 1998 GDP/capita indexed at PPS)
***   RHP estimate from Eurostat figures

society', mainly as represented by pressure groups and NGOs.[24] A number of issues on the agenda are there as a result.

A coalition of interested groups, organized by the UK-based Royal Society for the Prevention of Cruelty to Animals – RSPCA, acting in its role as 'the UK member organization of the Eurogroup for Animal Welfare'[25] set out to 'get animal welfare onto the WTO agenda'. They certainly succeeded in making it one of the issues the EU would like to find in an 'inclusive round'. This would cover both farming issues, such as battery hens and penned veal, and cruel trapping or hunting practices for fur or skins. The EU has already banned the import of the skins of baby seals and of animals caught in leg-hold traps, in both cases as a result of pressure exercised by the European Parliament, which was heavily lobbied by animal welfare groups. It is generally acknowledged that the most powerful lobby established in the Parliament is the Intergroup for Animal Welfare. It brings together members from all political parties with activists and meets regularly to develop policies and positions.

The EU's plans to press harder on animal welfare issues were set out in a formal Proposal on 27 July 2000.[26] (See also reference above under Agricultural Negotiations.)

A coalition including the World Wide Fund was active in promoting trade and the environment to be on the agenda of the next round. It is indeed on the EU wish list, but as an issue probably does not have the prominence its promoters were seeking.

Consumer Agenda

Consumers are formally represented in a number of the EU's consultative and policy setting committees by BEUC, universally known by the acronym of its French title – 'Bureau Européen des Consommateurs'. Consumer groups argue that they are not sufficiently considered in trade policy. They have an attentive ear in the Commission, which is reeling from a series of health scandals and certainly would want the power to continue to control trade. Consumer groups desire not to import or consume genetically modified organisms. This has already led to a revolt by some member states. Genetically modified maize (corn) and soya were approved for planting in the EU by the responsible expert committee[27] (1997), but Austria and Luxembourg, bowing to pressure from their own consumers, declared that they would not permit cultivation. Devolution of powers also threatens to produce a patchwork of approval within member states, with several German Länder and also Wales seeking to become 'GMO free regions'. Consumer groups also oppose the import of beef treated with growth-promoting hormones.

In both these cases, politicians and trade negotiators are torn between respect for the SPS agreement reached in the Uruguay Round, which they generally support, and the strongly expressed rejection of their voters, in the role of consumers. The United States is relying heavily on the SPS agreement and the fact that American consumers do not appear to have the same concerns to press its case.

Labour Standards

Although there were some representations from labour unions, the EU has decided not to pursue the question of labour standards through the WTO. Policymakers believe that the issue is best addressed through the International Labour Organization (ILO). As the interventions of Messrs Clinton and Gore in Seattle made clear, in this respect the EU position is very different from that of the USA.

THE NEXT WTO ROUND: EU OBJECTIVES

The EU remains committed to a full trade round and has proposed that it should be 'inclusive'. This means it would include the following issues (Lamy, 2000):[28]

- Market access, with a particular emphasis on agriculture, services and tariffs.
- New rules, on investment, competition and trade facilitation.
- Development, where the EU 'recognizes that the WTO has not helped all countries equally'. The EU's objective remains 'comprehensive free access to goods from least developed countries' but sees this as part of a generalized package and finds it 'disappointing that we could not agree together in Seattle'. The EU believes that one of the causes of failure in Seattle was that the WTO did not take adequate notice of the concerns of developing countries and that for a new round to succeed, these will have to be taken into account.
- Civil society: This means including the issues of 'the environment and the consumer agenda'. Pascal Lamy expressed his 'fear that public support for the trading system on both sides of the Atlantic is becoming frayed'. He continued to believe that an inclusive trade round, launched in 2000 'is the least bad way of achieving what has to be done'. He also saw it as providing the best opportunity for governments to respond to the concerns raised by citizen groups at Seattle.

CONCLUSIONS

The determination of trade policy is becoming increasingly political all over the world. This is certainly true in the EU. It is partly driven by the extent to which '...with the Uruguay Round the central domain of trade policy became domestic regulation and legal systems and the definition of domestic policy'.[29] 'Political' in this sense reflects first the need for member state governments and the European Parliament to reflect the will of consumers, especially when it is expressed through issue groups and NGOs. The weight of this opinion will certainly be felt in the attempts to resolve one existing major trade dispute – beef hormones – and one that threatens to erupt – the import of GMOs.

Politics also extends to the delicate balance between the national interests of the member states when they are assembled in the Council and the further balance between the Council and the EU's other institutions. In the last two Treaty revisions, Maastricht 1991 and Amsterdam 1998, Parliament has been accorded more powers. It is also noteworthy, however, that in areas to which the EU has extended shared sovereignty and that directly affect the lives of its citizens, Common Foreign and Defence Policy, and Justice and Home Affairs, the member states, in agreeing the reforms, have sought to exclude the other institutions from these areas by a complex system of 'pillars' and to manage them on an intergovernmental basis. Thus the Commission's determination to maintain, indeed extend, its control over the Common Commercial Policy is likely to lead to further inter-institutional tensions as trade policy affects citizens directly.

Decision-making in the EU is a long and complex process. The outcome of discussions on any given issue is difficult to predict because of the very different extent to which the three major institutions see themselves as 'European'. The Commission certainly sees itself as playing a leading role. This may mean that the policies it proposes are less than radical. They are tempered by the desire to be sure that they carry the member states with them. The Parliament also sets out to be 'European' – its members sit as Europe-wide political groups, not national delegations. On the other hand, they are all politicians, and to them, being 'European' may imply becoming more radical and amending the Commission's proposals to reflect better the strong feelings of their constituents. This is especially true on issues of the environment and of consumer protection. As the chapter shows, the Parliament's strong views in these two areas underlie the on-going dispute over hormone-enhanced beef and the looming one over the import of GMOs.

The Council, although it acts as a single body in co-decision, remains an assembly of 15 sovereign states, and ministers will naturally seek to advance their national interests. This makes decisions on trade issues difficult to achieve, even though they are subject to Qualified Majority Voting, because there tend to be polarized groups advocating liberal trade or protection. This can create 'blocking minorities'. (A proposal needs a two-thirds majority of votes in the Council to be passed.)

The EU sees itself as having a long and honourable history as a leader in the development of a liberal trade regime. It intends to continue this role. In considering the development of international trade policy, the EU may be seen as a practical example of advantages of moving to a full customs union (and of some of the problems this may entail). It can also serve as a yardstick by which to measure how far current agreements on international trade remain from the achievement of a true customs union.

NOTES

1. On French trade interests see Messerlin (1996).
2. *WTO Focus Newsletter*, January–February 2000, Geneva WTO.
3. Commission press release, 21 June 2000.
4. See Wrobel (1998).
5. On the effects of EMU see Mundell (1999).
6. Nicoll and Salmon (2001, pp. 193–214).
7. Westlake (1994).
8. Meunier and Nicolaidis (1999).
9. Edwards and Spence (1994).
10. Meunier and Nicolaidis (1999).
11. Meunier and Nicolaidis (1999, p. 483).
12. Jacob and Shackelton (1992).
13. See references to the EU–Japan automobile agreement by David Allen and Michael Smith (2000, p. 119).
14. Robin Pedler on competition policy (Pedler, 1996).
15. Stuart Eisenstat, article in *Financial Times*, 8 September 2000.
16. Robin Pedler (1994).
17. 'How to become a Top Banana', *Time*, 7 February 2000.
18. *Financial Times*, 2 October 2000.
19. Eisenstat, article in *Financial Times*, 8 September 2000.
20. wto.org/Englishtratop e/tpr e/tpl37 e.htm.
21. Cecchini (1988).
22. OCED (2000).
23. O'Connor (1999).
24. Pedler (1999).
25. RSPCA (1999).
26. Europa.eu.int/Commission/Services/Trade/Whats new, 27 July.
27. Bradley (1998).
28. Lamy (2000), Speech to US Council for International Business. Full text Europe.eu.int/ Commission/Services/Trade.
29. Ostry (2000).

REFERENCES

Allen, David and Michael Smith (2000), 'Annual review of the European Union, 1999/2000', *Journal of Common Market Studies*, **38**, September.

Bradley, Kieran (1998), 'The GMO committee on transgenic maize', in M.P. Van Schendelen (ed.) *EU Committees as Influential Policymakers*, Aldershot: Ashgate.

Cecchini, Paulo (1988), *The European Challenge 1992: the Benefits of a Single Market*, Aldershot: Wildwood House.

Edwards, Geoffrey and David Spence (1994), *The European Commission*, London: Cartermill.

Jacob, Francis and Michael Shackelton (1992), *The European Parliament*, London: Cartermill.

Lamy, Pascal (2000), Speech to US Council for International Business, New York City: 8 June.

Messerlin, Patrick A. (1996), 'France and trade policy: is the "French exception" passée?', *International Affairs*, **72**(2), April, 293–309.

Meunier, Sophie and Kalypso Nicolaidis (1999), 'Who speaks for Europe – the delegation of trade authority in the EU', *Journal of Common Market Studies*, **37**(3), September, 477–501.

Mundell, Robert A. (1999), 'The international impact of the Euro and its implications for transition countries', in Mario I. Bleger and Marko Skreb (eds) *Central Banking, Monetary Policies, and the Implications for Transition Economies*, Dordrecht: Kluwer, chapter 15.

Nicoll, William and Trevor C. Salmon (2001), *Understanding the European Union*, London: Longman.

OECD (2000), *Agricultural Policies in OECD Countries: Monitoring and Evaluation*, June, OCED.

Ostry, Sylvia (2000), 'The making sense of it all: a post-mortem on the meaning of Seattle', in Roger B. Porter and Paul Sauve (eds) *Seattle, the WTO and the Future of the Multilateral Trading System*, Kennedy School of Government, Harvard University.

Pedler, Robin (1994), 'The fruit companies and the banana trade regime', in Robin Pedler (ed.) *Lobbying the EU*, London: Cartermill.

Pedler, Robin (1996), *Business Guide to Lobbying in the EU*, London: Cartermill.

Pedler, Robin (1999), 'Public affairs in the EU – the growing role of NGOs', *International Journal of Communications Management*, March.

RSPCA (1999), *WTO Food for Thought*, London: Royal Society for the Prevention of Cruelty to Animals.

Westlake, Martin (1994), *The Council of the European Union*, London: Cartermill.

Wrobel, Paulo S. (1998), 'A free trade area of the Americas in 2005?', *International Affairs*, **74**(3), July, 547–62.

8. Japan in the WTO

Terutomo Ozawa

1 INTRODUCTION

Japan is at a critical crossroads in managing its economic affairs, both at home and abroad (*vis-à-vis* other countries). It has long been criticized for being insular, while at the same time taking advantage of the liberal global system of trade and investment, a system that was set up under the Pax Americana and that has come to be codified initially in the forum of the General Agreement on Tariffs and Trade (GATT) and more recently of its successor, the World Trade Organization (WTO). The criticism of Japan as a 'free rider' is muted at the moment (as of this writing), despite the growing – unprecedentedly huge – trade deficit of the United States, for which Japan is in no small part 'responsible'. This is because the US trade deficit and its accompanying capital inflows so far have actually assisted America's unprecedented economic prosperity to continue without inflationary pressure.

Japan is also often criticized for its inactivity in taking up any leadership for free trade and investment as an advanced country, and particularly as a triad power, within the multilateral framework of the WTO. Compared to the United States and EU, Japan has been a relatively 'reluctant' participant in voicing its own views as to how the world architecture of trade and investment should be redesigned, rebuilt, and managed. It has long been a compromiser and last-minute accommodator to US leadership in global capitalism. After all, the WTO, along with the International Monetary Fund (IMF) and the World Bank, is a forum of free market capitalism that the US as its hegemonic power has brought into existence to 'create the world in its own image'.

In fact, the number of trade disputes between Japan and the United States filed to the WTO as complaints is comparatively small, that is, significantly much smaller than those between the EU and the United States (see Chapter 6 in this volume). True, Japan recently has challenged the US at the WTO to clarify the ambiguous nature of the US antidumping law, which was 'arbitrarily' applied to steel imports from Japan, Brazil, and Russia for internal political reasons. Japan is also adamant in protecting its agriculture by stressing the 'multi-functionality' (for example, the environmental and cultural dimensions) of this primary sector. But, overall, cross-Pacific relations between the US and Japan are far less contentious and far less vociferous than their cross-Atlantic counterparts, who are troubled by trade wars over bananas, beef, and export subsidies (see Chapters 1 and 5 in this volume). Cross-Pacific trade issues are more often than not managed on a *bilateral* and *non-litigious* ('out-of-panel' settlement) basis outside the WTO's formal dispute solution mechanism.

Indeed, over the past few decades, the United States has been most insistently and continually pressuring Japan to remove protectionist and regulatory barriers to trade and inward foreign investment. There are good reasons for US bilateralism, as will be discussed below. The pressure exerted by the United States to modify Japan's trade and FDI-hosting behaviour has come to be known as *gaiatsu* [foreign pressure] in Japan, and policymakers themselves actually have come to use this pressure often as an 'excuse' to prise open some long-sheltered (hence, interest-group-vested) markets.

Presently, nevertheless, two significant developments in Japan's policy of trade and investment are in the making. First, internally, Japan is in the midst of institutional change, largely *on its own*, rather than being forced by *gaiatsu*; it is changing to become a more open, more strongly market-driven economy, albeit slowly and not as quickly as demanded by the United States. There are many encouraging signs of dramatic socioeconomic transformation as exemplified by sudden penetration of foreign multinationals into the core of Japanese industry, such as banking, insurance, retailing, and automobiles, the phenomenon unimaginable only a few years ago. The *keiretsu* groups, long considered barriers to entry, are steadily dissolving, and cross-shareholding is crumbling. Japan's Big Bang deregulation is integrating its financial sector more deeply with the rest of the world. At the company level, lifetime employment and seniority-based promotion and wages are now a thing of the past. Instead, merit-based compensation is becoming more widely adopted. In other words, Japan's erstwhile corporatist capitalism is in decline, and some key features of America's free market capitalism are increasingly being adopted. Second, Japan's external commercial (trade and financial) policy is more *regionally* and more *bilaterally* focused with its efforts to establish free trade and investment arrangements. For example, Japan's recent agreement with Singapore to sign a free trade pact signals this newly emerging trend. Japan also has been active in a new regional group, the 'ASEAN+3' (ASEAN plus China, Japan, and South Korea). This new regionalism is a desideratum, now that Japan's industrial production system straddles practically the whole region.

The leitmotiv of this chapter is that there are currently more powerful market forces at work than either Japan's WTO membership obligation or America's bilateral pressure itself, that are forcing the world's second largest economy to adopt more free market approaches in its national economic structure and management – namely to become 'more like the United States'.[1] After all, the WTO is in a crisis – and may even cease to function, as it is confronted with non-trade and investment political issues with which it is not equipped to grapple (see Chapters 1 and 2 in this volume). During the GATT days the organization had largely accomplished its original mission to re-move trade barriers in manufactures (except textiles). The marginal benefit of trade liberalization is becoming increasingly smaller, whereas its marginal political cost is growing larger in the form of social needs to deal with the side effects of trade and investment expansion. This is especially the case, now that the once-effective 'specificity rule'[2] has no longer been adhered to because of America's (Clinton and Gore's) political expediencies in tying labour standards, environmental regulations, and human rights with trade and investment issues. These expediencies were largely responsible for the mis-management of the 1999 start of the New Millennium round of trade talks in Seattle, which ended in a fiasco.

In short, notwithstanding the WTO crisis, there have been three major forces which are driving Japan's trade and investment regime to shift further towards American-style free market capitalism than ever before. These forces are: (i) an internal mandate for reform that has arisen from the successful consummation of catch-up growth and a decade-long stagnation, (ii) the imperatives of the Information Technology (IT) revolution and the New Economy (which promises a new round of Japan's catch-up growth), and (iii) the post-crisis move towards deregulation, market liberalization, and open regionalism in Asia and the rapid emergence of China as a superpower. These forces, though listed separately, are closely interwoven and reinforce each other in compelling Japan to renovate its economic institutions closer to the US model, especially in services.

2 INTERNAL MANDATE FOR REFORM

As is well known, Japan built a successful regime of catch-up growth in the post-World-War-II period. It came to be popularly known as the ''55-nen *keizai taisei* [1995 economic system]' (Hashimoto, 1996) in which a set of institutions conducive to rapid catch-up growth was brought into existence at the hands of economic planners and policymakers. Noguchi (1999) even calls it the '1940' system because of the policy legacies of national mobilization pursuant to the Pacific War in the form of 'centralism and production superi-ority'. Suzuki (2000) directly characterizes it as the 'catch-up-style Japanese system' or an '*ex ante* interventionist-style discretionary administration', a system, in his view, that 'had ended its role by the mid-1970s'. He urges a structural reform which leads to an '*ex post* check-style rules-oriented administration'.

It is thus widely recognized that Japan's catch-up regime had many unique characteristics. For starters, to achieve a rapid catch-up growth, the two national goals of 'production at all costs' and 'export drive to earn foreign exchange' were prioritized at the sacrifice of consumption and public services, such as housing (until only recently, the Japanese had been ridiculed for 'living in rabbit hutches'). In return for such sacrifice, however, a 'shared growth (SG)' approach (World Bank, 1993) was adopted as an implicit *social contract* to assure rapid growth, high employment, and a better future.[3] In other words, what I call the 'principle of inclusiveness' came to operate to minimize the pains of managed rapid growth under the following unique set of institutional arrangements:

- SG-1: the formation of *keiretsu* as an effective institution to reduce 'coordination failures' and capture externalities of industrial development, an institution which provided an economic environment where even absolutely 'weak' (initially) and/or small/medium firms can participate in *keiretsu*-organized activities on the basis of comparative advantages. This meso-industrial organization contributed to employment creation and transactional stability because of its inclusive nature of grouping.
- SG-2: state-sponsored bank-loan capitalism (instead of stock-market capitalism which Japanese policymakers thought would lead to an unacceptable income inequality) in which the so-called 'main banks' played the key role of corporate governance in financing, monitoring, and guiding (with managerial skills) highly leveraged, indebted non-bank enterprises.
- SG-3: life-time employment (guaranteed job security) at the large, if not small, companies, most of which were affiliated, either directly or indirectly, with the *keiretsu* groups.
- SG-4: the creation and retention of a 'private welfare' sector which was sheltered from international competition either under trade restrictions or because of strong domestic market orientation, a sector which eventually became *inner-focused (IF), sheltered, overstaffed* industries: banking, finance, construction, distribution, food and beverages, telecommunications, transportation, health care, and the like. This sheltered sector has been the political base of the Liberal Democratic Party, Japan's long-lasting polity regime.

Since all these features have already been explored in the existing literature (but only individually and separately in most cases), my purpose here is to conceptualize them as a holistic (interlinked) system of shared growth and consider its path-dependent consequences, as schematically illustrated in Figure 8.1.

Early on in the postwar period, *keiretsu* formation resulted in dynamic oligopolistic rivalries, especially under 'infant-industry' protection from import competition. The *keiretsu* groups were able to reduce 'coordination failures' in industrial investment projects (Matsuyama, 1997) and to internalize growth externalities (SG-1). All the necessary investment capital was strategically provided by their main banks (big city banks), which in turn secured needed liquidity from the Bank of Japan (which itself was then closely controlled as a developmental policy institution by the Ministry of Finance), while capital markets remained the secondary source of finance and their growth itself was intentionally stunted (SG-2) (Wallich and Wallich, 1976; Suzuki, 1987; Aoki and Patrick, 1994; Ide, 1998). This whole financial system can be characterized as 'bank-loan capitalism', which was specific to Japan's postwar catch-up strategy (Ozawa, 2000a).

In rebuilding and modernizing the war-torn heavy and chemical industries in particular, the *keiretsu* groups vied with each other in pursuing a so-called 'one set' principle (Miyazaki, 1980) by developing and controlling the overlapping sets of industries among themselves (for example, each group developed steel mills, petrochemical complexes, shipyards, and automobiles, and so on). This strategy worked when high growth continued during the golden age of capitalism of 1950–1974 (Marglin and Schor, 1990). The Japanese companies, especially large ones, were able to absorb an expanding body of labour force, especially new annual crops of university graduates as future managers, and guarantee job security under the life-time employment practice. Company unions, the bi-annual bonuses based on individual companies' performance, and a relatively small gap in compensation between management and the rank-and-file (egalitarianism) all contributed to cooperative industrial relations and high morale – hence high devotion and productivity – among employees (SG-3).

Those workers who did not enjoy the privilege of employment at big companies remained mostly in Japan's small business sector, especially in small-scale manufacturing and services, a sector that was either heavily protected and regulated under import restrictions or local-marketed-catering (that is, non-tradables) (SG-4). As illustrated in Figure 8.2, the existence of such an employment-retaining sector (inclusive of protected agriculture and fisheries) has eventually resulted in a new industrial dualism, an economic structure consisting of super-efficient outward-focused (OF) export-competitive industries (best represented by automobiles and electronics) and inefficient (low-productivity) inner-focused (IF) industries (such as telecommunications, transportation, agriculture, fisheries, food and beverages, distribution, con-

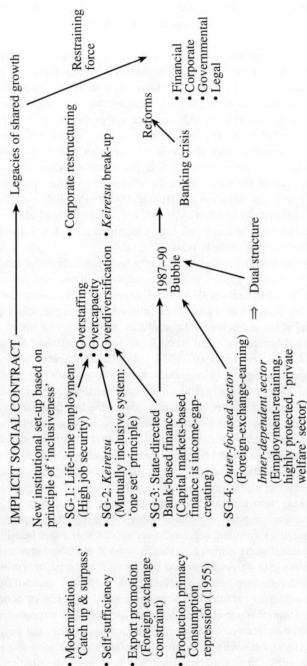

Figure 8.1   Path dependence in Japan's economic growth: internal mandate for reform

196

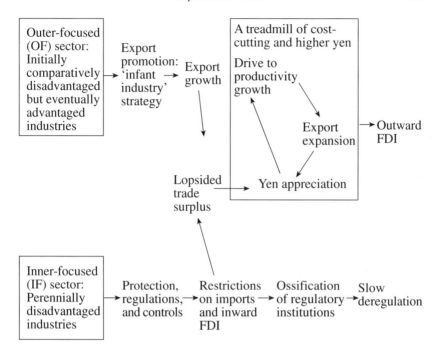

Source: based on Ozawa (1997).

Figure 8.2   Distorted structural dualism

struction, banking and insurance, medical/health care, legal services, and consumer services such as auto repair) (Ozawa, 1997).

Since imports and inward foreign investments were hindered in the IF sector, the OF sector was trapped in an inescapable treadmill of cost-cutting → trade surplus → yen appreciation → cost-cutting → trade surplus → further yen appreciation. Thus, the yen kept appreciating, becoming ever more overvalued in terms of purchasing power (that is, real exchange rate appreciation). The overvalued yen then compelled Japan's export industries to go overseas, swelling a rising outflow of foreign direct investment, while it discouraged foreign multinationals from setting up shop in Japan. The upshot was twin imbalances: a rising trade surplus combined with a lopsided balance in foreign direct investment. Japan's shopping spree involving the Rockefeller centre in New York City, the Pebble Beach Golf Club in California, Four Seasons' hotel chain, and other trophy acquisitions in the United States and elsewhere was once reported in the mass media as the act of 'ugly Japanese', creating public relations headaches for Japan.

Furthermore, this industrial dualism, combined with bank-loan capitalism, was an important contributory factor to the 1987–90 bubble, which, when it burst, finally culminated in a decade of banking malaise and economic stagnation during the 1990s. Yet these IF industries, notably agriculture, construction, and distribution, have been, and are still, the political strongholds ('cash cows') of Japan's ruling Liberal Democratic Party. And vested interests are opposed to institutional reforms. Hence, economic rationality is usually overruled by political expediency. Japan's unique catch-up regime organized through these special institutional setups has eventually become a barrier to commerce both at home and across borders.[4] This political dimension of the IF sector is critical in understanding the slow pace of reform efforts in Japan.

What were the consequences of these four features of shared capitalism in Japan? They ultimately caused *overstaffing, overcapacity, overdiversification*, and *overborrowing (excessive debt)* as soon as the Japanese economy slowed and stagnated, especially after the bubble burst. In fact, the *keiretsu* groups' efforts to have their own set of industries under the so-called 'one-set' principle and the main bank system caused a retention of comparatively advantaged industrial sectors, thereby hindering an international division of labour, as the Japanese economy matured. In other words, Japan itself as a whole became a 'one-set' economy with many inefficient (comparatively disadvantaged) industries which need to be discarded.[5] In addition, the government itself is now a burden (a key part of the problem) because of the 'excesses' of government involvement which cannot easily be rectified. The bureaucrats are quick and good at regulating but slow and procrastinating at deregulating because of their self-preservation instincts and vested interests.

In sum, the so-called '1955 economic system', which Japan instituted in the early postwar period, proved quite effective in enabling itself to catch up with – and even surpass in some areas – the advanced West. But it has clearly outgrown its usefulness. The system reveals glaring inadequacies in coping with the problems Japan currently faces as an advanced economy. A new economic system is badly needed. In fact, Japan has been struggling, over more than a decade, to scrap the old and build a new one. But the more effective Japan's catch-up system proved to be, the more strongly entrenched the interest groups (stakeholders) and the more difficult it was politically to dismantle the system. At the same time, however, Japan is not quite sure what new system to build. Nevertheless, there is a consensus that the 1955 system has to be dismantled. Indeed, it is particularly the IF sector, notably telecommunications, distribution, and banking and insurance, that is now being deregulated and made increasingly open to foreign ownership. In the meantime, inveigled by the relentless forces of global capitalism, especially with the imperatives of the New Economy, Japan is adopting some more features of American-style capitalism, if not wholeheartedly then willy-nilly as a matter of survival. (It is equally interesting to note that Germany, too, is reforming its institutions to become more like the US because of similar internal mandates, as discussed in Chapter 7 in this volume.)

3   THE IT REVOLUTION AND THE IMPERATIVES OF THE NEW ECONOMY

The global economy is currently in the grip of the IT revolution, a techno-logical and organizational revolution that has been unleashed, and that so far has most successfully taken root, in the United States over the last three decades, but especially during the 1990s. IT is the driving force of a New Economy. The most decisive force that is compelling the Japanese economy to become more akin to American-style capitalism is no doubt the impera-tives of an IT-driven New Economy.

Because the emergence of a New Economy was due to drastic deregulations and free market plays in the United States, its spread to Japan has already had a significant impact on Japan's old regime, especially in the areas of telecom-munications, distribution, and finance (that is, the former IF industries). It took the United States about 20 years to establish a New Economy by way of a series of deregulations (initiated during the Carter administration in the late 1970s and further pursued by the Reagan and Bush administrations, espe-cially dealing with *financial deregulations* in connection with the Savings and Loan crisis), *free trade policies* (such as the North American Free Trade Agreement (NAFTA) designed and negotiated by Bush but finalized by Clinton), a long period of painful *corporate restructuring*, its resultant *flexible labour* market, and a string of rapid *technological advances* in computers and telecommunications, all topped off by the invention and wide use of the Internet. Moreover, *capital markets* (venture capital, equities, IPOs, and M&As) have been an indispensable financial ingredient of the present US economic boom. All these events have rolled into one, generating 'a virtuous circle of stock market gains leading to increased wealth, consumption, invest-ment, productivity, and economic growth, leading in turn to additional gains in the stock market. This linkage of capital markets and the real economy has accelerated economic growth and wealth creation' (Mullins, 2000).

Thus, the IT revolution is not really a technological revolution *per se* but an *institutional* revolution involving both the real and financial sectors of the economy. The way it has come about in the United States ahead of any other country, it is the outcome of less government control and regulation, a more flexible labour market, and dynamic free capital markets, all combined in synergistic (some even describe 'speculative' or 'irrationally exuberant') interactions. In other words, a New Economy was created under this specific set of institutions so far unique to the United States.

3.1   A New Stage in the 'Flying-Geese' Sequence of Growth

In what way is the IT revolution impacting Japan's industrial structure and competitiveness? In this regard, the so-called 'flying-geese' (FG) model of economic development (originated in Akamatsu, 1935, 1962; expanded in Kojima, 1958, 1995; Kojima and Ozawa, 1984, 1985; Ozawa, 1992) is useful in analysing the distinctive characteristics of the New Economy brought about by the IT revolution. Here, most relevant is the stages paradigm of industrial upgrading and growth (Ozawa, 1993, 2000b, as reformulated from the FG model). It has so far envisaged the following four tiers of manufacturing in an evolutionary hierarchy of industries: climbing up from the bottom tier, (i) labour-driven industrialization (led by the 'Heckscher–Ohlin' industries such as textiles, toys, and sundries); (ii) resource-intensive, scale-driven heavy and chemical industrialization (involving the 'non-differentiated Smithian' industries such as steel and basic chemicals); (iii) component-intensive, assembly-based manufacturing ('differentiated Smithian' industries such as automobiles and electric/electronic goods); and (iv) R&D-driven, high-tech manufacturing ('Schumpeterian' industries such as new materials, mechatronics, and biotechnology).

These stages actually represent the path of industrialization the advanced Western economies have trodden over the past two centuries. Ever since the Industrial Revolution in England, industrialization in the rest of the world whenever successful has been essentially a derived phenomenon, in the sense that a follower or learner economy can emulate and learn from the already advanced (leader or teacher) economies. Continental Europe industrialized by following Britain through commercial contacts and conscious efforts for learning and emulation (Landes, 1969). Initially, so did the United States; 'America started off as a copier' and 'stole British technology' (Thurow, 1985), though America soon certainly introduced numerous innovations of its own, particularly in the area of mass production and marketing. So did Russia in its early modernization efforts (Gerschenkron, 1962). And likewise, Japan's economic miracle in both the pre- and post-World-War-II periods was based on this mechanism of learning and emulation under the hegemony of Pax Britannica early on and under that of Pax Americana more recently.

Japan has successfully climbed the ladder of industries by upgrading its production structure stage by stage, as illustrated in Figure 8.3. After World War II, it quickly modernized and revitalized its prewar industries ('Heckscher–Ohlin' and 'non-differentiated Smithian') as export-competitive spearheads (textiles, toys, steel, ships, synthetics) and then advanced to the stage of assembly-intensive, higher value-added industries (cars, machine tools, TV sets, VCRs, and other electronics) by innovating a new manufacturing system called 'the Toyota production system' or 'lean production' (Womack *et al.*, 1990; Ohno, 1978). More R&D-based, innovation-driven ('Schumpeterian') industrial development was the next stage Japan successfully entered, a stage of growth led by such R&D-driven industries as new materials, biotechnology, optoelectronics, and robotics.

What then comes after the Schumpeterian industry as the leading sector? Where should we place the information industry? The Internet economy or the New Economy does not fit into any of these past four phases, since it has emerged only recently. Hence, a new stage needs to be added to the previous sequence of growth. Here, what may be called the 'McLuhan' (after Marshall McLuhan) stage is conceptualized to represent the new Internet industry. This IT-driven New Economy is thus a brand-new stage for Japan to conquer (Ozawa, 2000b).

The 'McLuhan' information sector is a new, huge media complex composed of telecommunications companies (such as AT&T, British Telecom, and Northern Telecom) as upstream operators, and portal providers (such as Yahoo and America Online) as midstream operators, and e-commerce (dot-com) companies (Amazon.com, Ebay, Priceline, and hundreds of other online firms) as downstream operators. What they produce are 'information goods' – or interchangeably, 'abstract goods' or 'conceptual goods'. So far as the midstream and downstream operators are concerned, they are not as R&D-intensive as the 'Schumpeterian' industries which produce new 'physical goods' such as new materials, new drugs, and more advanced microchips. The 'McLuhan' industries do not require huge investments/expenditures in developing new services; nor do they need *formal* research laboratories equipped with a variety of physical research equipment unlike the traditional Schumpeterian industries. It is said that corporate R&D activities were becoming institutionalized in large corporations, so much so that Schumpeter (1942) himself predicted that entrepreneurship would be replaced by institutionalized R&D operations and that innovations would then be possible even under socialism. What is needed for the Internet is basically *imagination and ideas* – plus ample computer knowledge possessed by talented individuals. It should be noted, however, that the initial hardware of IT took the form of microchips and computers in the crevices of 'differentiated Smithian' assembly-based industries and 'Schumpeterian' innovation-driven industries. IT artefacts (that is, IT-supporting industries) themselves are still highly R&D intensive and are the indispensable auxiliary part of the 'McLuhan' economy.

Most interestingly, e-commerce will have its greatest impact on Japan's erstwhile most protected IF sector (notably, finance, distribution, *keiretsu*-controlled procurement, health care, transportation, education, and other

Figure 8.3

Old Economy ──────────────▶ New Economy

Stages of growth (a 'leading sector' model)

'Heckscher–Ohlin' stage: Labour-intensive, industries (e.g., textiles, apparel, sundries)	'Non-differentiated Smithian' stage: Scale-based, resource-intensive goods (e.g., steel, chemicals/synthetics, heavy machinery, ships)	'Differentiated Smithian' stage: Scope/scale economies-based, assembly-intensive goods (e.g., cars, TV sets, electronics)	'Schumpeterian' stage: R&D-based goods (e.g., new drugs, biotechnology, new materials, opto-electronics)	'McLuhan' stage: Information-dispersing, transaction-facilitating, 'virtuous space/market' - creating/providing industries (the Internet service providers, online commerce, B2B)

Market structure

Small & medium-sized businesses	Large businesses & *keiretsu* groups	Pyramidal (vertically integrated/linked) assembly-supplier chains	Large & medium size businesses	Small startups and spinoffs

Government role

Export promotion; 'H-O factor price magnification' effect; flexible labour; trading companies to assist small manufacturers	Import-substituting production ('infant industry' protection); physical infrastructure building (roads, high-ways, port facilities)	'Import protection as export promotion' (autos); Home-based exports	Government's science & tech policies	State leadership, deregulation, business restucturing, venture capital, M&As, stock option, IPO, entrepreneurship

IT Impact on the Old Economy/services [distribution, transportation, entertainment, health care, education, government]
- B2B e-commerce/exchanges (less inventory, procurement cost reduction)
- 'Build-to-order' (Dell Computer: B2C marketplace)
- Increased competition
- 'Extra brain-power': 'capacity to store, analyse and communicate information instantly, anywhere, at negligible cost' (*Economist*, 23–29 Sept., 2000).

Source: based and expanded on Ozawa (1993, 2000b).

Figure 8.3 The IT revolution (New Economy) and stages of growth

202

domestic market-focused services). Indeed, the more archaic, distorted, and inefficient an industry is, the greater the potential gains from the IT revolution – hence the faster the productivity growth.

Japan often boasts that Japanese subscribers (expected to reach the 20 million level by the end of 2000) to the mobile-Internet services delivered over the i-mode of cell phones outnumber any other country in the world. This domestic advantage puts Japan far ahead of the rest of the world in the present race to commercialize this fast-growing technology into third-generation (3G) cellular service, which is expected to 'bring Internet access at speeds seven times as fast as those of mainstream modems used in personal computers'.[6]

Surprisingly, however, it is not widely known that the United States forced Japan to deregulate the cellular phone market in 1994. Up until then, Japanese citizens were not even permitted to own cellular phones and their local companies were afraid of losing business to American rivals like Motorola, which had introduced cellular phones much earlier. Thanks to the *gaiatsu* exerted by the United States for deregulation, however, Japan opened up the market and leapfrogged to the front of the global race, catching up with, and soon even overtaking Europe, the early pace-setter in mobile phone services.

More importantly, America's New Economy shows that it thrives on robust capital markets. As aptly put by Michael Mandel (2000), 'If the IT revolution is an engine of the New Economy, its fuel is capital markets.' The lucky loops (cumulative causation) of entrepreneurial innovation → IPO → stock market boom → consumption spending → economic growth → entrepreneurial innovation is the core driving mechanism of American-style prosperity under the New Economy.

Many times in its recent history, Japan has benefited from being a latecomer. As seen in the FG paradigm of growth, Japan has successfully climbed up the ladder of industrialization, learning from, and emulating, the advanced West. In this regard, again, the US as the current leader of the New Economy is providing another unique opportunity for Japan to play catch-up. It is even possible to be able to surpass the US in the not so distant future, if Japan can mobilize itself once again as it has done so effectively in the past. Sensing this godsend opportunity, in September 2000, Japan's newly formed 20-member IT Strategy Council, chaired by the Sony Corp. president, and composed of other notable leading companies such as Softbank, Toyota Motor Corp. and IBM (Japan), announced an ambitious goal to surpass the United States in the Internet economy in five years. To achieve this goal, the Council urges the government to dismantle institutional obstacles (notably business-hampering regulations) to the growth of a New Economy.

In this respect, industry is ahead of the government. In fact, NTT (a formerly state enterprise called Nippon Telephone and Telegraph), the now partially privatized telecommunications giant, has recently even petitioned the government to step up the pace of relaxing regulations on foreign owner-ship (currently the maximum of 20 per cent), the government's one-third stake requirement, and the issue of new shares which requires governmental approval. These remaining restrictions are hampering NTT's expansion in overseas markets. In 2000, for example, when NTT acquired Verio, a US web-hosting company, the former's government ownership, even if partial, posed a political problem, although the US government approved the deal in expectation of further – eventual 100 per cent – privatization of NTT. Be-sides, instead of raising funds in the equity market NTT had to finance such acquisition through bank borrowings despite its huge existing debt. A New Economy thus calls for removal of regulatory barriers to the development of a high-speed mobile commerce (m-commerce) system in Japan.

Indeed, the Japanese, who are frustrated by a lost decade of growth, see a promise of revitalizing their economy in deregulations, and the government is criticized for its slow pace of implementation. Political backlash has been sharply registered in the unprecedentedly low approval rate of Prime Minister Yoshiro Mori, who was deeply unpopular among the public. It was against this backdrop that Prime Minister Mori barely survived a no-confidence vote in November 2000, when challenged within his own Liberal Democratic Party by a more reform-minded faction led by Koichi Kato but saved only by the latter's 'honourable retreat' at the end.

But will Japan wholeheartedly embrace the American model of a New Economy? How far will Japan really be able to reform its rigidified Old Economy system of institutions? Here, it is worth recapitulating the Ameri-can model of an IT-driven growth, that is, America's upward-spiral model of IT revolution → IPOs/M&As → stock market boom → wealth creation → economic growth → more Internet-based innovations → stock market boom. But it has resulted in skill shortages, ever-rising trade deficits, debt overhang, a rising income gap – and already a decline in high-tech stocks. It is even predicted that another banking crisis is in the offing because of a sharp rise in problem loans, the recent turmoil in the capital markets which made investment banking businesses riskier and money-losing, and the banks' huge lending exposure to the over-leveraged telecommunications sector.[7] The growth of a New Economy in the US has been robust, but it is thus built on eventually untenable factors, which may prove to be unravel-ling causes of US prosperity.

In the meantime, so long as the US economy is headed for a soft landing in the current business cycle, the current momentum of deregulation and re-structuring continues to nudge Japan further towards a more market-driven economy; Japan's huge hoard of $13 trillion in liquid private assets, its still high savings rate (27.8 per cent in 1999), and its robust current-account surplus ($107 billion in 1999) can easily support the growth of a New Economy without creating American-style bottlenecks, even if it emulates the US model.

However, the biggest obstacles to Japan's efforts to create a conducive environment for a successful New Economy lie in the still debilitated financial sector, the corporate sector burdened with excessive capacity and overstaffing, and the political system stuck in a rut of no leadership. Banks are still mired in bad loans, companies have only recently begun to discard money-losing businesses, and the ruling party's policies are still focused on the IF sector of the Old Economy.

The issue of corporate restructuring is closely tied to egalitarianism and the long-held implicit social contract for employment and job security. The Japanese public is, on the whole, still unwilling to see any mass layoffs of once-loyal company employees just for the sake of shareholder value. The present ruling party's power base is still in the rural areas and small businesses – that is, the long-sheltered IF sector. Japan's New Economy actually needs a new political leadership that can convert the IF sector, especially telecommunications, finance, and distribution, into a viable Internet-driven sector. Corporate Japan is groping for, and clearly in search of, a new business model compatible with both the imperatives of a New Economy and Japan's socio-cultural traditions.

Be that as it may, more than anything else, at the moment, the advent of the IT revolution is definitely serving as the most decisive force to remake Japan as a more open and more individualistic society. If this new information technology strategy focused on institutional reforms works, Japan's economic system will be much closer to American-style capitalism. Another great catch-up may have just begun. Ironically, not despite of, but rather *because of* the existence of the hitherto highly protected, inefficient, and yet-fully-to-be deregulated IF sector, Japan has an enormous potential to grow at a respectable rate. One study made by McKinsey, a US consulting firm, suggests that Japan could reach annual growth of 4.7 per cent (as against a paltry 0.6 per cent a year over the 1990–1999 period) and that it could eventually grow its way out of its ever-rising national debt (currently 130 per cent of GDP).[8]

4 POST-CRISIS LIBERALIZATION AND THE CHINA FACTOR IN ASIA

The recent financial crises have resulted in an accelerating pace of reform and restructuring in crisis-stricken countries (South Korea, Thailand, Indonesia, Malaysia, and the Philippines), not only because of the conditionalities of the IMF bailout programmes but also more importantly because of the internal imperatives of structural reform similar to those examined above in connection with the Japanese experience. These once stricken countries are now increasingly open to foreign multinationals' operations and takeovers, as seen in the recent rise in the incidence of cross-border mergers and acquisitions (Zhan and Ozawa, 2001; UNCTAD, 2000). But also, those countries that experienced no externally caused financial problems (Hong Kong, Singapore, Taiwan, and China) likewise learned important lessons from their brethren's plights and began to deregulate and marketize their economies, if gingerly. Throughout Asia, furthermore, there is at present not as much backlash, particularly from labour, against globalization as in North America and Europe. Non-governmental organizations (NGOs) are less organized and active. Asia as a whole is more pragmatic in dealing with the thrust of globalization and is willing to take advantage of it as a facilitator of further economic growth and transformation.

The Newly Industrializing Economies (NIEs) in particular are liberalizing their economic regimes in conjunction with promoting e-commerce and are eager to overtake Japan in this race. Hence, Japan can no longer afford to sit still or continue to procrastinate in eliminating any persistent remnants of the old *dirigiste* regime. Thus, new intra-Asian competition is now underway in creating a market-driven infrastructure to support a New Economy by way of deregulating and adapting to the imperatives of the IT revolution. Indeed, there are some rising fears that Japan is falling behind the online rush in the NIEs. Hong Kong and Singapore have sharply reduced telecommunications costs through drastic deregulation of the market. Both enjoy the advantages of their advanced information infrastructure and English skills. Hong Kong has built 'Cyberport', an IT business centre. Singapore has begun to wire up buildings in the country with high-speed Internet networks and aims to cover one quarter of them by 2005. Taiwan's cable television networks, with an 80 per cent coverage of the island's households, are capitalized on to offer cheap and fast online connection. South Korean households, over 60 per cent of which have a personal computer, are active online traders, accounting for nearly 70 per cent of all securities transactions. Furthermore, overseas Chinese business communities throughout East Asia, along with their mainland counterparts in China, are building up an Asian-wide cyber-network underpinned by a common language and culture. The Chinese entrepreneurs are comfortable with aggressive American business models, since many of them are US-educated and Silicon-Valley-trained.[9] Given these rapidly emerging Net economies in its neighbours, Japan could be left in the dust unless it also quickly adapts to the imperatives of the New Economy. As the *Nippon Keizai Shimbun* (Japan's equivalent of *Financial Times* or *Wall Street Journal*) editorializes, 'While still holding technological advantages in fields such as wireless access, the country needs to try harder to find a key role for itself in building Internet business models for Asia.'[10]

Another source of motivation for Japan to move closer to American-style capitalism – especially as an ally of the West in general and of the United States in particular within the WTO – is the China factor. 'The Genie is out' aptly describes the feelings of the Japanese toward emerging China. There have been many frictions, if not open and unmanageable so far, between Japan and China. For example, China is the largest recipient of Japan's foreign aid. Japan was offended when China listed the Beijing Capital International Airport on the Hong Kong stock exchange without telling Japan, which provided a ¥30 billion ($275 million) soft loan to this public facility. China's reply was that there was no need to thank Japan, since the loan was a form of repentance for Japan's war-time invasion of China. Japan was also annoyed by Chinese naval activity near Japanese territorial waters.[11] Hence, some even consider halcyon the Cold War period, a period during which China was 'contained'. From now on, Japan's political and economic relationships with China are expected to be quite delicate, and many thorny issues are bound to occur in the future.

In this regard, Japan needs a multilateral forum, such as the WTO or APEC, to solve bilateral problems with China. In this regard, Japan can no longer afford to confine itself to a self-centred regime of its own. In fact, it has recently become diplomatically involved, if not overtly but rather discreetly, with the marketization/democratization of its huge neighbour. For example, when Japan hosted the G7 plus Russia Economic Summit on the island of Okinawa in June 2000, it reportedly had manoeuvred, but failed, to invite China as an observer. Japan thus is walking a tightrope trying to help marketize and democratize China but at the same time remains highly apprehensive of China as a future rival – and as Asia's political hegemon.

Japan has also begun groping for Asian leadership by gingerly asserting a diplomatic status commensurate with its economic power in international governance organizations. At the annual meetings of the IMF and the World Bank in Washington DC in April 2000, for example, Japan tried to get a bigger voice for itself and other Asian nations in the fund's operations. In fact, by putting up a Japanese candidate Japan attempted to secure the IMF managing directorship, which has always been a European. It is well known that Japan has long been looking for a permanent seat on the UN security council. Reportedly Japan even jostled to seek the position of director general of UNESCO (United Nations Educational, Scientific, and Cultural Organization) by 'promising to put $1 billion into [it] and dangled financial aid before countries on the executive council'.[12]

Yet for the obvious reasons of self-interest and its limited geopolitical capacity, Japan's diplomacy is more sharply focused on the economic affairs in Asia by taking an initiative for what Fred Bergsten (2000) calls 'the new Asian regionalism' or 'the new regional arrangements being fashioned in East

Asia by Japan, China, South Korea and the ten members of the Association of South-East Asian Nations (ASEAN)'. The 'ASEAN+3' have announced a region-wide system of currency swaps, an Asian Monetary Fund (AMF), designed to deal with a future Asian financial crisis. This is the very system proposed earlier by Japan but then condemned by the West as a renegade plan against the IMF system. In addition, Japan is keen to expand the role of the Asian Development Bank in financing regional growth by increasing capital for the bank. But the US saw no need for capital hike and criticized to the effect that the bank's organization was characterized by a 'hodgepodge' and that it should use existing funds more efficiently.[13]

On the trade front, the Asian Free Trade Area was planned by the Philippines, but so far has failed to rally support. Instead of promoting such an intra-regional free trade agreement, Japan and some other Asian countries are increasingly involved in bilateral agreements. As noted, a free trade pact with Singapore was to be signed by December 2001. This will be a first for Japan and a second for Singapore, which has a bilateral trade agreement with New Zealand. Singapore has already announced an impending free trade agreement with the United States. Japan is particularly interested in establishing free trade with Mexico, now that the latter's *maquiladoras* have to pay tariffs (from 2 to 25 per cent) on imported components from countries other than the USA and Canada. Mexican and Japanese government-affiliated research institutions have agreed that such a pact would have merit. The matter has assumed more significance because Korea has signed an investment guarantee treaty with Mexico and is discussing free trade with Mexico and also Chile and New Zealand.

5   US BILATERALISM

As pointed out in the introduction, the US has long been putting pressure on Japan for trade and investment liberalization on a bilateral basis, while Japan had long emphasized multilateralism within the framework of the WTO – perhaps for the very reason of averting America's unilateral demands. There is one good reason why the US has stressed bilateralism, and why Japan has long been accommodating pressure from the US. During the Cold War period, the United States allowed – and even encouraged – Japan to pursue *dirigiste* development policy to reconstruct and expand its economy. In other words, Japan's *illiberal* way of conducting economic affairs discussed earlier was tolerated, and some of its distinctive institutional arrangements such as the *keiretsu* formation, the main bank system, and company unions were actually promoted by the occupying allied forces (that is, the United States) as instruments of quick economic recovery and reconstruction in the wake of

China's communist revolution and the suddenly emerged threat of communism in Japan's industrial trade unionism. (In February 1947, when Japan's communist-controlled trade unions called for a massive general strike with an intent to overthrow the Japanese government, General MacArthur, the Supreme Commander for the Allied Powers or SCAP, crushed such a move by sending out tanks to the streets, and communist labour leaders were purged under the so-called 'red purge'.[14]) The US did treat Japan as a special case, since it sacrificed economic interests in order to build up Japan as a strong bastion against communism. And this 'special' relationship is the very source of justification for the US actively managing economic relations with Japan on a bilateral basis.

Indeed, in the early postwar period the US adopted unilateral free trade without reciprocity, and such a US policy was even strongly supported by labour unions. In the early 1960s George Meany, then president of the AFL-CIO, declared that it was in the interests of the United States to freely import small Volkswagens from Germany and toys from Japan so that the Germans and Japanese could in turn purchase American goods. The American Federation of Labor and Congress of Industrial Organizations (AFL-CIO) even officially stated that 'without free trade...at least half of the American people would be doomed to a life of poverty. The nation would be consumed by crime, civil disorder, race riots, violence, forcing an end to all civil and industrial liberties' (as cited in Donahue, 1992: 23). Thus, in those days, the doctrine of comparative advantage and free trade was espoused and put into practice with the strong support and endorsement of labour unions. The logic of US trade policy in the early postwar years was that an increase in imports was more likely to help than to hurt the US balance of trade, since the rest of the world was so hungry for US goods and any foreign exchange they earned would be spent promptly (Evans, 1967).

But at the end of the Cold War (or perhaps ever since President Nixon's visit to China in 1972 and the subsequent start of China's open-door policy), US trade policy switched from unilateral free trade policy to reciprocity (the 'level playing field' principle). Japan began to be constantly pressured to open up its markets.

For example, the United States initiated a series of bilateral trade negotiations with Japan, starting with the Market-Oriented Sector-Selective (MOSS) talks (1985–86 during the Reagan administration) and proceeding to the Structural Impediments Initiative (SII) talks (1989–90 during the Bush administration) and the Framework (or Bilateral Comprehensive Economic) talks (from 1993 onward under the Clinton administration) (Mikanagi, 1996; Choppa, 1997). Interestingly, these major rounds of talks were organized, under different nomenclatures, with the change of guard at the White House, and were accompanied by significant modifications in the objectives of US trade policy. The MOSS round signalled a shift of US focus from restraining Japanese imports in the US to opening up *specific* Japanese markets for American exports (Mikanagi, 1996). In contrast, the SII talks involved *economy-wide* issues, such as macroeconomic policy (centred on savings and investment relationships which influence the external balance), the distribution system, Japan's land policy, and *keiretsu*. Then, the Framework talks reverted to, and refocused on, the sector-specific approach by aiming at tangible results as 'indicators' of market opening.[15]

Under these US pressures, however unwillingly, nevertheless, Japan started dismantling import barriers step by step, first only in those manufacturing industries in which it had developed competitiveness, while delaying liberalization of, and assisting through various means, those industrial sectors in which Japan's competitiveness was still weak. Since the financial sector, especially the banking industry, played such a critically strategic role as the financier of industrialization, it was among the very last sectors which began to be liberalized only in the recent past. The so-called 'Big Bang' financial liberalization programme, analogous to Britain's experience, was initiated as recently as April 1998 with a gradual spread of deregulations over the subsequent three years. In this respect, Japan has been following a stepwise sequence of liberalization – first in manufacturing, second in non-financial services, and finally in financial services, more or less all at its *own* pace. There are, however, still many remaining institutional and regulatory barriers confronting not only foreign multinationals but also domestic enterprises.

There is a rising backlash in Japan and elsewhere in Asia against the persistent US pressure for liberalization. Actually there have been two strands of backlash: the first occurred when the Japanese economy was riding high while the US economy was stagnating in the 1980s, and the second in the wake of the 1997–1998 Asian financial crisis. The first type took the form of a hubristic argument that it is the United States, and not Japan, which should be adjusting economic institutions to improve trade balances: 'many of Japan's trading partners' problems could be solved only if they would learn from rather than lecture Japan' (Saxonhouse, 1983: 270). On the back of what the World Bank (1993) admiringly called 'the East Asian miracle', Asian values suddenly began to be asserted as superior to Western (especially Anglo-Saxon) values in the 1980s.

Then, the recent Asian financial crises came as humiliations to Asian values, and the second type of backlash ensued. This is best described by Fred Bergsten (2000: 24),

Whatever the right and wrongs of its opinions, East Asia has decided that it does not want to be in thrall to Washington or the West when trouble hits in future. It is not rejecting the multilateral institutions, let alone opting out of the international capital markets or the globalisation of trade – which it knows would weaken rather than strengthen its prospects. It seems to want to work with, and within the framework of, existing bodies.

But East Asia also clearly feels that multilateral institutions, on which it was previously willing to rely, are no longer infallible. It notes that its aggregate economy and external trade are about as large as those of the United States and the EU, and that its monetary reserves are much larger [East Asia's official reserves amount to $668 billion, compared with $380 billion for the EU and $71 billion for the US]. Hence it wants its own institutions, and a central say in its own fate. As East Asia regains its strength, it is determined never to be totally dependent again.

In short, Japan, along with other Asian countries, thus pushes for bilateralism or at best plurilateralism within the framework of Asian regionalism to supplement its erstwhile reliance on WTO multilateralism. There are apparently concerns about this sudden rise of intra-Asian regionalism on the part of the United States. But Laura Tyson (2000), a former chair of the Council of Economic Advisors for the Clinton administration, put a positive spin on the situation by saying that 'regional trade deals under discussion in Asia could be a catalyst for a new round of global trade talks'.

6 SUMMARY

There are three major systemic forces at work compelling the Japanese economy to remake itself as a more market-driven one in the image of American-style capitalism. One such force is internally generated, while the other two emanate externally. The path-dependent mandate for reform (internally generated pressure) has so far been frequently impeded by anti-reform political expediencies but was still forceful enough to move Japan, if gradually, towards marketization. The conventional pressure from WTO commitment to free trade and investment (external pressure) has been rather weak. As a member of the WTO at the formal policy level, Japan is a minimalist in liberalizing its economic regime. On the other hand, another external force stemming from the post-crisis move towards deregulation and market liberalization in the rest of Asia is a stronger incentive for Japan to follow suit lest it be left behind in this age of globalization. The costs of doing business in Japan have grown unbearably high, so much so as to make itself an unfavourable location for economic activities relative to other Asian economies.

The recent opening up of China and its imminent emergence as a superpower, political as well as economic, also pushes Japan towards a closer alliance with the United States and other Western powers – hence there is an unavoidable necessity for Japan to become more like the United States. But more than anything else, the newly arisen imperatives of the New Economy to accommodate the needs of the Internet age, combined with the fast-paced IT revolutions occurring in Asia's neighbours, are most forcefully propelling Japan to dismantle the Old-Economy-compatible institutions and adopt a new economic regime. In this respect, a New Economy may promise Japan another round of 'catching up and surging ahead', not despite but rather because of the existence of its erstwhile sheltered IF industries (notably, telecommunications, distribution, and finance) for which information technology happens to be most effectively adaptable to restructure and rationalize business operations. This fortuitous opportunity exists, now that Japan has finally made a strategic decision to overhaul its information infrastructure, including the legal and regulatory system, for the era of e-commerce. This is compelling Japan to adopt American-style institutions for the New Economy, hence becoming more – if not totally – like the United States.

NOTES

1. This does not negate the fact that Japan's membership obligation no doubt did serve in the past as a compelling force to restructure its institutional setup to be more accommodative and congruous with liberal global capitalism.
2. The specificity rule says that first-best policy is to attach the source of a problem (say, a low labour standard) *directly* (via a labour law) instead of using a second-best policy (such as a tariff) which creates by-product distortions (for example, tariff-caused consumption distortions).
3. World Bank (1993) observes: 'To win the support of non-elites, the leaders of the HPAEs [High Performing Asian Economies] introduced mechanisms that drastically increased opportunities to share the benefits of growth. These mechanisms varied from economy to economy but included *education* (in all the HPAEs); *land reform* (in Japan, Korea, and Taiwan, China); *support for small and medium-size industries* (Hong Kong, Japan, Korea, and Taiwan, China); and *government provision of such basic amenities* as housing and public health services (Hong Kong and Singapore), Nearly all HPAE governments walked a delicate line regarding labor by limiting the power of unions and intervening to *check labor radicalism*, while at the same time encouraging a cooperative climate in which labor was rewarded for increases in productivity' (pp. 159–60). In specific reference to Japanese experiences, I am constructing a Japanese model of shared growth by emphasizing some unique institutional features as key elements in an integrated holist system.
4. Observing the Japanese system in 1982, Gary Saxonhouse (1983: 271) succinctly identified the following 11 illiberal elements: '(1) a major government role in formulating and facilitating an extremely high profile industrial policy; (2) special government impact on the financial system through an enormous volume of postal savings, through nonmarket forced placement of government debt, and through direct influence on the size and compositions of bank loan portfolios; (3) existence of large bank-centered industrial groups and the underdevelopment of equity markets and venture capital institutions; (4) existence of very large industrial group-associated general trading companies which dominate Japan's foreign trade and important elements of Japan's distribution system; (5) presence of legislation and administrative regulation continuing to reinforce, notwithstanding great changes in recent years, Japan's highly inefficient distribution system; (6) pervasive use of cartels and an absence of continuing antitrust enforcement; (7) despite great changes recently, continuing significant limitations for Japanese households on the forms and terms under which capital assets and liabilities can be acquired; (8) treatment of Japanese

labor as a fixed cost rather than as a variable cost over the course of the business cycle; (9) incomplete and delayed implementation of capital and interest rate liberalization and yen internationalization; (10) incomplete and delayed implementation of competitive bidding practices for procurement in both the public and the private sector; and (11) incomplete and delayed liberalization of service sector transactions.'

5. Mitsuhiro Seki (1999) characterizes Japanese industry as a 'full-set industrial structure'. He also traces the origin of this feature to Japan's geographical position and its late-comer status: '…Japan, isolated geographically in the extreme eastern end of Asia from its neighbors and uncolonized, was both forced and able to set out to independently develop industries in multiple fields. Japan's engagement in several wars, including the Sino-Japanese War (1894–1895), the Russo-Japanese War (1904–1905), and World War I, merely furthered the country's industrialization. Isolated from the rest of East Asia, its relations with its neighbors always tense, Japan was forced to provide for itself' (p. 323).

6. *Wall Street Journal*, 31 August 2000.

7. Warnings have appeared in recent news reports: 'Banks in trouble', *Economist*, 28 October 2000, pp. 65–8; 'The financing squeeze', *Business Week*, 30 October 2000, pp. 50–53; and 'Bond believers see prelude to a fall', *New York Times on the Web*, 19 November 2000.

8. As reported in 'Annual country report: Japan', *Financial Times*, 19 September 2000.

9. These developments are emphasized in an editorial of the *Nikkei Weekly* (28 August 2000: 6). It also observes: 'Asian information-technology leaders seldom talk about Japan. Companies owned by overseas Chinese are leading online business growth throughout Asia.'

10. *Ibid.*

11. This spat was reported in detail, for example, in 'Japanese find aid diplomacy fails to generate goodwill', *Financial Times*, 19–20 August 2000: 24.

12. *Wall Street Journal*, 15 October 1999.

13. *Wall Street Journal*, 9 May 2000.

14. Gibney (1992: 165–6) explains in detail: 'Charged with developing democratic trade unions, even at the cost of some unrest and disturbance, the Occupation consistently refused to intervene against planned strikes or slowdowns… The general strike called for 1 February 1947, however, was political in nature. Liberated from jail by Occupation order, Japan's Communist Party executive, led by a restless, dynamic, and brilliant Party activist, Tokuda Kyuichi, had concentrated its efforts on infiltrating and taking control of various nationwide union "struggle" committees… [The general strike's] purpose was rankly political – to bring down the Japanese government.'

15. The most recent spat involves a renewal of the 1995 auto-trade agreement which was designed to give US car makers greater access to Japanese dealers and US parts makers to original-equipment sales. Japan's position is that such a pact is no longer necessary since Japan's automobile industry is open to foreign ownership, as is represented by 36.8 per cent purchase of Nissan Motor by Renault, 34 per cent acquisition of Mitsubishi Motors by Daimler-Chrysler, 49 per cent stake in Isuzu Motors, 20 per cent in Suzuki Motor, and 21 per cent in Fuji Heavy Industries by GM.

REFERENCES

Akamatsu, Kaname (1935), 'Wagakuni yomo kogyohin no boeki suisei [The trend of Japan's foreign trade in woollen goods]', *Shogyo Keizai Ronso*, vol. and pages unknown, November.

Akamatsu, Kaname (1962), 'A historical pattern of economic growth in developing countries', *Developing Economies*, preliminary issue No. 1 (March–August): 1–23.

Aoki, Masahiko and Hugh Patrick (1994), *The Japanese Main Bank System: Its*

Relevance for Developing and Transforming Economies, New York: Oxford University Press.

Bergsten, Fred (2000), 'East Asian regionalism: towards a tripartite world', *Economist*, 15 July : 23–26.

Choppa, Leonard J. (1997), *Bargaining with Japan: What American Pressure Can and Cannot Do*, New York: Columbia University Press.

Donahue, Peter (1992), 'Free trade, unions and the state: trade liberalization's endorsement by the AFL-CIO, 1943–1962', *Research in Political Economy*, Vol. 13: 1–73.

Evans, John W. (1967), *US Trade Policy: New Legislation for the Next Round*, New York: Harper.

Gerschenkron, Alexander (1962), *Economic Backwardness in Historical Perspective: A Book of Essays*, Cambridge: Harvard University Press.

Gibney, Frank (1992), *The Pacific Century: America and Asia in a Changing World*, New York: Charles Scribner's Sons.

Hashimoto, Juro (1996), 'Keizai no '55nen-taisei o doha seyo [Demolish the 1955 economic system]', *Ekonomisuto*, 22 October: 64–9.

Ide, Masasuke (1998), *Japanese Corporate Finance and International Competition*, London: Macmillan.

Kojima, Kiyoshi (1958), 'Nihon keizai no gankokeitaiteki hatten to bocki no yakuwari [Flying-geese-style growth of the Japanese economy and the role of trade]', reproduced in Kiyoshi Kojima, (ed.) (1972), *Nihon Boeki no Kozo to Hatten [The Structure and Growth of Japan's Trade]*, Tokyo: Shiseido.

Kojima, Kiyoshi (1995), 'Dynamics of Japanese direct investment in East Asia', *Hitotsubashi Journal of Economics*, Vol. 36, No. 2 (December): 93–124.

Kojima, Kiyoshi and Terutomo Ozawa (1984), 'Micro- and macro-economic models of direct foreign investment: toward a synthesis', *Hitotsubashi Journal of Economics*, **25** (1): June: 1–20.

Kojima, Kiyoshi and Terutomo Ozawa (1985), 'Toward a theory of industrial restructuring and dynamic comparative advantage', *Hitotsubashi Journal of Economics*, **26** (2), December: 135–45.

Landes, David (1969), *The Unbound Prometheus*, Cambridge, UK: Cambridge University Press.

Mandel, Michael J. (2000), *The Coming Internet Depression*, New York: Basic Books.

Marglin, Stephen A. and Juliet B. Schor (1990), *The Golden Age of Capitalism: Reinterpreting the Postwar Experience*, Oxford: Clarendon.

Matsuyama, Kiminori (1997), 'Economic development as coordinating problem', in Masahiko Aoki, Hyung-Ki Kim and Masahiro Okuno-Fujiwara (eds), *The Role of Government in East Asian Economic Development*, Oxford: Clarendon Press: 134–60.

Mikanagi, Yumiko (1996), *Japan's Trade Policy: Action or Reaction?*, London & New York: Routledge.

Miyazaki, Yoshikazu (1980), 'Excessive competition and the formation of Keiretsu', in Kazuo Sato (ed.), *Industry and Business in Japan*, White Plain, New York: Sharpe: 53–73.

Mullins, David W. Jr. (2000), 'New Economy well worth the pain', *Nikkei Weekly*, 20 March: 7.

Noguchi, Yukio (1999), 'Leaving the "1940" system and moving into a new system', in Kozo Sato (ed.), *The Transformation of the Japanese Economy*, New York: Sharpe: 392–402.

Ohno, Tai'ich (1978), *Toyota Seisan Hoshiki* [*Toyota Production Formula*], Tokyo: Daiyamondo.

Ozawa, Terutomo (1992), 'Foreign Direct Investment and economic development', *Transnational Corporations*, **1** (1), (February): 27–54.

Ozawa, Terutomo (1993), 'Foreign Direct Investment and structural transformation: Japan as a recycler of market and industry', *Business & the Contemporary World*, **5** (2) (spring); 129–49.

Ozawa, Terutomo (1997), 'Japan', in John Dunning (ed.), *Governments, Globalization, and International Business*, Oxford: Oxford University Press: 377–406.

Ozawa, Terutomo (2000a), 'The "Flying-Geese" paradigm: toward a co-evolutionary theory of MNC-assisted growth', in Khosrow Fatemi (ed.), *The New World Order: Internationalism, Regionalism and the Multinational Corporations*, Oxford: Elsevier Science: 209–24.

Ozawa, Terutomo (2000b), 'The internet revolution, networking, and the "Flying-Geese" paradigm of structural upgrading', paper presented at the 26th annual conference of the European International Business Academy (EIBA), Maastricht, the Netherlands, 10–12 December 2000.

Saxonhouse, Gary R. (1983), 'The micro- and macroeconomics of foreign sales to Japan', in William Cline (ed.), *Trade Policy in the 1980s*, Washington, DC: Institute for International Economics: 259–304.

Schoppa, Leonard J. (1997), *Bargaining with Japan: What American Pressure Can and Cannot Do*, New York: Columbia University Press.

Schumpeter, Joseph A. (1942), *Capitalism, Socialism and Democracy*, New York: Harper.

Seki, Mitsuhiro (1999), 'The destruction of the full-set industrial structure – East Asia's tripolar structure', in Kazuo Sato (ed.), *The Transformation of the Japanese Economy*, New York: Sharpe: 321–39.

Suzuki, Yoshio (1987), *The Japanese Financial System*, Oxford: Clarendon Press.

Suzuki, Yoshio (2000), 'Strategies for overcoming Japan's economic crisis', in Masahiko Aoki and Gary Saxonhouse (eds), *Finance, Governance, and Competitiveness in Japan*, Oxford: Oxford University Press: 9–16.

Thurow, Lester C. (1985), *The Management Challenge: Japanese Views*, Cambridge: MIT Press.

Tyson, Laura A. (2000), 'The message from Asia: trade locally, think globally', *Business Week*, 4 December: 28.

UNCTAD (2000), *World Investment Report, 2000*, New York: UN Publications.

Wallich, Henry C. and Mabel I. Wallich (1976), 'Banking and finance', in Hugh Patrick and Henry Rosovsky (eds), *Asia's New Giant: How the Japanese Economy Works*, Washington, DC: Brookings Institution: 249–315.

Womack, James P., Daniel T. Jones and Daniel Roos (1990), *The Machine that Changed the World*, New York: Macmillan.

World Bank (1993), *The East Asian Miracle: Economic Growth and Public Policy*, New York: Oxford University Press.

Zhan, James and Terutomo Ozawa (2001), *Business Restructuring in Asia: Cross-Border M&As in the Crisis Period*, Copenhagen: Copenhagen Business School Press.

9. Openness, growth and development: trade and investment issues for developing economies

Nigel Pain[1]

I INTRODUCTION

Developing countries have expanded their share of international trade and investment significantly over the past decade. Numerically they now dominate the present 139 members of the World Trade Organization (WTO) (as of October 2000) and a further 30 countries are seeking to join, including China and Russia. Although this would seem to place developing countries in a position from which to exert a much stronger voice over trade negotiations, the last few years have seen many of them become increasingly disenchanted with the operations of the WTO and the global trading system in general. Several experienced considerable social and economic disruption during the financial turmoil in emerging markets in 1997 and 1998, casting doubt on the benefits of greater international integration. Many feel that the industrialized countries are delaying the implementation of their obligations arising out of the Uruguay Round agreements. The Ministerial talks in Seattle in 1999 were a failure, with developing countries feeling that their interests and concerns were being neglected in the negotiating agenda.

Inevitably this has reduced the enthusiasm of many governments for participating in further rounds of trade and investment talks and has raised hostility towards the WTO in parts of civil society. Yet international trade and investment liberalization are far from complete, suggesting that it may still be worthwhile to pursue reforms to the multilateral trading system that seek to improve market access. The objective of this chapter is to assess the evidence for the proposition that the interests of developing countries will be enhanced through greater international openness and to draw out some of the implications of that evidence for the issues confronting them in any future round of negotiations.

The tariff liberalization that has taken place over the past fifty years can be conveniently separated into four phases: the period 1947–61 following the inception of the General Agreement on Tariffs and Trade (GATT), the Kennedy Round from 1964–67, the Tokyo Round from 1973–79 and the Uruguay Round. Prior to the Uruguay Round the developing countries did not participate fully in all the multilateral negotiations. This is not to say that they did not benefit from them. The Most Favoured Nation (MFN) principle enforced under GATT meant that tariff reductions granted to one trading partner had to be granted to all GATT members. However, the focus of the negotiations was obviously on the principal issues of interest to the industrialized countries, and so textiles, clothing and agriculture tended to receive less attention than other manufactured products. Developing countries also benefited from the preferential access extended by many industrializing economies under the Generalized System of Preferences to the so-called 'Group of 77' countries, although again some key product lines were frequently excluded and quantitative restrictions were sometimes imposed.

In contrast developing countries participated actively in the Uruguay Round negotiations, and signed the Agreement in its entirety. One reason for this was a growing acceptance by many of them, and a heavy emphasis in the policy advice given by multilateral institutions, that openness and the liberalization of trade and investment policies were essential for successful development. It also reflected a gradual undermining of the intellectual consensus that had previously favoured import-substituting regimes as a means of stimulating industrialization (Kreuger, 1997).

Greater international integration is widely regarded as a pre-requisite for improved economic performance by developing countries. Opening up to international trade and reducing barriers to capital flows are both thought to improve the prospects for economic growth, with consequent improvements in per capita incomes. Trade and capital flows provide a means of closing what Romer (1993) terms 'idea gaps' and 'object gaps'. Foreign financial assistance can for instance enhance domestic savings and finance additional fixed capital. Foreign-owned firms can help to bring new knowledge into host economies. Exporting provides a means of financing the purchase of foreign capital equipment that is likely to be significantly cheaper, and of better quality, than that manufactured at home. Openness also has many other dimensions. An important one which is not considered in detail in this chapter concerns the timing and consequences of full capital account liberalization. This is not a direct part of a potential Millennium Round agenda, although many of the issues raised in the debate over the impact of capital account liberalization on development are similar to those raised in the literature on trade liberalization and development, as the discussions in Stiglitz (1998) and Rodrik (2000) make clear.

Successful development delivers improved living standards. This is not simply a matter of raising GDP per capita, but also involves other factors that lead to an enhanced quality of life, such as lower poverty and longer life

expectancy. However, in this chapter we concentrate on the relationship between openness and per capita incomes, partly to keep matters to a manageable
length. Arguably, higher incomes also provide one means of achieving the
broader social goals of the development process, as suggested in the recent
review of the wider relationships between trade liberalization and poverty by
Ben-David *et al.* (2000).

The structure of this chapter is as follows. In the next section we review the
role of developing economies in international trade and highlight differing
developments in individual regions. The experience of East Asia has clearly
been different from that of other regions, both in terms of movements in the
share of global trade and in terms of growth in real per capita incomes since the
early 1970s. In Section III we look at trends in the global pattern of foreign
direct investment (FDI). This reveals the growing share of new investments
now being located in developing countries, although as with international trade,
the gains do not appear to have been distributed evenly amongst all regions,
with Africa in particular having received comparatively little new investment.

It is clear that the interests of developing countries cannot easily be generalized, and they will not all share the same interests or concerns in different
aspects of future trade negotiations. The entry of China, and potentially the
Russian federation, into the WTO will also change the balance of interests
significantly, simply because of the size and political influence of both economies. The phasing out of quotas on textiles and clothing in industrialized
countries becomes much more significant if Chinese producers are also to
enjoy barrier-free entry. Discussions over the restrictions imposed on foreign
investors by host economies also become more important given the scale of
inward investment in China.

Section IV contains a review of the evidence linking trade and foreign
direct investment to economic growth and development. It considers the role
of international trade, and in particular the impact of exporting on performance, and then reviews the evidence on inward investment and growth in
developing economies. There is also a discussion of the lessons to be learned
from the experience of Mexico, where significant changes have occurred in
trade and investment policies over the past two decades. The evidence reviewed does suggest that greater international openness can help to raise per
capita incomes, but the gains from greater openness are by no means automatic. Openness is part of a development strategy, not a substitute for one,
and, as discussed in Section V, needs to be complemented by investments in
human capital and institutional reforms tailored to domestic needs and objectives rather than preferences imposed by industrialized countries. This does
not mean that developing countries should not seek to make their economies
more open to international trade, investment and knowledge, but simply that
the difficulties they face in adjusting to full liberalization should be taken into

account in any round of trade negotiations. It also needs to be recognized that many developing countries presently lack the administrative capacity to participate effectively in the WTO.

Section VI contains a discussion of some of the key issues on which any future trade negotiations are likely to focus, including the built-in agenda from the Uruguay Round to improve market access in agriculture and services and review the Agreements on Trade-Related Intellectual Property Rights (TRIPs) and Trade-Related Investment Measures (TRIMs). It also considers whether the agenda should be broadened to include labour and environmental standards and whether some developing countries should continue to receive 'special and differential treatment'.

From a perspective of openness and development it is clear that the main emphasis of any future trade round should be on measures that aim to reduce barriers to trade and enhance the contestability of product markets, whilst recognizing that it may take some time for many developing economies to build up the necessary institutional capacities to participate effectively in the WTO process. Measures to impose the labour and environmental standards of the industrialized countries on developing economies have little to do with enhancing market contestability, and should be discussed in more appropriate multilateral forums. The agreements reached in the Uruguay Round can be seen as ones in which many low income economies have taken on mandatory commitments in exchange for non-binding promises of assistance from industrialized countries, many of which have yet to materialize. If the next round is to be a true 'development round' this potentially destructive imbalance should be redressed, with negotiations guided by the basic principles of fairness and comprehensiveness (Stiglitz, 2000). Some other brief concluding comments are given in Section VII.

II   TRENDS IN INTERNATIONAL TRADE

Developing countries presently account for about 30 per cent of total world trade in merchandise products and in services.[2] The trends in their share of world trade are shown in Figures 9.1 and 9.2. It is clear that the share of developing economies declined over the 1980s, but began to recover during the 1990s. Based on the arithmetic average of the growth rate of imports and exports, the annual growth in the dollar value of developing countries' merchandise trade averaged 7.4 per cent between 1990 and 1999, compared to just 2.4 per cent from 1980 to 1990. In contrast the annual rate of growth in developed economies' trade slowed to 4.9 per cent in the 1990s, compared to 6.6 per cent in the 1980s. It is encouraging that the growth rate of developed economies' trade has begun to pick up at a time when they have participated

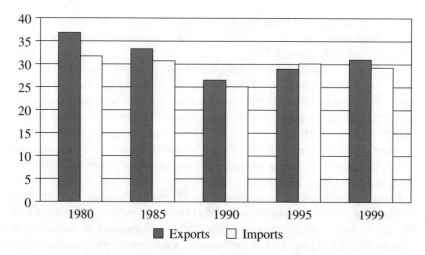

Figure 9.1   Developing country share of world merchandise trade (%)

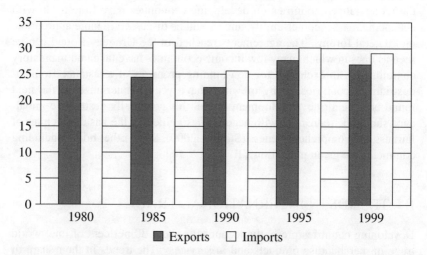

Source: Calculated from March 2000 data provided by WTO Statistics Division. Developing countries include the transition economies.

Figure 9.2   Developing country share of world services trade (%)

actively in trade liberalization, but it is impossible to judge the extent to which these developments are related.

The rate of growth of developing economies' trade in services also accelerated in the 1990s, although this may partly reflect improvements in statistical coverage. The average annual growth rate rose to 7.9 per cent from 6 per cent in the 1980s. Services have become an increasingly important part of developing countries' trade, with services exports accounting for around 17.5 per cent of the combined value of merchandise and services exports in 1999, compared to 10.5 per cent in 1980. Thus it should not be surprising that many developing economies continue to have a strong interest in further trade liberalization in services. Many are heavily dependent on services as a source of foreign exchange, reflecting specialization in tourism or transportation services. A General Agreement on Trade in Services (GATS) was one of the major results of the Uruguay Round negotiations, with national treatment and market access commitments being applied to a number of service sectors, although coverage was far from complete.

There have also been some important changes in the structure of merchandise trade in developing countries. Up until the early 1980s the merchandise exports of developing countries were dominated by primary products, such as fuels, raw materials and agricultural produce, while exports from the industrialized countries largely comprised manufactured goods. Manufactures accounted for only a third of developing country exports. However, growth has accelerated since then, and by the mid-1990s the share of manufactures in developing country exports had risen to over two-thirds. The share of fuels and minerals in total exports declined from around one-half in 1981 to one-sixth by the mid-1990s, partly reflecting the sharp decline in real fuel prices during this period.

Thus developing countries now have a strong interest in seeking to include industrial products in any further WTO negotiations, even though this is not part of the built-in agenda from the Uruguay Round. Tariffs and non-tariff measures such as quotas and antidumping actions constitute a significant market access barrier for many developing producers of manufactured goods, both in industrialized and in other developing economies. Developing economies may also have more to gain from further liberalization, since they tend to face higher tariff levels than producers in industrialized economies, as can be seen from Table 9.1, which reports average tariff levels in 1995.

There are two reasons for the higher tariffs faced by producers in developing economies. First other developing economies are a more important market than they are for producers in industrialized countries, and these economies have higher average tariff levels. Secondly, manufactured goods from developed countries are relatively concentrated in lines such as processed food products, textiles and clothing. These are products with relatively high tariff levels in the industrialized economies, and also significant non-tariff barriers, such as the tariff-rate quotas introduced in the Uruguay Round Agreement on Agriculture.

Analyses of further trade liberalization using applied general equilibrium models also suggest that developing countries stand to make important collective gains from further tariff liberalization, although inevitably there is little

Table 9.1   Import-weighted average tariffs in 1995 (%)

Exporting region	Importing region			
	High Income		Developing	
	Manufacturing	Agriculture	Manufacturing	Agriculture
High income	0.8	15.9	10.9	21.5
Developing	3.4	15.1	12.8	18.3

Source: Hertel *et al.* (2000).

agreement about the precise magnitude of the gains. The Organization for Economic Cooperation and Development (OECD) estimates that a full, global tariff liberalization for agricultural and industrial goods would ultimately raise world GDP at constant prices by 3 per cent, equivalent to $1.2 billion on its baseline projections (OECD, 1999). Output in the non-OECD area would rise by 4.9 per cent compared to 2.5 per cent in the OECD itself. In contrast Hertel (2000) estimates that full liberalization (including also some measures that affect services) would raise world welfare by $350 million. However, he agrees that the gains accruing to the developing countries would be significantly greater than their share of world GDP.

The above discussion highlighted some of the major trends in the trade patterns of developing economies. If these figures are decomposed by developing region it is clear that many countries will have different concerns and negotiating objectives in any future trade negotiations. Inevitably this reduces the chances of finding cohesive groupings of developing economies that can bargain collectively with the industrialized economies.

The export shares of five regions – Latin America, Africa, the Middle East, Asia and Developing Europe – are shown in Figures 9.3 and 9.4. The experience of many Asian economies has clearly been different from the others, with the developing economies in Asia having seen a sustained improvement in their share of world trade, both in services and merchandise trade. This has not been reflected in the overall share of world trade taken by developed economies because of the marked decline in the trade share of the Middle East and African economies associated in part with weak commodity prices, and the collapse in trade in the transition economies associated with the dissolution of the Council of Mutual Economic Assistance (CMEA) (Michalopoulos, 1999). However, even in Latin America, which appears to have had a relatively stable trade share, the picture is bleak if Mexico is excluded, because much of the overall growth in trade in the 1990s has been

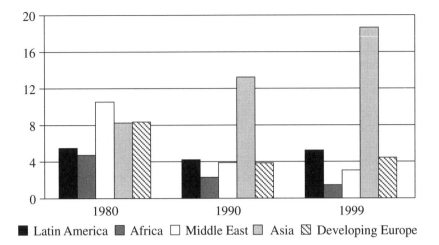

Figure 9.3   Developing regions' share of world merchandise exports (%)

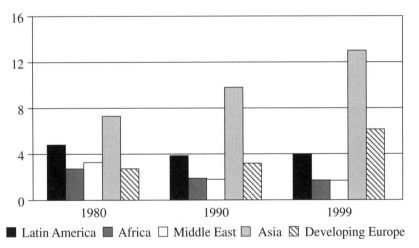

Source: calculated from March 2000 data provided by WTO Statistics Division. Developing
countries include the transition economies.

Figure 9.4   Developing regions' share of world services exports (%)

due to the impact of the rapid growth in Mexican trade associated with the
North American Free Trade Agreement (NAFTA).

The experience of Asia does not simply reflect the rapid development of
the four newly industrialized countries – Korea, Taiwan, Hong Kong and
Singapore – which are now probably better classified as developed economies

rather than developing ones. Their merchandise exports rose by 11 per cent per annum on average between 1980 and 1999, but the rest of developing Asia still achieved growth of 9.5 per cent per annum.

One important difference between the Asian economies and other developing regions is that a significantly higher proportion of their exports comprise manufactured products, as can be seen from Table 9.2. This matters because the volume of trade in manufactures has been growing much more rapidly than other types of trade. Within the manufacturing sector many of the Asian economies are also relatively specialized in some of the fastest growing export sectors, notably office machinery and telecommunications equipment. However, when looking at imports, it is not obvious that the interests of the Asian economies will be all that different from those of other developing regions, with manufactures accounting for around three-quarters of total merchandise imports in all of them.

Table 9.2   The commodity composition of merchandise trade in 1997 (%)

	Agriculture	Mining	Manufactures	Other
A. EXPORTS				
Latin America	24.7	23.2	51.9	0.2
Africa	17.5	48.4	27.3	6.8
Middle East	3.5	74.9	20.8	0.8
Developing Europe	12.3	30.2	55.2	2.3
Non-Japan Asia	11.4	8.9	77.8	1.9
B. IMPORTS				
Latin America	10.7	9.6	77.4	2.3
Africa	17.0	9.4	71.0	2.6
Middle East	13.9	6.1	76.7	3.3
Developing Europe	15.0	9.1	74.3	1.6
Non-Japan Asia	9.2	11.7	77.4	1.7
Memorandum				
World	10.9	11.3	74.1	3.7

Note: The regional coverage differs slightly from that used in Figures 9.3 and 9.4. Asia includes Australia and New Zealand, and Africa includes South Africa. 'Other' goods include gold, arms and ammunition and other SITC section 9 products.

Source: World Trade Organization Annual Report, 1998.

Growth has been exceptionally strong in many Asian countries for many years, and there has been a long debate about the mainsprings of growth in this region and about what can be learnt from the experience of these countries. One strand of the debate has focused on the early moves by some of the Asian economies towards greater international openness in the 1960s and early 1970s. Cross-country growth studies suggest that this is one of the main factors that can account for the comparatively rapid growth in Asia over the past three decades.

The links between openness and growth in East Asia are reviewed by Lloyd and Maclaren (2000). They argue that the perception that East Asia is an open region largely rests on its openness to merchandise trade compared to other developing countries. East Asian developing economies are generally less open than developed countries inside and outside Asia, and frequently less open to services and FDI than many other developing economies.

Whilst there has indeed been a focus on exporting in many of the countries, this has been only a part of the overall development strategy in many. Openness to ideas and foreign knowledge, and a resulting concern with product quality, have been at least as important, as have institutional structures. Barrell *et al.* (2000) discuss the different experiences of development in Korea and the former Soviet bloc. There were similarities in the growth process between South Korea in the 1970s and 1980s and Soviet Russia in the 1950s. Neither were pure market economies with independent firms undertaking actions in the interest of maximizing the returns to private shareholders. In both cases there was a clear development plan with quantity objectives, and barriers to inward investment that meant that foreign firms were virtually excluded. However, the difference, which is important for all the successful East Asian newly industrialized economies, is that the Korean plan involved high investment, helped by tax and credit incentives, and high levels of exports and imports. The high levels of investment went into plant and machinery whose productive potential was gauged by its ability to produce goods for the international market. Trade linkages with the rest of the world ensured that information flowed into the economies and made it essential that modern standards of product quality were quickly absorbed in order to ensure plan fulfilment. Complementary investments in education and training were also undertaken, raising the ability to absorb and adapt knowledge from other countries.

Russia did trade significantly, but largely with other members of the CMEA. Such trade rarely reflected underlying comparative advantages and soon disappeared once the transition process began. Michalopoulos (1999) highlights the case of the Bulgarian electronic and computer industry. In 1987 this employed more than 100,000 people and had intra-CMEA exports of $2 billion. By 1991 it had almost disappeared completely.

It is clear that there are no automatic links between greater openness and economic growth, although it does appear to be the case that those developing countries who have gained a greater share of world trade are also the ones whose per capita incomes have risen most rapidly. However, these countries are the exception rather than the rule. During the past 25 years there has been a divergence, rather than a convergence, between the levels of per capita income in the industrialized countries and many developing countries. This can be seen from Figure 9.5, which shows the average annual growth rate of per capita incomes, measured in US dollars at 1987 prices and exchange rates in selected regions from 1966 to 1998. Similar results are reported in IMF (2000) using purchasing power parity rates.

Real per capita incomes rose by an average 2.5 per cent per annum in the industrialized countries. This rate of growth was exceeded only in Asia, particularly East Asia, where incomes rose by an average 5.9 per cent per annum. China had a per capita income growth rate of 7.5 per cent per annum. Real incomes have risen in developing countries in the Middle East and Latin America, but at a slower pace than in the industrialized countries. Real incomes hardly changed at all in sub-Saharan Africa, and have actually fallen since 1973. The transition economies of Central and Eastern Europe are part of the Developing Europe bloc in Figure 9.5. Whilst real per capita incomes are estimated to have risen over the period as a whole, there has been a sharp decline since transition began. In total approximately three-quarters of all the

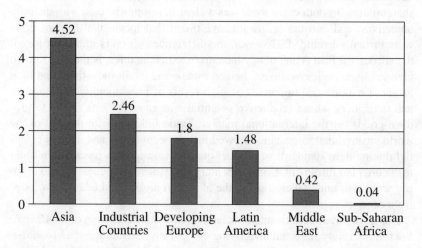

Source: *Global Economic Prospects and the Developing Countries 2000*, Table A2.2, World Bank.

Figure 9.5   Annual real per capita income growth, 1966–98 (%)

developing economies have recorded slower per capita income growth than the industrialized economies (IMF, 2000), although this group comprised only about 30 per cent of the total in terms of population, reflecting the relative success of China and, to a lesser extent, India, which had a per capita growth rate of 2.75 per cent.

III TRENDS IN GLOBAL FOREIGN DIRECT INVESTMENT

Recent patterns of cross-border investment reflect changes in the structure of the world economy. Advances in technology and telecommunications have changed the feasible span of managerial control and the motivation for dispersed production. Liberalization of trade and capital flows in many developed and developing economies has helped to improve market access for tradable products produced elsewhere.

Early supply-side models of foreign investment in developing economies emphasized the role of natural resources and differences in factor endowments. Investments in labour-intensive activities would be made by capital-rich countries in labour-abundant countries. Barriers to trade were also important, with foreign investment necessary to enter large markets protected from imports by high tariff levels and quotas. However, some countries such as India and Mexico which made considerable use of trade barriers to protect domestic producers, received relatively little investment for many years, suggesting that market size in itself was not always sufficient to attract investment.

Foreign investments in many developing economies are no longer dominated by the establishment of free-standing subsidiaries operating mining, agriculture and transportation facilities. The organization of many businesses has changed, with many multinational firms choosing to reorganize their activities on a regional or global basis, with activities increasingly outsourced to lower cost locations. This has focused greater attention on trade policies in different locations. Subsidiaries that are part of integrated production systems in open economies are thought more likely to benefit from technological upgrading and managerial attention (Moran, 1998). Export-orientated investments have been especially important in the high level of inward investment in developing economies in South and East Asia, as well as in small developed economies such as Ireland.

At the same time, widespread use of privatization and the removal of regulations prohibiting foreign ownership in financial services, infrastructure and power generation and supply have stimulated new inward investment in previously closed service and construction activities. Investments driven by privatization have been particularly important in Brazil and some of the

Table 9.3   *The global stock of foreign direct investment by recipient area*
              ($ billion)

	1914	1938	1960	1973	1985	1997
Developed countries	5.2	8.3	36.7	121.3	545.1	2312.4
	(37.2)	(34.3)	(67.3)	(72.9)	(69.7)	(67.3)
Developing countries	8.9	16.0	17.6	45.2	237.2	1124.3
	(62.8)	(65.7)	(32.3)	(27.1)	(30.3)	(32.7)
World	14.1	24.3	54.5	166.7	782.3	3436.7

Note: Figures in parentheses are FDI in host as a share of the world total. Figures may not always sum to global total because of rounding.

Sources: Dunning (1988, Table 3.2) and UNCTAD (1999, Annex Table B3).

transition economies. The increasing willingness of many governments to use build–operate–transfer regulations has also helped to create new opportunities for investment in infrastructure projects in countries such as China.

The long-term trends in the location of direct investment are shown in Table 9.3. In the first half of the 20th century some two-thirds of all investments were located in the developing economies. Over the last 40 years the picture has been quite different, with the vast majority of foreign direct investment taking place between the developed economies. Over two-thirds of all inward investments are now held within the developed economies.

The rate of growth of the nominal investment stock has accelerated from an average 3 per cent per annum between 1914 and 1960, to 9 per cent between 1960 and 1973 and around 13.5 per cent per annum between 1973 and 1997. Controlling for movements in the global price level during these periods, as proxied by the GDP deflator for the United States between 1914 and 1960 and the GDP deflator for the OECD economies since 1960, indicates that in real terms the growth of the global FDI stock has risen from 0.6 per cent per annum over 1914–60 to 4.25 per cent per annum during 1960–73 and 7 per cent per annum since that time.

In part the concentration of investments in the industrialized economies reflects the growing role of proprietary assets in the spread of foreign investment. The decision to establish foreign subsidiaries is influenced by the need to appropriate the rents accruing from the development of firm-specific knowledge-based assets and practices. Greater use is now made of customized production for local markets rather than mass production of homogenous goods. Investments of this type are more likely to be located in other industrialized economies rather than developing economies (Caves, 1996), although there are some examples, notably Singapore and Taiwan, where educational advances and skill upgrading have helped to attract technologically advanced investments and R&D centres (Lall, 1998; Tu and Schive, 1995).

Cross-border flows of capital, such as foreign direct investment, have also been stimulated by the liberalization of national capital markets. All the major economies have dismantled their capital controls since the collapse of the Bretton Woods system of fixed but adjustable exchange rates in 1971 and the subsequent move to a floating exchange rate regime. At the same time many developing economies have opened up their capital accounts, extending the geographical scope of capital market integration.

The size of the stocks of foreign direct investment in the world economy means that it can take many years for changes in the geographical pattern of new flows of investment to become apparent in the distribution of the stocks. The geographical distribution of existing investments suggests that direct investment cannot simply be characterized as the movement of production to lower wage economies. However, the stock data disguise an increasing tendency to locate new investments in the developing economies since 1990.

Trends in the location of new inflows of direct investment are reported in Table 9.4. Developing economies have received 36 per cent of all new investments during the 1990s, compared to just 18 per cent of new investment in the latter half of the 1980s. The growth of inward investment has been especially rapid in South and East Asia, led by the rapid expansion of new investment in China, which now has the third largest inward investment stock in the world, after the United States and the United Kingdom.

Reforms introduced since 1991 have stimulated inward investment in China, both by expanding the areas of the economy open to foreign investors and by allowing full current account convertibility so that profits could be repatriated more easily. This reinforced the attractiveness of the large domestic market and the effectiveness of the range of incentives on offer in the special economic zones. Coughlin and Segev (2000) provide a discussion of recent trends in FDI in China.

Excluding China, the developing economies received 26.75 per cent of all inward investment in the period from 1991–98. There has also been strong growth in inward investment in Latin America, with Brazil and Mexico being the most important hosts. Inward investment has been stimulated by privatization policies as well as by the opportunities opened up through regional integration via NAFTA and Mercosur. The interaction between trade policies and inward investment in Mexico is discussed in greater detail below. Again, Africa appears a notable exception, accounting for a declining share of total new investments in the developing economies.

Table 9.4   The regional pattern of foreign direct investment inflows

	1985–90 (average)	1991	1992	1993	1994	1995	1996	1997	1998
A. $ billions									
World	141.9	158.9	175.8	219.4	253.5	328.9	358.9	464.3	643.9
Developed economies	116.7	114.8	120.3	133.9	146.4	208.4	211.1	273.3	460.4
Developing economies	25.2	44.1	55.5	85.6	107.1	120.5	147.7	191.1	183.4
Africa	2.9	2.8	3.2	3.5	5.3	4.1	5.9	7.7	7.9
South and East Asia	12.4	21.2	27.7	49.8	61.4	67.1	79.4	87.8	77.3
Latin America	8.1	15.4	17.6	20.0	31.5	32.9	46.2	68.3	71.7
Transition economies	0.5	2.6	4.8	8.3	7.1	16.0	15.2	22.4	21.7
Other	1.4	2.2	2.3	4.0	1.9	0.3	1.1	4.9	4.9
B. Share of world (%)									
Developed economies	82.3	72.2	68.4	61.0	57.7	63.4	58.8	58.9	71.5
Developing economies	17.7	27.8	31.6	39.0	42.3	36.6	41.2	41.1	28.5
Africa	2.0	1.7	1.8	1.6	2.1	1.3	1.6	1.6	1.2
South and East Asia	8.7	13.4	15.7	22.7	24.2	20.4	22.1	18.9	12.0
Latin America	5.7	9.7	10.0	9.1	12.4	10.0	12.9	14.7	11.1
Transition economies	0.3	1.6	2.7	3.8	2.8	4.9	4.2	4.8	3.4
Other	1.0	1.4	1.3	1.8	0.7	0.1	0.3	1.1	0.8
Transition economies Share of developing (%)	1.8	5.8	8.6	9.7	6.6	13.3	10.3	11.7	11.8

Note: Transition economies comprise the separate UNCTAD data for Central and Eastern Europe, Central Asia, Croatia and Slovenia.

Source: Calculations from UNCTAD (1997, 1998 and 1999, Annex Table B1).

The emerging markets crisis led to an overall slowdown in the level of new investment in developing economies in 1998, although this was primarily confined to a few Asian economies and Russia. Most other developing economies experienced a further rise in inward investment. The overall share of new investments taken by developing economies was also affected by the rapid growth of investment in the developed economies, with strong equity markets helping to finance major cross-border mergers and acquisitions in the United States and Europe. These type of investments are not ones that most developing economies could hope or expect to attract.

FDI in the transition economies has accelerated since 1994. In the next four years inward investment amounted to 11.75 per cent of the total level of inward investment in developing economies and about 4.25 per cent of total global inward investment. The proportion of foreign investments going to the transition economies has risen steadily since the early part of the decade. Investment continues to be dominated by privatization-related flows. Inflows jumped up in 1995, coinciding with the peak of the privatization programmes in Hungary and the Czech Republic. Since that time there have been continuing high levels of investment in the Visegrad economies, augmented by rising resource-based investments in countries such as Kazakhstan and Azerbaijan. As a group the transition economies appear to be performing much as might be expected given that they began from a position with little inward investment. At the end of 1998 the stock of inward investment in these economies represented 2.45 per cent of the total global stock of direct investment. This was broadly in line with their share of global GDP. If flows remain at the level seen over the past four years, then the share of the total FDI stock should rise further.

IV   OPENNESS AND GROWTH

IV.1   International Trade: Theoretical Issues

There are numerous channels through which openness to trade, and in particular exports, might improve the prospects for growth. Traditional theories of trade under perfect competition have always indicated that trade can enhance allocative efficiency and welfare in the economy as a whole by allowing resources to be transferred from import-substituting activities into ones in which countries have a comparative advantage. Recent advances in trade and growth theory also stress the importance of imperfect competition, economies of scale, product diversity and the spread of ideas and organizational techniques across international borders.

Exporting is typically associated with an expansion in the size of the potential market facing the firm. Higher demand may thus allow an expansion in production and the exploitation of economies of scale, particularly in small countries or capital-intensive activities in which the minimum efficient scale of production is large relative to the size of the home market.

Exposure to greater foreign competition may also generate improvements in exporters' performance, by eliminating organizational inefficiencies, irrespective of whether firms can learn from exporting. The domestic price of tradable goods may also fall, relative to the level it would otherwise have been at, enhancing consumer welfare. However, competition may not be without costs. Baldwin and Caves (1997) argue that competitive pressures will enhance turbulence, which they define in terms of entry and exit rates and gross job creation and destruction. Greater competition implies that producers of differentiated products face a more elastic demand in the international market. This raises the relative sizes of quantity responses to disturbances from either foreign or domestic sources. In this case exporters might perform well if there are positive shocks, but poorly if there are adverse shocks. In a related paper Feeney (1999) illustrates that the benefits of learning-by-doing and specialization due to trade depend on the trade-off between the gains from diversifying country-specific risks and the losses from the greater risk of exposure to industry-specific shocks.

Enhanced allocative and organizational efficiency produces once-only effects from trade on per capita incomes. New theories of trade and growth identify a number of routes through which greater openness might have longer lasting effects on the rate of growth. A key feature of many of these models is the 'love-of-variety' preferences introduced by Dixit and Stiglitz (1977).[3] There are two distinct versions of this approach. In one, all varieties of a good enter a representative consumer's utility function and all are consumed. In the other, final goods are modelled as produced using varieties of intermediate inputs, with increasing returns in the number of varieties used.[4] The (non-Ricardian) versions of these models have increasing returns to scale, either because there is a fixed cost associated with the production of each variety, or because there are assumed to be increasing returns in the number of different varieties of intermediate inputs.[5]

In the model with differentiated varieties of finished goods, trade expands the number of varieties that are produced and hence expands utility, and potentially productive efficiency (Feenstra *et al.*, 1999). In the alternative model with differentiated varieties of intermediate inputs, trade again expands the number of varieties, but this is met through increasing returns and economies of scale in incumbent firms, generating rises in productivity per firm. Consumer welfare again rises, as lower costs of production are passed through to the prices of final goods.

In endogenous growth models such as those proposed by Grossman and Helpman (1991), the generation of new product varieties via trade makes it cheaper and easier to invent new varieties. Exposure to foreign markets might also improve the efficiency of the firm and raise growth either through learning from foreign rivals or through spillovers of technologies and knowledge. For instance, firms that participate in export markets might gain access to technical expertise regarding product designs and production methods from their foreign buyers (Clerides *et al.*, 1998; Egan and Mody, 1992). International knowledge spillovers arising from trade or cross-border investment expand the stock of ideas that may be used for research in each country. Successful R&D can then generate growth through expansion in the variety and quality of domestically produced goods and services. Thus the rate of technological progress is endogenous.

However, there is no guarantee that trade liberalization will promote growth in such models (Rodríguez and Rodrik, 2000). If countries become increasingly specialized in low-tech sectors in which little or no R&D takes place, then resources may be diverted away from the activities that help to promote long-term growth. Older, unresolved arguments over the need to protect 'infant industries' also suggest that there are circumstances in which the maintenance of trade restrictions might promote long-run performance.

Thus there may be a variety of channels through which exporting could generate improvements in the relative performance of exporting firms. Some of these channels, such as competition, economies of scale, entry and exit and knowledge spillovers, are already known to be general influences on productivity growth. There is a large literature on the relationship between exporting and growth. We begin by reviewing the aggregate cross-country evidence before turning to some more recent evidence from microeconometric studies of individual firms.

IV.2   International Trade: Macroeconometric Evidence

The widespread belief that openness is linked to growth has until recently had considerable support in the literature. Ben-David *et al.* (2000, Chapter 1, Annex Table 1) cite twenty empirical studies published between 1977 and 1998 which use cross-country evidence and trade policy indicators and which find that open and outward-orientated economies tend to enjoy faster economic growth. The indicators used include trade ratios, tariff levels and indices of price and exchange rate distortions. The strong policy implication is that countries should seek to dismantle barriers to trade, as emphasized frequently in the policy recommendations provided by most of the major inter-governmental organizations.

In a further study not included in the literature cited by Ben-David *et al.*, Frankel and Romer (1999) also report a significant positive association between international trade and per capita income using cross-sectional data for

150 countries in 1985. They find that a rise of 1 percentage point in the ratio of trade to GDP raises income by between 0.5 and 2 per cent. An important feature of their study is the recognition of the difficulty of attributing causality in cross-sectional regressions of this kind. If richer countries tend to trade more, or can afford to forgo many trade policy restrictions, then causality may run from income to policy. Frankel and Romer seek to overcome this by using information on geographical characteristics to construct an instrument for trade.[6] One other important point to note about their study is that it relates to trade shares, not trade policies. Some countries may have extremely liberalized policies and contestable markets but still experience low levels of trade relative to GDP because of their size or location.

Rodríguez and Rodrik (2000) have recently questioned the reliability of many of the results concerning the consequences of trade policies (as opposed to the level of trade) for growth. They argue that in some cases the indicators of openness are poor measures of trade barriers, or highly correlated with other variables that are themselves likely determinants of growth, such as the quality of institutions or macroeconomic stability. In other cases the econometric techniques used in some studies are argued to be inappropriate, and re-estimation using different techniques and controls for other policy and institutional variables results in significantly weaker findings. For example, one study they consider is that of Frankel and Romer. Re-estimating their model with additional dummies to control for geographic characteristics such as climate, Rodríguez and Rodrik find that the trade regressor becomes a statistically insignificant determinant of per capita incomes. Similar results are reported by Jones (2000), who finds that trade policy measures tend to become insignificant in cross-country growth regressions which include the broader measure of the quality of institutions developed by Knack and Keefer (1995).

IV.3   International Trade: Microeconometric Evidence

Until recently most econometric work on trade and growth has been undertaken with aggregate data. There is no guarantee in such studies that firms experiencing faster productivity growth are ones which have entered the export market. The growing number of firm-level econometric studies on newly available longitudinal data sets permits a direct assessment of the structure of the underlying causal relationships between trade and performance. Pain and te Velde (2000) provide a comprehensive review of the literature on the impact of exporting on corporate performance. Other aspects of the relationship between openness and plant-level growth in developing countries are reviewed by Tybout (2000).

The benefits of openness and exporting should show up in the performance of individual firms, as well as in the overall level of welfare and growth in the economy. The stylized facts in many developing economies appear consistent with these arguments; in most countries exporting firms tend to be larger, older and more innovative than other firms (Tybout, 2000). However, they are also consistent with a counter argument that a self-selection process is at work. It is only the better performing firms that are able to enter international markets because they are the ones able to bear the sunk costs associated with entry into foreign markets and the more intense competitive pressures there. We review the evidence from recent studies for a number of developing countries.

The impact of exporting on firm performance in East Asia has been studied for Taiwan and Korea. Aw *et al.* (1998) use quinquennial Census data for five export-intensive industries – textiles, apparel, plastics, electrical engineering and transportation equipment. Liu *et al.* (1999) undertake a study of the Taiwanese electronics industry, using a smaller, annual panel data set. The pattern of their results is consistent with findings for developed economies such as the United States (Bernard and Jensen, 1999), with considerable support for the self-selection hypothesis, and limited evidence of learning by exporting. On average exporters have significantly higher levels of productivity than non-exporters, and firms that enter the export market have higher productivity than non-exporters prior to entry. This is found for all of the industries studied. Firms that exit the export market have lower levels of productivity than continuous exporters, and the differential continues to widen after exit, although by an insignificant amount in some industries.

Continuous exporters do not appear to perform significantly better than non-exporters, and in some industries in Taiwan appear to perform significantly worse, when evaluated using total factor productivity. However, Aw *et al.* (1998, Table 4) do find that the total factor productivity differential between entrants and non-exporters continues to widen after entry in four out of five industries in Taiwan and Korea. In three cases – textiles, plastics and electronics in Taiwan – this effect is significant. This is the only real evidence of any potential gains from exporting.

The learning-by-exporting hypothesis has also been tested by Clerides *et al.* (1998) using plant-level data for Colombia and firm-level data for Mexico and Morocco. Although their methodology differs from the studies for East Asia, their evidence is consistent with them. Plants that become exporters have higher productivity prior to entry into export markets, but typically do not experience marked increases in relative productivity after entry. Separate estimates of cost functions for individual industries reveal only two – apparel and leather goods in Morocco, where past exporting experience has a significant negative impact on current average variable costs.

An interesting feature of Clerides *et al.* (1998) is that they also attempt to test for externalities from exporting in Colombia. The evidence across industries is mixed, but there is some support for the hypothesis that a firm is more likely to export if it belongs to an export-intensive industry or region. They also find that firms in export-orientated regions tend to enjoy relatively lower costs than firms in other regions, irrespective of export status, although in several cases these differentials are not significantly different from zero. This provides some weak evidence in favour of externalities from exporting.

Bleaney *et al.* (2000) investigate the learning-by-exporting hypothesis using survey data on a sample of medium-sized manufacturing firms in Belarus, Russia and Ukraine. In contrast to the other studies discussed here, their focus is on employment levels, rather than measures of productive efficiency. They report a significant positive correlation between current employment levels and past export status. Since they control for past employment levels, the evidence also implies that employment growth has also been higher in exporting firms, which is consistent with the hypothesis that exporting improves allocative efficiency.

Thus the overall evidence on the impact of greater international openness to trade is mixed. Whilst there cannot be an automatic presumption that increasing exports will generate faster economic growth, the learning-by-exporting hypothesis cannot be ruled out completely. However, most exporting firms appear to have experienced more rapid improvements in productivity prior to entry into export markets. Of course the pursuit of liberal trade policies by national governments, and the consequent encouragement of firms to enter international markets, may be an important factor that encourages domestic firms to make the investments that enhance their productivity, but there is no direct evidence of this.

The microeconometric evidence suggests that exporting plants have an absolute productivity advantage over non-exporting plants, implying that they are more likely to be close to the production possibility frontier for their industry. Part of the explanation for the faster productivity growth of non-exporters thus may simply be that they can benefit from eliminating technical inefficiencies as well as from technological advances. Part of the explanation for the faster growth of exporters in the year or so after entry into the export market may simply be that greater exposure to international competition quickly eliminates many remaining inefficiencies. If learning-by-exporting is more important for young or new plants, with older plants having successfully incorporated knowledge of best practices, then we would expect to see a permanent effect on the level of productivity following export market entry, but not a permanent effect on growth.

IV.4   Openness and Foreign Direct Investment

Openness to foreign direct investment can also improve the prospects for growth and development. Inflows of foreign investment can modernize and expand the stock of physical and human capital in the economy, helping to fill what Romer (1993) termed 'object gaps'. This is particularly important where domestic resources are insufficient to cover the investment required by the economy. It increases the productive capacity of the economy and can influence employment levels. By bringing access to foreign technology and management techniques, and by making available products and processes that embody foreign knowledge, FDI also helps to close 'idea gaps' and augment the stock of domestic knowledge. This can improve efficiency of production and raise the average productivity level of the entire economy (Barrell and Pain, 1997). If domestic firms adopt the new production processes, then there will be beneficial externalities from inward investment. FDI can also have an impact on growth levels through trade, if foreign firms are export orientated and improve the variety and quality of products produced in host economies, or provide domestic firms with information on how to access export markets. Barrell, Holland and Pain (2000) summarize the available literature on the impact of foreign direct investment in the transition economies.

However, again there can be no automatic presumption that inward investment will be beneficial (Moran, 1998). The introduction of labour-saving techniques may not be desirable in a country with a large supply of labour and little capital. Equally entry of a dominant foreign firm can harm competition, particularly if there are barriers to entry and the institutions required for effective domestic regulation have yet to be developed. Promises of protective tariffs to prevent imports from competing against a foreign investor for the domestic market will almost certainly reduce consumer welfare and reduce the potential benefits to be gained from inward investment.

The empirical literature on multinationals and development is extensive, with detailed surveys provided recently by Blomström *et al.* (2000) and Caves (1999). They suggest that spillovers from inward investment can be an important source of economic growth for developing economies, but there is no strong consensus on the associated magnitudes, and the impact can vary by country and by industry. This points to the significance of local conditions in host countries and the need to adopt policies that complement inward investment. A high level of local competence and a competitive environment have both been found to raise the absorptive capacity of host economies. Borenzstein *et al.* (1998) find that the effect of foreign direct investment on growth is much weaker in countries with relatively low levels of education attainment. Skilled labour can be utilized to help upgrade and adapt existing proprietary technologies. Balasubramanyam *et al.* (1996) find that the impact of inward investment on growth is much larger in countries with export-promoting policies, and hence open and contestable markets, than in countries with import-substituting ones. Domestic content requirements and protection from external competition appear to reduce the chances of receiving and benefiting fully from inward investment. Import-substituting regimes tend to attract stand-alone foreign plants operating at sub-optimal scale. Export-orientated regimes allow the foreign subsidiary to undertake just those tasks for which the host location is best suited.

The level of human capital and skills is particularly important in ensuring that there is not too large a gap between the capabilities of foreign companies and indigenous firms which hope to be able to benefit from their presence. Caves (1999) argues that in service sectors much depends on matching managerial capabilities. Services are commonly produced at the site of consumption and may therefore generate demonstration-type spillovers. But if foreign firms are much larger than domestic firms, the range of tasks undertaken and the degree of supervision required will be very different and the example provided by the foreign subsidiary may not be widely applicable.

In a cross-sectional analysis of per capita manufacturing exports from 33 developing countries in 1995, UNCTAD (1999, Box VIII.6) finds a significant positive association between exports and inward FDI per capita after controlling for the level of domestic R&D expenditure and the size of the domestic manufacturing sector. The reported results imply that a rise of 1 per cent in FDI per capita would be associated with a 0.45 per cent rise in the value of manufactured exports per capita, with the strongest effects being felt in high-technology exports. Barrell *et al.* (2000) report related evidence indicating that foreign firms have improved the export performance of the Visegrad economies and China in recent years.

IV.5   Trade Policies and Inward Investment: Lessons from Mexico

Foreign direct investment has expanded rapidly in Mexico during the present decade. Over the five years since the formation of NAFTA, inflows of direct investment have averaged 2.9 per cent of GDP per annum, compared to 1.2 per cent per annum over the previous fifteen years.[7] A distinguishing feature of these inflows is that over half of them have been in the manufacturing sector, a much bigger proportion than in the other major Latin American economies. Whilst entry into NAFTA and geographical proximity to the United States have clearly helped to make Mexico a more attractive investment location, there have also been important reforms to the policy framework (Graham and Wada, 2000). There are also several academic studies that demonstrate that foreign investors have had a beneficial impact on domestic firms in Mexico, suggesting that it may offer important lessons for the design and effectiveness of trade and investment policies.

For many years the emphasis in Mexico lay in regulating rather than promoting foreign investment. The domestic market was heavily protected by tariff barriers and foreign investment was seen as an alternative means by which foreign countries could attempt to gain control over the Mexican economy. Policy was governed by a 1973 statute limiting foreign involvement in most industries to minority participation subject to prior authorization from the federal government. With the exception of a jump in resource-based inflows in 1980–81, at a time when oil prices were strong, inward investment remained modest. High and volatile inflation in the 1980s, and the associated possibility of debt defaults, also acted to deter investors (Shah and Slemrod, 1995).

In the mid-1980s important market-orientated reforms began to be introduced in several sectors. Small to medium levels of investment for foreign majority participation became exempt from prior government approval, trade barriers began to be lowered and regulations governing special export zones were relaxed. The present inward investment regime was codified in the Foreign Investment Law which came into force in December 1993. The law was one of a series of measures designed to liberalize trade and capital markets prior to entry into NAFTA from 1994. In effect it helped to lock in many of the previous reforms that had liberalized the institutional framework of the country (Blomström and Kokko, 1997). The law opened more areas of the economy to foreign ownership, provided national treatment for most foreign investors, eliminated all performance requirements for foreign investment projects and liberalized the criteria applied for automatic approval of foreign investment projects.

Foreign firms have consistently identified bureaucracy, slow government decision-taking and lack of transparency as obstacles to investment in Mexico. Measures have thus been taken to improve the transparency of the regulatory system. An Economic Deregulation Council was established in 1995 to review all rules and regulations of the federal government. The thrust of this reform was to remove regulations, unless it could be shown there was a clear justification for government involvement, and to minimize any adverse impact on businesses.

For many years widespread use was made of special corporate tax incentives in Mexico (Feltenstein and Shah, 1995). Most of these have now been removed, with greater emphasis given to maintaining a competitive corporate tax rate. High inflation and high nominal interest rates in the 1980s left many firms facing financing constraints. Credits against future taxes were of less use than reductions in tax rates which immediately benefited cash-flows. Account was also taken of tax reforms in the major source of inward investment, the United States. Tax rates above those in the US act as a disincentive, but tax rates significantly below those in the US may simply transfer revenue to the US Treasury, since a higher proportion of an identical tax liability will be paid in the United States because of the way in which the United States taxes the foreign source income of its companies. Recognition of this has led to the elimination of most direct tax incentives in Mexico.

Inward investment may also have been encouraged by the obligations imposed on direct investment policy by provisions in the NAFTA Treaty designed to ensure that state and local governments accord national treatment to investors from NAFTA countries. Graham and Wada (2000) argue that this enhanced the credibility of investment liberalization, since violation of the NAFTA provisions could be subject to sanctions or require the payment of monetary damages.[8]

An important part of the successful transformation of the Mexican economy has been the measures introduced to stimulate export growth. These began many years before entry into NAFTA, and meant that the Mexican economy was well placed to exploit fully the improved access it received in the North American marketplace. Historically, inward investment in the Mexican manufacturing sector was often geared to serving the protected domestic market rather than markets abroad. Many measures were introduced to try and stimulate exports from inward investment projects, with performance requirements imposed on foreign investors in the late 1970s to force imports to be balanced by exports. These measures were not particularly successful, with the export propensities of US-owned foreign affiliates in Mexico remaining well below those in other developing countries, as can be seen from Table 9.5.

Table 9.5   Export propensities of US majority-owned foreign affiliates (%)

	1966	1977	1983	1993	1996
World	18.6	30.8	35.1	40.7	42.0
Developing countries	8.4	17.9	26.9	39.6	41.6
Mexico	3.2	10.5	19.8	32.1	52.6

Note: Exports as a ratio of total sales.

Source: UNCTAD (1999, Annex Table A.VIII.6).

Policy changes in the mid-1980s led to the Mexican government making more active use of priority development areas and targeted incentives for export-orientated investments. Import-substituting policies were ended in 1985 and the government announced that it was joining the General Agreement on Tariffs and Trade. At that time there were export controls on 85 per cent of non-petroleum exports (Hanson, 1998). By the end of 1987 export controls had been abolished completely and average tariffs on imports were half what they had been in 1985. Mexico had originally begun to permit export assembly operations following the Border Industrialization Programme in 1965. Plants located in a free-trade zone next to the border with the United States were granted certain exemptions if they exported all of their output in the so-called '*macquiladora*' programme. In 1972 the government began to allow the creation of free trade zones in other parts of the country. In 1988 the government began to allow plants in these zones to sell up to half of their output on the domestic market (Hanson, 1995). The combination of this reform, together with the gradual relaxation of controls over new investment, led to a rapid rise in the level of export-orientated investments. *Macquiladora* employment rose from 212,000 in 1986 to 430,000 in 1989 and 940,000 by 1997. There are now estimated to be some 107 export processing zones in Mexico, with the firms located in them employing around 1 million people.[9]

There were also changes in trade policies and performance requirements that acted to stimulate investment in particular sectors. Moran (1998) cites the informatics sector as an example. Up to 1985 inward investments were limited to joint ventures, operating in subscale plants with production primarily geared to a domestic market protected by import quotas. The acceptance of a major, wholly-owned, export-orientated investment from IBM in 1985 was followed by investment expansion packages from existing inward investors to expand their operations to allow higher levels of exports.

The rapid expansion in export-orientated investments has been reflected in a rise in the relative export propensity of US foreign affiliates in Mexico as shown in Table 9.5. The rising trend between 1983 and 1993 has subsequently accelerated markedly since the formation of NAFTA. The export processing zones continue to offer special incentives. Exemptions from import taxes are granted for equipment and goods to be re-exported and for certain inputs into production, such as machinery and equipment of exports.[10]

The use of export processing zones and trade policy reform has changed the economic geography of Mexico (Hanson, 1998). Industrial activity has shifted away from the largest centre of population, Mexico City, to northern states on the US border. Entry into NAFTA has accelerated the integration of Mexican plants into the corporate production systems of major US automobile and electrical manufacturers. Ford of Mexico has changed its entire production strategy, building new engine and vehicle assembly plants to serve the North American market. *Macquiladora* facilities were utilized to help integrate part production with operations in the United States (Mortimore, 1998). However, the rapid speed with which Mexico has been able to raise exports owes much to the institutional reforms introduced in the 1980s, liberalizing trade policies and improving incentives for export-orientated investments.

Research suggests that foreign manufacturers in Mexico act as export catalysts for domestic firms. In a study covering the period from 1986–90

Aitken *et al.* (1997) found that the probability of an indigenous firm exporting was positively correlated with proximity to multinational firms, but not with proximity to general export activity. This suggests that foreign firms have brought wider benefits to the economy, possibly by helping to upgrade the standards of local suppliers and management and by providing information about foreign markets. Mexico now has the fifth highest level of exports of all developing economies and is the largest developing country exporter of automotive products.

There have also been a number of studies of the impact of foreign-owned firms on the productivity of Mexican firms. The findings from these studies are summarized in detail in Blomström and Kokko (1998). Foreign presence does appear to have a positive impact on the rate of growth of local productivity. This effect is weaker in those industries in which the products and technologies of foreign companies have little in common with those of local firms. Spillovers and learning by example are much stronger in industries in which foreign and domestic firms are in competition with each other, suggesting that a limited foreign presence in a previously protected market may be more beneficial than a situation where foreign affiliates hold dominant market shares.

Mexico points to the importance of complementary trade and industrial policies in host countries as determinants of the magnitude and scope of spillovers and the export potential from inward investment. Reforms to improve the skills of the workforce and the technological capabilities of domestic producers may still be needed to generate the full benefits from openness. There remains concern about the level of linkages between foreign firms and domestic suppliers and about the level of domestically financed R&D (Lall, 1998). In some cases local supplier industries have found it difficult to raise technological levels to international standards (Mortimore, 1998).

Mexico has always had the natural advantage of geographical proximity to the large market in the United States, but this by itself did not lead to significant levels of inward investment. Investment promotion policies have had to be refocused and incentives carefully targeted. Reforms to the institutional framework governing trade and investment were also required. These created the market conditions which enabled Mexico to benefit rapidly from the formation of NAFTA.

IV.6   Openness and Growth: A Summary

A reasonable summary of the evidence on trade and growth and inward investment might be that it is consistent with the hypothesis that greater openness helps to raise per capita incomes, but there is a large amount of uncertainty regarding the magnitude of the effects and it is likely to depend on a range of host country and external characteristics. There is little evidence in favour of the opposite view that trade protection is beneficial for sustained economic growth, suggesting that reforms should more appropriately be biased towards trade liberalization. It should also be remembered that growth is not the same as welfare. If openness helps to raise the number of relatively high productivity firms in the liberalizing economy, then the overall level of allocative efficiency in the economy will improve, as will living standards.

There is nothing in the present literature to indicate what an appropriate level of openness might be. In general, smaller economies tend to have higher levels of trade relative to GDP simply because there are fewer domestic consumers for producers to trade with. It is quite possible that significant trade restrictions are costly but more modest restrictions are not (Collier and Gunning, 1999). There are clearly some economies such as North Korea which have fallen behind as a result of remaining closed to the outside world for the last fifty years, and others, such as Hong Kong, which have experienced sustained growth associated with their openness. However, these are extremes, and it may be difficult to generalize from their collective experience.

For practical reasons it may not be sensible for many developing economies to rush and eliminate all of their tariffs. This is because trade taxes are an important proportion of the overall level of tax revenue. Trade taxes were still over 30 per cent of total tax revenue in Africa in the mid-1990s, and 24 per cent of revenues in the Asia-Pacific region and 21 per cent in Latin America and the Caribbean (Oyejide, 2000). Whilst it is easy to broaden the legal definition of the tax base, collecting the revenues due can be done only when administrative capacities develop. Thus for many countries, particularly low income ones, it is unrealistic to expect that they will agree to the immediate abolition of all their remaining tariffs, even if they can be persuaded of the need to ensure their regimes of trade protection are as simple and transparent as possible. Equally the adoption of WTO mandated customs valuation procedures can often not be undertaken without investments in order to improve the administration of customs points (Finger and Schuler, 2000).

V OPENNESS AND INSTITUTIONS

Considerations over the risk attached to investment may be particularly important in determining the level of investment in developing economies. Evaluations of risk are typically driven by the general institutional framework of the economy, as well as the rules and regulations that govern the entry and operations of foreign investors. The prospects for political and macroeconomic stability together with the transparency of the legal regulations governing factors such as foreign ownership of land, tax liabilities and profit repatriation all matter to potential investors (Jun and Singh, 1996).

It is clear that being open to outside influences has been important in the success of a number of developing countries. However, as Rodrik (2000) argues, this by itself is not sufficient to ensure sustained growth. Strong public institutions are also important complementary determinants of economic performance. A set of political and economic institutions that encourages transactions at minimal cost and credible commitment helps to raise the efficiency of market-orientated economies (North, 1997). Secure property rights and the prompt enforcement of legal obligations are likely to be especially important. Even well-defined property rights may be of little immediate benefit if they do not confer 'control rights' over the associated stream of income from those assets.

Brunetti *et al.* (1997) investigate the relationship between foreign direct investment inflows and the findings from a survey of the institutional framework as perceived by private firms in 20 transition economies in 1997. They focus on five particular topics: the predictability of rules, political stability, security of property rights, reliability of the judiciary and the extent of corruption. All were individually found to be significant positive determinants of the level of FDI inflows between 1993 and 1995, apart from the predictability of rules. The security of property rights and political stability were also found to be significant determinants of per capita income growth over the same period.

A wholescale transformation of society is at the heart of the development process (Stiglitz, 1998 and 2000). Financial institutions are central to a functioning market economy, as are secure property rights, enforceable contracts and regulatory institutions. Systems of social insurance and conflict management also have to be established to help provide stability and cohesion at a time of systemic re-organization. Desirable institutional arrangements may vary from country to country, reflecting both societal norms as well as what is practicable given the present state of development (Rodrik, 2000). In a second-best world some transitional institutions and seemingly distortionary trade policies may be more effective than 'best practice' institutions initially, as removing one distortion may be counterproductive in the presence of other distortions. For instance policies of mass privatization and capital account convertibility in Russia in the 1990s created incentives for asset-stripping and capital flight because they were implemented at a time when reforms to the judiciary and the enforcement of property rights had barely begun. In contrast, closed capital accounts in China enabled the financial system to utilize domestic savings to provide support for domestic investors. Sequencing reform can be very important, and trade and capital market liberalization cannot be seen in isolation from other components of a development strategy. Rodrik (2000) argues that the key factor for many developing economies is not their international openness but the fact that they have successfully built institutions that have enabled them to manage the consequences of international openness.

If markets are competitive, and institutions are in place to ensure they remain competitive, greater international openness will raise average per capita incomes by enhancing allocative efficiency. However, this does not mean that there will be political support for such policies. If trade and investment are confined to small enclaves they may do little to spur development in the medium term (Stiglitz, 1998). There is also a question of the extent and mechanisms by which those who gain from openness will compensate those who lose. If such compensation is to occur within developing countries, then systems of social insurance or a progressive and enforceable tax structure are required. If compensation, in the form of official assistance, is to come from developed countries, then multilateral agreement over the indicators that should form the basis for the level of assistance will be needed. If compensation does not come at all, there is a risk that exclusion from the benefits of openness will lead to dissenting voices against liberalization.

The clear message from the literature is that openness to trade and investment and liberalized trade policies are only part, albeit an important one, of a development strategy, not a substitute for it. Developing economies can gain from openness provided they ensure a competitive market environment and are able to invest in the public institutions that facilitate the workings of open and competitive markets. In many cases assistance from the industrialized economies is essential for this to occur, and this needs to be recognized and accepted if future trade negotiations are to be successful and improve the prospects for development.[11]

A related issue is whether many developing countries have a sufficient administrative capacity to participate fully in multilateral trade negotiations. Sampson (2000) argues that many do not have sufficient resources to participate meaningfully in the large number of meetings that take place at the WTO. Again, technical assistance and training from the industrialized economies should help some countries to participate more effectively by developing the necessary mechanisms to analyse the implications of proposals under negotiation (Oyejide, 2000). These resource constraints also strengthen the case for any negotiations to have a tightly focused agenda in order to minimize the risk of exclusion from the negotiating process. Mechanisms to facilitate cooperation and joint action amongst the developing economies may also be needed, as it is unlikely to be feasible for all 139 (or more) members of the WTO to participate fully in every individual stage of the negotiating process.

In the remainder of this chapter we consider some of the key areas in which negotiations may take place and draw on the literature on openness and growth to highlight some of the key issues for developing economies. Although we do not discuss manufactures trade in any detail, it is clear from the discussion of the data in Section II that this is also likely to be an area of considerable interest to developing economies.

VI   TRADE POLICY ISSUES FOR DEVELOPING COUNTRIES

VI.1   Agriculture

A key feature of the Uruguay Round was the Agreement on Agriculture (AoA). This agreement had three main components – reforms to improve market access, reductions in export subsidies and cuts in domestic producer subsidies. As is clear from Table 9.1, the level of protection in agriculture tends to be considerably higher than in manufacturing, although the process of tariffication in the Uruguay Round has at least served to make the degree of protection more transparent. Agricultural liberalization primarily requires further reforms to end the high levels of agricultural support in many developed countries, notably in Europe and Japan. The AoA laid out a timetable for reductions in agricultural support, including an end to the Multi-Fibre Agreement, but much of this was end-dated and is due to be completed only by 2005.

The impact on developing economies of planned and any future reforms to agricultural policies is far from uniform. Producers of agricultural produce stand to gain significantly from improved market access in the industrialized economies. Economies such as Argentina, Brazil, Colombia, Chile and the Philippines all stand to make significant gains (Panagariya, 2000). However, because reductions in subsidies are likely to raise prices, countries that are net food importers might experience difficulties in implementing any agreement. As the experience of Indonesia showed in the Asian crisis, the forced imposition of reforms that raise domestic food prices significantly can cause significant political disruption, especially in the absence of democratic institutions for conflict management (Rodrik, 2000).

Any negotiations should allow for such difficulties as far as possible. Significant food aid might also be required for a period of time to augment existing social safety nets. Oyejide (2000) highlights the potential difficulties that many African economies may face, and it is clear from Table 9.2 that the share of food products in imports is higher there than elsewhere.

One area in which developing countries may also face pressures for reform lies in health and safety standards, as codified in the WTO agreement on sanitary and phytosanitary (SPS) measures. The principal aim of these measures is to maintain food product quality and safety, partly to assuage consumer concern in developed countries. Yet in effect standards are being imposed which many developing economies may not be able to meet without access to new production technologies and technical assistance. Openness is likely to be essential if knowledge of this kind is to be acquired.

VI.2 Services

One of the major results of the Uruguay Round negotiations was the GATS. The primary goal of this measure was to obtain market access commitments from as many countries and in as many service sectors as possible. Perhaps inevitably, the areas in which fewest commitments were made tended to be low-skill, labour-intensive activities, where developing countries tend to have a comparative advantage. One important area in which some progress has been made concerns the liberalization of market access in areas such as finance and telecommunications, helping to facilitate foreign direct investments in some developing economies.

Arguably the main priority of future negotiations should be to ensure that the GATS covers all service sector activities and expands market access commitments. Network effects are especially important for many service sector providers and a presence in the foreign market is often essential for trade to take place.

Developing countries can stand to make significant gains from service sector liberalization and this should allow them to offer some commitments in any future round of negotiations. Opening up their own service sectors, including government procurement, can help to reduce market segmentation and allow foreign suppliers to bring in new technologies. This is the route which many of the transition economies in Central and Eastern Europe have chosen to take. The alternative is to maintain inefficient production techniques which *de facto* amount to a tax on consumers. Areas such as telecommunications, energy supply and transportation may all be appropriate candidates for greater liberalization. However, for competition to flourish, especially in utility industries in which there is a semi-monopoly provider, there again needs to be complementary investments in regulatory institutions (Mattoo, 2000). This has to be recognized in drawing up the likely timescale for any reforms.

One important aspect of trade in services which should be part of any negotiations on services concerns the opportunities for migration by workers from developing economies into industrialized ones. Negotiators failed to make much progress on this issue during the Uruguay Round. Quotas, qualification requirements and the application of economic needs tests are frequently applied to prevent the entry of service suppliers. Liberalizing entry requirements in developed countries again provides potential gains to developing countries, not just because it may raise service exports, but because it can also raise the exposure of migrants to new ideas and working practices in the industrialized economies. Returning workers can augment the stock of knowledge in their home economies. Industrialized countries can gain by relieving labour market pressures from shortages of particular types of labour.

A widely cited example of the potential for exports of services from developing countries is the Indian software industry. Exports in 1999–2000 amounted to US$4 billion, and accounted for around 10.5 per cent of total export revenue in that period (NASSCOM, 2000). Software exports had been just $225 million in 1992–93. Approximately 58 per cent of exports in 1999–2000 were accounted for by on-site services, that is through the temporary movement of programmers, and hence were dependent upon the availability of visas in the major industrialized economies, particularly the United States. Liberalization of regulations has helped. The shortage of labour in the US IT sector led to a rise in the annual cap on the number of temporary work visas available to foreign nationals from 65,000 in the early 1990s to 115,000 in 1999 and 2000. Current proposals before the US Congress suggest a potential further rise to 200,000 by 2002.

Whilst this reduction in trade barriers has helped to raise the level of trade, the opportunities for development of the domestic market in India have remained limited. The technologies required for advanced IT equipment cannot yet be utilized fully because of inadequate and outdated telecoms infrastructure. Thus export revenue accounted for 70 per cent of the total revenue of the software industry in 1999–2000. In summary, the use of export zones and the availability of a low-cost pool of English-speaking skilled labour has helped to attract and retain software investments, and a reduction in barriers in the industrialized economies has allowed exports to expand. But it has not been sufficient to ensure that the full potential benefits of these investments have been felt throughout the economy.

VI.3 Standards

Standards have become an increasingly important issue in international trade. The Uruguay Round TRIPs agreement obliged all WTO members to enforce intellectual property rights, although some developing countries were allowed some years to adjust to this. The TRIPs agreement involved significant changes in national legislation, and also the creation of new institutions in many developing countries. This was the first clear attempt to harmonize regulatory standards across all WTO members, with the standards in question being those of the industrialized countries rather than the developing ones. It also marked a departure from the longstanding GATT principle of negotiations and agreements *not* to do certain things (Hertel *et al.*, 2000).

In any exercise of this kind it is difficult to strike the appropriate balance between encouraging domestic innovation and technology transfer against the possibility of the restricted diffusion of new products and processes. Given that most process and product innovations are achieved by producers in the industrialized countries, the protection of those patentable innovations is in itself likely to transfer incomes from developing countries to the industrialized ones. Set against this is the possibility that enhanced patent protection improves the incentives to undertake innovation as well as the incentives for foreign-owned firms to transfer new technologies into subsidiaries in developing economies. This may raise the overall level of allocative efficiency in the host economies, and hence living standards, even if there are fewer possibilities for the diffusion of technologies to developing country producers. However, the evidence on the importance of such factors is limited. Blomström *et al.* (2000) note that there is little evidence on the question of whether host country intellectual property regimes do have any bearing on the size or scope of spillover benefits from inward investment.

The trend towards discussion of standards has continued in recent years, with developed economies having attempted to force discussions over labour and environmental standards onto the Seattle agenda. Again the likely result would be to try and impose the standards of the industrialized economies on the developing economies. It should be clear that such measures have nothing to do with improving market access and contestability, and in effect simply deprive many developing countries of important elements of their comparative advantage in trade (Oyejide, 2000). This does not mean that such issues should not be discussed in multilateral forums, as there can be important international externalities. It is simply that they are best done so in more appropriate settings such as the International Labour Organization. The openness and growth literature does not highlight these factors as being important for development, and imposition of them, with a potential threat of trade sanctions if action was not taken, would impose significant compliance costs on developing economies.

VI.4   Trade-Related Investment Measures

The GATT was concerned with cross-border trade in goods. The WTO is concerned also with the treatment of foreign enterprises and natural persons. At present the treatment of foreign investment in the WTO agreements is fragmented. Market access for foreign investors in service sectors is part of the GATS, and TRIMs prevents host countries from imposing some performance requirements on foreign investors.

The rapid growth in foreign direct investment over the past decade means that there are now many governmental and non-governmental organizations pressing for further investment-related measures. The potential agenda is broad, ranging from the liberalization of market access in other industries, through governing the rules of 'locational tournaments' to attract foreign investors, to obtaining agreement on a comprehensive list of industrial policies to do with technology transfer, licensing requirements and the enforcement of joint ventures. All of these matter for the development process and it is important that there is a careful analysis of the costs and benefits of any industrial policy as well as consideration of the effects of excessive competition with other countries. But, as with standards, the extent to which these issues are trade related is questionable (Bora *et al.*, 2000; Panagariya, 2000). The failed negotiations between OECD member states for a multilateral agreement on investment provide an indication of the likely difficulties there will be in reaching agreements on these issues. If the wider aspects of investment liberalization are to be kept within the auspices of the WTO, it would seem preferable to establish an entirely independent framework for negotiation, with a timetable separate from that for further trade and market access negotiations.

VI.5   Special and Differential Treatment

It has been recognized for some time that many developing countries, particularly the low income ones, will always face difficulties in implementing many of the measures discussed in the multilateral rounds. This was reflected in the concept of 'Special and Differential Treatment' (SDT). During the Tokyo Round SDT provisions were used to grant some countries exemption from particular rules and enhance their market access via tariff preferences. The emphasis during the Uruguay Round was different, with a concentration on the construction of rules that would apply to all participants, with developing countries granted only additional time to implement obligations. Whilst this has the merit of ultimately generating a simplified global trading system, it raises the risk of over-burdening many developing countries because of their lack of the complementary institutional capacity.

Wang and Winters (2000) argue that the concept of special and differential treatment needs to be re-invented if a future trade round is to be successful. Tariff preferences granted by the industrialized economies may not be appropriate, partly because tariff levels are now so low in some products and partly because they may be accompanied by quantitative restrictions in others. A better approach would be to seek agreement over measurable criteria that could be used to classify economies according to their state of development, and then to relate the timescale and extent of SDT to their progress against these criteria. Oyejide (2000) makes a related argument, and suggests that the World Bank's criteria for classifying countries into high, middle and low income countries would be an obvious choice, as it already has widespread acceptance.[12]

VII CONCLUDING COMMENTS

The evidence from a wide range of studies suggests that a sound institutional and legal framework, along with timely and predictable enforcement of the rules embodied in that framework, is essential if reforms to trade and investment policies are to have significant effects in developing countries. Political and macroeconomic stability, security of property rights, reliability of the judiciary, strong regulatory institutions and an absence of corruption are especially important. Without a strategy that tailors market-based reforms to existing institutional and social capabilities, or one that provides the necessary financial and technical assistance to facilitate the development of new institutions, greater international openness is likely to be of little use. With it, liberalization of trade policies might well provide a successful stimulus to development.

In the absence of multilateral agreements, regional and bilateral preferential agreements can be expected to proliferate. The number of regional trade agreements in force has already risen from 62 in December 1994 to 113 by the end of 1999 (Sapir, 2000). Whilst regional trading arrangements can still improve market access for developing countries and pave the way for economic cooperation in many areas, they are also more costly for countries with limited administrative capacity as each tends to have its own set of regulations and standards. Inevitably developing countries seeking to become part of NAFTA or to reach a preferential trade agreement with the EU, and undertaking bilateral negotiations, have little bargaining power and are forced to accept the existing rules of the club. In some cases existing trading arrangements may be disrupted. For instance transition economies that succeed in becoming members of the European Union will not be able to maintain any bilateral trade agreements that differ from the collective trade policies pursued by the Union as a whole.

Countries excluded from the current spread of regionalism will undoubtedly suffer some trade discrimination. In principle these countries might be eligible for compensation under GATT and WTO rules. In practice discrimination is difficult and costly to prove, and there can be little doubt that the collective interests of the developing economies would be best served by seeking to maintain a common voice in tightly focused multilateral negotiations.

NOTES

1. I am grateful to Gavin Boyd and Anna Lanoszka for helpful comments and suggestions and to colleagues at the National Institute, notably Ray Barrell, Dawn Holland and Dirk te Velde for their contributions to the joint research from which some of the material in this chapter is drawn. I am also grateful to the ESRC for financial support (grant number L138251022).
2. In the discussion below, developing economies include the transition economies of Central and Eastern Europe. Developed economies follow the definition applied by the WTO in preparing its statistics on world trade by region and selected economies and comprise North America, the EU, EFTA, Japan, Australia, New Zealand and South Africa. The newly industrialized economies of South-East Asia and Mexico are all classified as developing economies.
3. An alternative approach is to use 'ideal variety' preferences, in which different varieties have different characteristics and consumers purchase the variety whose characteristics are closest to their ideal. The two approaches are broadly equivalent if the range of characteristics is such that all varieties compete with each other (Smith, 1994).
4. The models differ in their implications for the types of goods traded. One predicts increasing trade of final goods, whereas the other predicts increasing trade in intermediate goods.
5. In this case there are fixed costs of inventing the blueprint for each new variety.
6. The instrument is the fitted values from a regression of bilateral trade on distance, geographical area and dummies for common borders and landlocked countries. The fitted values for the individual pairs of countries are then aggregated to obtain an estimate of the geographic component of countries' overall trade.
7. Based on data from the 1999 IMF *International Financial Statistics Yearbook*.
8. However, as of the end of 1999, there were still some impediments to foreign investment in Mexico. Large investments require approval from the National Foreign Investment Commission, although these represent only around 5 per cent of all investment projects. Approval often requires that projects satisfy employment considerations or offer technological benefits. Mexico is also not yet a member of the Multilateral Investment Guarantee Agency.
9. UNCTAD (1999), Annex Table A.IX.3.
10. The largest incentives are still offered to companies which set up manufacturing plants within 20 kilometres of the northern and southern borders. Companies in these areas can gain exemptions of up to 100 per cent on import duties for a maximum of 10 years after they begin operations. To qualify they must manufacture products not produced elsewhere in Mexico.
11. Finger and Schuler (2000) estimate that the average cost per developing country of implementing the Uruguay Round commitments on customs reforms, intellectual property protection and sanitary and phytosanitary standards will be $150 million, which would exceed the annual development budgets in many countries. Finger (2000) likens the economics applied whilst negotiating the Uruguay Round to the economics of buying a yacht – discussions do not take place over the price as it is taken as given that all parties find it acceptable.
12. At present low income countries are classified by the World Bank as those with a per capita GDP of $760 or less in 1998. Middle income countries are those with a per capita GDP between $761 and $9860.

REFERENCES

Aitken, B., G.H. Hanson and A.E. Harrison (1997), 'Spillovers, foreign investment and export behaviour', *Journal of International Economics*, vol. 43, pp. 103–32.

Aw, B.Y., S. Chung and M.J. Roberts (1998), 'Productivity and the decision to export: micro evidence from Taiwan and South Korea', NBER Working Paper No. 6558. (*World Bank Economic Review*, forthcoming.)

Balasubramanyam, V.N., M. Salisu and D. Sapsford (1996), 'Foreign direct investment and growth in EP and IS countries', *Economic Journal*, vol. 106, pp. 92–105.

Baldwin, J. and R. Caves (1997), 'International competition and industrial performance: allocative efficiency, productive efficiency and turbulence', Harvard Economics Discussion Paper No. 1809.

Barrell, R. and N. Pain (1997), 'Foreign direct investment, technological change, and economic growth within Europe', *Economic Journal*, vol. 107, pp. 1770–76.

Barrell, R. and N. Pain (1999), 'Trade restraints and Japanese direct investment flows', *European Economic Review*, vol. 43, pp. 29–45.

Barrell, R., D. Holland and N. Pain (2000), 'Openness, integration and transition: prospects and policies for economies in transition', presented to IESG Silver Jubilee Conference on International Economics in the 21st Century: A Research Agenda, University of Sussex.

Ben-David, D., H. Nordström and L.A. Winters (2000), *Trade, Income Disparity and Poverty*, World Trade Organization Special Studies No. 5.

Bernard, A.B. and J.B. Jensen (1999), 'Exceptional exporter performance: cause, effect or both?', *Journal of International Economics*, vol. 47, pp. 1–25.

Bleaney, M., I. Filatotchev and K. Wakelin (2000), 'Learning by exporting: evidence from three transition economies', Centre for Globalisation and Labour Markets Research Paper 2000/6, University of Nottingham.

Blomström, M. and A. Kokko (1997), 'Regional integration and foreign direct investment', NBER Working Paper 6019.

Blomström, M. and A. Kokko (1998), 'Multinational corporations and spillovers', *Journal of Economic Surveys*, vol. 12, pp. 247–78.

Blomström, M., A. Kokko and S. Globerman (2000), 'The determinants of host country spillovers from foreign direct investment: a review and synthesis of the literature', in Pain (2000).

Bora, B., P.J. Lloyd and M. Pangestu (2000), 'Industrial policy and the WTO', *The World Economy*, vol. 23, pp. 543–60.

Borensztein, E., J. De Gregorio and J.-W. Lee (1998), 'How does foreign direct investment affect economic growth?', *Journal of International Economics*, vol. 45, pp. 115–35.

Brunetti, A., G. Kisunko and B. Weder (1997), 'Institutions in transition: reliability of rules and economic performance in former socialist economies', World Bank Policy Research Working Paper No. 1809.

Caves, R.E. (1996), *Multinational Enterprise And Economic Analysis* (Second Edition), Cambridge: Cambridge University Press.

Caves, R.E. (1999), 'Spillovers from multinationals in developing countries: the mechanisms at work', William Davidson Institute Working Paper No. 247.

Clerides, S.K., S. Laul and J.R. Tybout (1998), 'Is learning by exporting important? Micro-dynamic evidence from Columbia, Mexico and Morocco', *Quarterly Journal of Economics*, vol. CXIII, pp. 903–48.

Collier, P. and J.W. Gunning (1999), 'Why has Africa grown so slowly?', *Journal of Economic Perspectives*, **13**(3), pp. 3–22.

Coughlin, C.C. and E. Segev (2000), 'Foreign direct investment in China: a spatial econometric study', *The World Economy*, vol. 23, pp. 1–24.

Dixit, A. and J. Stiglitz (1977), 'Monopolistic competition and optimum product diversity', *American Economic Review*, vol. 67, pp. 297–308.

Dunning, J.H. (1988), *Explaining International Production*, London and Boston, Unwin Hyman.

Egan, M.L. and A. Mody (1992), 'Buyer–seller links in export development', *World Development*, vol. 20, pp. 321–34.

Feeney, J. (1999), 'International risk sharing, learning by doing and growth', *Journal of Development Economics*, vol. 58, pp. 297–318.

Feenstra, R.C., D. Madani, T.H. Yang and C.Y. Liang (1999), 'Testing endogenous growth in South Korea and Taiwan', *Journal of Development Economics*, vol. 60, pp. 317–41.

Feltenstein, A. and A. Shah (1995), 'Macroeconomic implications of investment incentives in Mexico', in A. Shah (ed.) *Fiscal Incentives for Investment and Innovation*, Oxford: Oxford University Press.

Finger, J.M. (2000), 'Implementation and the integrated framework', presented at WTO Committee on Trade and Development seminar on Implementation of the WTO Agreements, Geneva.

Finger, J.M. and P. Schuler (2000), 'Implementation of Uruguay Round commitments: the development challenge', *The World Economy*, vol. 23, pp. 511–26.

Frankel, J.A. and D. Romer (1999), 'Does trade cause growth?', *American Economic Review*, vol. 89, pp. 379–99.

Graham, E.M. and E. Wada (2000), 'Domestic reform, trade and investment liberalisation, financial crisis and foreign direct investment in Mexico', *The World Economy*, vol. 23, pp. 777–98.

Grossman, G.M. and E. Helpman (1991), *Innovation and Growth in the Global Economy*, Cambridge, Massachusetts: MIT Press.

Hanson, G.H. (1995), 'The effects of offshore assembly on industry location: evidence from US border cities', NBER Working Paper 5400.

Hanson, G.H. (1998), 'North American economic integration and industry location', *Oxford Review of Economic Policy*, **14**(2), pp. 30–44.

Hertel, T.W. (2000), 'Potential gains from reducing trade barriers in manufacturing, services and agriculture', *Federal Reserve Bank of St. Louis Review*, **82**(4), pp. 77–100.

Hertel, T.W., B.M. Hoekman and W. Martin (2000), 'Developing countries and a new round of WTO negotiations', presented at 12th Annual Bank Conference on Development Economics, Washington DC: World Bank.

IMF (2000), *World Economic Outlook May 2000*, Washington DC: International Monetary Fund.

Jones, C.I. (2000), 'Comment on Rodríguez and Rodrick', *NBER Macroeconomics Annual*, forthcoming.

Jun, K.W. and H. Singh (1996), 'The determinants of foreign direct investment: new empirical evidence', *Transnational Corporations*, vol. 5, pp. 67–106.

Knack, S. and P. Keefer (1995), 'Institutions and economic performance: cross-country tests using alternative institutional measures', *Economics and Politics*, vol. 7, pp. 207–27.

Krueger, A.O. (1997), 'Trade policy and economic development: how we learn', *American Economic Review*, vol. 87, pp. 1–22.

Lall, S. (1998), 'Exports of manufactures by developing countries: emerging patterns of trade and location', *Oxford Review of Economic Policy*, **14**(2), pp. 54–73.

Liu, J.T., M. Tsou and J.K. Hammitt (1999), 'Export activity and productivity: evidence from the Taiwan electronics industry', *Weltwirtshaftliches Archiv*, vol. 135, pp. 675–91.

Lloyd, P.J. and D. MacLaren, (2000), 'Openness and growth in East Asia after the Asian crisis', *Journal of Asian Economics*, vol. 11, pp. 89–105.

Mattoo, A. (2000), 'Developing countries in the new round of GATS negotiations: towards a pro-active role', *The World Economy*, vol. 23, pp. 471–90.

Michalopoulos, C. (1999), 'The integration of the transition economies into the world trading system', World Bank Policy Research Working Paper 2182.

Moran, T.H. (1998), *Foreign Direct Investment and Development*, Washington DC: Institute for International Economics.

Mortimore, M. (1998), 'Getting a lift: modernising industry by way of Latin American integration schemes. The example of automobiles', *Transnational Corporations*, **7**(2), pp. 97–136.

NASSCOM (2000), National Association of Software and Service Companies Annual Survey, available at http://www.nasscom.org.

North, D.C. (1997), 'The contribution of the new institutional economics to an understanding of the transition problem', World Institute for Development Economic Research Annual Lecture, United Nations University, Helsinki.

OECD (1999), 'Non-OECD countries and multilateral trade liberalisation: a background note on some key issues', Document no. TD/TC(99)18/FINAL, OECD, Paris.

Oyejide, T.A. (2000), 'Interests and options of developing and least-developed countries in a new round of multilateral trade negotiations', G-24 Discussion Paper No. 2, UNCTAD and Harvard University Centre for International Development.

Pain, N. (ed.) (2000), *Inward Investment, Technological Change And Growth: The Impact Of Multinational Corporations On The UK Economy*, Weybridge: Palgrave Press.

Pain, N. and D.W. te Velde (2000), *Exposure to International Markets and Corporate Performance*, report prepared for UK Department of Trade and Industry, London.

Panagariya, A. (2000), 'The Millennium Round and developing countries: negotiating strategies and areas of benefits', G-24 Discussion Paper No. 1, UNCTAD and Harvard University Centre for International Development.

Rodríguez, F. and D. Rodrik (2000), 'Trade policy and economic growth: a skeptic's guide to the cross-national evidence', *NBER Macroeconomics Annual*, forthcoming.

Rodrik, D. (2000), 'Development strategies for the next century', paper presented at World Bank Annual Conference on Development Economics, Paris.

Romer, P. (1993), 'Idea gaps and object gaps in economic development', *Journal of Monetary Economics*, vol. 32, pp. 543–73.

Sampson, G.P. (2000), 'The World Trade Organisation after Seattle', *The World Economy*, vol. 23, pp. 1097–118.

Sapir, A. (2000), 'EC regionalism at the turn of the millennium: toward a new paradigm?', *The World Economy*, vol. 23, pp. 1135–48.

Shah, A. and J. Slemrod (1995), 'Do taxes matter for foreign direct investment?', in A. Shah (ed.) *Fiscal Incentives for Investment and Innovation*, Oxford: Oxford University Press.

Smith, A. (1994), 'Imperfect competition and international trade', in D. Greenaway and L. Winters (eds) *Surveys In International Trade*, Oxford: Basil Blackwell.

Stiglitz, J.E. (1998), 'Towards a new paradigm for development: strategies, policies and processes', Prebisch Lecture, Geneva: UNCTAD.

Stiglitz, J.E. (2000), 'Two principles for the next round or, how to bring developing countries in from the cold', *The World Economy*, vol. 23, pp. 437–54.

Tu, J.-H. and Schive, C. (1995), 'Determinants of foreign direct investment in Taiwan Province of China: a new approach and findings', *Transnational Corporations*, vol. 4, pp. 93–104.

Tybout, J. (2000), 'Manufacturing firms in developing countries: how well do they do and why?', *Journal of Economic Literature*, vol. XXXVIII, pp. 11–44.

UNCTAD (1999), *World Investment Report 1999*, Geneva: United Nations.

Wang, Z.K. and L.A. Winters (2000), 'Putting "Humpty" together again: including developing countries in a consensus for the WTO', CEPR Policy Paper No. 4.

10. Designing a market enhancing WTO

J. David Richardson

1 OVERVIEW AND PRELIMINARIES

In Richardson (2000b) I argue that certain narrow new issues in global trade negotiations belong there quite naturally. I label these conformable issues 'market-supportive regulation'. Market-supportive regulation is regulation that enhances the 'market system', making it work better and for a broader constituency. That paper argues that ideally both market enthusiasts and society win from a commitment, more specifically to:

> Wise incorporation of market-supportive regulation into global trade negotiations, which is the key to generating a new wave of 'gains from trade' and to widely disseminating those gains within and among societies.

In this chapter I refine that argument. I emphasize two particular provocations. First, I believe that the World Trade Organization (WTO) is indeed the right forum for the new-issue experiments that I propose. Second, I believe that one very specific labour-relations policy, open trade in 'worker-agency services', is an excellent illustration of market-supportive regulation. My other illustrations are less provocative. They include a narrow subset of regulatory principles and practices from the domains of competition policies and technology policies.

But only a narrow subset. Only those regulatory principles that conform most closely to the market system – thereby enhancing it – belong on the WTO negotiating agenda. The rest would threaten the organization and hold back the progress of negotiations.

My provocations and terminology beg several questions.

Why not take a breather from global trade negotiations? The global backlash has been strong, and not just in Seattle; perhaps now is not the time. My answer is that the stakes in going forward are surprisingly high. It's still 'well worth it' for all WTO members, including the United States.[1] Furthermore, going forward on three specific new sub-issues has unappreciated value. It is a way to do two urgently needed things: to empower the global market system further and, simultaneously, to increase its constituency and thus enhance its broad legitimacy.

What privileges the 'market system' to lead me to recommend its further enhancement? First, I will argue that the market system is a remarkable social mechanism for reaching objectives of all kinds – necessary and noble, individual and communal, monetary and intangible – non-coercively. Second, and more important, I believe that the current market system needs an incentive to negotiate on issues of its own legitimacy, limits, and regulation. Its gains from negotiating new liberalization with new issues, standing side by side with procedural and material gains for worker organizations, technology users, and nascent and small firms, are what make my proposed way forward viable – because it is mutually beneficial, 'win–win'.

Why any new issues at all, however narrowly defined by the term 'market-supporting'? Why not WTO business as usual? Why not just say no to new issues?[2] I maintain that 'business as usual' is no longer an option. The broad, global backlash against it is here to stay.[3] There will be no results from multilateral negotiations this way, no chance to enjoy the new gains from global integration without some broadening of the perceived beneficiary base beyond business.

Why the WTO for my proposal – there are alternative forums and mechanisms? Part of my answer is that the WTO already oversees a market-supportive body of regulations; indeed that is its main purpose. Another part of my answer is that the WTO has already started implementing market-supportive regulation in the Trade-Related Aspects of Intellectual Property Rights (TRIPs) Agreement, and in telecommunications and other services (see Winham and Lanoszka (2000)). The last part of my answer is that alternative forums have proved incapable of handling new issues effectively (for example, the Organization for Economic Cooperation and Development (OECD) on investment) and unable to broaden the constituency of beneficiaries (for example, the North American Free Trade Area's failed attempt to draw in labour and environmental communities).

Why include incendiary labour issues, putting at risk easier and wiser incorporation of policies to buttress competition and technology diffusion? My primary answer is that without some more predictable means for typical workers worldwide to share in the gains from deeper global integration, there is no longer a political coalition to sustain it. Its mutual benefits, its win–win promises, are no longer adequate (Richardson *et al.* (1998)). My secondary answer is that well-designed regulations to govern worker-agency services actually alleviate market shortcomings; allowing open trade in worker-agency services would alleviate them even more.

But what do these idiosyncratic terms mean more exactly? Worker-agency services, market system, market-supportive regulation?

In Section 2 below, I describe what I mean by market-supportive regulation and by the market system, illustrating both in Sections 3, 4, and 5 by narrowly selected competition, technology, and labour policies. For labour, the internal policy that underlies external trade in worker-agency services is freedom of association and collective bargaining, one – but only one – of the internationally recognized 'core labour rights'. I finish with brief discussions of why domestic political constituencies might come to support incorporation of these narrow new issues into the WTO and how my proposal differs from those that emphasize political deal-making or economic 'democratization'.[4]

2   MARKET-SUPPORTIVE REGULATIONS AND THE MARKET SYSTEM

Market-supportive regulations are those that enhance the market system, making it more effective, stable, and sustainable. They are in fact vital organs for a healthy market system. But the terms in these brief statements need elaboration.

What I call the 'market system' is a peculiar mix of competition and cooperation. Everyone is familiar with the competition. But few reflect very deeply on the cooperation. Almost all the agents that compete are social groupings, whose internal organization is for the most part cooperative, not competitive. 'Firm' is the generic term for these agents – corporations, partnerships, labour unions, 'not-for-profits', and others.

Firms are both the suppliers of most products and services and also the principal buyers. Households, who are also cooperative social agents, are generally buyers only of final goods as consumers. These final goods are assembled from materials and components that have already been bought and sold many times by firms, through a long series of exchanges in both input markets and in internal, intra-firm transactions.

The market system is thus a complex, vertical and 'social' network of purchases and sales, contracts and conventions among firms – social agents. The market system is itself a mix of competition and cooperation, a social organism. The quality of the organism's competition and cooperation determines how effectively and efficiently it combines fundamental inputs such as worker services to produce final goods for those very workers. In other words, the quality of this social market system determines the standard of living of its workers.

Economic regulations condition this competitive-cooperative market system.[5] Among other goals, they aim to make the market system work better. Designed properly, they are market-supportive and simultaneously part of the social infrastructure.[6] They regulate the intensity of competition, the scope of cooperation, and define the due processes and legal boundaries for both, including the important boundary between coercive and voluntary transactions. Internal cooperation within firms is governed by such regulations as employment and company law. External competition and cooperation across firms is governed by such regulations as contract law and competition (antitrust) policy.[7]

Specific examples help to make this argument tight. For one example, company law enhances the market for corporate control; it establishes categories of voting rights and procedures for shareholders, and determines when and how a rival firm's managers can compete for the shareholders' allegiance (cooperation). For a second example, labour-relations law enhances the market for cooperative representation – agency;[8] it establishes workplace voting procedures for workers to be represented collectively by a union, and when and how another union could compete for certification to organize the workers cooperatively. For a third example, intellectual-property law aims to undergird the markets for artistic creation and productive innovation, indirectly compensating for externalities and for missing intergenerational markets.

In sum, the market system is thus socially populated, socially rooted, socially conditioned, and socially constructed. It is far, far away from the chaotically competitive 'law of the jungle' with which it is sometimes rhetorically confused.[9]

I argue that, correspondingly, a sustainable *global* market system will be socially constructed and conditioned, too, by policy design.[10] And I want to argue in the rest of this chapter that three kinds of limited, market-supportive economic regulations are natural companions to global markets, enhancing their performance and broadening their legitimacy, and natural friends of the WTO process.

3　MARKET-SUPPORTIVE COMPETITION POLICIES

Market-supportive competition policies are one of the best examples of regulation that conforms to the fundamental purposes of the WTO and that belongs under its umbrella. Multilateral trade negotiations and competition policies usually have very similar objectives.[11] The aim of both is more open, contestable, non-discriminatory market organization of economic activity. Contestability denotes the right to compete for market access by exporters, foreign investors (who would receive national treatment, with limited exceptions), and small and new home suppliers alike.[12] These groups are the beneficiaries and constituents of the WTO's incorporation of competition-policy baselines that we foresee and recommend.

I believe that the time is ripe for multilateral WTO negotiations over 'conditions of competition' – though they will take a long time to reach fruition and must properly begin in a very modest, procedural way. In previous writings, Edward M. Graham and I[13] recommended that first-generation initiatives include only the gradual commitment of all WTO members to implementing a baseline set of domestic competition policies concerning cartel practices and anti-competitive horizontal restrictions, and to creating guidelines for merger and acquisition. These baseline policies would be notified to the WTO, which would also oversee a process of consultations, but initially not formal dispute settlement.[14] To emphasize its modest, though market-supportive goals, we characterized this phase as 'cooperative unilateralism'.

Indeed Graham and I have argued that a 'conditions-of-competition' WTO agenda is becoming more and more natural and increasingly necessary. The concerns and ambiance of trade negotiation and grievance are rapidly changing. Concessions that concern regulatory practice pervade recent negotiations over insurance, financial services, intellectual property, telecommunications services, and Trade-Related Investment Measures (TRIMs). Contentions over new-economy industrial policies lie ahead in information technology, electronic commerce, agriculture, and technology-related investment requirements. Chinese and Russian accession to the World Trade Organization – or not – will ultimately rest on bargaining over internal accessibility policies, not border measures.

Social conditions of competition are the common theme in all these new concerns and ambiance. Who may compete with whom? Or displace them, or absorb them? Under what contingencies? With what kinds of government support? Using what processes, technology, contractual practices, employment relations?

Graham's and my initial proposals met significant scepticism, especially among American commentators, though less so among Europeans.[15] More recently, however, American antitrust officials have endorsed cautious moves in the 'cooperatively unilateral' direction we recommended. Specifically, they have embraced a Global Competition Initiative recommended by an expert panel (ICPAC, 2000) that would begin a process of plurilateral cooperation on competition policies. But it would be institutionally free-standing, a 'forum' focused initially on procedural cooperation and merger review, involving the WTO,[16] but not focused on it.

So why *should* the WTO be the focus? An important reason is that WTO-sponsored liberalization in key sectors such as services, telecommunications, and information technology will be the principal proving ground for how contestable global markets really are. A second reason is that baseline competition-policy commitments by large, would-be members of the WTO, especially China and Russia, will solidify the organization; without such commitments, all the more traditional WTO conventions 'at the border' will be seriously undermined by private practices 'behind' it (China, for example, still does not practise internal, inter-regional freedom of trade). A third reason is that the adoption of core competition policies in all WTO members helps to ease each member's transition toward more open borders. Enhancing internal contestability helps rationalize a country's internal market structure, allowing the fittest firms to prosper, absorbing weaker firms, and thereby finding it easier to cope with additional pressures from freer trade and investment. A fourth reason is that baseline competition policies protect an economy from the worst abuses of other policies that support markets by protecting technological property rights and rights of workers to associate and to be represented by an agent, policies to which we turn next.

4   MARKET-SUPPORTIVE TECHNOLOGY POLICIES

Like competition policies, market-supportive technology policies conform well to the fundamental purposes of the WTO. And the WTO has already embraced a first phase of technology issues in its TRIPs Agreement. At a basic level, technology is information. Reasonably complete, diffuse information is a pre-condition for markets to work well – effectively, fairly, with minimal discrimination. These three are virtually the same desiderata as the WTO pursues for global markets. Market-supportive information is the reason that the WTO insists on detailed, accurate 'notification' of policies by every member country (an unsung requirement and benefit of membership).

Markets work anyway, of course, in environments with imperfect or asymmetric information. But they don't necessarily 'work well'. A large microeconomics literature has shown this over the past twenty years. Imperfectly informed markets sometimes waste resources; they sometimes leave capable buyers isolated (rationed by discrimination); they sometimes violate the market system's self-imposed limitation to voluntary, non-coercive transactions.

I believe that imperfectly informed markets need regulatory support to enhance their performance and make them properly defensible. And this is also true globally. The current TRIPs Agreement embodies only half support at best.

The view that technology is basically information signals very clearly that technology is both a private good (an input) and a public good. Maskus (2000), in a definitive treatment of the TRIPs Agreement, conceives of intellectual property rights (IPRs) as 'fundamental inputs … public inputs …

public infrastructural investments'. As a private good, IPRs have the same value for information as property rights have for any good.[17] As a public good, technology-as-information markets are subject to the classic shortcomings of under-production and under-utilization.

I believe the time is ripe for significant, balance-oriented refinement of the TRIPs Agreement. My general reading is that the existing agreement is a good first phase in supporting the global market for producing new information, new ideas, and new technologies, but that ongoing second-phase TRIPs negotiations should more strongly support the global market for distribution. The existing TRIPs Agreement has focused more on generation than dissemination, more on supporting the market to produce innovation and less on supporting the business-to-business 'retail market' for technology users and traders. The two markets are very different, the agents (constituents) involved are very different, just as they are for electricity generation and distribution (US *Economic Report of the President* (1999), Ch. 5, pp. 211–18).

With this aim, in Richardson (2000b) I have proposed two families of market-supportive TRIPs refinements: market *facilitation* measures and *forbearance/standstill* on controversial carry-over issues.

1. *Facilitation.* There has been little formalization of the technical and financial assistance provision of the TRIPs Agreement (Part VII). New adopters of TRIPs regimens have been loath to pay their own administrative set-up costs, especially when short-term forecasts have these countries together paying out up to $5 billion annually in royalties and fees to IP-abundant countries (Maskus, 2000, Table 4.2, citing work by McCalman, 1998). A market-supportive way to cover up-front administrative fixed costs is to finance them by external loans from technology producers. The loans could then be serviced out of transitional 'facilitation fees' on cross-border royalties paid for host-country IP protection. Such an arrangement facilitates and finances mutually beneficial technical assistance, and licensing (technology distribution) as well. It is not foreign aid. It should be conceived as 'rent-reinvestment' rather than 'rent-shifting'. It could be tactically implemented by Patent Offices and by public–private consortia, rather than by diplomatic agencies. It would create natural forums for negotiating licensing and 'follow-on innovation', which aid in both the production and distribution of technology.

2. *Forbearance/standstill.* The current TRIPs Agreement preserves a great deal of national discretion (sovereignty). For example, there is national discretion on implementation definitions and procedures (such as 'working requirements'), publishing conventions for patents, exemptions (for example, for plant breeding, health-related and other non-commercial research, environmental and species preservation, non-commercial use), and treatment of parallel imports.[18] Such discretion has surprising market value in cultures and

environments where the very idea of property rights to technology is new. It allows experimentation with different standards and regulatory competition among them, in essence 'innovation' in the procedures of IP protection. Considerations like these suggest the value of regularizing such status-quo discretion, via a TRIPs standstill agreement, at least for a time, rather than pushing ahead with deeper, tighter TRIPs commitments along the technology-production lines emphasized in the existing TRIPs Agreement.[19]

I have also argued in Richardson (2000b) that technology aspects of the WTO's current TRIMs Agreement might also benefit from a standstill aimed at preserving national discretion (sovereignty). In particular, technology-transfer performance requirements on inward investors were not banned by the TRIMs Agreement.[20] Preserving a country's option to negotiate technology-transfer requirements for inward investors – a ban on any ban – is arguably supportive of the market for distributing technology. Unlike other performance requirements, these may 'pay off' in host countries.[21] Among other reasons, technology-transfer performance requirements encourage commercial negotiations over licensing, without dictating its terms. Otherwise anti-competitive, anti-market 'refusal to deal' can become entrenched. Many technologies are, in essence, akin to 'essential facilities' in the competition policies that govern transportation and telecommunications markets. And in such cases 'negotiated compulsion' *is* a familiar market-supportive tool of competition authorities (for example, compulsory divestiture, cease-and-desist orders, consent decrees over licensing) and of buyer-protection agencies (for example, compulsory warranties, truth in advertising).

But why the WTO for any of this? The most obvious reason is that the WTO has already committed to incorporating market-supportive technology regulations, not only in TRIPs and TRIMs, but also in its Information Technology Agreements, and maybe in coming e-commerce protocols. But most of the regulations support technology production. The time is ripe for a second phase, undertaking technology commitments along the distribution-oriented lines sketched above. If done wisely, the WTO will pull technology users into the group of beneficiaries from global integration and broaden its support base beyond the creative and well-heeled innovator community!

A less obvious reason for making the WTO the forum for technology-distribution agreements relates to competition policy. The TRIMs Agreement formally calls for competition policies to be taken into account when the agreement is subjected to its first WTO review. Furthermore, if the WTO adopted the subset of competition policy regulations proposed above, then it would almost surely have to refine the TRIPs Agreement as well. Perspective and practice on how competition policies need to be different, if at all, for technology-intensive activities, is still being worked out.[22] But the frontier of critical thinking in this area is clearly the tension between protecting the incentives to innovate and encouraging the distribution of its fruits.

5 MARKET-SUPPORTIVE LABOUR POLICIES

WTO agreement on a subset of market-supportive labour regulations is the most radical – and the most speculative – aspect of my thesis. It would encompass only one of the familiar core labour principles, specifically freedom of association and collective bargaining. It belongs in the WTO because it is basically a proposal for liberalization of trade in services – worker-agency services – the market services of agency that worker organizations and labour unions ideally provide.[23] It therefore falls sensibly under the rubric of the General Agreement on Trade in Services (GATS). Under my proposal, the International Labour Organization (ILO) would remain the forum for discussion of and commitment to the many important broader labour-market principles, beyond this one.

In Elliott and Richardson (2001), my colleague Kim Elliott and I evaluate, then endorse, open trade in worker-agency services. We see it as entirely conformable to the WTO's endorsement of open trade in other services. We understand such worker-agency services to encompass primarily: collective representation and bargaining over wages, benefits, and working conditions; workplace safety monitoring; grievance and dispute settlement; training, apprenticeship, and employee assistance; financial counsel (for example, for pensions) and management of other benefits (for example, child care). We emphasize the market-supportive character of these services. They alleviate market failures associated with collective action problems, workplace public goods,[24] imperfect information, and relationship-specific assets.[25] They discipline practices that border on coercion (recall that the market system presupposes voluntarism). They create countervailing market power to the anti-competitive market power of firms.

When entry and accessibility are present, that is, when alternative local and global suppliers can contest the right to represent workers as agents, they perfect the market for such services. They enhance their quality and variety, they encourage innovation in worker-agency services, they lower their cost.

We foresee the same sort of gains from open trade in worker-agency services as exist for other agency services. Open trade in accounting and legal services provides enhanced agency for users of information about firms (for example, investors in them). Open trade in distribution services provides enhanced agency for producers. Open trade in brokerage and underwriting provides enhanced agency for borrowers, entrepreneurs, and innovators.

Implementation of a market-supportive worker-agency agreement would necessarily proceed modestly and procedurally, because this is a radical idea in many dimensions. It would begin with a 'cooperatively unilateral' first phase, like that proposed for competition policy above. Only after reasonable success at that phase would we envision a TWAS (Trade-related Worker Agency Services) Agreement. It would cover freedom of association and the right to collective bargaining, and would include designated activities and/or sectors in which national treatment would be offered to foreign worker-agency organizations. Only after sufficient success in implementing this second phase would we propose widely cross-sectoral rights of establishment and national treatment for foreign worker-agency organizations, subject to a limited number of negotiated exceptions.

In the 'cooperatively unilateral' first phase, national discretion would be virtually unaffected – subject only to the commitment to implement baseline freedom of association and collective bargaining, to notify these commitments to the WTO as well as the ILO, and to submit to the kind of (non-binding) mediation, not dispute settlement, featured above in the first phase of market-supportive competition-policy commitments. Formal dispute settlement would be introduced only in the second-phase TWAS Agreement, which would be modelled on services commitments under the GATS.

Our focus on just the most market-supportive core labour right – freedom of association and collective bargaining – leaves a great deal of scope for both distinctive national labour-relations law, and for ILO initiatives to set and publicize best-practice standards on broader labour rights. Countries would have considerable flexibility, especially in the first phase, to regulate the locus of collective bargaining (plant, firm, industry, country); to determine conditions for strikes (sectoral restrictions, arbitration/mediation rules, worker-replacement strictures, and so on).

Our vision inevitably involves more than the traditional amount of competition among traditional unions and rival worker-agency institutions. It opens labour relations to cross-border competition, too. But our vision does not disparage traditional worker solidarity. In fact, it emphasizes the fact that some unions serve their combined membership better than others (with fewer internal inefficiencies or political diversions, and less corruption). It also emphasizes global worker solidarity – similar workers worldwide can collectively and globally modulate the competition among themselves in the same way that nationally unionized workers in a single plant or firm do.[26]

But why the WTO? The most important reason is that our proposed arrangements for trade in worker-agency services are market-supportive, market-opening, and indistinguishable from GATS protocols for other services. They open trade in labour-agency services to new entrants – specifically to traditional unions who are rethinking their objectives and economic roles under the heading 'new unionism', and to employee associations, expert consultancies, temporary-labour firms, and so on. Finally, certain familiar issues in labour relations such as contract compliance and certification/decertification have natural analogues in competition policy. We envision that a WTO competition-policy agreement could in at least several aspects be tailored to protect open and transparent competition to represent workers.

Critics, of course, will have much to say about the detail of this proposal. But they may have even more to say about its apparent fundamental weakness. 'Unions just aren't like that.' My answer is, 'Maybe some are not, but they should be.' Labour unions admittedly depart from market-supportive ideals, but so do firms. Mundane political objectives of labour unions can often conflict with market objectives (wages, benefits, working conditions), but mundane political objectives of firms similarly compete with their market objectives.[27] Labour unions can be undemocratic, but so can firms (for example, in voting vs. non-voting shares and in rights of minority shareholders). Labour unions can be corrupt, but so can firms.

6   WHERE THE LOCAL POLITICAL SUPPORT LIES

In democracies, no good idea is ever adopted without political support. Where would local political support come from for the thesis of this chapter, that the WTO should embrace a narrow subset of new issues to enhance global markets and buttress its own global legitimacy? At first, the answer seems to vary with a member country's standard of living.

Where would the local political support come from in richer countries? Not from the usual suspects. That would be looking for love in all the wrong places. The traditional private-sector trade community is sceptical about global competition policies, lukewarm toward information dissemination, and downright opposed to the global adoption of any core labour rights. At least for the moment … .

But small business ought to recognize the value of baseline competition-policy protection in foreign markets.

But educators and farmers and hospitals ought to recognize the value of baseline policies that facilitate distribution of technology.

But workers and their unions ought to recognize the value of multilateral support for the global association and bargaining rights that put them on the same footing as corporate owners of tangible and intellectual property rights.

And if small businesses, socially-oriented agencies, workers, and unions are *not* seeing any significant gains *for them* from further globalization of the traditional, naked kind, can anyone really blame them for thinking that multilateral liberalization serves only the profit-minded, capitalist owners of big business?

And where would the local political support come from in poorer countries? Not from corrupt elites. They will realize that their power is undermined by open markets – open markets that are sought by competition policy and that are enhanced by worker-oriented competition among unions and other labour agents. They will realize that their power is also undermined by the security of all kinds of property rights, including those to develop and fairly apply innovation and those to represent workers collectively.

But honest firms, and honest unions, and technology users, no matter how poor, are all potential gainers from these initiatives. So perhaps the answer to where the local political support lies does not vary across countries after all. Perhaps it can be summarized very crisply. Everywhere it comes from the 'margin' – the margin of persons and groups on the outer edge of gains from the narrow, naked globalization of commerce alone.

If, by contrast, the 'market system' – as I have described it – is what is on the WTO's negotiating table, are there not gains for large masses? *And* extra enhancement of global markets, too, as long as regulations are what I have called market-supportive? So that even commercial interests end up gaining, too, after all?

Surely there's more promise in positive WTO-based momentum on these new issues than the trickle-down of rising commercial tides, either within a country or among them!

7   CONCLUSION

I am persuaded that the WTO's incorporation of a narrow subset of market-supportive new issues would unleash large mutual gains to a broad constituency of businesses, worker groups, and others, and clear the way for more legitimate and more sweeping global market integration in the new millennium.

Others agree, at least in part. But my proposal for sequentially embodying market-supportive new issues in the coming WTO negotiations is importantly different from two others. One is the stance of real politique – concede new issues to 'buy off' the opponents of further global integration – 'feed the trade sharks' as one commentator put it.[28] The second is the populist stance of stakeholder economics, that somehow everyone has a civil or human right to voice or ownership in market institutions – therefore new constituencies have a natural democratic right to be at the commercial negotiating table with their new issues.

My problem with the first stance is that it is too crass, and yields too quickly to the near-zero-sum practice of tossing lesser bones to rival dogs.

My problem with the second stance is its fundamental misunderstanding of the limits of real democracy and the way that it has made itself prosperous by ceding conditional and exclusionary – apparently *un*-democratic – property rights to social market institutions.

NOTES

1. New research suggests sizeable gains to further global liberalization, even for relatively open countries like the United States. These gains are of many kinds – gains from goods *and* services, from stronger export engagement *and* deeper import dependence, and from inward *and* outward investment *and* technology transfer. Much of this new research has been carried out at the grass roots – firm-by-firm, worker-by-worker, county-by-county. It is surveyed in Richardson (2000a) and Lewis and Richardson (2001).

2. As recommended by, for example, a number of the chapters in Bhagwati (1999) and Bhagwati and Hudec (1996).

3. For evidence that the backlash characterizes even middle-class Americans, and not just Seattle street protestors, see Slaughter and Scheve (2001).

4. I plan a more detailed defence of the ideas in this chapter and in Richardson (2000b) in a forthcoming publication by the Institute for International Economics, including a discussion of how the WTO might practically incorporate the market-supportive new issues.

5. Many of the market's social groups have legal status that grants them the right collectively to own and exchange property, including intangible property (for example, intellectual property) and licences (for example, to represent a set of workers), and to differentiate and isolate their legal liability as group members from their liability as individuals.

6. This 'progressive' view of the way government regulation can support markets has deep roots in economic philosophy, the institutional school, and the social gospel, and surfaces frequently (Reich, 1991, World Bank, 1997, Holmes and Sunstein, 1999, for example), though is generally submerged by alarmist, populist accounts of the war between greed and governance. Garrett (1998, pp. 789ff.), for example, describes the potential for a 'virtuous circle between activist government and international openness'.

7. Not all economic regulations are market-supportive. Some are market-inhibiting – though often 'for a good cause' (for example, prohibitions on markets in socially dangerous goods and services, or limitations on current markets to avoid extinction of future markets, as in fisheries regulation). And still other regulations are distant from markets. So-called social regulation (Noll, 1997) is often motivated by non-material values and needs. Voting regulations, systems of education, criminal justice, national military service, and social-welfare and human-rights policies are all social regulations that are all less directly supportive of markets than the economic regulations above. Social regulations *are* important – vitally important – but they are not promising issues for impending negotiations that should aim to realize the large gains from further integration of global markets. Social regulations are too distant, too diversionary, not sufficiently conformable, orthogonal (Nivola, 1997, though Rodrik, 1997, Ch. 5 provides a counter-position).

8. Markets for agency are often missing because of well-known dilemmas such as coordination or collective-action problems.

9. So the prototypical 'economic man/woman' so common in elementary textbooks is really a rhetorical fiction. So, too, the mythical individual entrepreneur. Typical real market transactions involve competition and cooperation in a complex sequence among internally cooperative social groups.

10. Wright (2000) argues a similar thesis.

11. By contrast, bilateral and regional negotiations often have many other objectives, distant from competition policies, from coalition-building to regional security.

12. Contestability is not the same as market access, as usually described in trade negotiations.

As a right to compete, contestability is more akin to the idea of market 'accessibility'. Market access is then the fruit of successful competition. Antitrust specialists, unlike trade specialists, keep the concepts scrupulously distinct, for example in the counsel to 'defend competition, but not any given competitors'. Market accessibility is not hard to measure. Market accessibility is evaluated by all the new antitrust tests of entry barriers and foreclosure: effects of anti-competitive practices on prices; on competition upstream, downstream, and in adjacent regions and products; on the sunk costs of entry; and on the range of desirable attributes of a product or service.

13. See Richardson (1998a, b) and a series of papers brought together in Graham and Richardson (1997a, b). Other contributions include Graham (1994, 1995, 1996, 1998), Graham and Lawrence (1996), Graham and Richardson (1999), and Richardson (1995, 1997, 1999).

14. Only in a second phase did we imagine a commitment to negotiate a Trade-Related Antitrust Measures (TRAMs) Agreement, focused on first-phase baseline practices, and to bring normal dispute settlement to bear. Assuming satisfactory performance at this second stage, our third stage (TRAMs-plus) would extend the coverage to more controversial issues, including vertical practices and competition-policy 'safeguards' – exemptions for industries that are downsizing. The second and third stages of our proposal might be phased in at different rates by different member groups in the WTO, as in the case of TRIPs.

15. See Tarullo (2000) for a recent and extensive American scepticism. See Lloyd (1998), Lloyd and Vautier (1999), and Meiklejohn (1999), for less sceptical weighing of pros and cons. See Brittan (1997) and Van Miert (1998) for early European enthusiasm. Other recent and valuable discussions of the issues include Evenett *et al.* (2000) and the four Annual Reports of the Working Group on the Interaction Between Trade and Competition Policy (downloadable from www.wto.org under WT/WGTCP/number of report).

16. It would also involve the OECD, UNCTAD, the World Bank, governments, and practitioners and commentators in an advisory capacity. See, for example, Janow (2000).

17. Romer (1994) shows that the benefits (to a developing country, no less) from being able to import unique inputs, embodying new technology, are presumptively many times larger (20 times larger is his central calculation) than traditional calculations of the gains from trade. See also Lawrence and Weinstein (1999), who find evidence that imported inputs contributed importantly to Japanese and Korean productivity growth. See also Katz (1987). The message is, once again, that the stakes are still high for further global integration, even for developed countries like Japan and the United States.

18. Parallel imports are 'goods brought into a country without the authorization of the patent, trademark, or copyright holder after those goods were placed legitimately into circulation elsewhere' (Maskus, 2000, Ch. 4). Virtually no poorer countries regulate parallel imports. This allows them as pure buyers to 'shop for technology' from the cheapest source, consistent with static free-trade principles. The United States, as an important technology producer, restricts parallel imports in order to preserve the appropriate dynamic incentive (reward) for US innovators. The European Union adopts a halfway house between innovation incentives and free trade, banning parallel imports from outside its membership, but allowing them from within for the sake of the 'single market'.

19. The one exception to such discretionary forbearance might be negotiations to create a distribution-encouraging agreement disciplining parallel imports of public health-related products and technologies, as endorsed by Maskus (1999, 2000). The aim of such an agreement would be to allow some international price discrimination in relevant pharmaceuticals and related products, and to discipline the arbitrage that sometimes undermines it. The aim would be low prices in poor countries with significant public health needs, offset by higher prices in richer countries. The aim would be to expand markets to include users willing/able to pay only the marginal cost of public health-related goods. The 'progressivity' of the implicit financial transfers is obvious. The likely positive (global) welfare effects are less obvious, but are presumptively significant from the analysis of Malueg and Schwartz (1994).

20. It banned performance requirements covering compulsory local content and trade-balancing and foreign-exchange-balancing requirements (Schott and Burman, 1994, pp. 112–13).

21. They need not be imposed to be a powerful negotiating tool, and they will not be imposed if a valuable investor would go elsewhere. Moran (1998) argues persuasively that investor performance requirements for local content or joint ventures actually *inhibit* the global dissemination of technology. He is also critical of export and technology-transfer requirements, but not as persuasively. Both export and technology-transfer performance requirements, in fact, often serve as internal host-country antidotes to foreign investors negotiating exclusive, privileged, anti-competitive local market power (for example, exclusive rights to supply).

22. Gilbert and Shapiro (1997) and US *Economic Report of the President* (1999), Ch. 5.

23. See, for example, Stiglitz (2000), Part II. Pencavel (1991) is the most comprehensive treatment I know of labour unions as agents for their worker/principals, though he restricts his attention only to their wage, hours, and employment effects. See also Freeman and Medoff (1984), Freeman and Kleiner (1990), and Kochan (2000).

24. Workplace public goods are defined by Pencavel (1991, p. 6) as the unwritten rules and conventions that are too costly to write down in detail, and that benefit workers (and often employers) in a non-excludable, non-rival way.

25. Relationship-specific assets are essentially what a firm's incumbent workers provide. In general, contractual relationships add extra economic value to the intrinsic value of whatever assets the contracting agents bring to the relationship. But once negotiated, contracts are usually costly to break. In that case there is an incentive created for each agent, through opportunistic behaviour, to tilt the distribution of the extra value in their favour. This is called the 'hold-up' problem. Such opportunism, almost always present in contracts covering relation-specific assets, is more than a distributional question. It causes distortionary inefficiency in the form of under-investment in all relation-specific assets, including the employment relationship. On the general issues, see, for example Besanko *et al.* (1996), pp. 110–21. On their application to employment relationships, see Stiglitz (2000), pp. 16 passim.

26. For an account of labour agents' potential constructive role in modulating globalization, deregulation, and reform, see Freeman (1993), Section III and Stiglitz (2000), Part III.

27. See Pencavel (1998), pp. 30–40. For example, firms, like unions, can divert enormous resources from market activities to support political parties, candidates, and regulatory agencies whose decisions will guarantee the firms political access and political security.

28. Stokes (1999). See also Destler and Balint (1999) and Wright (2000) for more extensive proposals apparently motivated by real politique.

REFERENCES

Besanko, David, David Dranove and Mark Shanley (1996), *The Economics of Strategy*, New York: John Wiley.

Bhagwati, Jagdish (1999), *A Stream of Windows: Unsettling Reflections on Trade, Immigration, and Democracy*, Cambridge, Massachusetts: MIT Press.

Bhagwati, Jagdish and Robert E. Hudec (1996), *Fair Trade and Harmonization: Prerequisites for Free Trade?*, Volumes 1 and 2, Cambridge, Massachusetts: MIT Press.

Brittan, Sir Leon (1997), 'Competition policy and the trading system: towards international rules in the WTO', manuscript, remarks given for the Institute for International Economics, Washington, DC, 20 November.

Destler, I.M. and Peter J. Balint (1999), *The New Politics of American Trade: Trade, Labor, and the Environment*, Policy Analyses No. 58, Washington: Institute for International Economics, October.

Elliott, Kimberly Ann and J. David Richardson (2001), *Free Trade in Worker Agency Services*, Washington, DC: Institute for International Economics (forthcoming).

Evenett, Simon J., Alexander Lehmann and Berm Steil (eds) (2000), *Antitrust Goes Global: What Future for Transatlantic Cooperation?*, London: Royal Institute of International Affairs and Washington: Brookings Institution.

Feketekuty, Geza and Bruce Stokes (1998), *Trade Strategies for a New Era: Ensuring US Leadership in a Global Economy*, New York: Council on Foreign Relations.

Freeman, Richard B. (1993), 'Labor market institutions and policies: help or hindrance to economic development', Washington, DC, World Bank: *Proceedings of the World Bank Annual Conference on Development Economics 1992*.

Freeman, Richard B. and Morris M. Kleiner (1990), 'The impact of the new unionization on wages and working conditions', *Journal of Labor Economics*, 8 (January), pp. S8–S25.

Freeman, Richard B. and James L. Medoff (1984), *What Do Unions Do?*, New York: Basic Books.

Garrett, Geoffrey (1998), 'Global markets and national politics: collision course or virtuous circle?', *International Organization*, 52 (Autumn), pp. 787–824.

Gilbert, Richard and Carl Shapiro (1997), 'Antitrust issues in the licensing of intellectual property: the nine no-no's meet the nineties', *Brookings Papers on Economic Activity: Microeconomics*, Washington: The Brookings Institution.

Graham, Edward M. (1994), 'US antitrust laws and market access to Japan', in Henry B. Cortesi (ed.), *Unilateral Application of Antitrust and Trade Laws*, New York: The Pacific Institute/The Asia Institute.

Graham, Edward M. (1995), 'Competition policy and the new trade agenda', in Organization for Economic Cooperation and Development (ed.), *New Dimensions of Market Access in a Globalizing World Economy*, OECD Documents, Paris.

Graham, Edward M. (1996), 'Competition policy in the United States', in Carl J. Green and Douglas E. Rosenthal (eds), *Competition Regulation Within the APEC Region: Commonality and Divergence*, New York: Oceana Press.

Graham, Edward M. (1998), 'Contestability, competition, and investment in the new world trade order', in Feketekuty and Stokes (1998).

Graham, Edward M. and Robert Z. Lawrence (1996), 'Measuring the international contestability of markets: a conceptual approach', *Journal of World Trade*, 30 (October), pp. 5–20.

Graham, Edward M. and J. David Richardson (1997a), *Global Competition Policies: An Agenda*, Washington: Institute for International Economics, Policy Analyses in International Economics No. 51.

Graham, Edward M. and J. David Richardson (eds) (1997b), *Global Competition Policies*, Washington: Institute for International Economics.

Graham, Edward M. and J. David Richardson (1999), 'A US–EU road toward multilateralism in international competition policy', *Economic Perspectives* (An Electronic Journal of the US Information Agency), 4 (February), pp. 27–9.

Holmes, Stephen and Cass R. Sunstein (1999), *The Cost of Rights: Why Liberty Depends on Taxes*, New York: W.W. Norton.

Hufbauer, Gary C. and Rita M. Rodriguez (eds) (forthcoming), *Ex-Im Bank in the 21st Century: A New Approach?*, Washington: Institute for International Economics.

ICPAC (International Competition Policy Advisory Committee) (2000), *Final Report*, Washington: US Department of Justice, Antitrust Division.

Janow, Merit E. (2000), 'The Global Competition Initiative (GCI): possible next steps', manuscript.

Katz, Michael L. (1987), 'The welfare effects of third degree price discrimination in intermediate goods markets', *American Economic Review*, 77 (March), pp. 154–67.

Kochan, Thomas A. (2000), 'Building a new social contract at work: a call to action', Presidential Address to the Industrial Relations Research Association, January, manuscript.

Lawrence, Robert Z. and David E. Weinstein (1999), 'Trade and growth: import-led or export-led? Evidence from Japan and Korea', Cambridge, Massachusetts: National Bureau of Economic Research Working Paper No. 7264, July.

Lewis, Howard and J. David Richardson (2001), *Why Global Integration Matters Most!*, Washington, DC: Institute for International Economics: Globalization Balance Sheet Series.

Lloyd, Peter J. (1998), 'Multilateral rules for international competition law?', *The World Economy*, 21 (November), pp. 1129–49.

Lloyd, Peter J. and Kerrin Vautier (1999), *Promoting Competition in Global Markets*, Cheltenham, UK and Northampton, MA, USA: Edward Elgar.

Malueg, David A. and Marius Schwartz (1994), 'Parallel imports, demand dispersion, and international price discrimination', *Journal of International Economics*, 37, pp. 167–95.

Maskus, Keith E. (1999), 'Intellectual property issues for the new round', manuscript, October, to be published in Schott (2000).

Maskus, Keith E. *International Protection of Intellectual Property Rights: Evidence, Analysis, and Policy*, Washington, DC: Institute for International Economics, manuscript, August, forthcoming.

McCalman, Phillip (1998), 'Reaping what you sow: an empirical analysis of international patent harmonization', Canberra: Australian National University Working Paper in Economics and Econometrics 374.

Meiklejohn, Roderick (1999), 'An international competition policy: do we need it? Is it feasible?', *The World Economy*, 22 (December), pp. 1233–49.

Moran, Theodore H. (1998), *Foreign Direct Investment and Development: The New Policy Agenda for Developing Countries and Economies in Transition*, Washington, DC: Institute for International Economics, December.

Nivola, Pietro S. (ed.) (1997), *Comparative Disadvantages? Social Regulations and the Global Economy*, Washington, DC: The Brookings Institution.

Noll, Roger G. (1997), 'Internationalizing regulatory reform', in Nivola (1997).

Pencavel, John (1991), *Labor Markets Under Trade Unionism: Employment, Wages, and Hours*, Cambridge, Massachusetts: Basil Blackwell.

Pencavel, John (1998), 'The appropriate design of collective bargaining systems: learning from the experience of Britain, Australia, and New Zealand', *Comparative Labor Law and Policy Journal*, **20** (3), pp. 447–81.

Reich, Robert B. (1991), *The Work of Nations: Preparing Ourselves for 21st-Century Capitalism*, New York: Alfred A. Knopf.

Richardson, J. David (1995), 'Comment' on J. Michael Finger, 'Can dispute settlement contribute to an international agreement (institutional order) on locational competition?', in Horst Siebert (ed.), *Locational Competition in the World Economy*, Symposium 1994, The Kiel Institute, Tubingen: J.C.B. Mohr (Paul Siebeck).

Richardson, J. David (1997), 'Competition policies as irritants to Asia-Pacific trade', in David Robertson (ed.), *East Asian Trade After the Uruguay Round*, London: Cambridge University Press.

Richardson, J. David (1998b), 'Multilateralizing [competition policy] conventions',

Brookings Institution *Trade Policy Forum* on Private Practices and Trade Policy, Washington, DC.

Richardson, J. David (2000a), 'Exports matter ... and so does trade finance', forthcoming in Hufbauer and Rodriguez.

Richardson, J. David (2000b), 'The WTO and market-supportive regulation: a way forward on new competition, technological, and labor issues', *Federal Reserve Bank of St. Louis Review*, **82** (4), July/August, Proceedings of the Twenty-Fourth Annual Economic Policy Conference of the Federal Reserve Bank of St. Louis, pp. 115–29.

Richardson, J. David, Armando E. Rodriguez, Chi Zhang and Geza Feketekuty (1998), 'US performance and trade strategy in a shifting global economy', in Geza Feketekuty and Bruce Stokes (eds), *Trade Strategies for a New Era*, New York: Council on Foreign Relations.

Rodrik, Dani (1997), *Has Globalization Gone Too Far?*, Washington, DC: Institute for International Economics, March.

Romer, Paul (1994), 'New goods, old theory, and the welfare costs of trade restrictions', *Journal of Development Economics*, 43, pp. 5–38.

Schott, Jeffrey J. (2000), *The WTO After Seattle*, Washington, DC: Institute for International Economics.

Schott, Jeffrey J. and Joanna Burman (1994), *The Uruguay Round: An Assessment*, Washington, DC: Institute for International Economics.

Slaughter, Matthew J. and Kenneth F. Scheve (2001), *Worker Perceptions and Pressures in the Global Economy*, Washington, DC: Institute for International Economics, Globalization Balance Sheet Series.

Stiglitz, Joseph (2000), 'Development strategies and the labor market', Keynote Address to the Industrial Relations Research Association, Boston, Massachusetts, January, manuscript.

Stokes, Bruce (1999), 'Feeding the trade sharks', *National Journal*, July 24, p. 2180.

Tarullo, Daniel K. (2000), 'Norms and institutions in global competition policy', *American Journal of International Law*, 94 (July), pp. 478–505.

UNCTAD (United Nations Conference on Trade and Development) (1997), *World Investment Report 1997: Transnational Corporations, Market Structure, and Competition Policy*, New York and Geneva.

United States (1999), *Economic Report of the President*, Washington, February.

Van Miert, Karel (1998), 'The WTO and competition policy: the need to consider negotiations', manuscript, Speech/98/78, Geneva, April 21.

Winham, Gilbert R. and Anna Lanoszka (2000), 'Institutional development of the WTO', Chapter 2 of this volume.

World Bank (1997), *The State in a Changing World*, Washington, DC: World Development Report.

Wright, Robert (2000), 'Continental drift', *The New Republic*, January 17, pp. 18–23.

F13

F33

11. The world trading system: collective management potentials

Gavin Boyd

Study of the world trading system, as it operates under the auspices of, as well as outside of, the World Trade Organization (WTO), brings into view issues that set requirements for collective management, in the common interest, within regional contexts and at the global level. These issues are posed because of the largely ungoverned internationalization of market efficiencies and failures; imbalances in the spread of gains from foreign commerce; increasing disparities in the market strengths of firms; and shifts in the bargaining strengths and policy orientations of governments. Certain categories of issues relate to the WTO as a bargaining forum facilitating the negotiation of changes in economic openness, and as a regime in which the outcomes of interactions between governments depend in varying degrees on their observance of agreed although not fully internalized principles and rules. The principles and rules have been formulated as expressions of a spirit of cooperation, but the dominant bargaining processes are between the USA and the European Union, and with much adversarial legalism result in hard and precise agreements rather than affirmations of commitments to trustful and adaptive cooperation.

The structural and policy interdependencies of states are changing continually in the world economy, as firms competing for international market shares engage in foreign production and trade, and as governments make diverse attempts to increase structural competitiveness and to improve current accounts. Contrasts in cultures, institutions, and in corporate operations and in national policies have extensive effects, inviting analysis in terms of comparative interdependent institutional economics. The corporate and government rivalries tend to intensify when increases in economic openness are negotiated, and general awareness of this qualifies policy level endorsement of the simple rationale for trade and investment liberalization: competition policy problems, it is well understood, become larger and more difficult to resolve.

Reductions of trade barriers, through mostly unequal negotiations, principally between the EU and the USA, contribute to accelerations of concentration trends, as more competitive firms gain international market strengths at the expense of weaker rivals. Meanwhile the firms gaining dominance become more capable of overcoming the remaining trade barriers, often with the aid of investment bidding governments. Major causal processes in the evolution of the policy levels and the structural levels of the global political economy thus become evident. The two levels are linked, as the structural effects of corporate activities contribute to political changes, through shifting patterns of interest representation, and by evoking adaptive trade, industrial, investment, taxation, and competition measures. An overall trend is a weakening of economic sovereignty, reflecting common problems of political development, but governments in more integrated political economies can implement promotional measures that enhance economic sovereignty and structural competitiveness. In less integrated states the costs of deepening integration in the world economy, activating pressures from disadvantaged groups, tend to force adoption of protectionist measures. These, however, together with rising tax burdens associated with the costs of deepening integration, tend to encourage increased outward direct investment, in effect adding to those costs while reducing tax revenues.

As structural and policy interdependencies become more complex and more difficult to manage there are clear imperatives for wide-ranging cooperation. This tends to be considered more feasible in regional contexts than at the global level, and that is a factor in the attraction which the European Union has for neighbouring countries. It is also a factor, but with more ambiguity, in the attraction which free trade relationships with the USA have for Latin American countries.

Transregionally, there is a well recognized potential for collaboration between the European Union and the USA, based on high levels of structural and policy interdependence. These levels are changing, due primarily to high levels of US corporate dynamism, and there are serious frictions in Atlantic trade relations, but world commerce is dominated by this relationship. The degree of domination has been more prominent, in recent years, because of Japan's economic decline. If Japan were to become closely associated with the Atlantic relationship there could be strong Triad leadership for wide-ranging cooperation in the world economy. This can be affirmed with reference to the weaknesses of regional economic cooperation ventures in Latin America, Asia, and Africa.

MARKET EFFICIENCIES AND FAILURES

In the deepening integration in which countries are linked through transnational production, trade in financial assets, and arm's length as well as intrafirm trade in goods and services, market efficiencies and failures assume cross-border dimensions. These have consequences for interdependent growth and inflation. The efficiencies receive attention in policy statements and economic advice to governments advocating general increases in the openness of markets that widen the scope for economies of scale and specialization: these are the benefits of globalization. The failures are given much less recognition, and tend to be seen mainly in the context of disparities in the gains from international commerce.

The major efficiencies result from the operations of transnational enterprises extending their production and distribution activities across numerous countries, inducing host and home governments to provide market friendly environments, and drawing investment from diverse sources into what can be claimed to be highly cost-effective functions. Intensifying international competition, driving increases in efficiencies, meanwhile forces weaker firms into declines. At the same level, while labour remains immobile, the location decisions of transnational enterprises become sources of pressure for higher labour productivity and more active technology enhancing and generally supportive national policies. Overall technological progress, moreover, is aided because the leading firms consolidating their market positions are able to invest in frontier innovations at levels not possible for declining enterprises. The higher financing for innovation and also for organizational expansion is possible in part because of reduced exposure, through internationally dispersed operations, to the tax burdens of countries in which political competition has weakened fiscal discipline.

Oligopolistic strengths associated with the concentration trend, however, facilitate *pricing to market*, with the exploitation of weakened competition.[1] Meanwhile positive externalities, including technology diffusion, are offset by sectoral disruptions as related firms are disadvantaged by the relocation and restructuring strategies of the successful multinationals, especially following acquisitions. With the disruptions there is unemployment – a form of market failure often not recognized as such – and, while there are losses of human capital, there can be declines in business confidence which discourage new entrepreneurship.[2] Further, information failures tend to occur with the concentration trend, as firms in the ascendant can advantageously restrict flows of commercial intelligence, while indirectly lowering trust in what may be available. The creditworthiness of the successful firms, moreover, can be obscured because of the opaqueness of financial markets.

The financing of the most profitable firms is claimed to be an achievement of international financial markets, but it encourages short-termism and capital flight from slow-growing areas. More fundamentally, the funding of productive operations is affected by diversions of investment into trade in financial assets, which can be more profitable because of speculative appreciations and opportunities for tax avoidance.[3] The speculative activity can lead to financial crises – potentially devastating cases of market failure that evidence regulatory deficiencies and that can obligate government bailouts of distressed firms at public expense. What the speculative activity reveals, moreover, is not only unfounded investor optimism but a larger phenomenon of investor irrationality, on a scale which raises questions about efficiencies in financial markets.[4]

For the entire international political economy the efficiencies and failures associated with concentration trends and the expansion of financial markets are factors in the provision, and failures to provide, international public goods. Communication services, payment facilities, consulting activities, and orderly competition and cooperation between firms sustain coherent international patterns of production and exchange, but with deficiencies in service of the common good.[5] Potential complementarities in the development of corporate capabilities and strategies are not sufficiently sought and discovered; levels of trust and goodwill are generally low; restraints on the acquisition and use of oligopoly power are weak because of inadequate institutional development in business associations and deficiencies in the political will of governments. Further, stability in the increasingly linked real economies is endangered by the very risky speculation in financial markets.

Market forces are not overcoming the various market failures that are assuming cross-border dimensions. Corporate competition is pervasive, and it sustains the concentration trend, adds to the negative externalities associated with restructuring and relocation strategies, contributes to increases in information problems, and causes the neglect of public goods issues to become more serious. Imperatives for very extensive entrepreneurial cooperation can thus be seen, so that markets will become more comprehensively productive. Questions about the responsibilities of governments also demand consideration, not only because national policies aid many forms of corporate competition but also because spontaneous redirections of corporate behaviour, if they occur, are not likely to meet public goods requirements sufficiently.

GAINS FROM TRADE

The internationalization of market efficiencies and failures has effects in the spread of gains from trade, that is, in a broad sense, including gains from transnational production and commerce in financial assets. The most prominent imbalances are between the major industrialized states and the developing countries, and, in the Triad, between the USA and the European Union. All these imbalances have cumulative effects which alter relative bargaining strengths, generally to the disadvantage of Third World states whose prospects for outward-oriented growth are affected by discriminatory treatment of their low-technology exports.[6]

The disparities in gains from trade, while reflecting the consequences of internationalized market efficiencies and failures, also reflect the results of differences in bargaining strengths, and in their use. The bargaining strengths of successful firms increase as the concentration trend continues, and the bargaining strengths of large industrialized states and groups of states also increase. The economic involvement of governments, visible in the configuration of cross-border market efficiencies and failures, is also evident in uses of bargaining leverage that induce changes in economic openness that can open the way for more unequal competition in quests for market shares.

The general growth expectations implicit in the rationale for international trade liberalization thus have to be qualified in ways that indicate imperatives for overall governance, enlarging on the policy significance of market efficiencies and failures. Reductions of trade and investment barriers are conducive to growth because the scope for productive specializations by the most efficient firms is increased. Development by weaker firms is hindered, yet these may have long-term innovative potential, and may be victims of undetected anti-competitive activities. Further, the terms on which degrees of market openness are negotiated by governments, and the multiple forms of economic involvement by those governments, despite their losses of economic sovereignty, are continually altering the conditions of corporate competition, notably through tax favours and regulatory measures.

Of fundamental importance, moreover, in the consideration of disparities in gains from trade, are the effects of speculative asset appreciation, associated with high-volume and high-risk rent seeking in financial markets. Large investment flows can be drawn to a state experiencing speculation-led growth, despite the vulnerabilities that have to be reckoned with by other states. Firms benefiting from the speculation-led growth can strive more effectively to secure larger global market shares. This can greatly complicate the spread of gains from trade because the speculation-led growth will have strong import-drawing effects (unless the administration is firmly protectionist, in which case there will be inflationary pressures) while the nation's firms will be more inclined to serve foreign markets through transnational production than through arm's length exports.

Disparities in gains from trade resulting from generally productive operations, and disparities directly and indirectly due to large-scale rent seeking thus have to be recognized in comprehensive assessments of issues of governance in the world economy. Potentially destabilizing misallocations of investment in large-scale rent seeking have to be identified as challenges that demand much attention in discussions of requirements for collective management. If prospects for substantial reduction of speculative asset appreciation through national measures are not favourable, a system of collective management will have to be formed to ensure regulatory change under the pressures of external accountability.

INTERACTING GOVERNMENTS

Great differences in the bargaining strengths and strategies of governments, it must be stressed, and in their explicit and informal involvement in their national economies, as well as in the foreign operations of their firms, are evident in the real terms on which changes in market openness are negotiated, at the global and regional levels. In discussions of ways of structuring systems of collective management, questions about national entitlements to participate in decision making have to be considered. In the WTO the formal rule of one vote for each member state has secondary significance because agreements on market openness negotiated between the USA and the European Union invite acceptance by the rest of the membership, which is fragmented. The degree of Atlantic hegemony tends to increase as the European Union enlarges and as the USA initiates Latin American trade arrangements that begin to extend the North America Free Trade Area.

The unequal bargaining between governments is a pervasive factor to be recognized in a rationale for collective management: principles for determining the terms of national representation would be necessary elements of such a rationale. General acceptance of representation in a system of collective management on the basis of national economic size, or total population, would be difficult to achieve: transformation of the WTO into a structure with weighed voting for countries or groups of countries would accord with the interests of the international community but might not be agreeable to major states seeking to preserve the WTO simply as a bargaining forum.

At a very fundamental level the problems resulting from the bargaining strengths and strategies of the USA and the European Union will require changes in their policy processes. More integrative foreign economic policies will be necessary, and these will have to be supported and complemented by integrative orientations in the strategies of their firms. With such changes transformation of the WTO into a more representative structure with collective management functions would become more feasible. The imbalances in gains from trade and the internationalized market failures associated with those imbalances meanwhile would become less formidable problems.

In the USA assertions of corporate and labour interests, operating in the dynamics of policy processes very sensitive to constituency concerns, tend to motivate aggressive management of external trade relations in order to secure hard and precise agreements that can be used if necessary for litigation to enforce performance. The principle of reciprocity, which under the WTO is supposed to guide trade diplomacy, is relativized, and there is confidence in the nation's superior bargaining strength. The administration, while sensitive to the overall interests of the nation, has to be attentive to the demands of concerned groups, as it typically lacks the support of a well institutionalized political apparatus: the organizational weaknesses of the major political parties in effect cause the political process to function with agency style dynamics.[7] For this to be transformed into a source of high principled statecraft, exceptional leadership with much moral suasion will be necessary. Such an advance in political development is imperative in order to achieve harmonious and equitable US involvement in the world economy. Business associations, although fragmented by the divisive effects of a very individualistic culture, will have to become more public spirited, so as to provide supportive inputs into highly constructive foreign economy policy making and to inspire their members to work for equitable partnering with foreign enterprises, instead of viewing these as potential acquisitions.

Transformation of the European Union's policy processes, to express greater goodwill toward trading partners, build trust, and prepare the way for more harmonious development of the Union's structural interdependencies, will also require very dedicated leadership at policy levels and this will have to be supported by corporate associations with similar vision and commitment. In Europe's recent history the failures of totalitarian despotisms and the achievements of community-building leaders, especially Jacques Delors, together with traditions of close government–corporate relations, have contributed to receptiveness to concepts of cooperative rather than competitive capitalism.[8] Although the logic of market integration has stressed efficiencies driven by competition there is considerable awareness of the interests of workers in corporate stability, and of the social as well as economic value of managerial orientations toward sustained productive achievements rather than short-term rent seeking.[9]

A Union foreign economic policy guided by quests for structural partnering, complementing a similar US endeavour, could be a strong force for reform and development of the world trading system. The most significant results, in Atlantic relations, could be the development of more balance in structural competitiveness; reduced diversion of European investment into speculation-led growth in the USA; more amicable treatment of trade and investment disputes; and collaborative approaches to the problems of restructuring the WTO. With the emphasis on structural partnering, to be achieved primarily through the promotion of entrepreneurial cooperation for complementarities in direct investment planning, concerns about structural impediments to commerce would diminish.

The danger of a financial crisis in the USA, which overshadows the world trading system, would be gradually reduced by reorientations of European and American policies and corporate decision making toward building balanced, stable, and dynamic industrial complementarities. The strong rent seeking tendencies in the US political economy would be moderated, for the benefit of the real economy. This, moreover, would make monetary tightening for the restraint of speculation less necessary, and upward pressures on the exchange rate resulting from US growth would be lowered, to the advantage of US exporters. Improvement of the US current account, aided by some depreciation of the dollar as speculation-led growth slackened, thus reducing propensities to import, meanwhile, would help to reassure international investors, while restricting their scope for the exploitation of exchange rate volatility.[10]

POLICY LEARNING

The evolution of the world trading system, with its efficiencies, failures, imbalances, and uses of bargaining leverage, obligates new thinking about structural transformations in deepening integration. The rationale for general reductions of trade barriers in order to facilitate specializations that will have extensive growth enhancing effects becomes less persuasive, especially for countries with lagging structural competitiveness and inferior bargaining strengths. This is the case because increases in economic openness, even if resulting from fairly equal bargaining, tend to accelerate concentration trends: intensified competition pushes weaker firms into declines. International competition policy cooperation, if it develops, is expected to be an unequally negotiated process, with outcomes after protracted litigation and interactions during which the market positions of vulnerable firms will be weakened by the discriminatory explicit and tacit actions of stronger enterprises. Rational policies for states with inferior bargaining power are to delay trade liberalization agreements, while striving to enhance structural competitiveness. But departures from this logic may seem compelling; investment bidding opportunism can have short-term political rewards, although on balance there can be costs for national firms.

The structural policy endeavours of states with inferior bargaining power are likely to become more difficult because of the cumulative gains of strong firms acquiring larger international market strengths.[11] Hence participation in regional integration arrangements can be an appropriate choice if there are possibilities for collectively self-reliant industrial progress. If the regional arrangement is only a free trade system dominated by a state with superior bargaining strength, however, participation may well have serious disadvantages, because of the competitive advantages of firms in the dominant state and losses of market access in the external environment.

Regional options depend on locational factors as well as potentials for collective management and community formation. Proximity to the EU is a major factor in the choices of its immediate neighbours. For Latin American countries, however, entry into an expanding North American Free Trade Area which is not set to evolve into a community is a difficult choice, complicated by the effects of failures to build Latin American regional integration systems.[12] For industrializing East Asian countries the weaknesses of the Association of Southeast Asian Nations and the constraints on Japan's policies because of its recession and heavy dependence on the US market, severely limit trade policy options.

In the political economy of the world trading system, then, issues of multilateral liberalization are significant in quite diverse contexts. For prospective members of the European Union the terms of entry are far more important than the possible advantages of involvement in multilateral trade negotiations, and any such involvement has to be guided by EU preferences. For Canada and Mexico, very heavily dependent on the US market and receiving mainly US direct investment, participation in multilateral trade interactions is of secondary importance, and bargaining strengths in relation to the USA are declining. For most Latin American countries multilateral trade issues are less important than opportunities for freer trade with the USA, and, to a lesser extent, with the European Union.[13] Trade policy interactions with the USA also have more significance than multilateral negotiations for industrializing East Asian states and for Japan – more so than might have been anticipated before the East Asian financial crises of the late 1990s.

Policy learning based on consideration of the potential benefits of general trade liberalization thus tends to have limited and probably declining interest for many members of the WTO. For European Union states, moreover, trade issues within the single market have much greater prominence than opportunities for freer international commerce, and those opportunities are significant mainly in Atlantic relations. Gains to be expected from multilateral reductions of trade barriers, however, are major considerations for the USA, because of its central role in the world trading system and the magnitude of its trade deficits.

The USA's role is also distinctive because of problems regarding the *internal* spread of gains from foreign commerce – problems which raise questions about the rationale for multilateral trade liberalization, and which have to be confronted in Europe also. In the free trade rationale there is tacit recognition that increased economic openness puts downward pressure on labour in industrialized states as their commerce expands with Third World areas. This recognition has to be supplemented with references to the additional downward pressure on wages in industrialized states as their firms expand foreign production. Further qualifications, it must be stressed, have to be made because of the effects of sectoral disruptions associated with import penetrations that pose difficult adjustment problems and with corporate relocation and restructuring strategies.[14]

In-depth assessment of the structural factors determining the real effects of free trade tends to become more and more important in American, European, and Third World policy learning. Enhancing the benefits within national political economies and between them, while reducing the domestic costs and the international imbalances, is clearly a task of great complexity: it cannot be expected to result from the independent pursuits of market shares by the vast numbers of contending firms, aided in diverse ways by unequally competing governments. Regulatory imperatives are evident, but the fundamental requirement, it must be stressed, is wide-ranging corporate cooperation. The concerns of workers in industrialized states, as Rodrik has demonstrated, are well founded, and so are those of workers in less industrialized states as these experience structural changes in the course of ungoverned globalization. The costs of adjustment – in welfare and retraining programmes – tend to fall more heavily on workers, particularly in industrialized states, as firms reduce taxation by extending foreign operations. Meanwhile political processes in industrialized states tend to become more polarized between gainers and losers, and this can be to the advantage of political parties operating as large distributional coalitions.[15]

In the necessary in-depth assessment, finally, the free trade rationale has to be adjusted to take account of the effects of high-volume trade in financial assets. This must be reiterated, in view of the basic interests of savers in countries from which investment is flowing to high-risk growth areas, and more importantly in view of the dangers of large-scale destabilization, because of the dynamics of speculative asset appreciation. The dangers increase as the commerce in financial assets expands, because of its profitability and scope for tax avoidance. Real economies are affected by the resulting misallocations of investment, and meanwhile these contribute to the overall concentration trend in the world trading system.

THE WTO AND THE IMF

The problems in the structural evolution of the world trading system demand fundamental change in the World Trade Organization, through enhanced representation arrangements, the introduction of weighed voting, and an orientation toward the development of structural complementarities, in conjunction with the negotiation of reductions in trade and investment barriers. This transformation of the organization could be aided by the International Monetary Fund (IMF) through surveillance and advocacy endeavours to promote reform in international financial markets and advances in the coordination of sound macro-economic policies by the USA, the EU, and Japan. The IMF is well placed to begin these tasks without delay, and the political will to apply energies to these endeavours could be formed with Atlantic leadership, especially if the European Union becomes represented in the Fund as a single unit. Conditions for reform of the WTO, which no doubt would be a longer-term process, would then be more favourable. Institutional development of the IMF could be activated in support of its enhanced roles in financial market reform and Triad macroeconomic coordination.

The IMF operates under strong US influence, due to the weighing of votes, and its lending to distressed Third World countries has special significance for US financial institutions whose loans to such countries have been at risk. Conditions attached to the IMF lending have obliged receiving governments to avoid restraining imports – despite the gravity of their balance of payments problems – and to become more open to foreign direct investment, especially in financial sectors. Although this conditionality has been criticized by Western economists, on grounds of equity and because it forces irrational dependence, Third World countries have lacked the solidarity that would be needed for leverage to induce change.[16] Economic advice from the IMF has appropriately stressed requirements for financial market reform in the distressed countries, but the Fund's assessments of their problems have discreetly avoided references to the predatory operations of US and other institutions in Third World financial markets.

European Union representation as a single unit in the IMF would be an advance in its institutional development that would broaden the scope of its responsibilities, on the basis of European concerns about problems of stability in world financial markets. The Union's vulnerability to the destabilizing effects of a crisis in the USA is increasing as Atlantic financial links become stronger. The British economy is extremely vulnerable, but British policy, influenced by the importance of financial ties with the USA, could hinder a European drive for single representation in the IMF and the formation of a political will to orient the Fund toward stabilizing functions in the global economy. At the same time British policy could also hinder European Union initiatives for restructuring and institutional development in the WTO unless these were favoured by the USA.

The European solidarity that is clearly required to reorient the IMF toward the urgent tasks of financial market reform and macroeconomic cooperation would be vital for the development of a more functionally representative WTO. Divisive factors in the EU's WTO involvement tend to encourage US unilateralism, based on strong bargaining strength and motivated by concerns about unsustainable trade deficits – that is, in the absence of a European foreign economic policy orientation with firm cooperative intent. In the dynamics of Atlantic interactions, a united and highly constructive European stance, through learning and accountability effects, could induce reciprocation in US policymaking, overcoming its tendencies toward pragmatic disjointed incrementalism and aggressive unilateralism. To promote such partnering, and institutionalize it, the formation of Atlantic policy communities could be a high-priority EU objective. This would be an opportunity for a vital expansion of the European Commission's functions and those of the European Central Bank. The European sponsorship of the transregional policy communities, moreover, could occasion recognition of a need for high-level knowledge-intensive inputs that could be provided by a European Council of Economic Advisers, constituted as an independent institution. As a dialogue partner such a council could have a dynamic relationship with the US Council of Economic Advisers, which tends to be pressed into the service of presidential political interests.[17]

A restructured and refocused IMF, drawing on the expertise of Atlantic policy communities, could become the principal source of advocacy for the reform and stabilization of international financial markets. The rationale for this advocacy would have to stress imperatives for tight regulation of trading in corporate securities and substantial taxation of such trading. Additional elements of the rationale would have to be the interests of workers in corporate stability, and the complementarity between these interests and those of central banks in restraints on speculative asset appreciation, and in maintaining the effectiveness of monetary transmission mechanisms, through restrictions on the growth on securities sectors.[18] A fundamental theme, expressing the vital importance of the widened IMF mandate, would be the urgency of overcoming potentially very destructive speculation in world financial markets, as well as their diversions of investment from service of the real economies.

Triad macroeconomic policy coordination, promoted by the Fund in conjunction with its reforming efforts in financial markets, would contribute to greater order and dynamism in the world economy. Fund advice has been repeatedly urging Triad fiscal discipline in order to restrain expansionary pressures generated by political competition, and thus facilitate increases in interdependent growth as well as reductions in sovereign debt burdens that invite speculation in financial markets. As increases in the costs of globalization tend to obligate higher welfare spending, however, especially in Europe, Fund advice has to relate more comprehensively to fundamentals. This will mean intensive encouragement of policy learning about imperatives for functional order in world trade and finance that basically obligate broad structural cooperation. The lesson to be imparted is that without such partnering the imbalances in gains from commerce between states and within states will have disruptive and growth-retarding effects, and these will probably make collective remedial responses more difficult.

The rationale for a restructured and refocused IMF may be challenged on the ground that international market discipline is a vital form of pressure on governments for effective macromanagement: if industrialized states fail to curb destabilizing speculation, the severe consequences will force them to work for stability in the future, and if industrializing states mismanage their financial sectors the gravity of the results will then obligate reform. Constructive thinking about the IMF, however, rests on the logic of institutionalized external accountability as a source of pressure for government performance in contexts of high and intricate policy and structural interdependence. Such external accountability can counter tendencies toward inward looking and politically expedient policymaking.[19]

The logic of building structures of external accountability can be reinforced with observations about international market discipline. The discipline of international financial markets, it must be stressed, is not altogether functional in the interests of real economies. Successful speculators can in effect penalize profitable firms that are not committed to short termism and that are not chosen as targets for tacitly collusive upward bidding, and subsequently those targets can be replaced by others. Perception of the discipline in international financial markets, moreover, is difficult not only because the current strategies of the speculators are constantly changing and are not revealed, but also because these markets are tending to become more opaque, especially because of the use of highly sophisticated financial instruments designed to hedge against but also exploit volatility.[20] What may be identified as market discipline represents the effects of failures as well as efficiencies in financial markets. Where the failures occur because of the regulatory deficiencies and confidence-lowering defects of governments, other administrations thus disadvantaged must be able to operate through structures of external accountability.

The discipline in international markets for goods is commonly attributed to competitive pressures. Failures in these markets, however, tend to become larger as they assume greater cross-border dimensions, thus affecting growth and employment in many states. Individually, moreover, such states often lack the bargaining leverage that would be necessary for effective representation of their interests. This is especially apparent when moderately sized industrializing states have to reckon with increasing oligopolistic strengths in international high-technology markets – that is in the absence of regional or high-level competition authorities.[21] With continuing concentration trends, international discipline in markets for goods becomes more oligopolistic.

Expanded responsibilities for the IMF can thus be seen, primarily regarding financial markets but also with respect to the interdependencies of real economies inadequately serviced by those markets. The operations of international financial markets, while contributing to concentration in those markets, also contribute to concentration trends in global markets for goods. Altogether, then, the contributions which the Fund could make to sound structural evolution in the world trading system could be substantial. For these contributions to be made, however, a vigorous European role in the Fund would no doubt be necessary.

THE WTO AND THE WORLD ECONOMY

Without highly constructive political entrepreneurship, supported by corporate associations, the World Trade Organization must be expected to evolve as a conflicted bargaining forum, dominated by changing mixes of cooperation and aggressive unilateralism in Atlantic relations. The balance of bargaining strengths in those relations will shift as the European Union continues to enlarge, but the Union's capacity for macromanagement may be weakened by strains, especially between Germany and France, over issues in its system of governance. Japan's role in the Trilateral pattern will remain peripheral, because of heavy dependence on the US market and the constraints due to slow recovery from the financial crises of the late 1990s. Prospects for the emergence of viable Third World regional integration systems are significant only in Latin America, and may diminish if the USA negotiates preferential trade arrangements in that area.

The main processes of structural change in the world economy will continue to result, more and more, from the transnational production operations of international firms, mainly those based in the USA, and these will no doubt strengthen their presence in Europe, without being significantly affected by stresses in Atlantic trade relations. With the expansion of international financial markets, meanwhile, portfolio investment flows will tend to be larger than foreign direct investment flows. The USA's attraction of mainly passive investment, because of high speculation-led growth, will be the central process in international finance, sustaining considerable emphasis on diversions of funds away from productive use. Dangers in this complex process, however, will increase, because stock appreciations have been tending to rise well above sustainable levels in the USA, and, in conjunction with the large US trade deficits, are challenging investor confidence.

The negotiation of further international trade liberalization under WTO auspices will be very difficult. For the USA very substantial increases in access to foreign markets will be necessary to facilitate export expansion, and this urgent need will encounter European resistance. European structural competitiveness will continue to lag, and in Europe the benefits of monetary union will tend to be seen mainly in terms of regionally based growth. Japan will be tacitly reluctant to support multilateral trade liberalization proposals, because of its concerns with increasing domestically based growth for complete economic recovery. Many Third World states, moreover, will see advantages in the adoption of delaying tactics, because of anxieties about US leverage. Further, European, Japanese and Third World policymakers will be very much aware of the prospect of internal dissent in the USA, caused especially by opposition from organized labour, and of the USA's altered status in the WTO because of its failure to prevent the mob violence that disrupted the Seattle WTO Ministerial meeting in 1999.

US interest in multilateral trade liberalization will undoubtedly be complemented by endeavours to expand regional trade links. Opportunities for the development of these in Latin America have become more encouraging because of disputes between Brazil and Argentina that have weakened Mercosur, and because the European Union has been neglecting the development of its economic ties with Latin America. The danger of protests by organized labour discourages US trade liberalization initiatives directed at Latin America. If Mexico develops preferential trade links with other Latin American states, however, these may well provide scope for the Southern expansion of US commerce through Mexico. Yet in the development of its Latin American commerce, through direct and indirect links, the benefits for the USA's trade balance may only be moderate because of the priority given by US firms to the service of Latin American markets through transnational production.

Stronger US corporate emphasis on transnational production for foreign markets is a trend to be expected because of the hostility of US labour unions to trade liberalization initiatives, and the probability that such initiatives, even if the domestic opposition can be overcome, would promise only slow results. Accordingly, while any US liberalizing endeavours in the multilateral context are not likely to elicit enthusiastic European, Japanese, or Third World responses, investment bidding to attract US enterprises is likely to increase, especially in the developing areas, and particularly in Latin America. General awareness of the opposition of US unions to free trade, if increased by dramatic indications of the strength of that opposition, will tend to increase the investment bidding, in Latin American and other areas. This, however, will not result in openness to proposals for a multilateral investment agreement. The investment bidding governments, especially in Third World areas, value their freedom for discretionary treatment of incoming foreign direct investment, and are unwilling to accept WTO or any other disciplines in this regard. The failure of Triad initiatives for a Multilateral Investment Agreement, which had evidently encouraged the Seattle rioters and weakened the interest of the Clinton administration, revealed conflicts in Atlantic relations that have made renewed Triad collaboration in this area very unlikely.

European Union promotion of multilateral trade liberalization is a complex process in which the organizational interests of the European Commission and its status in the Union tend to benefit from adversarial management of commercial issues, especially in Atlantic relations, that is while it seeks to expose Union firms to challenging competitive pressures. For member states the overall gains to be anticipated will be uneven, with Germany being especially advantaged. Most members will probably have stronger interests in their investment bidding strategies, which in the longer term will contribute mainly to the expansion of the US corporate presence in the Union. For firms constituting this presence the potential benefits of further Atlantic trade liberalization, although significant, are evidently not worth the costs of strains that could be caused in relations with their host governments by pressing for freer Atlantic commerce.[22]

Because of the size of its trade deficits the USA may be obliged to impose restrictions on imports, particularly from countries with surpluses in bilateral commerce. The restraints could move the current account into balance without substantially affecting investment inflows, and would in any case be welcomed by labour groups and firms in sectors experiencing strong import penetration. Multilateral interactions on trade liberalization issues, however, would become more conflictual, depending on the reactions of targeted states and others. Meanwhile, demands for further protectionist measures would undoubtedly be made by groups in less competitive US sectors, provoking adverse foreign reactions.

Actual or threatened US import restrictions, it must be stressed, would add to the incentives for US firms to expand their foreign production activities further, for more secure penetration of international markets, as well as to take advantage of likely increases in investment bidding. Any indications of heightened dangers of a financial crisis in the home economy, moreover, would also add to the incentives to spread transnational production more widely, particularly in Europe, where vulnerability to the effects of a US financial crisis, although increasing, is still at moderate levels.[23]

The central significance of the USA in the world trading system, as it is shaped by structural changes, is posing more sharply issues for Europe, Japan, and many other states. These issues will affect assessments of and attitudes toward multilateral trade negotiations, and will tend to obligate expansion of the negotiating agendas, especially because of the increasing prominence of underlying structural concerns – concerns that are becoming more closely linked with problems of international competition policy cooperation. These problems, it must be noted, will become more intractable, and yet more susceptible to unequal bargaining solutions, as multilateral trade interactions become more conflictual.

Altogether, the probabilities that can be projected from trends in fundamentals necessitate intense focus on possibilities for constructive American statecraft, with concerted entrepreneurial cooperation. The potentially great importance of a new integrative thrust in the European Union's foreign economic relations thus deserves much attention because of the inspiration which it could communicate and the learning which it could activate at government and corporate levels. Reciprocal policy learning and entrepreneurial learning, with broad and very active accountability, has become necessary because of the dimensions and stresses of Atlantic policy interdependencies and structural interdependencies. In this way engagement with fundamentals, receptive to Japanese involvement, could become a basis for partnering with Latin American and East Asian countries. This would be a major advance toward restructuring the principal commercial linkages in the world economy, and thus reconstituting the World Trade Organization, with broader yet more manageable responsibilities.

Drawn from fundamentals, the thinking for institutional development of the WTO on a basis of alliance capitalism for structural partnering could offer a way forward for collective governance of the global political economy. This would overcome problems of internationalized market failure and of imbalances in the spread of gains from commerce, domestically and across borders, while inspiring more integrative bargaining over questions of market openness. Quests for hard and precise agreements on trade and investment liberalization would decline, and the trend toward adversarial legalism in multilateral interactions would diminish. With the general increases in trust and goodwill, meanwhile, regional integration systems in Third World areas could be given encouragement and support, to generate the growth effects of single markets.

The problems of the world trading system, it must be reiterated, demand comprehensive understanding of the overall effects of corporate strategies and national policies, without unwarranted assumptions about evolutionary progress toward any kind of equilibrium, or about requirements to sacrifice social justice concerns in the interests of economic efficiency. Such concerns have been appropriately criticized in the Special Issue of the *Cambridge Journal of Economics*, November 2000, on Social Justice and Economic Efficiency. Well founded social justice and efficiency considerations converge, it must be stressed, to provide a basis for wide-ranging integrative cooperation, restraining concentration trends to provide wider scope for concerted entrepreneurship, directing investment entirely into productive activity, and facilitating the development of social capital in civic societies.

The structural partnering that can be hoped for in Atlantic and then in Triad economic relations, inspired by concepts of advanced alliance capitalism, could give new inspiration and encouragement to Russian policymakers and corporate elites. For the rebuilding and development of their political economy they have received much advice about the efficiencies of market forces in competitive rather than cooperative capitalism. For them the principal policy implications have concerned the degrees to which the national economy should be opened to foreign trade and investment, and on what terms, given the disadvantages of weak bargaining strength. There is an understandable emphasis on strengthening the role of the state in the economy. From the Atlantic side this should receive enlightened responses that will moderate Russian anxieties about Western economic penetration and inspire confidence in the possibilities for equitable structural partnering. On the Russian side there is scope for knowledge-intensive contributions to Western policy learning and corporate learning about imperatives for more order, stability, and social justice as deepening intregration continues in the world economy.

Problems in the structural evolution of the world trading system are challenging Atlantic elites to engage in more constructive dialogue with China also. China's entry into the World Trade Organization involves acceptance of Western demands for economic liberalization. Reduction of the government's explicit role in finance, production, and exchange thus entails greater reliance on informal methods of coordination and control, which can be seen to offset the competitive advantages of foreign firms, and their forms of tacit collusion, as well as the formal and informal assistance they receive from their governments. The Chinese involvement in world trade is exceptional because its exports of low-cost consumer items help to keep down inflation in the USA, thus in effect allowing US monetary policy to be more tolerant of speculative asset appreciation. China's financing of outward-oriented industrial growth at rising technological levels thus becomes more feasible, that is in conjunction with inflows of foreign direct investment, informal guidance of which is vital for the regime's structural policy. Basic change in the orientations of Western elites, demonstrating credible commitments to equitable structural partnering, and cultivating trust in integrative cooperation, is clearly needed for the development of a fully productive Chinese role in the world trading system.

Very demanding international public goods imperatives have to be recognized by US and European elites. The highly constructive knowledge-intensive responses that are necessary will have to be made on a long-term basis, and will have to be well institutionalized. For this to be appropriately planned, initiatives will have to be taken to build very active Atlantic policy communities, linked in consultative networks with a European Council of Economic Advisers and an outward-oriented US Council of Economic Advisers.

NOTES

1. See references to pricing in Rangan and Lawrence (1999).
2. The most serious declines in business confidence have been in Europe, where they have been responsible in a large measure for outflows of investment to the USA.
3. On the speculative appreciations see Wolf (2000).

4. See symposium on financial market instability, *Oxford Review of Economic Policy*, 15, 3, Autumn 1999 and Schleifer (2000).
5. See Kaul et al. (1999).
6. Third World countries are disadvantaged in the WTO. See Das (1999).
7. See Deardorff and Stern (1998).
8. See Cohen and Boyd (2000) and Blair and Roe (1999).
9. See Blair and Roe (1999).
10. A key problem is the sustainability of the US trade deficit. See Mann (1999).
11. See trends indicated in UNCTAD (2000).
12. See Appendini and Bislev (1999).
13. See Appendini and Bislev (1999) and Wrobel (1998).
14. See *Cambridge Journal of Economics*, 24, 6, November 2000, Special Issue on Social Justice and Economic Efficiency.
15. On the problems for workers see Rodrik (1999). See also Boix (1999).
16. The lack of solidarity is reflected in Das (1999).
17. See Stiglitz (1998).
18. See Blair and Roe (1999) and, on the growth of securities sectors, see Enoch and Green (1997), especially chapters 5, 6 and 13.
19. European Union representation in the Fund as a single unit would oblige the USA to manage its involvement in the Fund with increased sensitivity to Union views and preferences. See discussion of Fund dynamics in Henning and Padoan (2000).
20. See Enoch and Green (1997), especially chapter 13.
21. On problems of competition policy cooperation see *The World Economy*, **21**(8), November 1998, symposium on Competition Policy, and Lloyd and Vautier (1999).
22. A Transatlantic Business Dialogue of European and US senior executives has urged the USA and the EU to seek cooperative solutions to Atlantic trade disputes – *Financial Times*, 6 December 2000.
23. Except in the case of Britain: see Wolff (2000).

REFERENCES

Appendini, Kirsten and Sven Bislev (1999), *Economic Integration in NAFTA and the EU*, New York: St Martin's Press.

Blair, Margaret M. and Mark J. Roe (1999), *Employees and Corporate Governance*, Washington DC: Brookings Institution, Part II.

Boix, Carles (1999), *Political Parties, Growth and Equality*, Cambridge: Cambridge University Press.

Cohen, Stephen S. and Gavin Boyd (eds) (2000), *Corporate Governance and Globalization*, Cheltenham, UK and Northampton, MA, USA: Edward Elgar.

Das, Bhagirath Lal (1999), 'Strengthening developing countries in the WTO', *International Monetary and Financial Issues for the 1990s*, Vol. XI, Geneva: UNCTAD.

Deardorff, Alan V. and Robert M. Stern (eds) (1998), *Constituent Interests and US Trade Policies*, Ann Arbor: University of Michigan Press.

Enoch, Charles and John H. Green (1997), *Banking Soundness and Monetary Policy*, Washington DC: International Monetary Fund.

Henning, C. Randall and Pier Carlo Padoan (2000), *Transatlantic Perspectives on the Euro*, Washington DC: Brookings Institution.

Kaul, Inge, Isabelle Grunberg and Marc A. Stern (eds) (1999), *Global Public Goods*, Oxford: Oxford University Press.

Lloyd, P.J. and Kerrin M. Vautier (1999), *Promoting Competition in Global Markets*, Cheltenham, UK and Northampton, MA, USA: Edward Elgar.

Mann, Catherine L. (1999), *Is the US Trade Deficit Sustainable?*, Washington DC: Brookings Institution.

Rangan, S. and Robert Z. Lawrence (1999), *A Prism on Globalization: Corporate Responses to the Dollar*, Washington DC: Brookings Institution.

Rodrik, Dani (1999) in Richard E. Baldwin, Daniel Cohen, Andre Sapir and Anthony Venables (eds), *Market Integration, Regionalism and the Global Economy*, Cambridge: Cambridge University Press, chapter 5.

Schleifer, Andrei (2000), *Inefficient Markets*, Oxford: Oxford University Press.

Stiglitz, Joseph (1998), 'The private uses of public interests: incentives and institutions', *Journal of Economic Perspectives*, **12**(2), Spring, 3–22.

UNCTAD (2000), *World Investment Report 2000*, Geneva: UNCTAD.

Wolff, Martin (2000), 'After the crash', *Foreign Policy*, September/October, 46–52.

Wrobel, Paulo S. (1999), 'A free trade area of the Americas in 2005?', *International Affairs*, **74**(3), July, 547–62.

Index